THE COURTS AND THE PEOPLE:

The Courts and the People: Friend or Foe?

The Putney Debates 2019

Edited by
DJ Galligan

·HART·

OXFORD · LONDON · NEW YORK · NEW DELHI · SYDNEY

HART PUBLISHING

Bloomsbury Publishing Plc

Kemp House, Chawley Park, Cumnor Hill, Oxford, OX2 9PH, UK

1385 Broadway, New York, NY 10018, USA

29 Earlsfort Terrace, Dublin 2, Ireland

HART PUBLISHING, the Hart/Stag logo, BLOOMSBURY and the Diana logo are
trademarks of Bloomsbury Publishing Plc

First published in Great Britain 2021

Copyright © The editor and contributors severally 2021

A catalogue record for this book is available from the British Library.

ISBN: PB: 978-1-50994-179-7
       HB: 978-1-50994-003-5
       ePDF: 978-1-50994-005-9
       ePub: 978-1-50994-004-2

Typeset by Compuscript Ltd, Shannon
Printed and bound in Great Britain by CPI Group (UK) Ltd, Croydon CR0 4YY

MIX
Paper from
responsible sources
FSC® C013604

To find out more about our authors and books visit www.hartpublishing.co.uk. Here you will find
extracts, author information, details of forthcoming events and the option to sign up for our newsletters.

Preface

ON 28 OCTOBER 1647, the weekly meeting of the General Council of the New Model Army held in St Mary's Church, Putney turned into a debate about matters of constitution. Stretching over several days, the meeting ranged across critical matters of great moment. The civil war had been won, the king was in captivity, parliament in disarray, and the New Model Army in charge. Competing ideas of *constitution* were expressed and the Levellers' proposed *Agreement of the People* was, after animated debate, consigned to committee from which it never re-emerged.

Nearly four centuries later, in 2017, the Putney Debates were revived. The constitutional controversies aroused by the referendum in 2016 on Britain's membership of the European Union were the stimulus. A signal that beneath the calm and seemingly settled constitutional order of the United Kingdom, the views of members of parliament, the courts, officers of government, and most of all the people differ widely and are often defended passionately. The need for better instruction and more informed debate accessible to the public became plain. The new Putney Debates were instituted as an annual event with the aim of contributing in a modest way to those ends. Each year a subject is selected for examination, and speakers are invited to make brief but informed presentations followed by debate among themselves and with the audience. The proceedings are recorded on film and accessible to the public.

This volume results from the 2019 debates on the subject of the courts, their place in the constitutional order, their relations with the people, and the division of power between the courts and the other institutions of government. The following chapters, with one exception, began with the presentations at Putney in March 2019. I would like to record my thanks to the contributors for the considerable time and labour spent in converting a five-minute presentation into a substantial chapter. While the emphasis is on courts in the United Kingdom, a comparative element is included with contributions from Europe and the United States.

The debate was made possible by the sponsorship of the Foundation for Law Justice & Society, an independent institute, which has now ceased activities but was at the time affiliated with Oxford University and based at Wolfson College. My thanks to the Trustees for their support and to the administrative staff, Ms Judy Niner and Mr Phil Dines, for ensuring the debates ran smoothly and are recorded for posterity. I wish also to thank Hart Publishing, a division of Bloomsbury, for publishing the volume. It has been a pleasure to work with the editors, Ms Rosemarie Mearns, Ms Kate Whetter and Ms Linda Staniford.

Denis Galligan
Editor

Table of Contents

List of Contributors

John Adams is Adjunct Professor at Rutgers University, New Brunswick, USA.

Catherine Barnard is Professor of European Law and Employment Law at the University of Cambridge and Fellow of Trinity College, Cambridge, UK.

Daniel Butt is Associate Professor at the Department of Politics and International Relations at Oxford University and Fellow of Balliol College, Oxford, UK.

Nick Friedman is Fellow and College Lecturer in Public Law at St John's College, Cambridge, and University Lecturer, Faculty of Law, University of Cambridge, UK.

Denis Galligan is Professor of Socio-Legal Studies Emeritus at Oxford University and Professorial Fellow Emeritus at Wolfson College, Oxford, UK.

Graham Gee is Professor of Public Law at Sheffield University, UK.

Ezequiel Gonzalez-Ocantos is Associate Professor at the Department of Politics and International Relations at Oxford University and Professorial Fellow at Nuffield College, Oxford, UK.

Bogdan Iancu is Associate Professor in Comparative Constitutional Law and Theory at the University of Bucharest, Romania, and Fellow of the Foundation for Law, Justice & Society, UK.

Paul Magrath is Head of Product Development and Online Content at the Incorporated Council of Law Reporting, UK.

Amir Paz-Fuchs is Professor of Law at Sussex University and Fellow of the Foundation for Law, Justice & Society, UK.

Robert J Sharpe is Distinguished Jurist in Residence, Faculty of Law, University of Toronto; Visiting Professor, Oxford University; and Retired Justice, Court of Appeal for Ontario.

Katarina Sipulova is Senior Researcher at the JUSTIN Faculty of Law, Masaryk University, Czech Republic.

The People and the Courts:
An Introduction

DJ GALLIGAN

I

THE AIM IN the following chapters is to examine the place of the courts in the constitutional order, an order that consists of powers and relationships. Power is the subject matter of relationships among the people, between the people and the agencies of government, and among the agencies themselves. Relations between the people and the courts have centre stage, with other sets in supporting roles. The issues under review are the nature and purpose of the power of courts, the reasons and justification for it, the constraints and limits, and how power is used in practice. The different ways of conducting the analysis are evident in the chapters. Some start with a political theory from which the constitutional order follows. Political theories tend to be less concerned with the world as it is but rather how it ought to be ordered according to a set of ideals. Others are inclined towards a social understanding which means examining relations as practised and experienced, aiming to draw out the sentiments and dispositions that guide the parties in their perceptions and understandings. Yet another approach is the historical where the aim is to uncover the foundations of the relationship and to chart the route from the past to the present, guided by the adage that in order to know where we are today, we need to know how we got here. A final approach is the comparative, the idea that nations confront common issues is the design and practice of the constitutional order, from the study of which we gain knowledge of constitutions generally and acquire insights into particular cases. Some of the chapters here are squarely within one or other of the approaches, while others combine elements of each. My purpose in this introduction is not to give a brief description of each chapter but to sketch the setting and to show how each contributes.

***

The setting of the 2019 Putney Debates was one of criticism, and by some condemnation, of the courts. The courts are condemned for being part of an elite separate from the common people and criticised for lacking knowledge of or showing concern for the common people. In the opening chapter Robert

Sharpe confronts both these issues and sets out to show how the courts, properly framed, are the friends rather than the foes of the people. On his account, the primary duty of judges is to apply the law in deciding the cases before them, while the law is on the side of the people. First, the law protects their peace and security, saves them from oppression by the powerful and guarantees that even unpopular cases will be dealt with according to settled standards. Secondly, if the law becomes remote from the people, distant from their lives and experiences, and instead reflecting the interests of groups and guilds, the courts are there to keep it in line with 'contemporary social mores and perceptions', in 'harmony with prevailing social values'. Legal values follow from social values, the most fundamental of which is the right of each person to be treated with dignity and respect, which generates juridical equality and the right to be treated equally before the law. The courts make sure the legal interpretation of social values keeps pace with contemporary understanding. Thirdly and critically, the law 'serves and belongs to the people' and 'must remain within the broad channels of public acceptability if it is to be respected'. And finally, public acceptability imposes its own constraints, for the courts have a duty to uphold the rights of individual persons and vulnerable groups. So in a few deft sentences the courts are bolted securely into the constitutional order. The rule of law protects the people and provides social goods of fundamental importance, of which the courts are the guardians. In order to earn that place, discharge their duties and be effective guardians, courts need to have independence.

The rule of law is not the only constitutional value, and here democracy enters the arena. The two do not at first sight seem happy companions. Relations between them are best approached, first, by saying what we mean by democracy, secondly, showing how courts fit in, and thirdly, noting the problems that result. Democracy has its origin in the idea of the people, the *demos*, ruling themselves. On that foundation all sorts of structures are erected, each claiming the credentials of democracy. Just as equity was said to be as long as the lord chancellor's arm, democracy appears to be in the eye of the beholder. It is enough for present purposes to settle on a rather middle-of-the-road notion that power in some sense comes from the people, is to be used to serve the well-being of the people, and is to be accounted for to the people. If that is the governing idea enthroned at the summit of society, the route down to practice passes through several circles, each contributing to the whole yet each offering a choice of pathways.

The constitutional order is the first circle conceived and designed to give effect to the governing idea. It is itself open to copious variation. Two ideas are most prominent. One is that each person counts, and is entitled to equal concern and respect, which translates into juridical equality and rights to be treated in certain ways. The other is that the people are the source of the authority of agencies to which they delegate much of their native authority, while reserving some matters for their own resolution. Descending to the next circle, the people's task is to settle the content to these general ideas. Again there are various options from which to choose. One is how far to extend equal treatment, whether it goes beyond equality before the law to include more substantive equality and social and economic rights. Another task is to settle what portion of authority to delegate to officials and on what terms. From there we progress to the next circle where agencies are created, power is allocated and relationships formed. Here the issues are how much power to delegate, how much to keep in their own hands, what kinds of agencies and offices to create, and the distribution of power among them. The terms have to be settled of the relationships among the people, between the people and government, and among the agencies of government. We then descend to the practical working of the system to consider the sentiments and dispositions of the people, in all their diversity, and of the officials, whether politicians, administrators or judges. The constitutional order enters into practice through, and depends upon, the sentiments of understanding and dispositions of action and restraint on the part of citizens and officials. Sentiments and dispositions give life to the structure of power and relationships; they are the means to secure the balance, moderation, equilibrium on which the mighty edifice rests.

Returning now to Robert Sharpe's outline of the place of the courts, although cautious in intent and reasonable in reach, it promotes a particular pathway through the circles of power, relationships and constitutional choices. It leads to outcomes some support and others contest. Other pathways from the peak through to practice are open and arrive at different destinations as to the scope of power of the courts, its purposes and its limits. The need for a referee, someone to apply the rules, is anodyne and hardly contestable. But when the rules include 'contemporary mores and perceptions', keeping 'pace with fundamental values' and settling the framework of 'real democracy', the landscape becomes more rugged and room for disagreement and division rife; the figure of the neutral referee no longer feasible. The point is not to question the values on which the political order is built and which the constitutional order protects: basic rights, freedom of thought and expression, prohibiting discrimination and marginalisation, and encouraging 'the full participation of citizens'. These are the values within the political order and the foundations of the constitutional order. Once the values are settled the contest is over who decides their meaning and scope. Whoever decides that marks the boundaries between the courts, other agencies and the people. The site of contest most common is between the courts and the democratic process. Invariably legitimacy is invoked, the claim that courts lack legitimate authority. A fine word 'legitimate', as Edmond the illegitimate sarcastically declares and tends to mean whatever we want.[1] The better course is to ask how the governing idea may be interpreted to justify the courts in deciding the very nature of the constitutional orders.

A powerful body of opinion objects it does not. The objection neatly put by Nicholas Friedman is that the judges are not elected by the people. Daniel Butt

---

[1] William Shakespeare, *The Tragedy of King Lear*, Act 1.2.18.

explains it 'as a crisis of democratic legitimacy' and the need 'to reduce the power of unelected judges'. One of the dilemmas of democracy is that 'courts should not act in a way that compromises the democratic character of the polity'. According to Catherine Barnard, democracy means that matters of major importance are decided by a majority of the people. The matters listed in Robert Sharpe's account certainly count as major. The reliance on the democratic process – elections, majorities, accountability – is based on a normative idea as to how power ought to be distributed and patrolled in the constitutional order. The claim as to what the courts should not be doing is justified by reference to the governing idea that the people are in charge of their own affairs. The people determine the nature of the polity and its values, and relegate the courts to a lesser place within the polity. Just what that place is, is hard to say, and the courts are left in a hazy landscape, the range of their role diminished but uncertain.

II

The landscape has not always been hazy or the place of the courts uncertain. As Bogdan Iancu shows in his chapter, the charter of the courts set in the eighteenth century, faded and stained, still in the twenty-first century exerts its influences. Baron Montesquieu gave the classic account: judges are 'only the mouthpiece of the law, inanimate beings that can moderate neither its force nor its rigours'. Far from being a relic of the past, the sentiment lives on in many places and jurisdictions. Just a few years ago, a study of administrative courts in Poland demonstrated the reluctance of judges to take account in their judgments of principles stated in the constitution of Poland and in European Union law.[2] When presented with our findings a hefty proportion of the judges defended their approach on the mouthpiece-of-the-law maxim. Their duty, they said, is to apply the rules of law neutrally and strictly and to avoid the hazards of abstract principles. Perhaps that was an older generation of judges and sentiments are now different. But plainly the force of eighteenth-century attitudes is not wholly spent and the undercurrent of judges as neutral functionaries still flows. The idea that judges might engage actively in the political process is unthinkable and would amount to constitutional heresy.

The heresy and the unthinkable are fast becoming the orthodox and the normal. Ezequiel Gonzalez-Ocantos describes the new dispensation; his words, robustly put, are worth reciting: 'Courts around the world have left behind

---

[2] DJ Galligan and M Matczak, 'Empirical Study of Judicial Discretion in Polish Administrative Courts' in R Coman and J-M De Wade (eds), *Judicial Reform in Central and Eastern European Countries* (Vanden Books, Brugge, 2007).

decades of subservience, incompetence, conservatism, and quite frankly, political irrelevance, to become architects of fundamental rights and key public policies.' Perhaps a slight overstatement of judicial shortcomings but let that pass. Far from being passive mouthpieces of law made by others, the courts are now in the heat of the 'political battleground'; they are at 'the centre of the most salient debates' and hand down decisions that 'antagonise and constrain those in government'. Judges around the world have woken up to the power they wield and wreak havoc on old orthodoxies. The new dispensation puts courts right at the centre of the political arena. A number of factors account for the transformation. One is the idea that we all have fundamental rights of a range and variety previously unimagined which precede and have priority over the political process. Such rights are declared in constitutional texts and the courts are charged to uphold them, a charge the courts could not perform without being thrust into the political process. A good example is the position in the United Kingdom after the Human Rights Act 1998 compared with before. A second factor runs parallel. The transformation, the rights' revolution, breeds and indeed depends on judges and lawyers themselves being socialised into the new dispensation. Old sentiments of deference to the political agencies are replaced by new sentiments as to the social relations between the people and government. And on the need for the courts to patrol the relationship and uphold the terms. From first entering legal training, through years of legal practice, to ascending to the bench, lawyers learn the new constitutional order, accept the foundations as compelling and acquire a sense of duty towards it.[3]

A third factor, according to Ezequiel, is the 'intensification of the transnational dialogue between courts'. The experience of courts across jurisdictions, the exchange of experience and mutual support, encourage and embolden national courts wherever they are. Courts such as the Inter-American Court of Human Rights and the European Court of Human Rights and others promote awareness of rights and encourage judges in domestic orders to the full rendering of fundamental rights. The passage is not easy and resistance comes from several quarters, the agencies of government, special groups and interests. Sectors of the people themselves resist. Not everyone thinks judges are best suited to settle critical matters, which no matter how neatly dressed in legal language, are political in nature and of 'high concernment'. That is not a bad thing, Ezequiel argues, because 'contestation can be an invaluable source of improvement for the work that judges perform in our societies'. Niccolò Machiavelli would rejoice to see defended so vigorously his claim of discord not concord being the route to good government. Although just where the people are in Ezequiel's account is not clear.

---

[3] For further analysis of the socialisation process, see DJ Galligan, *Law in Modern Society* (Oxford, Oxford University Press, 2007) ch 6.

However convincing the case for courts in a constitutional order committed to fundamental rights, the issue of 'democratic legitimacy remains'. Daniel Butt puts it this way: 'there is more to good law-making than democratic legitimacy, and there is more to democratic legitimacy than majority rule'. The more consists of the courts' 'scrutinising legislative and executive action'. The motivation is attributable to the rise of rights and the 'widely shared belief that these rights are of fundamental importance'. But a critical question remains. We might all agree that a wide array of rights are at the foundations of the constitutional order and that such rights are by nature open to varying interpretation. Yet we might disagree as to who is to have the final say on the meaning and scope of rights. Some argue for the political process, others for the courts. The political process means as a last resort the majority of the people (normally acting through representatives); the judicial process that a majority of a panel of less than a dozen judges settles the matter. After analysing the dilemma, Daniel concludes that 'judicial action could be legitimate if it had its own form of democratic support'.

The people are at last back on stage. We have seen that the democratic process is founded on the people being in charge of their own affairs. How the courts fit in, how they relate to the people, is so far left untouched. On some accounts there is no relationship. If judges are mere mouthpieces neutrally applying rules to facts, a mere technical process, there is no need for a relationship. Just as there is no need for one with the clerk filling in forms or the statistician arranging numbers. Once we put aside that image and study the cases, especially the controversial ones, adjudication reveals itself as a complex process of reasoning, drawing distinctions, settling boundaries and expressing preferences. Whether we call the process one of interpreting legal principles or deciding matters of policy does not mitigate the fact that in either case judges are engaged in settling questions of social, economic and political moment. For that courts need the authorisation of the people and that depends on a relationship with the people.

Daniel Butt then goes on to follow one trail that leads to a promising account of the relationship, that of *transformative constitutionalism*. In a lecture at Oxford some years ago the Chief Justice of the South African constitutional court, Pius Langa, laid out a constitutional order based on 'human rights, democracy and peaceful co-existence and development opportunities for all South Africans'. In practical terms transformative constitutionalism advances three goals: substantive equality; a legal culture in which decisions are justified in terms of the rights and values rather than on the authority of one or other agency of government; and transformation as a permanent ideal, a work in progress guiding 'dialogue and contestation'. To this vision of the constitutional order the courts are centre stage, a position they occupy by express authority of the people. No need here for contrived signs of consent, no need for the fictions and contortions of a social contract, no longer is consent 'figurative and metaphorical' as Adam Smith described it. Consent is now full-blown, an 'actual historical contract between the people of South Africa'. Daniel goes on to describe the process by which the post-apartheid constitution was made, involving the participation of the people, the agreement on basic principles and, one should add, a constitutional court that gave life to the noble ideals – a process the Chief Justice described as an actual historical contract. A process that could go beyond rights to bring about 'the full-blooded pursuit of social justice'.

III

The image of the courts as warriors in the thick of the political battleground, not just speaking the law but making it, holds much appeal. It seems to catch the place courts are coming to occupy in many constitutional orders, even if not stated or admitted. Yet the trail is neither straight nor without peril and a few notes of caution are in order. One is that the old problem of authority has not entirely gone away. The authority for judges to have a much extended role is said to be the consent of the people. If the people consent to the new order, reservations about courts entering the political arena are banished. They now enter with the clear and express consent of the people, not just a leading elite but the people as a whole. Here some doubts creep in. Does the people mean everyone or is it a majority? If a majority, then what about the dissenters? A case can be made for majority opinion serving day-to-day politics and law-making. But settling the very foundations of the constitution is of a wholly different order. The case has to be made, not assumed, for the majority's authority to settle the basic rules of the system, which include the majority rule itself. Dissent might reasonably be based on the view that the political process rather than the judicial is still the right setting for deciding policy and making law. And in addition, even if there were real unanimity at the time of the original settlement, how would that transfer to the next generation?[4] One answer could be, as Jeremy Bentham urged, that each generation review and revise the constitution. Long before Bentham, in the 1640s when the English constitution was in tatters, the Levellers proposed that everyone sign up to an 'Agreement of the People' to indicate true consent. Their wish never came to pass. Over a century later, the freemen of Pennsylvania in the constitution of 1776 opted for regular review and revision of the constitution. For that and other aspects of genuine rule by the people they were mocked and reviled by sensible opinion as 'upstarts drunk with liberty'.[5] Consent normally is inferred from conduct and the South African people, or a majority of them, appeared by their conduct to embrace and endorse the new constitutional settlement. Whether the inference is justified, how deep consensus ran, how much filtered down to the villages and townships, what divisions were brushed aside, is less clear.

---

[4] A point Daniel notes in passing.
[5] Described in GS Wood, *The Creation of the American Republic 1776–1787* (Chapel Hill and London, University of North Carolina Press, 1969, 1998).

A second word of caution concerns the checks and controls on judicial power. The standard criticism already at large is that courts are neither elected by the people nor answerable to them. And for that reason the power entrusted to them ought to be limited. We can imagine how a marked increase in power would be received and the more severe censure it would incur, a censure hardly eased by pleading the courts' power comes from the people. Power, we know, has a native tendency to grow, which left unchecked leads to unwanted and unjustified ends. To check and control power is, after all, one of the virtues of regular elections of political leaders, while the mighty edifice of public law is erected to contain the use and abuse of power by officials. The dilemma is plain: while avowing the need for independence, judges would be engaged in settling issues of high social, economic and political moment. An obvious solution would be to render judges more rigorously accountable to the people. The trouble is that would weaken the detachment from the political process judges need to have. Such detachment is, after all, the reason for appointing them guardians of the constitutional foundations. Whether there is an alternative solution that both preserves independence in the discharge of constitutional duties and renders adequate accountability to the people is best left until we see what the authors of later chapters say about the subject.

Another note of caution concerns the relationship between the courts and the other agencies of government, particularly the legislative branch. How is power to be divided between the two? Not only regarding the legislative branch, for a judiciary more heavily armed is likely to exact closer supervision of the executive and administrative agencies as well. Although they are normally accountable to the legislative body, the rigour varies and already courts have erected around them an array of legal principles. How then are the boundaries between courts and the legislative and administrative agencies of the political process to be marked? Courts armed with the powers of transformative constitutionalism potentially will turn a simmering row into open war. The old line of defence and division based on political agencies having the added authority of being elected by the people has gone because the courts would have the same democratic credentials. They would be as much the agents of the people as the legislative branch and its delegates. Both now would compete in the political arena without clear constitutional guidance as to the division of labour. However, prophecies of gloom about constitutional matters rarely turn out to come true. The relationships constituting the constitutional order are constantly on the move, sometimes backwards but quite often forwards. As ideas alter, sentiments are revised and dispositions generated, from which action follows. That is the sequence through which ideas pass, being altered and adjusted in the process, by which competition and conflict are contained, and out of which emerges practical action. The transformative approach to the constitutional order, if it filters into the ideas of the people, will progress through the sequence and perhaps end in practical constitutional measures broadly acceptable.

One final matter to note in passing is the competence of the different organs of government, a matter I touch on in my own chapter. In designing and establishing the agencies of government, the people, usually through representatives, try to match task and competence. The legislative agency is designed to draw guidance from the political arena, to receive and take account of the many strands of opinion, and to settle high policy. The courts, on the other hand, work to a different tune. There is a defined dispute to settle between defined parties. Argument and evidence are restricted and limited to the issue in contest, the outcome a resolution of the dispute according to legal principles. I liken the first to a bustling bazaar into which all interests freely enter, any opinion is freely stated and the submission of evidence is unrestricted. The other, the court process, is more an auction in which the parties try to outbid each other for the item on sale. Just two brief comments. One is that the courts are institutionally unsuited to settle major matters of policy and ought therefore to refrain from entering the political arena. The other comment, fairly much the opposite, is that the courts are capable of adjusting. Capable of extending their reach to hear evidence and argument from sources beyond the parties; to take and assess guidance from experts and specialists; and to reach rational and reasonable conclusions. Both, as we should expect, are contested issues calling for a volume of their own.

IV

The time has come to return to and develop the governing idea on which the analysis so far has proceeded. The idea simply put is that people are in charge of their own affairs, from which follow subsidiary ideas to guide the observer through the circles of political and constitutional order. The ideas are somewhat ambiguous in nature. Some are ideals of a normative nature, ideals about how the constitutional order ought to be; others are more empirically inclined drawing on how the people organise relationships and what they expect from them. Suppose we follow the more empirical route and see where it leads. We start with a model based on the idea or concept of the people being in charge of their affairs. The model catches a slice of human endeavour, snaps an aspect of social life common among peoples. The governing idea is given a social foundation. As I explain in my chapter, a model is not a generalisation of practice but an idea, a mental construction, formed by reflecting on practice. Once formed it is a frame through which to view and interpret practice. The model rests on the premise that the people have the common purpose of securing and advancing their well-being, partly by the endeavours of each, partly by cooperating with others. Cooperation leads to the formation of social relationships of many kinds. The people learn that some common ends, some aspects of well-being, are best reached through the formation of special agencies, which together constitute a system of government.

Several ideas follow. One is that relations between the people and agencies of government are those of principal and agent. The principal expects the agencies to do certain jobs on its behalf. Each agency is designed to perform certain tasks and power is allocated accordingly. The tasks divide roughly into deciding policies and making laws, administering and implementing the laws, and adjudicating disputes. The division of labour is not exact and the lines between one set of tasks and another are bound to be blurred, open to opinion and tending to shift about. In designing agencies and assigning tasks, the people are guided by a set of home truths. Power in agencies is necessary to serve their well-being. But power, they know, has an unruly habit of growing and expanding beyond its limits. Power is prone to abuse and misuse. The people know power attracts special groups and interests and is at risk of capture. In short, assigning power to government agencies serves the people's interests but creates risks for which they need to be on the look-out and against which they need to protect themselves.

Out of this hinterland of common purposes a constitutional order is delivered. Good government consists in securing and advancing the well-being of each and all. The people design agencies to achieve that aim. The creating and empowering of agencies is the first step to a constitutional order. The jobs to be done are plain. At the front line to decide policies and to make laws, to have them applied and to settle disputes; the second line is to see the front-line jobs are done well. The aims are clear but the design of suitable agencies and the allocation of tasks is rather rough and ready. How to attain the aim is as much guesswork and trial and error as confident deliberation. The critical point is that this process of setting-up agencies of government and allocating tasks is more elemental than and prior to refined ideas about the terms of the social relations that form around and guide them. Once a society reaches beyond the most primitive form of association and starts to rely on collective action, a notion of government is hatched. As it matures, the case for creating and empowering agencies strengthens. Soon it is clear that courts and other primary institutions are necessary if the society is to progress and prosper. The form they take and relations among them are influenced by all sorts of factors and events, one of which are ideas about the nature of government and how it ought to be organised. When (and if) ideas of the people being in charge of their own affairs come to dominate, they are inserted into a constitutional firmament and into a structure of government already in place. When ideas of democracy take hold, they enter into the realm of sentiments and dispositions, find accommodation and common cause with existing sentiments and dispositions, from which emerges practical action. The political process based on democratic ideas takes a central position in the constitutional order, not to the exclusion of the other prior and fundamental sentiments and dispositions, but as partners.

That does not cancel earlier sentiments and dispositions as to the need for agencies to administer justice. They remain part of the firmament, prior to and prevailing over sentiments and dispositions of self-rule. Adjustments may have to be made to accommodate the new prominence of democratic ideals and hence the political process. The line between the political process and the administration of justice may have to be redrawn. But the foundations stay in place and the courts remain secure in their constitutional role of administering justice. The potential for competition between the political agencies and the courts is heightened. The political process claims power over all matters of policy while the courts insist that in the administration of justice elements of policy are immanent and unavoidable. The application of even clear-line rules, the interpretation of more open rules and abstract standards, the individuation of pockets of discretion are part, an ineradicable part, of adjudication. The boundaries between the adjudicative process on the one hand and the political process on the other hand are neither fixed nor firm. While they are there in outline, the boundaries are marked by signposts rather than fences, guidelines rather than directives. Which leads on to the point that the system depends on the sentiments and dispositions of the agents themselves, the socialisation to which Ezequiel refers, not only of judges but all officials. It depends on an understanding of the process, whether adjudicative or political or administrative; a sense of how each process contributes to and fits within the whole; and finally but crucially, a sentiment of self-restraint, the willingness of each agent to impose restraint on the exertion of power. A well-working constitutional order relies on the eternal trinity of good laws, suitable institutions, and the sentiments and dispositions of both officials and the people, especially that of self-restraint.

V

The independence of the courts, judicial independence for short, was a major theme of the 2019 Putney Debates and is taken up in several of the following chapters. According to the model set out above, the constitutional order is founded on the people, on their common purposes, and on the contribution of government agencies. Judicial independence occurs within and is a quality of the relationship between the people and the courts. As the place assigned to the courts within the relationship varies, ranging from mouthpiece to warrior, the meaning and scope of independence are likely to vary. Putting aside the competing positions as to the nature of the relationship and the place of the courts, the common ground seems to be that courts serve the people: (i) by administering justice; (ii) which means interpreting the legal rules and standards; (iii) in which they are guided by the opinion of the people; (iv) for which they account to the people.

Again Robert Sharpe's chart of the landscape of judicial independence is a good place to start. The rule of law is dependent on the administration of justice, which in turn depends on an independent judiciary. At its most simple, judicial independence means allowing the courts to do their job of administering justice; independence is a means to that end. There is nothing exceptional about that because all officials need to be able to do their job properly and without interference. Some conditions apply to all offices, others are particular to judges. Nick Friedman sums it up as: 'a degree of freedom in deciding a case, from control by or pressure from the other branches of government, litigants, and the public at large'. A useful distinction Amir Paz-Fuchs draws is that between the independence of courts as institutions and the independence personal to each judge. Both dimensions need to be preserved and protected.[6] Robert lists the practical measures: security of office and finance, suitable qualifications, and control in organising the business of the courts. That the judiciary be separate from the executive and legislative branches is given particular weight. In addition to the external protections, the judges have to protect themselves by refraining from actions, such as taking part in politics. In the calm surroundings of settled constitutional orders, consensus is high as to what judicial independence means and how to attain it.

Bogdan Iancu in his closely argued chapter questions the unreflective transfer of the consensus to the less mature constitutional orders such as Poland and Romania. One size does not fit all, and the meaning, range and protection of independence, the resolution of competing values, 'require complex trade-offs' particular to each constitutional order. In his study of the courts in Israel, Amir adds another cautionary warning not to confuse or conflate judicial independence and the scope of judicial power. Yet are the two wholly unrelated? The meaning and content of judicial independence do seem to be determined in part by the scope of judicial power, which ranges from mouthpiece to warrior. At the mouthpiece-end independence is fairly straight and settled; for the warrior judges, up to their necks in matters of principle and policy, the terrain is uncharted. As judges travel along the line, from mouthpiece to warrior, the meaning of independence and the measures of protection seem to travel with them. The course the journey has taken in Israel illustrates the point. Amir shows how the 'constitutional revolution' sparked by the Basic Laws of 1992 empowered the courts to judge whether legislation has 'a disproportionately harmful effect on human rights'. The added power of the courts did not change the meaning or scope of independence. Nor would it change if the power to strike down legislation were lost. Amir's analysis of the tension and on notions of independence merits close reading.

Let us leave the subject plainly ripe for further discussion with a question. Would the people concede to Daniel's judge, engaged in delivering transformative constitutionalism, or Ezequiel's judge, 'the architect of fundamental rights and key public policies', the same level of independence as the judge whose ambition is to be a reliable mouthpiece? On Nick's account of independence the judges must be free from control or influence from the public at large. If judges are resolutely engaged not just in interpreting law but making law by deciding key issues of policy and the scope of human rights, the people would reasonably

---

[6] A distinction discussed in DJ Galligan, *Judging Judges* (Foundation for Law Justice & Society Policy Brief, 2012).

expect to be involved. They would reasonably claim a right to take part in the process and exert influence in persuading the judge of their point of view. The judge is, after all, the people's agent, making decisions of immense importance for them as principals.

VI

This brings us back to the relationship between the people and the courts where these issues are more suitably considered. It is suggested above that part of the relationship is that judges in judging are guided by the people and accountable to them. The authority of judges, remember, is provided for in the constitutional order, their purpose being to administer justice on behalf of the people. They are neither elected nor are they expected to represent special interests or sectors. So what is the relationship? There are three dimensions: the authority of the courts, the use of that authority and controls on the use of that authority. All three are contentious, excite widely different views and arouse passions to match. Here we must be content with a brief comment on each. The authority of the courts at one end is based on the deep democratic foundations of transformative constitutionalism. At the other end is the pragmatic view, notably put by David Hume, that the courts are there in place, while the people who come and go acquiesce in that power because it serves their interests. Numerous camps occupy the territory in between; one of some popularity is the social contract, the *as if* there were a social contract camp. Whatever camp one joins, the next issue is how the courts use authority. Again the camps are numerous and scattered. One appoints courts the guards patrolling the boundaries of democracy. If, as Robert Sharpe writes, 'democracy can only exist within a legal and political framework', then someone has to be in charge of the framework. That splits into sub-camps, ranging from the courts 'deployed to protect equal rights of participation', as Nick Friedman puts it, a kind of procedural approach, to full-blooded supervision of the substance of the political process.[7] Each camp relies on an understanding of the constitutional order of which, as the earlier discussion shows, there are many.

Perhaps the judges have their own opinions about relations with the people and how that guides the use of authority. Robert, himself a senior judge, makes plain his view that the courts are charged with upholding democracy and to do whatever that takes. In a study of the federal system of the United States, John Adams shows with clarity how the Supreme Court has cleared a pathway, twisting and turning but intact, between the rule of law and the political process. Relations between the two are moderated by the court's keeping 'an eye to public

---

[7] For discussion of the procedural approach and its defects, see DJ Galligan, 'Judicial Review and Democratic Principles: Two Theories' [1983] *Australian Law Journal* 69; reprinted in Mark Tushnet (ed), *Bills of Rights* (Routledge, London, 2007).

opinion' from which it has never departed too far or for too long. However, public opinion, one might note, is rather a wild horse which once mounted has its own will and way. John's analysis prompts questions for further study. One is to unravel the concept of public opinion. Another to show how through the bustling bazaar of opinions courses one common to all. What is the contemporary equivalent of the Pennsylvanian upstarts of 1776 drunk with liberty, and the grandees of property and status, between whom there was no common ground? The common ground between those storming the Congress as I write and the many other groups and sectors of diverse interests and values? A final question is how the courts not only respond to but lead and shape public opinion; how they 'channel the public will', as Nick puts it.

The Israeli experience is strikingly different. Niceties of public opinion appear to have a minor place in the sentiments and dispositions of the courts. Amir recounts the courts' resolve in the name of the rule of law, which includes 'democratic principles', to penetrate deeply into the territory of the legislative and executive branches. British judges are more cautious. Some at least, as Nick explains, would be concerned that the public 'might prove resistant to the idea of judicial law-making' and its passions against the courts inflamed. The evidence for such sentiments and dispositions of the people is left unstated. And it might do no harm to mention to the public and remind the judges of the common law.

VII

The administration of justice is the core of the relationship between the people and the courts. To administer justice properly the courts need to have a sphere of independence, to be free from interference in doing the job. No matter how administering justice is defined or the exact boundaries drawn, both contested issues, a certain independence is needed to do it properly. Yet courts are easy targets, often under attack and their independence endangered. Katarina Sipulova, in her illuminating study of the courts in the nations of central Europe, shows the forms attack takes and how it can be resisted. She reminds us of a now familiar theme. The more courts are visible and powerful, the more political they become. The more they use that power to 'constrain the executive and function as checks against illiberal policies', the more enticing a target they are. Katarina records the 'wave of political backlash against courts and judges all over the world' and the ways and means used. The courts may be sitting ducks to attack but are hawks in resistance. The two main lines of resistance are *on-bench* and *off-bench*. The first involves judges making strategic decisions, the second exerting extra-judicial pressure. The second takes two forms, judges acting together and each judge acting alone. A third brigade to summon into action is the international order. It stretches beyond the transnational judicial networks encountered in Ezequiel's chapter to embrace political opposition, supranational institutions, institutions of civil society, the media and the public. The judges have a formidable armoury to mobilize in counterattack. How effective each is and how solid the whole are matters for further empirical study. The score among the nations of central Europe is variable. The alliance between the judges, the media and the public depends, Katarina concludes, on the 'ability of courts to garner sufficient public trust and support'.

The judges themselves can do a lot to boost public trust. In his chapter, Nick sets out three concepts – transparency, mystification and popularity – each a means for cultivating the people's perception and acquiescence. Transparency is the key concept in Catherine Barnard's fine study of the European Court of Justice (ECJ). She begins by asking why a court dedicated to preserving and advancing the values of democracy, fundamental rights and the rule of law should be so loathed, at least by some sectors of society, especially but not only in Britain. The answer is because the court has avoided the gaze of the people.[8] As the Duchess Eleanora, paraded through the streets to be led into exile, warns her husband, the Duke of Gloucester, to watch out for nothing is to be dreaded more than the gaze of people, 'the giddy multitude' lining the streets who 'gaze and nod their heads and throw their eyes on thee'.[9] The Duke knows better, knows he must bow to the gaze and explain his actions. So must the courts. They must earn their place in the eyes of the people. On that the ECJ has failed. Catherine mounts a telling case to show that, regardless of its proud record of creating a European constitutional order, the ECJ has avoided the gaze of the public. A people kept at bay, its gaze avoided, is unlikely to have confidence in the institution. Transparency is the remedy, the route to popularity. If the people see what the court is doing, know the reasons for its actions, their confidence may be gained. Catherine urges the ECJ to move beyond the thin mean sense it now practices to embrace transparency in a full and generous sense. 'Judgments must live and breathe in a broader social and political context.' The judges must listen to the people and encourage the people to listen to them.

Paul Magrath adopts a similar approach in addressing the issue in the British context. Mystery is to be banished and replaced by transparency. Paul shows keen insight into both the need for judges to promote public understanding of what they do and the ways and means open to them. Open justice 'goes to the very heart of the idea of the rule of law'. The judgments of the courts are the first and most decisive step to transparency. They must 'speak as clearly as possible to the public'. To that foundation judges may add through their writings, lectures and relations with the media, both traditional and social, the blogging judge soon to be a familiar figure. All in the interests of explaining and justifying what they do, how they go about administering justice on behalf of the people. Paul concludes by contrasting the old Doctrine of Reticence, of judges aloof

---

[8] Further on the people's gaze, see JE Greene, *The Eyes of the People: Democracy in an Age of Spectatorship* (Oxford and New York, Oxford University Press, 2010).

[9] William Shakespeare, *Henry VI Part II*, Act 2.4.22.

from the people and beyond their gaze, with a new doctrine, a new dispensation, a new social relationship of mutual encounter. We might name it the Doctrine of Engagement.

In a suitable finale, Graham Gee returns to judicial independence and offers a masterly case study of one dimension of the issue in the British context. Judges and lawyers, he writes, are justly proud of 'the long and rich tradition of judicial independence in the UK'. While relations between the courts and the people have dominated preceding chapters, relations between the courts and politicians add a dimension of importance and interest. Judges and lawyers must work with politicians to 'cultivate the conditions in which judges are equipped, individually and institutionally, to decide legal disputes impartially, according to law and free from improper pressure'. Some observers are concerned the relationship is fraying and the ministers of state are to blame. The office of Lord Chancellor, in particular, has come under scrutiny. Viewed traditionally as the 'guardian of judicial independence', the office was transformed by statutory changes in 2005. Some of the legal elite of judges, lawyers and others question whether the office still serves that purpose. Such misgivings, Graham argues, are not justified. They are based on three misunderstandings: of the traditional role of the Lord Chancellor's office, of the present role, and of the actions of a recent occupant in responding to attacks by the press on a decision of the Supreme Court. The care of the argument and the attention to detail merit close reading, leaving the sceptics with a high bar to meet.

Here just one or two points are noted. One is that much of the criticism of the office as now defined and of a particular occupant is outdated. It assumes 'the judges cannot speak on their own behalf'. If that is the assumption, then as other chapters show, Paul's in particular, it truly is outdated. Judges are entitled and expected to speak and write and broadcast in explaining, justifying and defending their judgments and their independence. Another general point is that there are limits on the extent to which serving politicians, including the Lord Chancellor, are able to 'serve as effective guardians of judicial independence'. They have a part to play, have many ways of directly and indirectly protecting the principle. They know, or ought to know, that judicial independence is central to the administration of justice and so at the foundation of the constitutional order. And, knowing this, politicians have a strong incentive and a duty to respect, guard and promote the principle. The extent of such duty, how it is best discharged and its limits are matters of high concernment and await further study.

1

The Case for Judicial Independence in the Age of Populism

ROBERT J SHARPE

T HE RISE OF populism challenges the legitimacy of most liberal-democratic traditions and institutions. The courts and the judiciary cannot escape the distrust of elites that fuels populism. In this chapter, I will consider why, when I was a judge, I enjoyed the protection of judicial independence. I will examine the case for judicial independence, its relationship to the underlying principles of the rule of law and the justification for the power of judicial review. I will discuss what judicial independence actually protects, and the limitations judicial independence implicitly imposes on judges. I will argue that along with judicial independence goes judicial accountability and I will consider how judges are made accountable.

I. THE COURTS: FRIENDS OR FOES?

It will not surprise you to learn that as a sitting judge, I considered myself to be a friend of the people, not a foe. However, I realised that if I did my job properly, there would be times when some people would see me as a foe, not a friend. I heard many cases involving unpopular litigants and causes. If I concluded that the law favoured the unpopular side, I was duty bound to decide accordingly. I was sometimes asked to rule that powerful individuals – the police, ministers of the Crown – had acted illegally. If I concluded that they had, I was duty-bound to say so, knowing that my decision was likely to attract public criticism. I even got asked to rule that the democratically elected representatives of the people sitting in parliament had enacted a law that violated a fundamental right or freedom protected by our constitution. If I concluded that the law did so, I had to rule accordingly.

These decisions are difficult to make and are often controversial. When I made them, I knew that my decision might not have met with popular approval.

I might have been criticised by the media and by powerful individuals. I might have even been labelled as an 'enemy of the people'.[1]

But if I made these difficult and controversial decisions because that is what the law required, I maintain that I could not be an 'enemy of the people'. The 'enemy of the people' cry springs from a dangerously short-term perspective. The people may not like result I reached in this case or that. But do not the people believe in the law as an institution to secure and protect their peace and security? Do the people not depend upon the law to stand between them and the rich and the powerful? And because the people can never be sure that, one day, it will not be their case that is unpopular, do not the people want independent judges to decide cases according to the law?

II. THE LAW AND PUBLIC OPINION

Judges have to have the courage to make unpopular decisions if that is what the law requires. They cannot bend to public opinion or populist revolt against a particular litigant or cause. Accused criminals, immigrants, asylum-seekers and members of minority groups often lack popular support and attract opprobrium. But they have legal rights and judges are duty bound to insist that those rights be properly respected.

This does not mean that judges cannot take popular opinion into account. Judges have to ensure that the law keeps pace with contemporary social mores and perceptions. The Supreme Court of Canada has stated that the courts have a role in changing the common law 'to bring the law into harmony with prevailing social values'.[2] But there is a difference between bowing to raw public opinion hostile to vulnerable minorities and ensuring that the law reflects the social understanding of fundamental legal values, such as the equality of all citizens and the right of everyone to be treated with dignity and respect. Ensuring that the law keeps pace with a contemporary understanding of those fundamental values makes to law truer to itself.[3]

Many such cases involve changing social perceptions regarding gender equality and the role of women. To take a familiar example, until 1928, when courts interpreted statutes conferring legal rights on 'persons' – the right to vote or to sit in Canada's Senate – women were excluded.[4] In a 1908 decision, the House of Lords dismissed the claim that a statute conferring the

---

[1] For discussion of the 'Enemies of the People' headline, see the conclusion, below, and J Rozenberg, *Enemies of the People? How Judges Shape Society* (Bristol, Bristol University Press, 2020).

[2] *R v Stone* [1999] SCR 290, para 239.

[3] See R Sharpe, *Good Judgment: Making Judicial Decisions* (Toronto, University of Toronto Press, 2018) 90. I have drawn freely on my book at various points in this chapter.

[4] R Sharpe and P McMahon, *The Persons Case: The Origins and the Legacy of the Fight for Legal Personhood* (Toronto, University of Toronto Press, 2007).

right to vote on 'all persons' who had graduated from certain universities included female graduates. The Lord Chancellor caustically observed: 'It is incomprehensible to me that anyone acquainted with our laws ... can think, if anyone does think, that there is any room for argument on such a point.'[5] Twenty years later, Lord Sankey, sitting on the Judicial Committee of the Privy Council on an appeal from Canada,[6] recognised that as the word 'persons' was capable of including women, it was social custom and practice, not the law, that excluded them. He held that a woman was a 'qualified person' under the Canadian Constitution to be appointed to the Canadian Senate. He refused to apply the long line of authority restricting the meaning 'person' to males, writing that the Privy Council 'must take great care ... not to interpret legislation meant to apply to one community by rigid adherence to the customs and traditions of another'.[7] The denial of personhood to women was the product of social and political forces, not the law; it was, as Sankey put it, 'a relic of days more barborous than ours'.[8] Sankey's judgment was rightly applauded in the Canadian and English press as a significant advance towards gender equality[9] and it remains a leading authority in Canadian constitutional law on how, with changes in social conditions, the precise meaning of the words of the constitution evolve over time.[10]

Judges, particularly those who sit on apex courts, have to display both wisdom and the qualities of 'prodigious judicial statecraft'[11] when dealing with public opinion. The law serves and belongs to the people and it must remain within the broad channels of public acceptability if it is to be respected and obeyed. In the common law tradition, the law is constantly evolving to meet the changing needs of society. But judges must never bow to public opinion that denigrates vulnerable groups or seeks to disregard individual rights guaranteed by the law. Judges enjoy judicial independence precisely because they must be equipped to resist populist or authoritarian pressure to ignore the law and take what may seem to be a more expedient path.

III. THREATS TO JUDICIAL INDEPENDENCE

I recognise that in a democratic society, particularly in an age of populism, it is not surprising to find that the power of unelected judges is contested.

---

[5] *Nairn v University of St Andrews* [1909] AC 147, 160.

[6] *Edwards v Attorney General for Canada* [1930] AC 128.

[7] ibid 138.

[8] ibid 128.

[9] Sharpe and McMahon (n 5) 181–82.

[10] Sankey's judgment is particularly notable for coining the 'living tree' metaphor for constitutional interpretation: 'The *British North America Act* [Canada's 1867 Constitution] planted in Canada a living tree capable of growth and expansion within its natural limits' (*Edwards*, n 6, 136).

[11] B Dickson, 'Operations and Practice: A Comparison of the Role of the Supreme Court in Canada and the United States' (1980) 3 *Canada–United States Law Journal* 86.

Judicial independence has long been accepted as a core constitutional principle yet judicial independence is frequently threatened. Some of these threats are anonymous, such as when judges are threatened with death, bodily harm or harm to their families or their property. Other threats are verbal when judicial decisions are attacked in a way that undermines respect for the judiciary. Perhaps most worrying are threats that come from government. Several of the chapters in this book cite threats to judicial independence in Eastern Europe and Latin America. But jurisdictions with long traditions of judicial independence are not immune. In the United States, there have been calls for laws to allow judges to be sued or imprisoned for unpopular decisions and threats of 'court packing' and jurisdiction stripping. Judges in both the United States and the United Kingdom complain that the erosion of judicial salaries and pensions through inflation and cuts as well as inadequate funding of the courts threaten judicial independence.

That not all of these threats succeed is a testament to the power of the ideals of judicial independence and the rule of law. A striking example occurred in Pakistan in 2007 when President Musharraf attempted to remove Chief Justice Chaudhry out of fear that the Supreme Court would stand in Musharraf's way in running for re-election. The Pakistani legal community courageously fought the move, both in the courts and in the streets. Eventually, Musharraf was swept from power at least in part on account of the public's indignant reaction to the cynical disrespect he had shown for the ideals of judicial independence and the rule of law.[12]

IV. WHY PROTECT JUDICIAL INDEPENDENCE?

The role of the courts and the principle of judicial independence rests on a vision of the proper relationship between citizens and between citizens and the state. The central component of that vision is the rule of law. Despite its importance, the rule of law is difficult to define[13] but in two leading judgments the Supreme Court of Canada[14] identified three essential components. The first is that the law is supreme and governs the actions of both the state and private persons. There is one law for all and the actions of government officials, like those of ordinary citizens, are governed by the law. Second, the rights and obligations of citizens are defined by law rather than arbitrary rule. As the Supreme Court of Canada explained: 'the rule of law requires the creation and maintenance of an actual order of positive laws which preserves and embodies the more general principle

---

[12] R Sharpe and M Bradfield, 'Crisis in Pakistan' in A Dodek and L Sossin (eds), *Judicial Independence in Context* (Toronto, Irwin Law, 2010).

[13] T Bingham, *The Rule of Law* (London, Penguin Books, 2011) identifies eight aspects of the rule of law.

[14] *Re Manitoba Language Rights* [1985] 1 SCR 721; *Reference re Secession of Quebec*, [1998] 2 SCR 217.

of normative order'.[15] The third essential element is that the exercise of public power must be based upon an existing and identifiable legal rule. Public officials cannot act without the support of positive law that authorises their conduct.

The rule of law reflects a noble vision of society and the relationship between the citizen and the state. Citizens must be accorded basic legal rights to ensure peace and security in their daily lives as well as certain fundamental rights, essential for effective democratic participation. The law disciplines the powerful by defining the extent and the limits of executive and legislative power and regulating the economic affairs of the wealthy. Elected officials have earned the support of the people but they do not have carte blanche to rule as they please. The people put them there for a purpose. The people gave them power on the basis of a certain understanding of the rules of the game. Those rules of the game, defined by the constitution and the law, demand ultimate respect for the people and for the rights of the people.

The rule of law cannot exist without an independent judiciary. The courts serve as the place where the citizen may go to challenge the arbitrary or oppressive actions of the state. The courts are the safe haven where the most impoverished or abused citizen may find support for his or her legal rights when they conflict with those of the rich and powerful in society. A court of law is the forum where errant, oppressive or corrupt police officers and government officials may be brought to account. The courts also set the standard for the behaviour of other public institutions. Where justice is not dispensed with impartiality in the courts, there is no hope for citizens to be treated with objectivity, fairness and honesty by other institutions.

The law must be interpreted and applied in the spirit of this noble rule of law vision. That can only happen with an independent judiciary committed to upholding rule-of-law values and equipped to resist the pressures of those whose interests would be served by setting those values aside. Human experience teaches us that those with power, whether political or economic, will push their power to the limits and beyond. If we want the rules of the game to be respected, we are going to need a good referee to enforce them.

V. IS JUDICIAL POWER LEGITIMATE AND JUDICIAL REVIEW

This brings us to the debate over the legitimacy of judicial power and judicial review.[16] To some, judicial power and judicial review are suspect.[17] Judges lack

---

[15] *Re Manitoba Language Rights* (n 17) 749.

[16] I use the term 'judicial review' to refer both to the power of the courts to review administrative decisions and the power of the courts to determine the constitutionality of legislation to determine the constitutionality of legislation. In Canada, the Constitution Act, 1982, s 52, gives courts the power to strike down legislation, but I include in this category of judicial review the power of the UK courts under the Human Rights Act, 1998, s 4, to declare laws enacted by parliament to be incompatible with the rights guaranteed by the Act.

[17] See J Waldron, 'The Core of the Case Against Judicial Review' (2006) 115 *Yale Law Journal* 1346.

a democratic mandate and, it is argued, this means that their powers should be sharply curtailed. Interference with the decisions of democratically elected officials thwarts the popular will and, critics contend, judicial review is therefore illegitimate.

I agree that judges must act judiciously when confronting issues of governmental action, but I do not agree that that in a democracy, judges have no role in controlling the actions of elected officials on grounds of illegality. My point here is quite simple. A healthy, well-functioning democracy needs rules and it needs a referee to interpret and enforce those rules. There is more to democracy than raw majority rule. Democracy can only exist within a legal and political framework that allows for free and open debate and protects the values of individual dignity, autonomy and freedom of choice. Real democracy involves a legal framework that respects freedom of thought and expression, guards against discrimination and marginalisation of minorities, and encourages the full participation of all citizens. That legal framework, necessary to protect democracy, has to be respected and it has to be enforced, especially when it is resisted by powerful forces, be they public or private. The task of maintaining the rule of law and the rules of a healthy democratic society is that of the courts, exercising independent judgment, free from political pressure. Democracy, the rule of law and judicial review are partners, not foes. Judicial protection of democracy's essential legal framework makes judges the friends, not the enemy, of democracy.[18]

The rule of law ideal requires impartial, independent judges, not beholden to any group or interest, accorded the status and protection necessary to enable them to stand above the political fray, immune to the pushes, pulls and swings of popular opinion and the influence of powerful private interests. As stated in a leading study of judicial independence and accountability in Canada, judges necessarily occupy a 'place apart'.[19] Conferring power upon unelected judges has been criticised as creating a democratic deficit by undermining the capacity of elected representatives sitting in parliament to govern in accordance with majority will. But viewed in another light, empowering unelected judges to enforce the rules of democracy can be seen as a democratic necessity. As Canadian Chief Justice Dickson stated: 'The ability of each citizen to make free and informed decisions is the absolute prerequisite for the legitimacy, acceptability, and efficacy of our system of self-government.'[20] A later Supreme Court decision refers to this as the 'democratic imperative' that everyone be

---

[18] JH Ely is a strong proponent of this view in *Democracy and Distrust: A Theory of Judicial Review* (Cambridge, MA, Harvard University Press, 1980). P Monahan echoes this view, with his own refinements, in *Politics and the Constitution: The Charter, Federalism and the Supreme Court of Canada* (Toronto, Carswell, 1987). See also A Barak, *The Judge in a Democracy* (Princeton, NJ, Princeton University Press, 2006) esp 24–26, 33–35. See also Rozenberg (n 1).

[19] ML Friedland, *A Place Apart: Judicial Independence and Accountability in Canada* (Ottawa, Canadian Judicial Council, 1995).

[20] *R v Big M Drug Mart Ltd* [1985] 1 SCR 295, 346.

encouraged to participate fully in public life.[21] Justice Aharon Barak of the Israeli Supreme Court wrote extra-judicially that '[w]ithout judicial independence, there is no preservation of democracy and its values'.[22] Unfortunately, majorities of the day are often hostile to minorities and are prone to use, or abuse, their power to suppress opinions that threaten the status quo. Baroness Brenda Hale, sitting in the UK Supreme Court, explained: 'Democracy values everyone equally even if the majority does not.'[23]

These judicial statements are not self-serving justifications for unduly 'activist' judicial review. To the contrary, they recognise the need to reconcile judicial power with democracy. Democracy cannot exist in a vacuum. It does not consist of raw, untrammelled majority rule. Like all other human institutions, democracy needs rules and it needs a stable framework. This means that judicial power is essential to democracy for it is through the exercise of judicial power by an independent and impartial judiciary that the rules of democracy are maintained and enforced. The decision[24] that provoked the infamous 'Enemies of the People' headline attacking the judiciary for having usurped the power of the people to decide their own destiny actually reinforced democracy and the sovereignty of parliament. It ensured that the crucial decision to leave the European Union was made not by executive fiat, but by the people's representatives sitting in parliament. Similarly, the decision of the Supreme Court[25] to nullify the prorogation of parliament in 2019, contested by some as an improper assertion of power by unelected judges, served to thwart an attempt to remove from parliament the capacity to scrutinise the terms of withdrawal from the EU. As Joshua Rozenberg concluded in his recent book, *Enemies of the People?*: 'Far from being the enemies of the people, judges are just about the only friends we have.'[26]

Critics of judicial review fail to pay sufficient heed to the fact that judicial power is 'soft power' and therefore less to be feared than the power of public office or wealth. Courts depend upon the legislature for resources and for the enforcement of their decrees. Judges lack the means to map out a political agenda or to achieve political goals. In the famous words of Alexander Hamilton, the judiciary has 'no influence over either the sword or the purse. ... It may truly be said to have neither FORCE nor WILL, but merely judgment.'[27] The judiciary is 'the least dangerous branch' of government.[28] Judges do not initiate the cases they decide and while they may decide many important issues, they essentially

---

[21] *Mouvement laïque québécois v Saguenay (City)* 2015 SCC 16, para 75.

[22] Barak (n 21) 77.

[23] *Ghaidan v Godin-Mendoza* [2004] UKHL 30, para 132.

[24] *R (Miller) v Secretary of State for Exiting the European Union* [2016] EWHC 2768 (Admin).

[25] *R (Miller) v Prime Minister: Cherry v Advocate General* [2019] UKSC 41.

[26] Rozenberg (n 1) 190.

[27] *Federalist No 78*.

[28] A Bickel, *The Least Dangerous Branch: The Supreme Court* (New Haven, CT, Yale University Press, 1986).

are restricted to reacting to the cases that come before them and lack the means overtly to develop or achieve a political agenda.

VI. THE CONSTITUTIONAL PROTECTION OF JUDICIAL INDEPENDENCE

Since 1701 and the Act of Settlement,[29] judicial independence has been a cornerstone principle of the British constitution. Before 1701, judges were appointed 'at pleasure' and could be removed from office by the monarch if he or she disagreed with their rulings. The Act of Settlement provided that judges enjoyed the security of salaries established by law, tenure of office during good behaviour, removable only for conduct rendering them unfit for judicial office. upon the joint address of both Houses of Parliament.

The principle of judicial independence is now seen to be an essential element of all modern constitutional democracies. The United States Constitution, Article III establishes the judiciary as an independent and separate branch of government and vests the judicial power of the United States in the Supreme Court and in such inferior courts as the Congress may establish from time to time. The judges of those courts hold their offices during good behaviour (interpreted to mean that judges have tenure for life) and their salaries cannot be decreased. In Canada, judicial independence is guaranteed by both the original Constitution Act, 1867,[30] and by the Charter of Rights and Freedoms, 1982.[31] Judicial independence is also recognised and protected by widely accepted international norms and standards.[32]

What exactly do we mean by judicial independence? One of the clearest statements of the meaning of judicial independence is found in the United Nations Basic Principles on the Independence of the Judiciary (1985), Article 2: 'The judiciary shall decide matters before them impartially, on the basis of facts and in accordance with the law, without any restrictions, improper influences,

---

[29] An Act for the further Limitation of the Crown and better securing the Rights and Liberties of the Subject, 12 and 13 Will 3 c 2, s III: 'judges commissions [are] made *quamdiu se bene gesserint* [during good behavior] and the salaries ascertained and established; but upon the address of both Houses of Parliament it may be lawful to remove them'. See now Constitutional Law Reform Act 2005, s 3(1): 'The Lord Chancellor, other Ministers of the Crown and all with responsibility for matters relating to the judiciary or otherwise to the administration of justice must uphold the continued independence of the judiciary.'

[30] ss 96–99 and the preamble with its reference to a 'Constitution similar in Principle to that of the United Kingdom'.

[31] s 11(d) guarantees individuals charged with a criminal offence 'a fair and public hearing by an independent and impartial tribunal'.

[32] The European Convention of Human Rights, Art 6: 'In the determination of his civil rights and obligations or of any criminal charge against him, everyone is entitled to a fair and public hearing within a reasonable time by an independent and impartial tribunal established by law.' The Universal Declaration of Human Rights, Art 10 provides: 'Everyone is entitled in full equality to a fair and public hearing by an independent and impartial tribunal, in the determination of his rights and obligations and of any criminal charge against him.'

inducements, pressures, threats or interferences, direct or indirect, from any quarter or for any reason.'[33]

There are four central elements of judicial independence.[34]

The first is that judges enjoy tenure or security of office and are removable only for a cause related to their capacity to perform the judicial function. If we disagree with a judge's ruling, we appeal it to a higher court, we do not remove the judge. Judges may be removed only for misconduct or disability that makes them unfit for judicial office. The reason is that giving the judge tenure of office fortifies his/her duty to decide according to law rather than yield to political pressure or popular opinion. If judges could be removed at will, public confidence in their capacity to render independent and impartial rulings based upon the law would be seriously undermined.

The second essential element is that judges enjoy financial security so that they need not fear diminution in remuneration because of judgments that are unpopular or unfavourable to the government. Financial security also ensures that judges are paid sufficiently and have the security of a proper pension to avoid any dependence on or pressure from outside forces, whether actual or perceived.

Third, judicial independence ensures judicial control over court administration, especially the assignment of judges to particular cases. The government funds the courts and is responsible for their maintenance. But the government is also the most frequent litigant. The power to influence decisions by administrative means must be curtailed to maintain public faith in the independence of the judiciary.

Fourth, respect for judicial independence requires a merit-based appointments process that 'safeguard[s] against judicial appointments for improper motives'.[35] Public confidence in the judiciary would suffer if judges were appointed for partisan political reasons or at the bidding of the rich and powerful.

Implicit in judicial independence is the need to maintain a separation between the judiciary on the one hand and the executive and legislative branches of government on the other.[36] The separation of the judiciary from the executive and legislative branches is a central feature of the rule of law, the constitutional ideal that the affairs of government are to be conducted according to the law and the constitution as interpreted and applied by an independent judiciary.[37] While separation of powers is an American doctrine not fully embraced by the British constitution, recent constitutional reforms rest on the need to maintain a clear line between the legislative and executive functions of government and the

---

[33] www.un.org/ruleoflaw/blog/document/basic-principles-on-the-independence-of-the-judiciary/.
[34] *Valente v The Queen* [1985] 2 SCR 673.
[35] United Nations Basic Principles, Art 10.
[36] *Reference re Remuneration of Judges of the Provincial Court (PEI)* [1997] 3 SCR 3, para 125.
[37] ibid para 10.

judiciary. Particularly notable was the creation of the Supreme Court and the changes to the office of the Lord Chancellor.

Until 2009, the United Kingdom's court of last resort was the Appellate Committee of the House of Lords. The members of the Appellate Committee were all senior and highly qualified judges, but they sat and decided cases in their capacity as members of the House of Lords. While, in practice, that arrangement fully respected judicial independence, it fell well short in appearance. The creation of a new Supreme Court, completely separate and independent from parliament and the legislative branch, established judicial independence in the letter as well as the spirit of the law.[38]

The same package of reforms completely redefined the office of Lord Chancellor. Until 2007, the Lord Chancellor stood at the head of the judiciary, but at the same time was a member of cabinet and presided over sittings of the House of Lords. Most Lord Chancellors regularly sat as judges in the Appellate Committee of the House of Lords. The Lord Chancellor was responsible for making judicial appointments and for dealing with judicial misconduct. While this arrangement worked well for a very long time, that depended upon a subtle understanding of the purpose and limits of the office that was not captured in positive law. The office has been radically altered. The Lord Chancellor has been stripped of judicial power, judicial appointments are controlled by the Judicial Appointments Commission and the Lord Chancellor occupies a role more akin to that of a minister of justice.[39] However, the Lord Chancellor remains subject to the obligation to uphold the independence of the judiciary.[40]

These reforms reflected the importance attached to judicial independence in the United Kingdom. Judicial independence has been a centrepiece of the Untited Kingdom's constitutional arrangements since 1701 but until 2005, there were historical anomalies in the letter of the law with respect to the apex court and the head of the judiciary. Those anomalies have now been removed and the current arrangements respect both the letter and the spirit of judicial independence.

VII. JUDICIAL INDEPENDENCE: A MEANS TO AN END

I realise that judicial independence sounds very good for judges – a secure job with a secure salary and control over one's work is beyond the dreams of most members of society. I also recognise that some judges make the mistake of seeing judicial independence as a charter of rights for judges. That is quite wrong. Judicial independence is instrumental, it is not valued for its own sake

---

[38] Constitutional Reform Act 2005, Part 3, s 23.
[39] ibid Part 2.
[40] Constitutional Reform Act 2005, s 3(1). For discussion of how the Lord Chancellor carries out this role, see G Gee, 'Defending Judicial Independence in the British Constitution' in Dodek and Sossin (n 15).

and it does not exist to benefit judges. Guaranteeing judicial independence has the *effect* of conferring significant legal rights on judges, but that is not its *purpose*. As one commentator observed, 'we value and stress judicial independence for what is assures to the public, not for what it grants judges themselves'.[41] Protecting judicial independence is simply a means to a very different end.[42] Judicial independence serves to secure the institutional arrangements required to ensure that judges decide cases on the basis of the evidence and the law without interference from powerful forces or the swings of public passion. Tenure of office, security of remuneration and control over judicial assignments are guaranteed to judges so that they can, both in fact and in appearance, without fear or favour, render impartial justice according to law.

VIII. THE CONSTRAINTS JUDICIAL INDEPENDENCE IMPOSES ON JUDGES

Although judicial independence certainly benefits judges, those benefits do come with a cost. Judicial independence implicitly imposes significant duties and limitations upon judges. To carry out their role and to occupy their place apart, judges have to refrain from the activities of engaged citizenship. If judges are to be independent, they must accept the curtailment of their right to freedom of expression and their right to participate in ordinary political activity or engage in debate on matters of public interest. At one time, under the highly restrictive Kilmuir Rules,[43] judges were forbidden from saying anything: 'every utterance which [the judge] makes in public except in the course of the actual performance of his judicial duties, must necessarily bring him within the focus of public criticism'. This has been relaxed and judges are now permitted to speak in public outside the courtroom, but restrictions remain. They 'must avoid public statements either on general issues or particular cases which cast any doubt on their complete impartiality, and above all, they should avoid any involvement either direct or indirect, in issues which are or might become politically controversial'.[44] The price of judicial independence remains judicial silence on controversial matters.

On the bench, judges must act according to the very principles judicial independence is intended to protect. Judicial independence does not imply that judges are free to decide cases on a whim or on the basis of their personal views.

---

[41] G Watson, 'The Judge and Court Administration' in *The Canadian Judiciary* (Toronto, Osgoode, 1976) 183.

[42] *R v Lippé* [1991] 2 SCR 114, 139: 'judicial independence is but a "means" to this "end". ... Independence is the cornerstone, a necessary prerequisite, for judicial impartiality.'

[43] A Barnett, 'Judges and the Media – The Kilmuir Rules' [1986] *PL* 383, 384–85.

[44] Lord MacKay of Clashfern, *The Administration of Justice* (London, Stevens & Co, 1993) 25–26. For further discussion, see Lord Neuberger of Abbotsbury MR, 'Where Angels Fear to Tread', Holdsworth Club 2012 Presidential Address, 2 March 2012, www.judiciary.uk/wp-content/uploads/JCO/Documents/Speeches/mr-speech-holdsworth-lecture-2012.pdf.

It exists to ensure the opposite, namely that judges strive to decide according to relevant evidence and the law. Judges must accept and respect that rationale. Judges in the UK take an oath to 'do right to all manner of people after the laws and usages of this realm, without fear or favour, affection or ill will'.[45] A judge is not free to decide a case on the basis of what seems to the judge, all things considered, to be the best possible outcome. The judge is not allowed to consider all things. The judge is to consider only those things that have a sufficient legal pedigree, even if this requires the judge to decide the case in a way that does not accord with the his/her personal or political views. Judicial independence protects the rule of law not the rule of judges. Judges who fail to follow their oaths and who decide cases on the basis of personal views or factors extraneous to the evidence and the law act contrary to and undermine the principle of judicial independence.

I would be very concerned about a judge who has never felt compelled to decide a case in a way that goes against the judge's personal views. That is simply an unpleasant but familiar part of the job. We are prepared to put our personal views to one side because that is what we have promised and because, at the end of the day, we must accept that it is necessary to tolerate occasional outcomes that we personally regard as wrong or unjust in order to preserve the overarching ideal of a legal order that exists separately and independently from the personal views of judges.

In their private lives, judges must avoid controversy or any hint of dishonesty. The Supreme Court of Canada has described the judicial function as 'absolutely unique' with the judge as 'the pillar of our entire justice system'. The public 'demand[s] virtually irreproachable conduct from anyone performing a judicial function'.[46] This high standard necessarily involves 'a certain loss of freedom' on the part of judges to pursue goals and objectives that are open to persons who are not judges.[47] Judges are not permitted to engage in business or undertake any other form of employment. Judges may engage in civic, charitable and religious activities, but are cautioned to 'avoid any activity or association that could reflect adversely on their impartiality or interfere with the performance of judicial duties'.[48] Judges may not solicit funds, even for charitable causes,[49] nor may they be involved in organisations likely to be engaged in litigation. They must refrain from partisan political activity or attending political gatherings.

These restrictions on judges are natural corollaries of judicial independence. They are the conditions required to ensure that judicial independence and impartiality is maintained both in fact and in appearance.

---

[45] www.judiciary.uk/about-the-judiciary/the-judiciary-the-government-and-the-constitution/oaths/
[46] *Therrien (Re)*, 2001 SCC 35, paras 108 and 109.
[47] ibid para 111.
[48] Canadian Judicial Council, *Ethical Principles for Judges* (Ottawa, Canadian Judicial Council, 2004) Principle 6.C.1(a), 28.
[49] ibid Principle 6.C.1(b), 28.

IX. THE LIMITS OF JUDICIAL INDEPENDENCE

Judges must realise that the protection of judicial independence does not provide them with an inexhaustible well of support. The protection of judicial independence is contingent upon judges remaining within the broad limits inherent in the judicial role. If they do, they can count on what political scientists refer to as 'diffuse support' for the judiciary as general principle. Diffuse support will persist in the face of an unpopular decision where 'specific support' is lacking.[50] However, the more the judges push the limits of judicial power, the more they are likely to encounter challenges to the idea of judicial independence. Judicial decisions on matters raising contentions moral and social issues such as abortion, physician-assisted death, prostitution, government-funded healthcare and social welfare schemes take courts into territory not contemplated when judicial independence was established as an essential element of constitutional democracy. This is not the place to argue the propriety of judicial review in these contentious areas, only to note that an adverse knock-on effect on public attitudes towards judicial independence may be expected. As Beatson LJ put it in relation to judicial independence, the more judges engage in issues of public policy, the greater the risk 'that the judiciary will be seen by others, in particular the media used to painting issues in stark colours, as having policy preferences' and the more they 'will be seen as just another "player" in the political and policy-formation processes'.[51] The more they make decisions not clearly rooted in the text of the constitution, past judicial practice and precedent, the more likely they are to encounter resistance from politicians, anxious to guard their turf, and from the public, sceptical of claims of judicial neutrality and objectivity. The closer judges hew to adjudication on matters traditionally seen as falling within the province of the judiciary, the more they can expect judicial independence to be respected.

This does not mean that for judicial independence to survive, judges should become timorous souls, reluctant to defend human rights out of fear of likely criticism. It does mean, however, that judges should ensure that their decisions are well supported by legal principles rather than their personal or political preferences. Like others who wield public power, judges will get the respect they deserve. The power of judicial review should always be exercised with humility and careful attention to the inherent institutional limits of courts as policy-makers.

X. JUDICIAL ACCOUNTABILITY

Judicial independence does not render judges unaccountable for the manner in which they perform their duties. Judicial independence and judicial accountability

---

[50] SB Burbank, "Reconsidering Judicial Independence: Forty-Five Years in the Trenches and in the Tower", https:ssrn.com/abstract=3373992, 12–13.

[51] Sir Jack Beatson, 'Judicial Independence and Accountability: Pressures and Opportunities', Nottingham Trent University (16 April 2008) www.judiciary.uk/wp-content/uploads/JCO/Documents/Speeches/beatsonj040608.pdf.

are really two sides of the same coin. Judicial independence protects judges from removal from office because of unpopular decisions, but that does not mean that the judiciary can escape the scrutiny to which other public officials are exposed. With independence comes accountability.

Judicial independence was hotly contested during the debates over the US Constitution. One critic counselled against making judges 'independent of the people, of the legislature, and of every power under heaven' because individuals 'placed in this situation will generally soon feel themselves independent of heaven itself'.[52] This view has not faded with the passage of time. Popular opinion is increasingly sceptical of those who have and exercise authority, and judges cannot escape public scrutiny. The modern culture of transparency demands justification from all who wield power and the demand for transparency extends to judges and judicial power. The maintenance of judicial independence is contingent upon measures to ensure judicial accountability.

A litigant, or indeed any member of the public, may lay a complaint against a judge for misconduct in office. This is an important feature of judicial accountability. Judges are intensely concerned about any public criticism and, no doubt, the very threat of a complaint is enough to keep most judges in line. On the other hand, it would be wrong to look to complaints of judicial misconduct as the sole means of ensuring judicial accountability. Complaints only deal with misconduct that is so seriously contrary to the impartiality, integrity and independence of the judiciary that it has undermined the public's confidence in the ability of the judge to perform the duties of office or in the administration of justice generally.[53] More than a complaints procedure is required to ensure judicial accountability.

The first such measure is the open court principle: in the frequently quoted words of a leading English case, 'justice must not only be done, it must also be seen to be done'.[54] The open court principle ensures that there is no secret justice and that the work of judges is transparent. It means that, barring exceptional circumstances, the courts are open to public view and, in particular, the media. In the leading English case,[55] reference was made to the writings of Jeremy Bentham who famously wrote: 'In the darkness of secrecy, sinister interest and evil in every shape have full swing. ... Where there is no publicity there is no justice.' Bentham also argued: 'Publicity is the very soul of justice. ... It keeps the judge himself while trying under trial.' Open courts, exposing the work of the courts to the public and keeping the judge 'under trial' serve as guarantees of judicial accountability.

---

[52] Quoted in *Oxford Handbook of Law and Politics* (Oxford, Oxford University Press, 2008) 101.

[53] *Therrien v Minister of Justice et al* 2001 SCC 35; *Moreau–Berube v New Brunswick (Judicial Council)* 2002 SCC 11; *Re Baldwin* (10 May 2002) Ontario Judicial Council, *Re McLeod* (20 December 2018) Ontario Judicial Council, www.ontariocourts.ca/ocj/ojc/public-hearings-decisions/.

[54] *R v Sussex Justices, ex parte McCarthy* [1924] 1 KB 256.

[55] *Scott v Scott*, [1913] AC 419, 477.

Related to the open court principle is the requirement for reasoned decisions.[56] Judges are not permitted simply to announce their decisions like oracles with mystical authority. Judges are required to explain their decisions by giving reasons for judgments, exposing to the litigants, to the higher courts and to the public the path they have taken to arrive at a decision. The requirement of reasoned decisions is the way the legal system enforces the obligation of judges to base their decisions on the law and not on their personal views or opinions. If the judge cannot provide a reasoned justification for the decision, the decision may be set aside on appeal and will be subjected to professional and public scrutiny and criticism.

Requiring reasons makes judges accountable to three audiences.

First and foremost are the parties to the dispute. They are entitled as a matter of simple justice to an explanation of why one has won the case and the other has lost. Judges frequently say that the most important person to think of when writing reason is the losing party. When judges give their reasons, they are speaking to the parties, and in particular, the losing party. As an English judge, renowned for his engaging and accessible style of judicial writing, observed: reasons give 'proof' that the judge 'has heard and considered the evidence and arguments' and that the judge 'has not taken extraneous considerations into account'.[57]

The second audience, for all but judges on apex courts, is the appellate court. Judges know that their decisions may be appealed and set aside if they do not follow the law. Judges are obliged to explain their decisions in a manner that facilitates appellate review. They are obliged to explain precisely why they decided the case as they did so that the appellate can exercise its oversight role and ensure that the decision comports with the law.

While the decisions of apex court judges are not subject to appeal, they are subject to minute and intense scrutiny from the third audience, the public, the media, the legal profession and legal scholars. This intense focus on the decisions of apex courts arguably makes them even more accountable than the lower courts despite the absence of an appeal. As a Canadian legal scholar observed: 'reasons provide a basis for ... public and political debate about the justice of a particular decision and of the underlying law that authorized it'.[58] All judges have to be mindful that the integrity and authority of the courts will suffer if their decisions are perceived as not being based upon legally acceptable principles. The public is entitled to an explanation of how and why judicial power was exercised.

---

[56] Sharpe (n 3) 134–45.
[57] A Denning, *The Road to Justice* (London, Stevens & Sons, 1955) 29.
[58] H Stewart, 'The Trial Judge's Duty to Give Reasons for Judgment in Criminal Cases' (2010) 14 *Crim LR* 19, 23.

Reasons for judicial decisions are necessary to bridge the gap between judicial power and democratic legitimacy: reasons require unelected judges to demonstrate to the public that the judicial process is legitimate and based on sound principle and rationality. By providing reasons, judges expose to public view the basis for their decisions and provide the means for public scrutiny, accountability and, where appropriate, criticism.

The obligation to provide reasons fosters public confidence in the judicial process by forcing judges to be transparent. The 'legal culture of justification'[59] comports with the more general culture of justification that pervades modern democratic life.[60] Reasons shed light on why a decision was made and that, in turn, assures the public that the decision was not arbitrary. The Supreme Court of Canada sees the need to provide reasoned judgments as 'central to the legitimacy of judicial institutions in the eyes of the public'.[61]

In my view, the modern culture of transparency calls for courts and judges to take active steps to ensure their work and their decisions are understood by the public. Apex courts have adopted proactive communications policies that enhance public understanding of their work.[62] In both Canada and the United Kingdom, oral argument of appeals is live-streamed. Media relations officers can assist journalists tasked with having to issue on-the-spot reports of complex decisions by providing press summaries or briefings. Judges have engaged in public education and participated in publicly broadcast press interviews, some of which involve tough questioning.[63] These are healthy steps that recognise the public's interest in judicial proceedings and the public's right to know how the courts operate and who the judges are.

XI. ATTACKS ON THE JUDICIARY

Judges are human and do not like to be publicly criticised for doing their job. Because our tradition of judicial independence precludes judges from responding to public criticism, they feel vulnerable to public attack. They cannot respond to public criticism and must depend upon others to defend them from unjustified attacks. But judges must accept that they work in an open society, that they exercise public power and that they are subject to public scrutiny.

---

[59] D Dyzenhaus, 'The Politics of Deference: Judicial Review and Democracy' in M Taggart (ed), *The Province of Administrative Law* (Oxford, Hart Publishing, 1997) 279–307.

[60] J Rawls, *A Theory of Justice* (Cambridge, MA, Harvard University Press, 1971) 133.

[61] *R v Sheppard* 2002 SCC 26, para 5.

[62] Lord Reed, 'The Courts and the Public: Accessibility and Communication' Canadian Institute for Advance Legal Studies 'Cambridge Lectures' (5 July 2019); Chief Justice Beverley McLachlin, 'The Relationship Between the Courts and the Media', 31 January 2012, www.scc-csc.ca/judges-juges/spe-dis/bm-2012-01-31-eng.aspx.

[63] See eg Lady Hale's BBC *HARDtalk* interview, www.bbc.co.uk/programmes/w3csy9dg.

The *Daily Mail*'s infamous 4 November 2016 'Enemies of the People' headline serves as an extreme example of the type of public vilification that judges fear. Three senior and highly respected judges were condemned for ruling that the government would require the consent of parliament before it could trigger Britain's departure from the European Union. I certainly do not condone that headline or the failure of the Lord Chancellor and the government to defend the judiciary from a scurrilous attack. Nor do I doubt that the attack had the capacity to corrode public confidence in the judiciary. However, I think it is very important for judges to keep public criticism of this kind in proper perspective. We enjoy the prestige and the perks of judicial office and, almost all of the time, we enjoy the respect of the public. We must accept that we occupy a public office that confers upon us significant powers and that, in the age of transparency, we are accountable for the manner in which we exercise those powers. Judicial independence does not shield us from public scrutiny. Nor should it. The public is entitled to know what we do, why we have done it and to let us know if they disagree. It takes courage to make a decision we know will be unpopular and that is precisely why we are given the protection of judicial independence. There are times when judges must simply grin and bear the sting of public criticism. Judicial independence cannot spare judges from the pain of public censure but it should fortify their determination to decide according to the law.

2

Judicial Independence and Perceptions of Legitimacy

NICK FRIEDMAN

THE PROTECTION OF judicial independence is a shared enterprise. The executive, the legislature, the media, the academy and the public all have roles to play in safeguarding the courts' ability to restrain abuses of government power and settle disputes without fear or favour. The courts are not passive participants in this endeavour. In this chapter, I focus on what they themselves can do to protect their own independence. I argue that one of the most powerful ways they can do so is to cultivate the public's perception of their legitimacy, and I sketch three strategies by which they might achieve this goal.

My argument is as follows. In section I, I discuss the institutional weakness of courts relative to the other branches of government and explain why this threatens their independence. In light of this weakness, I argue in section II that the judiciary's independence turns crucially on the public's perception of its legitimacy. In section III, I discuss a critical feature of judicial decision-making that figures prominently in arguments about its legitimacy, namely its dependence on moral and political evaluation. In section IV, I define and develop three strategies by which courts can cultivate their legitimacy in the eyes of the public, which I call the strategies of transparency, restraint and popularity. These strategies are distinguished from each other by the way that each communicates or depends on the evaluative nature of judicial decision. I conclude with some reflections on the promise and perils that these strategies may hold for judicial independence.

Two preliminary matters are in order. The first concerns the nature of judicial independence. For present purposes, I adopt a common understanding of judicial independence as a degree of freedom, in deciding a case, from control by or pressure from the other branches of government, litigants, and the public at large.[1] So understood, judicial independence encompasses a judge's state of mind while deciding a case, as well as the material institutional conditions

---

[1] F Cross, 'Judicial Independence' in G Caldeira et al (eds), *Oxford Handbook of Law and Politics* (Oxford, Oxford University Press, 2008) 558, 561; TS Clark, *The Limits of Judicial Independence* (Cambridge, Cambridge University Press, 2010) 11.

required to foster that mental state, including security of tenure, financial security and some judicial control over the administration of courts.

The second concerns the nature of legitimacy, which might be understood normatively or empirically. As a normative concept, legitimacy is concerned with the justification of judicial decision-making according to principles of political morality, which includes articulating the conditions and limits of its proper exercise. (Of course, theorists disagree about which moral principles are relevant and the relative weight they bear.) One might apply these principles to a specific judicial decision (and so say that the decision is or is not legitimate), or to a more general justification of the existence and structure of judicial decision-making power in some legal system (and so say that the system's judiciary is or is not legitimate). Either way, the normative concept implies that a judicial decision, or judicial authority more broadly, might be legitimate even if the public broadly thinks it is not.

As an empirical concept, legitimacy is concerned with the public's *perception* of whether judicial decision-making is justified. By this measure, judicial decision-making is not legitimate unless the public broadly agrees that it is. As with the normative concept, citizens surely have diverse perceptions of what confers legitimacy on an institution. Furthermore, again like the normative concept, one can distinguish between a perception that a particular decision is justified – commonly described as 'specific support' or 'satisfaction with policy outputs' – and a broader perception – commonly described as 'diffuse support' or 'institutional loyalty' – that the existence, structure and longer-term exercise of judicial decision-making power is justified, even if it occasionally results in decisions that the public dislikes.[2] One relatively concrete measure of this broader perception, which is commonly relied on by political scientists and on which I will rely here, is 'institutional commitment'; that is, the public's 'willingness to maintain and defend the structures or norms of a regime even if they produce unfavorable consequences'.[3] In studies of judicial legitimacy, evidence for this willingness is typically drawn from opinion surveys asking whether the public would accept fundamental changes to the courts' role or structure, such as whether courts should be abolished, or have their powers or jurisdiction curtailed, or whether they can be trusted to make good decisions.[4] There is strong multi-country evidence, including in the United Kingdom, that large

---

[2] JL Gibson, GA Caldeira and LK Spence, 'Measuring Attitudes Toward the United States Supreme Court' (2003) 47 *American Journal of Political Science* 354, 356; JL Gibson and GA Caldeira, 'Blacks and the United States Supreme Court: Models of Diffuse Support' (1992) 54 *Journal of Politics* 1120, 1121; GA Caldeira and JL Gibson, 'The Etiology of Public Support for the Supreme Court' (1992) 36 *American Journal of Political Science* 635, 637. See also Clark (n 1) 17. See also D Easton, *A Systems Analysis of Political Life* (New York, Wiley 1965) 273.

[3] D Easton, 'A Re-assessment of the Concept of Political Support' (1975) 5 *British Journal of Political Science* 435, 451; Gibson and Caldeira (n 2) 1121.

[4] Gibson and Caldeira (n 2) 1127–30; J Gibson et al, 'On the Legitimacy of National High Courts' (1998) 92 *American Political Science* 343.

portions of the public are unwilling to accept such changes to their courts.[5] One can infer from this some measure of legitimacy afforded to the judiciary as an institution. As I discuss below, political scientists frequently test the correlation between such unwillingness and other beliefs or knowledge expressed by survey participants, and in that way try to understand some determinants of the public's perceptions of judicial legitimacy.

One can evaluate judicial decision-making against either the normative or empirical concept; that is, one can assess the gap between what courts actually do and what is legitimate for them to do, either according to principles of political morality or to the opinions of the spectating public. In what follows, I largely forgo normative evaluation. I consider judicial decision-making in light of the public's perception of its legitimacy, understood (as in the empirical work on which I draw) as expressed unwillingness to accept fundamental changes to the structure and powers of the courts. In the context of judicial independence, this concept of legitimacy is arguably the more fundamental, since it bears directly on whether the public will tolerate limitations by other branches of government on a judge's freedom to decide.

I. THE INSTITUTIONAL WEAKNESS OF COURTS

All political institutions are and must be concerned with their perceived legitimacy. Legitimacy is a special concern for courts, however, because of their institutional weakness relative to the other branches of government.

First, courts lack sharp institutional tools for imposing their will on those branches or the citizenry at large. The executive, as Alexander Hamilton argues in *The Federalist Papers*, 'holds the sword of the community', while the legislature 'not only commands the purse, but prescribes the rules by which the duties and rights of every citizen are to be regulated'.[6] The judiciary, by contrast, has 'merely judgment'.[7] It 'has no influence over either the sword or the purse; no direction either of the strength or of the wealth of the society; and can take no active resolution whatever'.[8] By today's standards, Hamilton overstates his case: courts frequently do influence the government's policing and spending powers; and some of the most potent arguments in favour of judicial power concern its potential contribution to improving social conditions and redistributing wealth. However, Hamilton rightly notes that courts can accomplish none of this without the executive's willingness to enforce their orders and the legislature's willingness to finance them – especially orders which are adverse to those

---

[5] Gibson et al (n 4).

[6] A Hamilton, 'The Judiciary Department' (*Federalist No 78*) in A Hamilton et al, *The Federalist Papers* (New York, Palgrave Macmillan, 2009) 236.

[7] ibid.

[8] ibid.

bodies or the political interests of those currently populating them.[9] On account of this incapacity, Hamilton famously describes the courts as the 'least danger- ous' branch of government.[10]

Second, while courts cannot impose their will on anyone without the coop- eration of the other branches, they are liable to have the will of those branches imposed on them. In a government based on the separation of powers, judi- cial authority is subject to a range of checks and balances by the executive and legislature. The details differ among jurisdictions, but they typically include the appointment and removal of judges, control over the courts' jurisdiction, size and budget, and setting the conditions of and eligibility criteria for judicial service.

In stable democracies, the exercise of these powers to check judicial over- reach evidences the separation of powers in action, as when Franklin Roosevelt halted the US Supreme Court's aggressive invalidation of his New Deal legisla- tive programme by threating to increase the court's size and fill it with liberals. However, as demonstrated by recent movements to suppress judicial independ- ence in Poland, Hungary and elsewhere, these same powers are vulnerable to abuse by authoritarian-leaning executives.[11] For the reasons discussed above, the courts have few means by which to resist this improper interference with their functions. Thus, while it is important that all three branches of government have some independence from one another, there is good reason to focus on the inde- pendence of the courts.

Third, the source of the courts' legitimacy (in both the normative and empir- ical senses) is more tenuous than it is for the other branches because judges are not elected by the people. This concern, which is of special relevance for present purposes, raises what Alexander Bickel calls the 'counter-majoritarian difficulty'.[12] The difficulty arises when an unelected judge 'declares unconstitu- tional a legislative act or the action of an elected executive'.[13] In such cases, the judge 'exercises control, not in behalf of the prevailing majority, but against it'.[14]

Since Bickel, the charge of counter-majoritarianism has been central to debates on the legitimacy of judicial review.[15] Jeremy Waldron, for example, argues that the practice is

> politically illegitimate, so far as democratic values are concerned: By privileging majority voting among a small number of unelected and unaccountable judges,

---

[9] ibid.

[10] ibid.

[11] KL Scheppele, 'Autocratic Legalism Symposium: The Limits of Constitutionalism – A Global Perspective' (2018) 85 *University of Chicago Law Review* 545, 551–53.

[12] AM Bickel, *The Least Dangerous Branch: The Supreme Court at the Bar of Politics* (Indianapolis, Bobbs-Merrill, 1962) 16.

[13] ibid 16–17.

[14] ibid 17.

[15] B Friedman, 'The Birth of an Academic Obsession: The History of the Countermajoritarian Difficulty, Part Five' (2002) 112 *Yale Law Journal* 153.

it disenfranchises ordinary citizens and brushes aside cherished principles of representation and political equality in the final resolution of issues about rights.[16]

Importantly, Waldron's target is the kind of strong-form, human-rights-based judicial invalidation of legislation found in the United States, Canada and South Africa. However, similar normative claims have been asserted with respect to the United Kingdom, often repackaged (under the banner of parliamentary sovereignty) as descriptive claims of positive constitutional law.[17] Here, the charge of illegitimacy is levelled not only at the 'disapplication' or reading down of domestic legislation pursuant to the UK's European obligations, but also at the invalidation of executive action, especially in areas with strong public policy dimensions or otherwise thought to be the peculiar responsibility of democratically accountable actors. As indicated by the conservative scholarly and public reactions to the Supreme Court's judgments in the *Miller* litigation – in which the court successively ruled (not on human rights grounds) that the government could not withdraw from the European Union without parliament's approval and declared the subsequent prorogation of parliament unlawful – the 'anti-democratic' charge is frequently levelled at judicial review as such, whether rights-based or not, whether aimed at legislation or executive action.[18]

Of course, the courts' democratic credentials are more complex than this. John Hart Ely, for example, argues that judicial review actually promotes democracy when it is deployed to protect equal rights of participation in the political process.[19] Sandra Fredman extends this point, arguing that courts support democratic accountability by forcing elected representatives to publicly explain and justify their actions, as well as by 'steering decision-making away from interest bargaining towards value-oriented deliberation'.[20] In a similar

---

[16] J Waldron, 'The Core of the Case against Judicial Review' (2006) 115 *Yale Law Journal* 1346, 1353. See also HLA Hart, 'American Jurisprudence Through English Eyes: The Nightmare and the Noble Dream' (1976) 11 *Georgia Law Review* 969, 971 (arguing that judicial review is 'particularly hard to justify in a democracy').

[17] See eg R Ekins, 'Protecting the Constitution – How and Why Parliament Should Limit Judicial Power' (Policy Exchange 2019) https://policyexchange.org.uk/wp-content/uploads/2020/01/Protecting-the-Constitution.pdf, accessed 7 August 2020. In other words, the claim that judicial review is illegitimate as a matter of political morality becomes (or reinforces) a claim that judicial review (or some form of it) violates the ultimate principle of the UK's constitution, namely parliamentary sovereignty. See also J Sumption, *Trials of the State: Law and the Decline of Politics* (London, Profile Books, 2020).

[18] *R (Miller) v Secretary of State for Exiting the European Union* [2017] UKSC 5, [2017] 2 WLR 583; *R (Miller) v Prime Minister* [2019] UKSC 41, [2019] 3 WLR 589. For an example of such scholarly reaction, see R Ekins and G Gee, *Miller, Constitutional Realism and the Politics of Brexit* (Oxford, Hart Publishing, 2018) 249 (describing the litigation as an 'attempt by members of the political and legal elite to use the courts to delay political action implementing the result of the referendum'). For an exemplary media reaction, see J Slack, 'Enemies of the People' *Daily Mail*, 3 November 2016, www.dailymail.co.uk/news/article-3903436/Enemies-people-Fury-touch-judges-defied-17-4m-Brexit-voters-trigger-constitutional-crisis.html.

[19] JH Ely, *Democracy and Distrust: A Theory of Judicial Review* (Cambridge, MA, Harvard University Press, 1980).

[20] S Fredman, *Human Rights Transformed: Positive Rights and Positive Duties* (Oxford, Oxford University Press, 2008) 105.

vein, Ronald Dworkin argues that judicial review provokes and frames a well-informed national debate – of the kind that is prized by republican ideals of government – about important choices of political morality.[21] As a general matter (and as these competing accounts suggest), the case against judicial review turns on particular, contestable and sometimes unstated understandings of the democratic ideal.

At bottom, however, these democratic defences of judicial authority only take us so far. In Bickel's words, 'nothing in the[se] further complexities and perplexities of the system ... can alter the essential reality' that courts suffer from some form of democratic deficit, which is at its widest when they invalidate legislative and executive action.[22] This deficit is precisely what makes judges vulnerable to headlines calling them 'enemies of the people',[23] and it is the reason why courts have to be critically concerned with shoring up their institutional power by other means. As I discuss next, one of their best tools for that purpose is to cultivate the public's perception of their legitimacy.

The foregoing discussion of the judiciary's relative institutional weakness among the branches of government should not be read as denying that courts exercise incredible power. It is true, as Bickel put it, that '[t]he least dangerous branch of the American government is the most extraordinarily powerful court of law the world has ever known'.[24] Nor should it suggest that courts are incapable of their own forms of overreach. It does, however, counsel caution about potentially misleading claims that we are living in an age of 'juristrocracy'[25] or 'judicial supremacy'.[26] Notwithstanding the substantial and contingent power that some courts have accumulated at certain times in this or that legal system, this locution sits uneasily with the vulnerability of courts in the face of strong political headwinds, which we have seen both within the United Kingdom and without. The fact is that courts are institutionally quite weak, and judges themselves are painfully aware of this.

II. INDEPENDENCE THROUGH LEGITIMACY

In light of these institutional weaknesses, one may wonder why the executive and legislature ever respect – as they frequently do in liberal constitutional democracies – the independence of the courts. The literature offers two sets

---

[21] R Dworkin, *Freedom's Law: The Moral Reading of the American Constitution* (Oxford, Oxford University Press, 1996) 345.

[22] Bickel (n 12) 17–18.

[23] Slack (n 17).

[24] Bickel (n 12) 1.

[25] R Hirschl, *Towards Juristocracy: The Origins and Consequences of the New Constitutionalism* (Cambridge, MA, Harvard University Press, 2004).

[26] LD Kramer, 'Judicial Supremacy and the End of Judicial Restraint' (2012) 100 *California Law Review* 621; R Ekins, 'Judicial Supremacy and the Rule of Law' (2003) 119 *LQR* 127.

of explanations, each of which complicates the rough picture of judicial independence that I described at the outset: they reveal, somewhat ironically, that a court's independence from the other branches of government and the public depends on how well it satisfies certain expectations of those constituencies.

One set of explanations focuses on the political benefits that the judiciary can secure for the other branches of government.[27] For example, elected officials may delegate to the courts the resolution of 'political controversies that they cannot or would rather not address'.[28] Alternatively, the legislature may be unsure ex ante about the impact that some rule may have or whether it infringes a complex constitutional principle, and thus may leave it to the constitutional expertise of courts to invalidate such rules ex post, as evidence of their implementation comes to light.[29] Indeed, one of the leading attempts to justify the constitutionality of judicial review of administrative action in the United Kingdom supposes that parliament generally intends for the powers it grants to the executive to be exercised in accordance with the rule of law, but leaves it to the courts to work out the requirements of that ideal on a case-by-case basis.[30] Finally, in the context of competitive democracy, today's governing majority may be willing to accept judicial constraints on its power in the expectation that it will benefit from those constraints in the future when it is in the minority.[31] Indeed, a number of empirical studies demonstrate a strong link between political competition and judicial independence.[32]

It is worth noting two features of the foregoing explanations. First, they are strongest as explanations of why the other branches of government benefit from and comply with certain exercises of judicial power. They are weaker as explanations of why these branches benefit specifically from *independent* judicial power. To be sure, it is clear enough why today's majority, hoping for protection when it is a minority tomorrow, would promote norms against interfering with the courts; it is less clear how such norms benefit a majority that merely delegates to courts certain decisions which, presumably, it would prefer them to resolve on a favourable basis. Second, to the extent that these factors help to secure judicial independence, they suggest that it is contingent on an institutional landscape and political calculations that lie mostly beyond the courts' control.

---

[27] G Vanberg, 'Constitutional Courts in Comparative Perspective: A Theoretical Assessment' (2015) 18 *Annual Review of Political Science* 167, 170–76; K Whittington, 'Legislative Sanctions and the Strategic Environment of Judicial Review' (2003) 1 *ICON* 446.

[28] MA Graber, 'The Nonmajoritarian Difficulty: Legislative Deference to the Judiciary' (1993) 7 *Studies in American Political Development* 35, 36; Whittington (n 27) 455–56.

[29] Whittington (n 27) 451–54; JR Rogers, 'Information and Judicial Review: A Signaling Game of Legislative-Judicial Interaction' (2001) 45 *American Journal of Political Science* 84.

[30] M Elliott, *The Constitutional Foundations of Judicial Review* (Oxford, Hart Publishing, 2001).

[31] JM Ramseyer, 'The Puzzling (In)Dependence of Courts: A Comparative Approach' (1994) 23 *Journal of Legal Studies* 721; Vanberg (n 27) 173–75.

[32] T Ginsburg and M Versteeg, 'Why Do Countries Adopt Constitutional Review?' (2014) 30 *Journal of Law, Economics, and Organization* 587; MC Stephenson, '"When the Devil Turns ...": The Political Foundations of Independent Judicial Review' (2003) 32 *Journal of Legal Studies* 59.

A second set of explanations focuses on the political costs that elected officials incur when they interfere with judicial independence.[33] Of particular relevance here are explanations focused on public support for the courts, understood, as I noted earlier, as unwillingness to accept fundamental changes to their role and structure. If there is widespread unwillingness among the public in this sense – as, in fact, there is in many constitutional democracies[34] – then it will be politically unpopular for the elected branches of government to restrict their power.[35] For this reason, a judiciary seeking to bolster its independence has to be critically concerned with establishing and maintaining the public's perception of its legitimacy.

The literature suggests that this perception is a product of two factors.[36] First, when a court decides a case in a way that the public likes, it experiences a short-term boost in specific support (as described above). If, over time, a court consistently delivers outcomes that are favourable to the public, this builds the court's reservoir of diffuse support or perceived legitimacy.[37] Second, the public's perception of the courts' legitimacy depends on their perception that judges follow fair, impartial and legalistic decision-making procedures.[38] As I discuss later on, there is a deep tension between these sources of perceived legitimacy: the fair, legalistic result may not always accord with the public's view of what justice requires.

Both factors seem to be meaningfully (albeit not completely) within a court's control, though it is not immediately obvious how a court should seek to control them. The first factor suggests that courts can build their institutional support by consistently delivering popular outcomes. However, as I discuss later, it is unclear how judges can learn the public's preferences on salient issues in an appropriate, accurate and timely way. The second factor might suggest that courts can build support for their work by following decision-making procedures that are fair, impartial and legalistic, or at least promoting a perception that their decisions meet these criteria. Interestingly, empirical evidence shows that that public support for courts tends to increase the more the public knows about them.[39] However, the literature is less clear about exactly which knowledge

---

[33] Vanberg (n 27) 176–79.

[34] J Gibson et al, 'On the Legitimacy of National High Courts' (1998) 92 *American Political Science Review* 343.

[35] JA Segal and HJ Spaeth, *The Supreme Court and the Attitudinal Model Revisited* (Cambridge, Cambridge University Press, 2002) 94; G Vanberg, 'Legislative–Judicial Relations: A Game-Theoretic Approach to Constitutional Review' (2001) 45 *American Journal of Political Science* 346, 347.

[36] JD Ura and A Higgins Merrill, 'The Supreme Court and Public Opinion' in L Epstein and SA Lindquist (eds), *The Oxford Handbook of US Judicial Behavior* (Oxford, Oxford University Press, 2017) 434, 442–43; VA Baird, 'Building Institutional Legitimacy: The Role of Procedural Justice' (2001) 54 *Political Research Quarterly* 333.

[37] Ura and Merrill (n 36) 434, 442–43.

[38] Vanberg (n 27) 179; Baird (n 36); Gibson et al (n 34) 345; TR Tyler and K Rasinski, 'Procedural Justice, Institutional Legitimacy, and the Acceptance of Unpopular US Supreme Court Decisions: A Reply to Gibson' (1991) 25 *Law & Society Review* 621, 621–22.

[39] Caldeira and Gibson (n 2).

might produce this result. Indeed, increasing awareness of judicial practices will build legitimacy only if those practices are favoured by the public.[40] If those practices are instead perceived as unfair, subjective or political, then the courts might do better with less transparency and more myth-building.[41]

As this last point highlights, the public's support depends not only on what courts actually do, but also on what they say about what they do. I tackle the former issue next and turn to the latter issue thereafter.

III. THE NATURE OF ADJUDICATION

It was common in the days of Blackstone and Coke to say that judges never make the law; they merely find the law and declare what it has always been.[42] This model of adjudication, variously known as the 'declaratory theory' or the doctrine of 'formalism', posits that formal textual sources like statutes and precedent overwhelmingly control the result in legal disputes, such that the judge's job is simply to find those sources, subject them to accepted techniques of statutory interpretation and legal reasoning to determine what the applicable rule, properly understood, has always been, and apply that rule to the facts.[43] On this view, language is determinative; judicial reliance on non-legal norms, such as those of morality or politics, is unnecessary and improper.

Towards the end of the nineteenth century John Austin had already begun to denigrate this 'childish fiction employed by our judges, that common law is not made by them, but is a miraculous something made by nobody, existing, I suppose, from eternity and merely declared from time to time'.[44]

However, it was the American Legal Realists, in the first half of the twentieth century, who decisively refuted the declaratory theory. The Realists argued that the law frequently underdetermines the result in legal disputes.[45] This relative indeterminacy has at least two sources. First (and for the Realists, foremost), accepted methods of legal reasoning can be used to generate legitimate but

---

[40] SC Benesh, 'Understanding Public Confidence in American Courts' (2006) 68 *Journal of Politics* 697, 699.

[41] JK Staton, *Judicial Power and Strategic Communication in Mexico* (Cambridge, Cambridge University Press, 2010) 7. See also G Casey, 'The Supreme Court and Myth: An Empirical Investigation' (1973) 8 *Law & Society Review* 385.

[42] W Blackstone, *Commentaries on the Laws of England*, vol 1 (Cavendish, 1766) 69; *Calvin's Case* (1609) 7 Co Rep 1, 77 ER 377, 409.

[43] A Beever, 'The Declaratory Theory of Law' (2013) 33 *OJLS* 421; F Schauer, 'Legal Realism Untamed' (2012) 91 *Texas Law Review* 749, 752–54; B Leiter, 'Legal Formalism and Legal Realism: What Is the Issue?' (2010) 16 *Legal Theory* 111, 111.

[44] J Austin, *Lectures on Jurisprudence, or, The Philosophy of Positive Law*, vol 2, 4th edn, ed S Austin and R Campbell (London, John Murray 1873) 655.

[45] Schauer (n 43) 752–61; B Leiter, 'American Legal Realism' in MP Golding and WA Edmundson (eds), *The Blackwell Guide to the Philosophy of Law and Legal Theory* (Oxford, Blackwell, 2008); H Dagan, 'The Realist Conception of Law' (2007) 57 *University of Toronto Law Journal* 607, 611–17.

conflicting rules from the same legal sources.[46] Karl Llewellyn argued, for example, that any case can be read in either a 'loose' sense – abstracting from its facts to derive a broadly applicable general principle – or in a 'strict' sense – by stipulating detailed factual conditions required to trigger the rule's application, effectively confining the case's holding to its particular facts.[47] Llewellyn similarly argued that judges frequently rely on conflicting canons of interpretation which serve to limit, or alternatively expand, the reach of a statute.[48] As Brian Leiter summarises the Realist view, 'judges respond primarily to the stimulus of the facts of the case'.[49]

Second, language in general, and the rich normative language of the law in particular, is pervaded by vagueness. This is perhaps the view most frequently associated with the Realists (in part because it is the focus of HLA Hart's criticism of them).[50] Max Radin's commentary on statutory interpretation exemplifies the view.[51] For Radin, '[a] statute is ... a statement of a situation, or rather of a group of possible events within a situation, and as such is essentially ambiguous'.[52] Referring to two well-known interpretive techniques, Radin argues that 'to interpret a law by its purposes requires the court to select one of a concatenated sequence of purposes, and this choice is to be determined by motives which are usually suppressed'.[53] And likewise, '[t]o interpret it by its results is to prophesy probable consequences for one or another of several interpretations, and the basis of the calculus is equally undisclosed'.[54]

The upshot of all this is that judges are called on to exercise law-making discretion much more regularly than the declaratory theory supposes, and when they do, they inevitably rely on non-legal considerations.[55] The Realists differ as to the nature of those considerations. One prominent view among them is that judicial discretion is (and ought to be) guided by moral and political norms.[56] These norms are either expressly claimed to be embedded in positive

---

[46] On the prominence of this claim in Realist scholarship, see Leiter (n 45) 51–52; Dagan (n 45) 217.

[47] KN Llewellyn, *The Bramble Bush* (Oxford, Oxford University Press, 2008) 68–72; K Kress, 'Legal Indeterminacy' (1989) 77 *California Law Review* 283, 297–99.

[48] KN Llewellyn, 'Remarks on the Theory of Appellate Decision and the Rules or Canons about How Statutes Are to Be Construed Symposium on Statutory Construction' (1949) 3 *Vanderbilt Law Review* 395, 401–06.

[49] Leiter (n 45) 52 (arguing that the this is the 'Core Claim' uniting the Legal Realists).

[50] HLA Hart, *The Concept of Law*, ed PA Bulloch and J Raz eds, 2nd edn (Oxford, Clarendon Press 1994). Leiter (n 45) argues that this type of indeterminacy was less important to Realists than Hart supposes (63–64).

[51] M Radin, 'Statutory Interpretation' (1929) 43 *Harvard Law Review* 863. See also J Dewey, 'Logical Method and Law' in WW Fisher III et al (eds), *American Legal Realism* (Oxford, Oxford University Press, 1993); Dagan (n 45) 613–17.

[52] Radin (n 51) 868.

[53] ibid 878.

[54] ibid.

[55] Schauer (n 43) 754–56; Leiter (n 43) 112.

[56] Schauer (n 433) 754–55; H Dagan, 'The Real Legacy of American Legal Realism' (2018) 38 *OJLS* 123, 142–43.

legal sources or operate silently in the background as the judge negotiates flexible legal materials to reach the outcome she thinks just. At least as a descriptive matter, that view has been decisively vindicated by contemporary empirical work. There is now an extensive 'attitudinalist' literature demonstrating the influence of a judge's own political ideology on her judicial decision-making.[57] In a well-known study of the House of Lords, for example, David Robertson concluded that the Lords enjoyed wide discretion in their use of legal materials, and that their choice of how to use them was influenced by their personal ideologies.[58]

Since the Realist intervention, the leading figures of Anglo-American jurisprudence have basically agreed that moral and political values play (and ought to play) a role in judicial decision-making. Hart, for instance, concedes that legal language sometimes has an 'open texture', such that 'the law fails to determine an answer either way and so proves partially indeterminate'.[59] Hart argues that the law in such cases is not merely subject to reasonable disagreement but is 'fundamentally incomplete'.[60] In order to decide such cases, a judge must exercise law-making discretion, and when she does, her duty is to 'to make the best moral judgment [s]he can'.[61]

Joseph Raz too, argues that in such 'unregulated disputes ... no particular solution to the dispute is required by law, though the law may ... give some general guidance'.[62] In such cases the court 'makes law by filling in the gaps',[63] and when engaging in such 'law-making judges do rely and should rely on their own moral judgment'.[64] In more recent work, Raz discusses what he calls the 'Janus-faced' quality of legal interpretation: it has both a backwards-looking aspect which 'aim[s] to elucidate the law as it is' and a forward-looking aspect which 'aim[s] to develop and improve it'.[65]

Dworkin, who disagrees with Hart and Raz on most of their major theses about the nature of law, fundamentally agrees with them on this point. For Dworkin, legal interpretation involves a dimension of 'fit', in that it is constrained by 'the brute facts of legal history' such as the specific wording of legislation

---

[57] SA Lindquist and FB Cross, *Measuring Judicial Activism* (Oxford, Oxford University Press, 2009) 40–43; Segal and Spaeth (n 35).

[58] D Robertson, *Judicial Discretion in the House of Lords* (Oxford, Clarendon Press 1998). *Cf* C Hanretty, 'The Decisions and Ideal Points of British Law Lords' (2012) 42 *British Journal of Political Science* 1.

[59] Hart (n 50) 252.

[60] ibid.

[61] ibid 252, 254.

[62] J Raz, *The Authority of Law: Essays on Law and Morality*, 2nd edn (Oxford, Oxford University Press, 2009) 181.

[63] ibid 182.

[64] ibid 199.

[65] J Raz, *Between Authority and Interpretation: On the Theory of Law and Practical Reason* (Oxford, Oxford University Press, 2009) 353–54.

and case law.[66] But it also involves a dimension of 'justification'.[67] When multiple interpretations are consistent with the same legal history, as they often will be, the judge must decide which interpretation shows the law 'in a better light from the standpoint of political morality. His own moral and political convictions are now directly engaged.'[68]

Theorists today disagree about the sources, extent and implications of legal indeterminacy, and about whether and how to constrain certain forms of value-laden decision-making by judges. While formalism (as noted below) has experienced something of a renaissance among conservative scholars and judges in the United Kingdom and the United States, there is a broad consensus among legal scholars that moral and political evaluation are a frequent occurrence in adjudication, so much so that it has become a cliché to remark: 'we are all legal realists now'.[69]

The fact of value-laden law-making in adjudication raises two important questions for the cultivation of judicial legitimacy. The first concerns whether there are techniques of interpretation or legal reasoning that might limit the scope of moral and political evaluation in judicial decisions (to the extent that such evaluation is thought undesirable). The second concerns whether or how judges should convey the role of such evaluation (whatever its scope or desirability) to the public. I explore these controversial matters in the remainder of the chapter.

IV. STRATEGIES FOR CULTIVATING LEGITIMACY

On account of their relative weakness among the branches of government, I have argued that courts must be critically concerned with cultivating the public's perception of their legitimacy. That perception is a product of two key factors: whether the public perceives that the courts follow fair, impartial and legalistic decision-making procedures; and whether the public is consistently pleased by the outcomes that the courts deliver. Since these factors are meaningfully within judicial control, they suggest certain strategies by which the courts can cultivate their legitimacy. In this section, I elaborate these strategies. The first two, transparency and restraint, are primarily public relations strategies which judges can and do pursue in their written judgments

---

[66] R Dworkin, *Law's Empire* (Oxford, Hart Publishing, 1998) 52. See also R Dworkin, *Justice in Robes* (Cambridge, MA, Harvard University Press, 2006) 15.

[67] Dworkin, *Justice in Robes* (n 66) 15. See also Dworkin, *Law's Empire* (n 66) 52, 255–56.

[68] Dworkin, *Law's Empire* (n 66) 256. See also Dworkin, *Justice in Robes* (n 66) 12–15. Dworkin's position is complicated, and placed in conflict with Hart and Raz, by his insistence that these moral principles are necessarily part of the law and that they yield one right answer in every legal dispute. To this extent, as others have noted, Dworkin might be taken as advancing a sophisticated version of the declarative theory. Leiter (n 43) 112.

[69] MS Green, 'Legal Realism as Theory of Law' (2005) 46 *William and Mary Law Review* 1915, 1917.

and extra-judicial statements. They are distinguished from one another by the way that each seeks to convey the role of moral and political evaluation in judicial decision-making. The third strategy, popularity, is primarily focused on the substantive outcome of judicial decisions (though undoubtedly its efficacy depends on this substance being communicated to the public). It not only depends on but aims at a certain kind of political evaluation by judges.

In what follows, I offer certain judicial statements and other empirical evidence as examples of what these strategies might look like in action. Although in some cases judges are surely advocating certain modes of adjudication as part of a conscious strategy to cultivate perceptions of their legitimacy, I do not mean to imply that this is always or even largely so. Undoubtedly many judges who advocate transparency or restraint, or who strive for popularity, do so because of normative beliefs about the legitimacy of judicial power. However, I invite the reader to construe these judicial behaviours in strategic terms, so as to grasp the different means by which judges might consciously seek, should they so wish, to cultivate their legitimacy in the public eye.

1. Transparency

Moral and political evaluation in adjudication does not necessarily mean, in my view, that judicial decision-making is neither impartial nor legalistic (at least not in any thick sense of those terms). Still less does it mean that adjudication is unfair or that judges are unconstrained by legal sources, political pressures and the limiting institutional features of courts. However, the evaluative aspect of judging does raise critical questions about whether my perspective would be broadly shared by the public. The strategy of transparency takes the risk. It not only proclaims the declaratory model a false picture of adjudication, but it advertises value-laden judicial law-making as a virtue.

This strategy is favoured by some on the English bench. In extrajudicial writing some decades ago, Lord Reid famously remarks on

> a time when it was thought almost indecent to suggest that judges make law – they only declare it. Those with a taste for fairy tales seem to have thought that in some Aladdin's cave there is hidden the Common Law in all its splendour and that on a judge's appointment there descends on him knowledge of the magic words Open Sesame. Bad decisions are given when the judge has muddled the password and the wrong door opens. But we do not believe in fairy tales anymore.[70]

Lord Neuberger and Lady Hale are among transparency's more prominent recent advocates.[71] Lord Neuberger argues that '[j]udges are and always have

---

[70] Lord Reid, 'The Judge as Lawmaker' (1972–73) 12 *Journal of the Society of Public Teachers of Law* 22, 22.

[71] Lord Neuberger, '"Judge not, that ye be not judged": Judging Judicial Decision-Making' (FA Mann Lecture, 2015) www.supremecourt.uk/docs/speech-150129.pdf, accessed 8 August 2020.

been lawmakers',[72] and that judges 'must approach the task of judging in a manner which embraces, rather than eschews, our humanity. We should do so more openly', he says, 'and more honestly'.[73] Lady Hale, for her part, recognises that each judge 'comes to the task with a set of values and perspectives that may lead you to pick different bits of the materials to reason towards an outcome'.[74] She argues that these different values contribute positively to adjudication, as '[y]ou will not get the best possible results if everybody comes at the same problem from exactly the same point of view'.[75]

Transparency is commonly advocated by those who subscribe to a 'living' theory of constitutional interpretation, of the kind that is well established in the United States, Canada and the European Court of Human Rights (ECtHR).[76] As articulated by the ECtHR, this doctrine treats constitutional documents (such as the European Convention on Human Rights) as 'living instrument[s] which ... must be interpreted in the light of present-day conditions',[77] not in light of 'what was thought to be acceptable state conduct when the Convention was drafted, or what specific rights the drafters of the Convention intended to protect'.[78] Justice William Brennan – an influential advocate of living constitutionalism in the United States – urged transparency in the doctrine's deployment, arguing that a 'faithful' constitutional interpretation 'must account for the existence of these substantive value choices and must accept the ambiguity inherent in the effort to apply them to modern circumstances'.[79]

---

[72] ibid para 41.

[73] ibid para 54.

[74] Lady Hale, Evidence before the Constitution Committee, Autumn 2011, quoted in A Paterson and C Paterson, 'Guarding the Guardians? Towards an Independent, Accountable and Diverse Senior Judiciary' (Centre Forum, 2012) 39, https://strathprints.strath.ac.uk/40759/1/guarding_the_guardians.pdf, accessed 14 September 2020.

[75] ibid 41.

[76] For a US overview, see JM Balkin, 'Framework Originalism and the Living Constitution' (2009) 103 *Northwestern University Law Review* 549, 559–66. For a Canadian overview, see W Waluchow, 'Constitutions as Living Trees: An Idiot Defends' (2005) 18 *Canadian Journal of Law and Jurisprudence* 207, 222. See also A Kavanagh, 'The Idea of a Living Constitution' (2003) 16 *Canadian Journal of Law and Jurisprudence* 55; G Letsas, 'The ECHR as a living Instrument: Its Meaning and Legitimacy' in A Føllesdal et al (eds), *Constituting Europe: The European Court of Human Rights in a National, European and Global Context* (Cambridge, Cambridge University Press, 2013). Interestingly, the theory traces its judicial roots to Llewellyn and Justice Oliver Wendell Holmes (commonly regarded as a proto-Realist). See KN Llewellyn, 'The Constitution as an Institution' (1934) 34 *Columbia Law Review* 1, 16; *Gompers v United States* 233 US 604, 610 (1914) (per Holmes J); *Missouri v Holland* 252 US 416 (1920). On Holmes's complex relationship to Legal Realism, see N Duxbury, 'The Birth of Legal Realism and the Myth of Justice Holmes' (1991) 20 *Anglo-American Law Review* 81. Holmes argues that the provisions of the US Constitution are 'organic, living institutions', the meaning of which is 'gathered not simply by taking the words and a dictionary, but by considering their origin and the line of their growth' (*Gompers*, 610). The declaratory theory, as Justice Holmes derisively describes it, posits law as some 'brooding omnipresence in the sky'. *Southern Pacific Co v Jensen* 244 US 205, 222 (1917).

[77] *Tyrer v UK* (1979–80) 2 EHRR 1 (ECHR) para 31.

[78] Letsas (n 76) 108.

[79] WJ Brennan, Jr, 'The Constitution of the United States: Contemporary Ratification' (1986) 27 *South Texas Law Review* 433, 437.

Perhaps unsurprisingly, given the absence of an entrenched constitutional text, the doctrine of living constitutionalism is less well established in the United Kingdom than it is in these other jurisdictions. However, the UK courts do regularly recognise the role of this doctrine in the ECtHR's jurisprudence, which they consider themselves bound to follow.[80] They have also recognised that '[c]onstitutional provisions, especially those protecting fundamental rights, generally fall to be interpreted in the light of the developing values of the societies for which they were made'.[81] Perhaps more significantly, the UK courts adopt what is arguably an analogous 'living' approach to the interpretation of ordinary statutes. According to the presumption of 'updating construction', the courts will generally presume that parliament intends its statutes to be 'always speaking', such that the courts must apply 'a construction that continuously updates its wording to allow for changes since the Act was initially framed', including changes in social conditions, technology or shared values.[82] As is clear from some of the leading cases on updating construction – in which, for example, the term 'family' was updated to include same-sex couples,[83] and the term 'domestic violence' was updated to include non-physical threats and intimidation[84] – the doctrine makes ample space for the influence of moral values, and yields a concomitant need for judges to be transparent about that.

The strategy of transparency has at least two benefits. First, as this brief discussion indicates, it is relatively straightforward to understand and present. Its description of adjudication matches the widely accepted fact about adjudication discussed in the preceding section, namely that it involves moral and political evaluation. This strategy does not rely – as the strategy of restraint arguably does – on complex conceptual manoeuvres or public relations doublespeak to mask a contradiction between, on the one hand, judges claiming to be value-neutral and legalistic, while, on the other, engaging in value-based decision-making with profound moral and political implications.[85]

Second, transparency helps to justify judicial power in the face of the countermajoritarian charge. John Rawls, for example, argued that adjudication is the quintessential form of public reason: part of what distinguishes courts from and justifies their role in relation to the democratically elected branches of government is that they offer detailed reasons for their decisions, which are subjected to searching public criticism.[86] Of course, the notion of public reason helps to

---

[80] *Kennedy v Information Commissioner* [2015] AC 455, 472; *Brown v Stott* [2003] 1 AC 681, 727.

[81] *Lendore v Attorney General of Trinidad and Tobago* [2017] 1 WLR 3369, 3391; *Edwards v Attorney General for Canada* [1930] AC 124, 136.

[82] FAR Bennion, *Understanding Common Law Legislation: Drafting and Interpretation* (Oxford, Oxford University Press, 2009) 52–53; *Fitzpatrick v Sterling Housing Association Ltd* [1999] 4 All ER 705; *Yemshaw v Hounslow LBC* [2011] 1 WLR 433.

[83] *Fitzpatrick* (n 82).

[84] *Yemshaw* (n 82).

[85] I elaborate this point in the conclusion.

[86] J Rawls, *Political Liberalism*, expanded edn (New York, Columbia University Press, 2005) 231–40.

justify adjudication only if the reasons made public are the reasons on which judges actually rely; in other words, only if judges behave transparently.

The downside of advertising the value-laden aspects of adjudication is that this may not be well received by the public. Patrick Atiyah flagged this risk some time ago, speculating that 'most English judges believe that it would shake public confidence in the judiciary, and therefore that it would be a bad thing, if the public came to understand that the judges do actually have a creative legislative role.'[87] More recently, Lord Neuberger expressed similar concern that the public might prove resistant to the idea of judicial law-making, which would increase the risk of attacks on the courts.[88]

These fears are understandable. Value-laden adjudication sits uneasily with public expectations that judicial decision-making be impartial and legalistic (at least in a thin sense of those terms). If that is so, then it may be better to conceive of and develop the strategy of transparency not as an attempt to meet those expectations, but rather as an attempt to change them. Its advocates should seek not only to reveal the truth about adjudication, but also (with the assistance of academics, sympathetic politicians, and others) to shift the public's criteria of judicial legitimacy. The alternative, which I discuss next, is to take those criteria as given and to portray adjudication, as far as possible, as a technical, value-free enterprise.

2. Restraint

Restraint, as a public relations strategy, takes Lord Neuberger's worry to heart. If the public's expectations of impartial and legalistic adjudication are contravened by value-laden judicial discretion, it may be that judicial legitimacy is better served by promoting something like the declaratory model. This strategy tells the public that this model is not only desirable but at least partially feasible, as long as judges adopt a restrained approach to the questions they adjudicate, the legal resources on which they rely to answer them and/or the modes by which they interpret those sources.

Judges on the US Supreme Court frequently advocate an implausibly blunt version of the declaratory model. Chief Justice John Roberts, in his confirmation hearing, compared the judge's role to a baseball umpire: 'my job', he said, 'is to call balls and strikes and not to pitch or bat'.[89] This umpire analogy was recently repeated by Justice Brett Kavanaugh, in one of the less remarkable portions of his bitterly contested confirmation process. Justice Kavanaugh said that a 'good judge must be an umpire – a neutral and impartial arbiter who

---

[87] PS Atiyah, 'Judges and Policy' (1980) 15 *Israel Law Review* 346, 360.

[88] Neuberger (n 71) para 21.

[89] Confirmation Hearing on the Nomination of John G Roberts, Jr to Be Chief Justice of the United States: Hearing Before the Senate Committee on the Judiciary, 109th Congress 56 (2005).

favours no litigant or policy'; he 'must interpret the law, not make the law'.[90] Republican presidents have consistently nominated judges expressly on the basis that they profess adherence to the declaratory model.[91]

In the United Kingdom, Lord Sumption has recently advocated a somewhat more nuanced view of judicial restraint. While he seems to accept that judges make law, he argues that judges stray into moral or political evaluation only when they address matters which they ought to leave alone. He takes particular aim at the principle of legality, according to which judges construe legislation consistently with the rule of law and fundamental rights. With respect to the rule of law, Lord Sumption argues that judges have adopted an expansive view of that concept that intrudes on legitimate government policy and 'depends on a subjective judgment, in which a judge's personal opinions are always influential and often decisive'.[92] With respect to human rights, he argues that identifying their existence and content 'is essentially a matter of opinion' involving 'a personal moral judgement' with which 'there is room for reasonable people to disagree'.[93] In arguing that such rights 'ought [not] to be made by judges', Lord Sumption advances a classic statement of the declaratory model: 'Judges exist to apply the law. It is the business of citizens and their representatives to decide what the law ought to be.'[94]

One tool for achieving judicial restraint is the interpretive methodology of originalism. The doctrine is best known by its American proponents, though, as I will show, it has some English ones as well. In both nations, originalism is always advocated with an eye on the countermajoritarian dilemma, and usually for the same combination of reasons: a belief that human rights are controversial because morality, in which they are grounded, is controversial, coupled with

---

[90] 'Judge Brett Kavanaugh's Opening Statement: Full Prepared Remarks and Video' *New York Times*, 4 September 2010, www.nytimes.com/2018/09/04/us/politics/judge-brett-kavanaughs-opening-statement-full-prepared-remarks.html, accessed 8 August 2020.

[91] Senate Confirmation of Sandra Day O'Connor as an Associate Justice of the Supreme Court of the United States (September 21, 1981) www.reaganlibrary.gov/research/speeches/92181d, accessed 8 August 2020; Remarks at the Swearing-in Ceremony for William H Rehnquist as Chief Justice and Antonin Scalia as Associate Justice of the Supreme Court of the United States (26 September 1986) www.reaganlibrary.gov/research/speeches/092686a, accessed 8 August 2020; Statement on Remarks at the Swearing-in Ceremony for Anthony M Kennedy as an Associate Justice of the Supreme Court of the United States (18 February 1988) www.presidency.ucsb.edu/documents/remarks-the-swearing-ceremony-for-anthony-m-kennedy-associate-justice-the-supreme-court, accessed 8 August 2020; Remarks by President Trump and Justice Gorsuch at Swearing-in of Justice Gorsuch to the Supreme Court (10 April 2017) www.whitehouse.gov/briefings-statements/remarks-president-trump-justice-gorsuch-swearing-justice-gorsuch-supreme-court/, accessed 8 August 2020; Remarks by President Trump at Swearing-in Ceremony of the Honorable Brett M Kavanaugh as Associate Justice of the Supreme Court of the United States (8 October 2018) www.whitehouse.gov/briefings-statements/remarks-president-trump-swearing-ceremony-honorable-brett-m-kavanaugh-associate-justice-supreme-court-united-states/, accessed 8 August 2020.

[92] Sumption (n 17).

[93] ibid.

[94] ibid.

a belief that moral controversies ought to be decided by democratically account-able officials.

In an instructive survey of the US discourse, Lawrence Solum describes origi-nalism as a diverse family of interpretive theories united by their commitment to two claims: that 'the original meaning of the constitutional text was fixed at the time each provision was framed, ratified, and made public'; and that 'consti-tutional practice should be constrained by this fixed original meaning'.[95] While American exponents of originalism initially argued that this original meaning is to be found in the intentions of the framers of the US Constitution, contem-porary originalists (owing to a range of difficulties in ascertaining such intent) argue that the Constitution's provisions should be interpreted as they would have been understood by the public at the time of their ratification.[96]

The doctrine's proponents argue that it significantly limits the indeterminacy of legal sources and, with it, the scope for value-laden judicial law-making. In a well-known concurring opinion, for example, Justice Antonin Scalia argues that: 'Indeterminacy means opportunity for courts to impose whatever rule they like; it is the problem, not the solution.'[97] The solution, he thinks, is original-ism, because it eschews 'vague ethico-political First Principles whose combined conclusion can be found to point in any direction the judges favor'.[98] In a canon-ical extracurial writing, he decries judicial decisions 'rendered not on the basis of what the Constitution originally meant, but on the basis of what the judges currently thought it desirable for it to mean'.[99] In public remarks honouring Justice Scalia after his death, Justice Neil Gorsuch argues that the judge's job is 'to decide what a reasonable reader at the time of the events in question would have understood the law to be – not to decide cases based on their own moral convictions or the policy consequences they believe might serve society best'.[100] Explicitly invoking Blackstone, he says that 'judges should be in the business of declaring what the law is using the traditional tools of interpretation, rather than pronouncing the law as they might wish it to be'.[101] These 'traditional tools', he says, 'do a remarkable job of eliminating or reducing indeterminacy', which is 'often (wildly) exaggerated'.[102]

---

[95] LB Solum, 'Originalism versus Living Constitutionalism: The Conceptual Structure of the Great Debate' (2019) 113 *Northwestern University Law Review* 1243, 1265–66. For a foundational challenge to the notion of originalist intent, see P Brest, 'The Misconceived Quest for the Original Understanding' (1980) 60 *Boston University Law Review* 204.

[96] Solum (n 96) 1250–51.

[97] *McDonald v City of Chicago, Ill* 561 US 742, 795 (2010).

[98] ibid 804.

[99] A Scalia, 'Originalism: The Lesser Evil (Essays in Constitutional Interpretation)' (1989) 57 *University of Cincinnati Law Review* 849, 852.

[100] NM Gorsuch, 'Of Lions and Bears, Judges and Legislators, and the Legacy of Justice Scalia Lecture' (2015) 66 *Case Western Reserve Law Review* 905, 906.

[101] ibid 907, 910.

[102] ibid 917. Justice Gorsuch has consistently adopted originalist thinking in his opinions. See eg *Gamble v United States* 139 S Ct 1960 (2019); *Kisor v Wilkie* 139 S Ct 2400 (2019).

On this side of the Atlantic, and for the same reasons, a number of judges advocate an original intent theory of the kind that their US counterparts have since abandoned. Lord Sumption, for example, takes issue with the ECtHR's interpretation of the Convention as a 'living instrument', a methodology which serves only 'to declare rights which are not there' based on the Court's own view of what morality requires.[103] His preferred mode of interpreting the Convention is one of original intent, according to which it means only what its signatories agreed it would mean, as evidenced by the language they chose and the history of their negotiations.[104]

Other British judges have argued for an original intent approach to parliamentary legislation. Lord Sales, for example, argues that courts should construe a statute according to 'Parliament's intention when it chose how it would legislate',[105] failing which the courts would simply 'import normative content of which they approve, even if it is not plausible to think that the legislating Parliament would have accepted it'.[106] Like Lord Sumption, Lord Sales is concerned with the principle of legality. When courts apply the principle, he argues the relevant question ought always to be 'whether any supposed fundamental "right" ... can plausibly be taken to have had such a level of acceptance among parliamentarians ... as to form part of the legislative context in which they meant to act'.[107] Likewise, Lord Hoffmann has declared that, 'like Justice Scalia, I am an originalist', agreeing with Justice Scalia's view that the US Constitution ought to be interpreted as it would have been understood by its historical audience.[108] The alternative, for Lord Hoffmann, 'is updating and amendment, not interpretation'.[109] Echoing something like Jack Balkin's 'framework originalism',[110] Lord Hoffmann argues that the interpretive doctrine of updating construction, discussed above, can in fact be reconciled with an originalist stance, as a constitution or statute may express an intention that its meaning be updated in light of future circumstances.[111]

Many scholars (including me) doubt that interpretive methodologies such as originalism really do restrain, rather than merely occlude, a judge's reliance on moral and political norms. They also contest (as I do) the desirability of

---

[103] Sumption (n 17).

[104] Sumption in N Barber et al (eds), *Lord Sumption and the Limits of the Law* (Oxford, Hart Publishing, 2016) 20–21.

[105] P Sales, 'Legislative Intention, Interpretation, and the Principle of Legality' (2019) 40 *Statute Law Review* 53, 54. See also P Sales and R Ekins, 'Rights-consistent Interpretation and the Human Rights Act 1998' (2011) 127 *LQR* 217, 218, where they argue that 'the traditional object of interpretation ... is to determine the intention of the enacting legislature'.

[106] Sales (n 105) 60.

[107] ibid 62.

[108] Lord Hoffmann, 'Judges, Interpretation and Self-Government' in Barber et al (n 104) 68–69.

[109] ibid 69.

[110] Balkin (n 76).

[111] Hoffmann (n 108) 69–70.

eliminating such reliance.[112] I will not engage these matters here. Of present concern is the way that such strategies are or can be deployed as part of a public relations exercise designed to cultivate the public's perception of judicial legitimacy. In this regard it is instructive to note the way that originalism has been taken up in conservative movement politics in the United States, which aptly demonstrates how restraint, as a public relations strategy, works in practice. Reva Siegel and Robert Post document a process, beginning with the Reagan administration and the launch of the Federalist Society, by which this rarefied matter of constitutional methodology has come to frame the public debate around the judicial role, 'emerg[ing] as a new and powerful kind of constitutional politics in which claims about the sole legitimate method of interpreting the Constitution inspired conservative mobilization in both electoral politics and in the legal profession'.[113] Whether this conservative movement has shaped or been shaped by public views about the judge's proper role, Jamal Greene's review of the evidence concludes that 'a substantial portion of the American public [now] reports an affinity for originalism'.[114] Thus, whether it is adopted in the sincere belief that value-free adjudication is possible or for more strategic aims, the result is the same: enhanced judicial legitimacy in the public eye.

3. Popularity

There is yet another strategy that the courts might follow to cultivate the public's perception of their legitimacy: the strategy of popularity. This strategy not only assumes that judges do tend to engage in political evaluation; it expressly advocates that they ought to do so, with the ultimate aim of delivering decisions that accord with the ideological preferences of a majority of the public.

Empirical studies of the relationship between judicial decisions and public political opinion are overwhelmingly focused on the United States. A substantial body of such research on the US Supreme Court affirms that a strategy of popularity is feasible. While the court occasionally issues decisions that defy the preference of a majority of Americans on some issue (such as abortion or gun control), studies conclusively show that the court, in the long run, is consistently ideologically aligned with a majority of the American public. When Americans are asked whether the Supreme Court is 'too liberal, too conservative, or about right?', their most common response for decades has been that the Court is 'about right'.[115] About as many choose 'too conservative' as 'too liberal'.[116]

---

[112] For a concise, recent summary of the criticisms of originalism, see J Greene, 'Selling Originalism' (2009) 97 *Georgetown Law Journal* 657, 660–72.

[113] Robert Post and Reva Siegel, 'Originalism as a Political Practice: The Right's Living Constitution' (2006) 75 Fordham Law Review 545, 548.

[114] Greene (n 95) 695, and the authorities cited therein.

[115] Ura and Merrill (n 36) 435.

[116] ibid 436.

This shows, as Ura and Merrill conclude, that the court has 'position[ed] itself in the center of Americans' collective political attitudes'.[117] As public sentiment shifts, so too does the court.[118]

The US Supreme Court's decisions in the most recent term add anecdotal support and colour to these studies.[119] Out of ten major cases covering controversial social issues such as LGBT employment rights, contraceptive coverage in employer-based health insurance plans, abortion restrictions and protections for undocumented immigrants, the court – according to an opinion survey by a cohort of US universities – resolved eight of them as a majority of Americans would have wanted.[120]

While most empirical work has focused on the US Supreme Court, I note that studies of other nations' apex courts tell a similar story: the decisions of these courts tend to align with the policy preferences of a majority of the public.[121] Collectively, this empirical evidence from within and without the United States suggests that the countermajoritarian dilemma, at least in some respects, is overblown: courts channel the public will much more effectively than the dilemma gives them credit for.

Another set of evidence reveals that the strategy of popularity is beneficial. When the Supreme Court successfully rides the wave of public sentiment, it reaps rewards in the form of enhanced legitimacy among the public. For a long time, the court has enjoyed widespread support among the American public.[122] As Barry Friedman argues, part of the reason why the justices have the incredible power they do is because the American public supports their having it.[123] Empirical research has tied this support to the public's assessment of the court's performance: the more an individual approves of the Supreme Court's decisions, the more likely they are to express support for the court as an institution;[124] when the court deviates from the prevailing public mood, its support wanes.[125] Thus, while long-run diffuse support helps cushion the blow of occasional decisions that the public dislikes, the court cannot consistently deliver such decisions

---

[117] ibid 439.

[118] CJ Casillas et al, 'How Public Opinion Constrains the US Supreme Court' (2011) 55 *American Journal of Political Science* 74.; KT McGuire and JA Stimson, 'The Least Dangerous Branch Revisited: New Evidence on Supreme Court Responsiveness to Public Preferences' (2004) 66 *Journal of Politics* 1018. See also B Friedman, *The Will of the People: How Public Opinion Has Influenced the Supreme Court and Shaped the Meaning of the Constitution* (New York, Farrar, Straus and Giroux, 2009).

[119] A Thomson-DeVeaux and A Wiederkehr, 'The Supreme Court's Big Rulings Were Surprisingly Mainstream this Year' *FiveThirtyEight*, 13 July 2020, https://fivethirtyeight.com/features/the-supreme-courts-big-rulings-were-surprisingly-mainstream-this-year/, accessed 8 August 2020.

[120] ibid.

[121] See Vanberg (n 27) 180 and the authorities cited there.

[122] Ura and Merrill (n 36) 439.

[123] Friedman (n 118) 11.

[124] Ura and Merrill (n 36) 442.

[125] RH Durr et al, 'Ideological Divergence and Public Support for the Supreme Court' (2000) 44 *American Journal of Political Science* 768.

without sacrificing its perceived legitimacy. Indeed, more recent studies suggest that the court's legitimacy might be even more sensitive to the public's views on individual cases than scholars have previously thought.[126]

While scholars have demonstrated consistency between the court's decisions and majority preferences on the relevant issue, and have also shown the legitimacy that this consistency imbues, they are less sure (as I noted earlier) about the mechanism by which the court achieves this consistency. There is broad agreement that the justice's own ideologies significantly influence their decisions,[127] but there is much debate around the causal impact of public opinion on individual justices and/or the outcomes of the court's decisions. As Gibson summarises the evidence, 'it is simply not clear whether the Court responds to public opinion, or shapes public opinion, or whether it responds to the same sort of factors that themselves shape public opinion'.[128]

One view, known as the 'strategic behaviour' hypothesis, is that the court actively cultivates its perceived legitimacy by consciously tacking to the political centre.[129] The hypothesis is inspired by the kind of argument I set out earlier: that the court's relative institutional weakness vis-a-vis the other branches of government gives it a strong incentive to cultivate its legitimacy however it can, including expressly aiming at crowd-pleasing results.[130] Several studies support the hypothesis with empirical evidence, arguing that the court not only reflects, but is sensitive and strategically responsive to, changes in the political views of the public.[131]

Again, the mechanisms by which the court learns these views are not well understood, though scholars have suggested some possibilities. Tom Clark, for example, suggests that the court learns these preferences indirectly, by looking for signals from the elected branches about the court's standing with the public.[132] Others have suggested that the justices are 'political creatures, who are broadly aware of fundamental trends in ideological tenor of public opinion'.[133]

---

[126] BL Bartels and CD Johnston, 'On the Ideological Foundations of Supreme Court Legitimacy in the American Public' (2013) 57 *American Journal of Political Science* 184; see also DP Christenson and D Glick, 'Chief Justice Roberts's Health Care Decision Disrobed: The Microfoundations of the Supreme Court's Legitimacy' (2015) 59 *American Journal of Political Science* 403.

[127] See n 57 above.

[128] JL Gibson, 'Thomas R. Marshall, *Public Opinion and the Supreme Court*' (1990) 54 *Public Opinion Quarterly* 289, 290. See also L Epstein and AD Martin, 'Does Public Opinion Influence the Supreme Court? Possibly Yes (but We're Not Sure Why)' (2010) 13 *University of Pennsylvania Journal of Constitutional Law* 263.

[129] MW Giles et al, 'The Supreme Court in American Democracy: Unraveling the Linkages between Public Opinion and Judicial Decision Making' (2008) 70 *Journal of Politics* 293, 294; Casillas et al (n 118) 75.

[130] McGuire and Stimson (n 11818) 1019; Casillas et al (n 118) 75–77.

[131] McGuire and Stimson (n 118); Casillas et al (n 118).

[132] Clark (n 1) 7.

[133] W Mishler and RS Sheehan, 'The Supreme Court as a Countermajoritarian Institution? The Impact of Public Opinion on Supreme Court Decisions' (1993) 87 *American Political Science Review* 87, 89.

Whether the justices are indeed strategically following public opinion, and whatever the mechanisms by which they might be doing so, the literature clearly shows that a court, if it does manage to follow the strategy of popularity with some success, will thereby enhance the public's perception of its legitimacy.

V. CONCLUSION

These, then, are some strategies by which courts might persuade the public of their legitimacy and, in that way, bolster their ability to act independently from (and against) the other branches of government. As I have argued, each strategy in isolation has its own advantages, drawbacks and implementation challenges. By way of conclusion, I note the dangers of pursuing some of them in combination.

Of the three strategies I have discussed, restraint and popularity seem most likely to enhance public perceptions of judicial legitimacy, since they each tap into a known source of those perceptions: the former feeds the public's expectation of impartial and legalistic decision-making, the latter feeds the expectation of ideologically favourable outcomes. Does this suggest that a court's quickest path to enhanced legitimacy is pursuing both strategies in tandem?

The experience of the US Supreme Court is a cautionary tale. In a landmark study in 1957, Robert Dahl remarked that Americans seem divided within and between themselves as to what they expect from the court: they are 'not quite willing to accept the fact that it *is* a political institution and not quite capable of denying it; so that frequently we take both positions at once'.[134] Since the originalist renaissance, the court itself has seemingly, and quite successfully, taken both positions at once, and by doing so it has accumulated power of a magnitude that other nations' apex courts rarely enjoy. On the one hand, the conservative wing of the court has adopted what might be construed as a conscious public relations strategy, supported by politicians and grassroots activists, to convince the public that value-free adjudication is possible and that they alone will deliver it. On the other hand, the court has delivered, year after year, decisions that accord with the prevailing political preferences of the American public. As I have noted, it remains unclear whether the court is doing that as a matter of overt strategy, but the available evidence is certainly consistent with that view.

It should be clear, however, that there is a deep tension between these two strategies: one denies the role of political evaluation in judicial decision-making and the other promotes it. The more successfully a court pursues the one strategy, the more it undermines the other. Indeed, recent empirical data suggest that the court may be walking too fine a line. Although it still enjoys (as it always

---

[134] R Dahl, 'Decision-making in a Democracy: The Role of the Supreme Court as a National Policy-maker' (1957) 6 *Journal of Public Law* 279, 279 (emphasis in original).

has) higher levels of support than the other two branches of government, that support appears to have dropped significantly in the last twenty years (and especially since 2009).[135] The cause, Friedman speculates, is 'a loss of faith that [the court is] up to anything other than simple ideological politics'.[136]

Transparency and popularity are more coherent allies, since the former not only publicises but, at least to some extent, celebrates the role of moral and political considerations in judicial decision-making. Together, these strategies paint an honest picture of what judges really do. However, if the courts open their hearts to the public in this way, there is no guarantee that the public will like what it sees. Indeed, since transparency at least superficially conflicts with the public's existing desire for impartial and legalistic judicial decisions, it seems less likely to enhance the courts' legitimacy than undermine it.

If transparency is to be a successful path to legitimacy (either alone or combined with popularity), it must therefore seek not merely to meet but also, as I have argued, to change the public's expectations about the nature and value of judicial decision. In trying to change the public's mind about judging, transparency's advocates might borrow some of the tactics deployed by the conservative movement in the United States. In some ways, the American public's support for originalism is encouraging: it is far from intuitive that the meaning of constitutional terms was fixed two hundred years ago, still less that this meaning should bind us today, and yet the doctrine's advocates have packaged the idea into an accessible and appealing set of slogans that can provide the basis for grassroots political mobilisation. If judges want to build their legitimacy while being true to what they do, they (and we) will have to shift our expectations of what we want them to do.

---

[135] B Friedman, 'Letter to Supreme Court (Erwin Chemerinsky Is Mad. Why You Should Care)' (2016) 69 *Vanderbilt Law Review* 995, 1004–05. *cf* Ura and Merrill (n 36) 435–36.
[136] Friedman (n 135) 1006.

3

The Judicialisation of Politics and Threats to Judicial Independence: When Should We 'Cry Wolf'?

EZEQUIEL GONZALEZ-OCANTOS

I. IS JUDICIAL INDEPENDENCE UNDER THREAT?

ONE OF THE overarching questions that motivated the 2019 Putney Debates was whether judicial independence is currently under threat. This question has gained relevance in the United Kingdom of late as a result of the judicialisation of the Brexit process immediately after the EU referendum. On 24 January 2017, the Supreme Court of the United Kingdom handed down a decision in what the *Guardian* called 'the most important constitutional case ever to be heard by the Supreme Court'.[1] In June of the previous year, a private claimant had thrown the High Court of England and Wales into the muddy waters of the Brexit saga, demanding that Theresa May's Conservative government seek parliamentary approval before triggering any process that would culminate in Britain's exit from the European Union. Needless to say, this was an approval that the Prime Minister had hitherto insisted was not necessary. After the High Court ruled against the government, the *Daily Mail* lunched an unprecedented rhetorical attack against the judges with the now infamous 'enemies of the people'[2] headline. Partly because the Secretary of State and Lord Chancellor, Liz Truss, failed to rebuke the use of this vitriolic language as severely as some commentators had hoped, the episode prompted concerns about the future of judicial independence in this country. It is important to note that while the Supreme Court subsequently upheld the lower court's judgment, it was not subject to the same degree of abuse.

The United Kingdom is certainly not the only country where judges find themselves increasingly thrown into the political maelstrom as a result of cases

---

[1] *The Guardian*, 23 January 2017, goo.gl/i1FvZy (accessed 2 March 2017).
[2] *Daily Mail*, 3 November 2016, goo.gl/ay0Kz5 (accessed 2 March 2017).

that force them to make deeply consequential interventions in the most fundamental institutional or distributive debates of the day. In this sense, clashes between, on the one hand, the political branches of government, major parties or the partisan press and, on the other, the courts, are more common and more visible than ever before.[3] In order to answer the question of whether judicial independence is currently under threat, it is therefore imperative to begin by examining the historical processes that have made these clashes more likely. My presentation at the Putney Debates, which kick-started the discussion about the extent to which judicial independence is indeed at risk, was in part devoted to this task. My aim in this chapter is to highlight in greater depth the conditions that favour the 'judicialization of politics' in contemporary democracies. Most of the examples I use to support the argument come from Latin America, the region of the world I study and know best, which has served as a fascinating laboratory of judicial activism since the 1980s. Towards the end, however, I present some embryonic ideas about the more complicated question of how to deal with attacks on judicial independence, and the extent to which rhetorical attacks such as the one lunched against the High Court are indicative of growing threats to judicial authority.

II. THE JUDICIALISATION OF POLITICS

At least since the end of the Second World War, but especially after the onset of the third wave of democratisation in the late 1970s, courts around the world have left behind decades of subservience, incompetence, conservatism, and quite frankly, political irrelevance, to become architects of fundamental rights and key public policies. Judges no longer behave primarily as formalistic arbiters in procedural or private disputes, and no longer see 'political questions' as lying outside their remit. Moreover, individuals and groups of all walks of life increasingly turn to the courts, framing their grievances in legal terms as questions of rights violations or deficits in rights effectiveness. The growing use of courts as political battlegrounds has put judges at the centre of some of the most salient debates of our age, and given them the opportunity to hand down deeply consequential decisions that antagonise and constrain those in government. Judges now intervene in politics to serve as arbiters between the branches of government in heated debates over policy and the reach of presidents' or legislatures' institutional prerogatives. In addition, courts often expand the content of

---

[3] G Helmke and J Staton, 'The Puzzling Judicial Politics of Latin America: A Theory of Litigation, Judicial Decisions and Interbranch Conflict' in G Helmke and J Ríos-Figueroa (eds), *Courts in Latin America* (New York, Cambridge University Press, 2011); G Helmke, *Institutions on the Edge: The Origins and Consequences of Inter-branch Crises in Latin America* (New York, Cambridge University Press, 2017).

constitutionally recognised fundamental rights, and in some cases, create new entitlements.

The decisions judges make can have massive effects on budgets, or fundamentally shape the distribution of power and resources in politics and society. We see this happening in places as diverse as Colombia, South Africa, India and, more recently, the United Kingdom. Courts in these countries regularly make health policy, environmental policy, housing policy, or intervene in debates about how states should conduct their international relations. A few examples from Latin America help illustrate the trend towards the judicialisation of politics. High courts in this region have handed down rulings that challenged the retrenchment of welfare benefits during periods of neoliberal adjustment;[4] opened the door for the prosecution of former military officers responsible for human rights violations;[5] mandated far-reaching reforms to national healthcare systems or the decontamination of large river basins;[6] and protected the rights of sexual minorities and internally displaced populations.[7] In addition to these progressive interventions in sensitive policy areas, one of the most extreme instances of judicial involvement in 'mega politics' is the judicialisation of grand corruption currently underway in several Latin American countries, especially in Brazil with the famous 'Car Wash' operation.[8] Like never before, courts in this region of the world are investigating and punishing corrupt economic and political elites for their participation in transnational bribery schemes mounted around large public infrastructure projects. These anti-corruption crusades have proven extremely disruptive of democratic politics. In some cases, judicial decisions led to the exclusion of leading candidates from presidential races. In others, they spurred cycles of popular mobilisation against a political class revealed to be deeply corrupt or pushed voters into the arms of anti-establishment outsiders with dubious democratic credentials.

---

[4] C Rodríguez-Garavito, 'Latin American Constitutionalism: Social and Economic Rights: Beyond the Courtroom: The Impact of Judicial Activism on Socioeconomic Rights in Latin America' (2011) 89(1) *Texas Law Review* 1669; D Kapiszewski, *High Courts and Economic Governance in Argentina and Brazil* (New York, Cambridge University Press, 2012); D Brinks and W Forbath, 'The Role of Courts and Constitutions in the New Politics of Welfare in Latin America' in R Peerenboom and T Ginsburg (eds), *Law and Development of Middle-Income Countries: Avoiding the Middle-Income Trap* (New York, Cambridge University Press, 2014).

[5] E Gonzalez-Ocantos, *Shifting Legal Visions: Judicial Change and Human Rights Trials in Latin America* (New York, Cambridge University Press, 2016).

[6] B Wilson and JC Rodríguez-Cordero, 'Legal Opportunity Structures and Social Movements: The Effects of Institutional Change on Costa Rican Politics' (2006) 39(3) *Comparative Political Studies* 325; S Botero, 'Judicial Impact and Court Promoted Monitoring in Argentina' (2018) 50(2) *Comparative Politics* 169.

[7] J Díez, *The Politics of Gay Marriage in Latin America* (New York, Cambridge University Press, 2015); C Rodríguez-Garavito and D Rodríguez-Franco, *Radical Deprivation on Trial: The Impact of Judicial Activism on Socioeconomic Rights in the Global South* (New York, Cambridge University Press, 2015).

[8] E Gonzalez-Ocantos and V Baraybar, 'Lava Jato Beyond Borders: The Uneven Performance of Anticorruption Judicial Efforts in Latin America' (2019) 15(1) *Taiwan Journal of Democracy* 63.

What explains this trend? The judicialisation of politics is partly the result of changes in the formal architecture of judicial branches; informal value changes that put the defence of human rights at the forefront of juridical analysis or transform traditional conceptions of the judicial role and professional norms; and the intensification of patterns of transjudicial communication between courts at different levels. Let us review these factors in some detail.

One obvious answer to the puzzle of why courts have become more central political actors in contemporary democracies is that formal institutions have changed, enabling and encouraging judicial activism. For example, in the aftermath of the third wave of democratisation, Latin American countries institutionalised a liberal rights discourse in their constitutions. As a result, the number of rights listed in these documents has increased dramatically over the years. Similarly, several constitutions now offer a more robust constitutionalisation of international human rights treaties, a phenomenon analogous to the transposition of the European Convention of Human Rights into UK law via the Human Rights Act of 1998. Such reforms offer a clearer legal basis for judges to acquiesce to the demands of vulnerable populations, handing down pro-rights jurisprudence that some commentators deem 'activist'.

Another important aspect of formal institutional change has been the creation of high courts with the specific mission to serve as the trustees of fundamental rights. This is true, for instance, in Colombia, Costa Rica, Chile and Peru, where reformed constitutions mandated the establishment of constitutional courts or special constitutional chambers within existing supreme courts. Such changes responded to calls to provide better safeguards for fundamental rights, as well as to the need to empower independent bodies capable of adjudicating institutional and policy conflict in increasingly complex polities. Similar reasons led to the creation of the UK Supreme Court under the Blair government. Scholars suggest that this institutional innovation was motivated, on the one hand, by growing concerns about the lack of independence of a court housed in one of the two legislative chambers, arrangements that were seen as out of sync with emerging European human rights standards, and on the other, by the need to count with a body that could adjudicate interjurisdictional disputes credibly amidst a more devolved administrative structure.[9]

Formal changes are, of course, a crucial factor behind the judicialisation of politics, as judges who have more expansive mandates and robust safeguards are normally more inclined to defy the status quo or intervene in sensitive policy areas. But an exclusive focus on formal institutions misses another interesting layer of the story: the promises of formal institutions are usually made effective by informal social and political processes. In this sense, informal changes in the way judges understand their role in the political system and read the cold text

---

[9] A Le Sueur (ed), *Building the UK's New Supreme Court* (Oxford, Oxford University Press, 2004).

of the law, ie changes in the prism or lens through which constitutions and legal codes acquire meaning in practice, were crucial for the rise of the court as a central political actor around the world.

I tend to think of judges as groups of individuals, in some cases highly bureaucratised ones, who are subject to intense professional socialisation processes at university and on the bench. These socialisation processes instill certain values and normalise particular behavioural patterns. Through such processes, judges develop a lens that filters how they read they law and reproduces a series of decision-making routines. This lens in turn conditions how they understand their professional mission as it relates to interpreting the law: 'is it OK to quasi-legislate?'; 'can I challenge laws passed by the government?'; 'should I care about compliance with international human rights law?'

In Latin America the lens that was dominant until the 1990s was characterised by a staunchly formalistic version of legal positivism.[10] The hegemony of these legal preferences stifled the willingness and the ability of judges to take rights seriously or make innovative readings of the law. Crucially, the formalistic positivist lens was structurally biased in favour of conservative interests, programming judges in a way that made progressive victories in court, as well as acts of political defiance, highly unlikely.[11] As long as the hegemony of such legal preferences remained unchallenged, no dose of formal institutional change could be strong enough to upend the passive role of courts in Latin American democracies.[12] For example, when international human rights treaties acquired constitutional status, many judges did not know what to do with them, simply because they had been trained in a "sovereigntist" legal tradition suspicious of international law.[13] And even when positive law reinforced the incorporation of new rights in other ways, there was still limited textual basis for telling a president to clean up a river basin because citizens in that area had a fundamental right to a clean environment, or to grant everyone free HIV medications because that is what is required by the fundamental right to health. Making such argumentative leaps required more than formal institutional changes; it required a special kind of judicial training and a renewed sense of institutional mission. A precondition for the kind of rights activism we observe today was therefore the availability of judicial actors willing to transform their routines, innovate, escape their comfort zone and rule in ways that were likely to upset more powerful actors. After all, iconoclastic pro-rights decisions undermine legislative supremacy, put pressure on the budget, touch the prerogatives of powerful establishment actors and may upset superiors in the judicial hierarchy.

---

[10] J Couso, 'The Transformation of Constitutional Discourse and the Judicialization of Politics in Latin America' in J Couso, A Huneeus and R Sieder (eds) *Cultures of Legality: Judicialization and Political Activism in Latin America* (New York, Cambridge University Press, 2010).

[11] L Hilbink, *Judges Beyond Politics in Democracy and Dictatorship: Lessons from Chile* (New York, Cambridge University Press, 2007).

[12] L Hilbink 'The Origins of Positive Judicial Independence' (2012) 64(4) *World Politics* 587.

[13] Gonzalez-Ocantos (n 5).

It is certainly not easy to shake up bureaucracies and transform the way they do things, or the values they are programmed to defend. It demands the implementation of intense resocialisation processes that break inertia, question taken-for-granted routines and introduce a new sense of possibility. What were the sources of the informal changes in legal knowledge, skills and normative commitments that made pro-rights activism possible? How did the practice of constitutionalism acquire a rights dimension that was previously absent, thus fuelling the judicialisation of politics? It is here where we need to look for factors beyond the judiciary. I tend to emphasise two different types of political processes that have led to changes in routines of legal interpretation, making judges more knowledgeable, attentive and respectful of fundamental rights, and more willing of intervene politically.

Strategic litigation is the first key input in this story of change. Strategic litigants are important in 'rights revolutions'[14] or the judicialisation of politics because they bring new topics and questions to court, making innovative jurisprudence possible. They also introduce new frameworks of rights adjudication, and new ways of thinking about issues. In doing so, they exert a disruptive exogenous force. As one former Mexican Supreme Court judge told me, litigants are 'the unknown soldiers of jurisprudence'.

In the 1980s and 1990s Latin American citizens and civil society organisations started to pay more attention to the courts and see litigation as a viable avenue for social change. One important background condition for this reorientation in tactics of social contention was associated with broader changes in the ideological context. Specifically, with the end of the Cold War and the rise of democracy, a liberal understanding of human rights became part of the mainstream political vocabulary. The spread of this discourse was important for the judicialisation of politics because it gradually legitimised new tactics to promote progressive transformations. To put it somewhat bluntly, progressive activism was no longer about making the revolution. As a result, going to court became a conceivable and appropriate form of engagement, even for some on the far-left who had previously considered litigation to be a 'bourgeois' activity. This shift in the mindset of civil society actors had an ancillary effect: it generated incentives for organisations to invest in professionalized legal teams, thus adding a new item to their repertoires of contention. The following is a quote from an interview with a Mexican activist-cum-NGO leader, referring to the development of these new capabilities in the 1990s:

> When we founded the *Academia Nacional de Derechos Humanos*, the idea was to defend human rights, but not to litigate. Causes, but no cases. This in part responded to the logic of the PRI regime. In that regime you did not litigate; you denounced, you negotiated, you talked. But eventually we realized that we had to find a way to take care of the cases that were brought to our attention. … It took us many years

---

[14] C Epp, *The Rights Revolution: Lawyers, Activists, and Supreme Courts in Comparative Perspective* (Chicago: University of Chicago Press, 1998).

to put together a legal team because there were no good lawyers available, especially lawyers that understood international human rights law. ... We had to nurture a new generation of lawyers."[15]

In sum, by the 1990s civil society actors across Latin America (and beyond) began to think about avenues for progressive social change in rather different ways, accommodating themselves to the growing hegemony of a liberal rights-centred discourse in a post-Cold War environment. But how exactly did strategic litigation affect the role that judges were willing to play in democracy once the ideational and professional infrastructure to make political use of the courts was in place?

Litigants can transform the judiciary from a passive, indifferent actor, into an active, competent and reliable ally, thus helping to realise some of the promises of a new version of constitutionalism. At a very basic level, sheer exposure to civil society and its demands makes judges more cognisant of their social embeddedness, and of their institutional responsibility in addressing really existing social demands. In other words, by 'knocking on the doors' of the judiciary, civil society actors remind judges that they are not an isolated bureaucracy. And this exposure can shape the institutional goals of the judiciary in dramatic ways. The following is a quote from an interview with an Argentine federal judge who recalls the impact of the 2001 financial crisis on the judicialisation of economic grievances, and how this transformed his views on constitutionalism:

> I became sensitive to the context. I couldn't apply the rules without taking a look at this context. For example, if a guy steals a sandwich in a post-1990s context of exclusion, I can't blindly apply the criminal code. ... I am obviously aware of the changes that society underwent during those years. This clearly opens your eyes to alternative legal discourses. ... The new constitutionalism developed strongly during the 2001 crisis. There were a lot of young lawyers that started to invoke the Constitution ... to request medicines for patients in critical conditions, etc. They began to see the rights in the Constitution ... and mobilized against the state, against pharmaceutical companies. ... So there are things that happened in Argentina that are linked to these changes in legal discourses and judicial behaviour.[16]

In another interview, a Brazilian prosecutor also highlighted the role of civil society and strategic litigation in changing judicial values:

> The Brazilian constitution of 1988 reformed the public prosecution service. It was no longer designed to act solely in criminal cases, but it now had the mission to defend democracy, human rights. The prosecution service therefore had to open its doors and deal very closely with civil society. For over 18 years, I've been talking to members of civil society every week.[... This made prosecutors more sensitive to civil society demands, in health, education, environmental issues, anything related to collective rights.[17]

---

[15] Author's Interview, Mexico City, 19 July 2010.
[16] Author's Interview, Buenos Aires, 20 May 2011.
[17] Author's Interview, Brasilia, 5 August 2015.

These are, of course, not your average Argentine or Brazilian judicial actors, but they are part of a group of rights-oriented professionals who simply did not exist before. Their testimonies illustrate how even the routines and values of 'old foxes' within the judicial branch can be disrupted by strategic litigation and social change, leading to new, bolder and transformative patterns of decision-making.

There is, however, a more fundamental way in which civil society can trigger this type of judicial change. NGOs and social movements often purposely try to resocialise judges in order to induce structural changes in the legal criteria used to adjudicate cases. This can permanently condition how judicial actors respond to political and social questions, biasing them in favour (or against) interventionism. In other words, civil society activists can become conveyor belts of new forms of juridical praxis, leading judges and prosecutors to accept and embrace new sources of law, techniques of legal argumentation and institutional missions. For example, in a book I wrote a few years ago I documented how litigants managed to transform judicial values so as to enable the judicialisation of human rights violations perpetrated during dictatorships and armed conflict in Latin America.[18] I show that waves of human rights trials such as those underway in Argentina, Peru or Chile, are more successful, ambitious and sustainable in countries where civil society actors deployed their skilful legal teams to diffuse knowledge and acceptance of international human rights law. Litigants in several countries created out-of-court, informal pedagogical spaces in which they literally taught judges about an alternative body of law. Judges then used this knowledge to defy amnesty provisions, build strong cases against powerful defendants and eventually put human rights criminals in jail. The following is an excerpt from a funding request by an Argentine NGO to the International Commission of Jurists in 1992, explaining why these resocialisation initiatives were needed:

> The course's goal is to analyse the use of international and regional human rights conventions in Argentina's domestic law. ... Both judges and lawyers, and even universities, scholars and legal journals frequently ignore [them]. ... For this reason, [we deem] it convenient to organise a regional seminar that brings together legal scholars, judges, lawyers, university professors and advanced law students ... with the goal of analysing this problem and diffusing the conclusions among the aforementioned groups. ... [The meeting] will constitute the first step of a movement that will translate into workshops, seminars, research, publications and judicial rulings conducive to a comprehensive domestic use of the norms of international human rights law.

This inflow of knowledge was accompanied by a renewed professional commitment, which ultimately gave judges both the motives, the courage and the tools to become effective agents of truth and justice for victims of state repression.

---

[18] Gonzalez-Ocantos (n 5).

Without these pedagogical efforts, courts in Argentina would not have been able to produce the most ambitious programme of prosecutions for crimes against humanity the world has ever seen.

In addition to strategic litigation, a second key driver of informal changes in value orientations and professional missions is the intensification of the transnational dialogue between courts. International courts in Europe, Latin America and Africa have become much bolder in recent decades, issuing rulings that decisively expand the sphere of fundamental rights and constrain state sovereignty. Thanks to growing opportunities for cross-border communication afforded by technological change and the creation of transnational judicial networks, the doctrines expounded in these international decisions sometimes trickle down, empowering and emboldening domestic courts in their own mission to champion fundamental rights.

For example, some of my recent research looks at the impact of the Inter-American Court of Human Rights, which was set up to police compliance with the American Convention of Human Rights.[19] Since the late 1990s, there has been a dramatic surge both in Inter-American Court rulings defending fundamental rights, and more importantly, in the use of these rulings as a source of law in domestic decisions. Inter-American jurisprudence has thus contributed to the consolidation of 'activist' rights-oriented jurisprudence across Latin America. The intensification of transjudicial communication is in part the result of the Inter-American Court's own efforts to promote continental discussions about the obligations of national judges under the American Convention.

The agency of international courts is crucial to promote greater awareness of international (human rights) law among local judges, and thus increase the chances of them issuing bold, rights-oriented jurisprudence. Regulating the use of international human rights jurisprudence is politically sensitive and directly affects the autonomy of domestic courts, reducing their room for discretion. Domestic courts are therefore sometimes reluctant to turn to non-national sources of law. As a Colombian Constitutional Court clerk explained to me:

> Self-regulation on these matters is unlikely because power is at stake. On the one hand, forging a consensus among constitutional judges [on the status and use of international human rights law] is difficult because this source of law bolsters the power of those with more progressive positions [inside the court]. It is no secret that the Inter-American Court of Human Rights favours pro-rights criteria. On the other hand, the absence of clear rules widens the court's margin of appreciation in relation to the Inter-American system. My power is greater when I'm free to decide when to use this jurisprudence.[20]

---

[19] E Gonzalez-Ocantos, 'Communicative Entrepreneurs: The Case of the Inter-American Court of Human Rights' Dialogue with National Judges' (2018) 62(4) *International Studies Quarterly* 737; E Gonzalez-Ocantos and W Sandholtz, 'Constructing a Regional Human Rights Legal Order: The Inter-American Court, National Courts, and Judicial Dialogue, 1988–2014' (forthcoming) *International Journal of Constitutional Law*.

[20] Author's Interview, Bogota, 24 August 2016.

The Inter-American Court of Human Rights was acutely aware of these sources of resistance, and did not seek to impose specific standards from above. Instead, it deployed a variety of subtle, non-confrontational tactics to rattle national courts, eventually encouraging them to reconsider the domestic status of international law and their role in the protection of fundamental rights. In many cases, such discussions triggered productive self-regulation efforts that led to greater use of human rights jurisprudence and greater consistency in the criteria used to protect fundamental rights. As Mohallem explains, local courts also reached the conclusion that this type of transnational judicial dialogue was useful to 'create an additional layer of support if they are under pressure from domestic executive or legislative branches'.[21]

In Europe, the European Court of Justice (ECJ) relied on similar tactics to encourage domestic judges to defy national sovereignty and assist in the construction of a European legal order. Specifically, the ECJ promoted the use of the 'preliminary ruling' mechanism outlined in Article 177 of the Treaty of Rome, which formally empowered national courts to seek advice from its supranational counterpart on questions of European law. In the 1960s, when the ECJ developed an interest in routinising these referrals as a means to expand its opportunities to make consequential rulings, the preliminary ruling mechanism remained an obscure clause and few local courts had considered using it.[22] Moreover, there was no consensus concerning the place of European law in domestic legal systems. The ECJ therefore responded by cautiously incentivising referrals. For example, some of its rulings were 'carefully crafted appeals to judicial ego',[23] aimed at inviting national courts to participate in a transjdudicial dialogue. The ECJ presented itself as the 'protector of the prerogatives of lower national courts',[24] ruling that the resolution of certain issues required a partnership between courts at different levels. In addition, it planned outreach activities to engage judges in discussions about how to operationalise referral practices.[25] Like in the Americas, these subtle tactics ultimately transformed the choice architecture of national courts and promoted reactions from local judges that ultimately led to unprecedented patterns of decision-making.

So far, I have discussed a variety of interrelated social and political processes both at the national and international levels that created the conditions for greater judicial involvement in political debates. Judges across the world are now willing and able to hand down rulings with profound budgetary, institutional

---

[21] M Mohallem, 'Horizontal Judicial Dialogue on Human Rights: The Practice of Constitutional Courts in South America' in A Muller (ed), *Judicial Dialogue and Human Rights* (Cambridge, Cambridge University Press, 2017) 93.

[22] K Alter, *Establishing the Supremacy of European Law* (Oxford, Oxford University Press, 2001).

[23] AM Burley and W Mattli, 'Europe Before the Court: A Political Theory of Legal Integration' (1993) 47(1) *International Organization* 41, 63.

[24] ibid 64.

[25] ibid 58–62; L Helfer and AM Slaughter, 'Toward a Theory of Effective Supranational Adjudication' (1997) 107(2) *Yale Law Journal* 272, 303.

and policy implications. What does this all mean for our discussion about contemporary threats to judicial independence?

III. THE POLITICISATION OF THE JUDICIARY

When courts get involved in deeply political debates, their actions are rarely uncontroversial, and in some cases, they can even prove extremely divisive. Where some people see bold and courageous champions of minorities, fundamental rights and good government, others see reckless and destructive institutions acting inappropriately or out of character. Crucially, the more often political battles are fought in the courts, the more that is at stake in the judicial docket. And the more that is at stake in the judicial docket, the more courts become a coveted bounty, and a target of criticism and abuse, for politicians and civil society groups with an interest in shaping policy outcomes. In other words, it is only to be expected that the judicialisation of politics sometimes leads to the politicisation of the judiciary.

Political parties subject to corruption investigations, trade unions invested in the outcome of employment law cases, religious groups concerned with the direction of reproductive rights, or NGOs fighting to bring the perpetrators of horrendous human rights violations to court, all naturally want to have a say on who the judges are, and most importantly, how the judges think. In fact, because of lifetime or long-term appointments in the judiciary, this is often the most effective way to entrench policy preferences and outcomes in the state apparatus, and thus protect them from changing political winds.

In an age of judicialised political battles we therefore see more public and intense debates about judicial reform; more backlash against international courts such as the International Criminal Court, the European Court of Human Rights or the Inter-American Court of Human Rights; more ambitious and sophisticated forms of judicial lobbying; more heated confirmation hearings; and more forceful and nasty questioning of specific judicial rulings. All of these phenomena could be interpreted as threats to judicial independence, and some of them clearly are. But my view is that these reactions are only to be expected given how political life normally unfolds in a democracy, and that we should be cautious when 'crying wolf'.

To be sure, attacks on the courts, even merely rhetorical ones, are sometimes worrying, and we should all definitely remain on high alert. While in the contemporary world democracies are unlikely to die a sudden death, via, for instance, a military coup, they are still at risk of dying very slow deaths through a gradual process of democratic erosion. As the recent trajectories of Venezuela, Turkey or Hungary suggest, such processes tend to begin with incumbents weakening checks and balances, such as judicial independence.[26]

---

[26] S Levitsky and D Ziblatt, *How Democracies Die: What History Tells Us About Our Future* (London, Penguin Books, 2017).

These risks notwithstanding, I think we need to be realistic, and understand that in a democracy there is bound to be some degree of contestation and
scrutiny of relevant decision-makers, including the courts. This means that we
should be cautious not to universally catalogue these reactions as threats to judicial integrity. In fact, *legitimate* acts of public contestation may not just target
the content of judicial decisions, but also the very right of courts to make such
decisions in the first place. This was partially what we saw during the debate
around the *Miller* case in the United Kingdom. After all, as the previous discussion of the value changes that catalysed the judicialisation of politics makes
clear, the norms that dictate which questions are appropriate for judicial consideration, and which ones are not, are contingent, value-laden political constructs
in their own right.

It is certainly hard to know when it is necessary to rebuke attacks on the
judiciary in order to defend the rule of law, and when to avoid expressing unnecessary indignation or outrage in the face of challenges to judicial authority. As
I alluded to above, complacency is definitely not an option in this day and age.
However, pushing this outrage or indignation too far can severely undermine the
quality of public debate by censoring legitimate criticisms. Democracy needs
challengers and, to some degree, it also needs iconoclasts. It needs voices that
are prepared to make democratic critiques of democracy. These are the voices
that John Stuart Mill called 'the salt of the earth'. Without them, he thought,
politics, and life more generally, 'can become a stagnant pool'.

Allowing and accepting contestation of judicial decisions, whether it
is well- or ill-mannered, measured or vitriolic, is partly what is required by
democratic principles. Seeking to confine debate about judicial decisions and
judicial power, for example, to legal experts, might have the benefit of limiting the pool of challengers to actors that have a stake in the game and are
therefore less likely to pose existential threats to the judiciary. Unfortunately,
such solutions are unsatisfactory, first, because they are fundamentally elitist, and second, because they ignore the fact that in contemporary judicial
dockets there is much more at stake than the development of good and sound
jurisprudence. In a world where courts are bold and expansive in the way that
they interpret their institutional prerogatives, livelihoods, values, worldviews
and democratic mandates, are also at stake. As more actors are affected by
daily court rulings, more voices should be entitled to give opinions about what
judges say and do.

In addition to these principled reasons for being wary of overreacting in the
face of public challenges to judicial decisions, it is also the case that contestation
can be an invaluable source of improvement for the work that judges perform in
our societies. It is important to remember that even under the best institutional
arrangements, courts are not exempt from corruption, ill-judgement or ignorance. Judges must therefore be scrutinised very closely, and should be prepared
to face the spotlight. In this sense, research shows that courts are better at dealing
with complex social and political questions, and also mitigate their democratic

deficit, when instead of detaching themselves from the broader social context, judges actively listen to, and incorporate, other points of view.[27]

Finally, while republican indignation in the face of attacks or challenges to judicial power and authority certainly has an important role to play in the survival of democracy and the rule of law, it needs to be deployed with great caution. For this republican indignation to be effective, it cannot be used all the time because otherwise we run the risk of becoming numb to the very real possibility of democratic erosion and decay. It is only when attacks or challenges to judicial power and authority directly violate fundamental norms or balanced constitutional structures that we should 'cry wolf'.[28] I suspect that despite being unpleasant and malicious, the 'enemies of the people' headline does not meet such criteria. In fact, a study I conducted in the aftermath of the Supreme Court's decision suggests that the hostile media coverage of the case did not dent the public legitimacy of the judiciary.[29] My co-author and I found that 71 per cent of the British public *strongly or somewhat believed* that the Supreme Court's decision ought to be accepted and not challenged, indicating the continuing ability of the institution to issue decisions that settle political conflicts. Crucially, our study shows that framing the court as elitist does not affect levels of mass acceptance of its decision-making prerogatives.

To conclude, this discussion hardly exhausts the debate about the extent to which judicial independence is indeed under threat in contemporary democracies, or how we should react to the use of caustic language against the courts. My goal in this chapter was admittedly quite modest. First, I sought to contextualise the growing salience of courts in political life in order to better understand why the issue of threats to judicial independence has become a relevant one. Second, I tried to emphasise that given the rise of the court as a political battleground, any debate about threats to judicial independence must begin with an acknowledgement of the fact that politics, perhaps even more so politics under democracy, is fundamentally conflictual, messy, boisterous and at times simply unpleasant to watch. As a result, we should be cautious when deciding what we denounce as a threat and what we let pass.

---

[27] R Gargarella (ed), *Por una justicia dialógica: El Poder Judicial como promotor de la deliberación democrática*, (Buenos Aires, Siglo XXI, 2014); Botero (n 6).

[28] For example, when presidents with hegemonic ambitions want to change rules of judicial appointment and dismissal, or when they want to remove the ban on indefinite re-election.

[29] E Gonzalez-Ocantos and E Dinas, 'Compensation and Compliance: Source of Public Acceptance of the UK Supreme Court's Brexit Decision' (2019) 53(3) *Law & Society Review* 889.

4

Judicial Independence and Transformative Constitutionalism: Squaring the Circle of Legitimacy[1]

DANIEL BUTT

I. INTRODUCTION

COURTS IN THE United Kingdom and the United States face a crisis of democratic legitimacy. In both jurisdictions, political actors are looking askance at recent and prospective judicial interventions in the policy process and are engaged in, or considering making, changes to the constitutional balance to reduce the power of unelected judges. At the time of writing, the United Kingdom is still engaged in the complex process of withdrawal from the European Union. The status of the 1998 Human Rights Act, which incorporates the European Convention on Human Rights into British domestic law and effectively handed a new power of judicial review to the British courts, is part of the ongoing exit negotiations. This follows well-publicised clashes between the government and the UK Supreme Court in the run-up to the Brexit deadline of 31 October 2019, which culminated in the court declaring that the British Prime Minister, Boris Johnson, had acted illegally in proroguing parliament. The 2019 Conservative Party manifesto suggested that wide-ranging reform was on the government's agenda, promising 'We will update the Human Rights Act and administrative law to ensure that there is a proper balance between the rights of individuals, our vital national security and effective government', and 'We will ensure that judicial review is available to protect the rights of the individuals against an overbearing state, while ensuring that it is not abused to conduct politics by another means or to create needless delays.'[2] The politicisation of the courts in the United States is, of course, nothing new, but popular

---

[1] I am grateful to Denis Galligan and Ezequiel Gonzalez-Ocantos for very helpful comments on a draft of this article.
[2] 'Get Brexit Done: Unleash Britain's Potential', *The Conservative and Unionist Party Manifesto 2019*, 48.

interest in the composition and powers of the Supreme Court, and the US judiciary more broadly, reached fever pitch during the Trump presidency, following the confirmation of Neil Gorsuch, Brett Kavanaugh and Amy Coney Barrett. The prospect of a long-term conservative majority on the Supreme Court bench has meant the resurrection of debates over court expansion and jurisdiction stripping.[3] In both states, it is fair to say that either the independence of the judiciary from other branches of government or the scope of judicial power is under real threat.

Whether this is a good or a bad thing is, of course, open to debate. It is clear that courts sometimes act as significant actors in contemporary politics, effecting outcomes that executives and legislatures are seemingly unwilling or unable to bring about, despite their lack of a direct electoral mandate. Yet for every *Roe v Wade* there is a *Dred Scott v Stanford*. In many times and many places, courts have proven to be unreliable guardians of either individual rights or the common good: sometimes protecting powerful elite interests, at other times folding in the face of hostile public opinion. Those who have sought to defend a strong judiciary have therefore typically faced two powerful objections: what gives the court the right to overrule the public in deciding matters of political consequence? And why would we think they would be likely to make good decisions in any case? This chapter argues that both questions can be addressed by forging a politically salient role for the courts grounded in active public support for and participation in the constitutional process. It first outlines an account of what is termed the 'judicial trilemma', whereby there appears to be an inherent trade-off between three desirable features of courts in democracies, relating to the scope of their powers, their independence from other political actors and their democratic legitimacy. It suggests that this apparent trilemma can be resolved through a revised understanding of democratic legitimacy, whereby a democratic public is both actively involved in forging and supporting the constitutional order which affords courts the responsibility for upholding individual rights. It denies that such 'second-order' legitimacy can be found in either the United States or the United Kingdom at present, but argues that a model for such an approach can be found in the ideal of 'transformative constitutionalism' pioneered in post-apartheid South Africa.

II. THE JUDICIAL TRILEMMA

Jean-Jacques Rousseau begins *The Social Contract* with a famous observation of the state of humanity in civil society: 'Man is born free; and everywhere he is in chains.' He sets his work a specific challenge, 'What can make it legitimate?

---

[3] For discussion, see RD Doerfler and S Moyn, 'Making the Supreme Court Safe for Democracy', *New Republic*, 13 October 2020.

That question I think I can answer.'[4] All democratic institutions must face this challenge: why should they get to tell other people what to do, when they draw up, enact, and enforce coercive law, and why should those affected do what they say? Such questions of legitimacy are particularly difficult for courts to answer. Although there are undoubtedly many problems with the real-world processes which lead to legislatures and executives wielding political power, both are typically rooted in some form of direct election. When this is not true, as in cases such as the UK House of Lords, a hybrid of political appointment and hereditary privilege, the institutions in question are generally limited in relation to other political actors, such as directly elected assemblies or chief executives, who can point to their own democratic mandate and so cast themselves as executors of the will of the people. For the most part, judges and courts have no such grounding of their political authority. Yet in some times and places they have exercised a great deal of power: sometimes in the place of, and sometimes in opposition to, other political actors with more obvious sources of legitimacy.

There is variation between different polities as to the degree of power that courts are able to exercise and the extent to which they are, in practice, able to operate independently of other political institutions. Common law systems have tended to be more open to the propriety of some form of judicial review of legislation than civil law systems, although there is clearly an important difference between a polity such as the United States, where the principle of the separation of powers is a key feature of the constitutional order and where the power of judicial review was institutionalised following the 1803 Supreme Court ruling in *Marbury v Madison*, and the United Kingdom, which has historically affirmed the legislative supremacy of parliament and where judicial review has been primarily confined to the administrative acts of officials and public bodies within the law. Recent years, however, have seen British courts exceeding these traditional limits and acting in a way that has more directly challenged the decision-making powers of both government and parliament, not least on account of the incorporation of the rights of the European Convention on Human Rights into domestic law by the Human Rights Act 1998. This reflects a general trend in many jurisdictions around the world to entrench the rights of their citizens in formalised bills of rights, in both domestic and international contexts – a development that Charles Epp famously labelled 'the rights revolution'.[5] Such developments enhance the power of the judiciary because it falls to judges to hear claims from individuals that their rights have been infringed; this in turn can afford the courts a considerable degree of latitude as to how these rights should be interpreted. In some cases, interest groups have deliberately sought to cast their political agendas in terms of rights to bring

---

[4] J-J Rousseau, 'The Social Contract' in *The Social Contract and Discourses*, ed GDH Cole (London, Dent, 1913) 1.1, 5.

[5] CR Epp, *The Rights Revolution: Lawyers, Activists, and Supreme Courts in Comparative Perspective* (Chicago, University of Chicago Press, 1998).

them within the purview of the courts and challenge majoritarian decisions. In other cases, democratically elected political institutions have been ready, even eager, to let the courts decide on particular issues. This can take place for a number of reasons, ranging from the unwillingness of popularly elected politicians to take stands on certain controversial issues, to a recognition that, in an age where there is widespread disillusion with other governmental institutions, courts in many countries have retained a degree of public trust, and so can legitimate unpopular policy outcomes

Judicial power in democracies, then, seemingly gives rise to what might be termed the *judicial trilemma*. There seems to many (though not to all) to be good reasons for courts to satisfy three distinct desiderata; yet all three cannot be achieved simultaneously. Or so it would appear. These might be summarised as follows:

(1) Scope: courts should be able to wield some significant degree of political power.
(2) Independence: courts should be willing and able to act in a counter-majoritarian fashion to uphold individual rights.
(3) Legitimacy: courts should not act in a way that undermines the democratic character of the polity.

Quite what it means for a given desideratum to be met in a given context will depend on the nature of the polity in question, but also on one's background theory of constitutional democracy. The 'significant degree' of political power in (1), for example, could be satisfied by a range of different models of judicial review of legislative and/or executive action, whereby courts are able to overrule other political actors in order better to protect individual rights. Courts need not necessarily possess the constitutional ability to act in a quasi-legislative manner by effectively passing their own legislation, requiring that certain policy outcomes be brought about, but they must at least be able to check the activities of other political institutions, typically by reference to some national or international schedule of rights. It may well be thought that to be meaningful, such power should not simply concern scrutiny of the administrative activities of the executive within the law, important though this is, but should extend to at least some degree of assessment of the compatibility of legislation with the rights of citizens, whether this is prior to or following the passage of law. The independence of the judiciary under (2) must be understood not purely in de jure but in de facto terms: it is not enough for the courts to have the formal power to overrule other political actors if they are not realistically able to do so in practice. While one does witness substantial anticipation of possible judicial challenges in the formulation of legislation in some countries, one would expect to see some degree of genuine frustration of the intentions of other political institutions by the courts on at least some occasions in circumstances where (2) is realised.

The most complicated of these desiderata is the third, owing to the contested nature of democratic legitimacy. Legitimacy is an extensively debated concept, but the basic idea here is that the outputs of the political process should stand in the right kind of relation to the will of the people if they are to possess authority, and not simply represent coercion imposed by brute force.[6] It does not follow straightforwardly from this that the judiciary must be subservient to the legislature, or even to the apparent wishes of the majority. One vision of the historical constitutional order of England, for example, see courts as institutions that are justified not primarily in terms of their contribution to democracy (not least because they were established long before democracy was plausibly imaginable), but to broader ideas of the common good, understood in terms of the protection, welfare and advancement of all: an idea that finds support in the recent *Miller* judgment.[7] But simply advancing, or seeking to advance, the common good is not sufficient to satisfy (3). It is true that the courts have long coexisted with other political institutions, but contemporary elected elements of the British government possess a claim to democratic authority that surpasses their historical antecedents, given the more recent development of full-blown representative democracy, most particularly following the passage of the Representation of the People Acts 1918 and 1928. If judicial actions are to be legitimate and not merely coercive, on this view, they must have some characteristic which confers authority upon them with reference to the rule of the people.

So far so good, but this idea of democratic authorisation is itself open to more than one interpretation. The most straightforward is to equate it with following the preferences of the majority. To do so would be to open up an obvious tension between desiderata (2) and (3), and so suggest that there are occasions when courts both should act against the majority (when, for example, doing so upholds constitutional rights), and should not do so (as doing so would be to act undemocratically). This leads some to oppose the very idea of significant judicial power, and to support bringing all major decision-making under the purported control of the majority, by reducing the scope of judicial power (1) or limiting its independence (2). Bringing the courts to heel, however, is not without cost and does not in itself resolve the problem of democratic legitimacy. Judicial power has not increased for no reason: the enhanced role of the courts in scrutinising legislative and executive action has, as stated, arisen in part owing to the rise to prominence of political activism relating to individual rights, and this in turn reflects the emergence of a widely shared belief that these rights are of fundamental importance. The rise of international human rights law in the aftermath of the Second World War has coincided with processes of democratisation in countries formerly under colonial or communist control, and that often experienced appalling human rights abuses. One may also point, to some extent, to the idea that postindustrial politics has been characterised by a shift

---

[6] The theoretical literature on legitimacy is extensive, but see particularly AJ Simmons, *Justification and Legitimacy: Essays on Rights and Obligations* (Cambridge, Cambridge University Press, 2001).

[7] *R (Miller) v Secretary of State for Exiting the European Union* (2017) UKSC 5.

from broad questions of societal class and wealth redistribution to issues which often cut across traditional political cleavages, and are often of great importance to particular minority groups. The claims of these groups are typically framed in terms of rights, and courts have been asked to uphold these rights against less sympathetic majoritarian legislatures. Much of recent political history has been marked by struggles for equality and against discrimination, initially on the basis of race and gender, and more recently on grounds such as sexuality, disability and age. Such struggle has often taken the form of a fight for legal entitlement, typified by the civil rights movement in the United States. Many now believe that governmental action should properly be limited by respect for such rights. So, for example, legislatures would act wrongly if they sought to act in ways that violated basic rights, even if they did so at the behest of a majority of the populace.

Suppose we grant that the protection of individual rights, whether understood in a relatively narrow way, in terms of classic 'negative rights' such as freedom of speech and assembly, or more expansively in relation to social, cultural and economic interests, should indeed be a priority for modern-day democracies, or, more strongly, that such rights limit the permissible scope of democratic decision-making. It does not follow from this alone that the responsibility for ensuring that rights are prioritised or the limits of permissible democratic decision-making respected should belong to the courts. Some writers, such as Jeremy Waldron, have maintained that such functions should be exercised by legislative assemblies themselves.[8] If someone has to act in this way, it may as well be legislative majorities, who at least possess a certain kind of democratic mandate. One question here, of course, is whether we think that such legislative majorities are likely to do a good job of protecting such rights – or, at least, a better job than the courts. But two further issues arise. First, there is no guarantee in many polities that a legislative majority will in fact equate to an overall majority of those voting in elections, let alone a majority of those eligible to vote. In the United Kingdom, for example, the only government since the Second World War to have the nominal backing of a majority of those who voted was the 2010 Conservative–Liberal Democrat coalition government. The Labour administration elected in 2005 had an overall majority in the Commons of sixty-six seats, despite capturing only 35.2 per cent of the popular vote, equating to just 22 per cent of the electorate. Admittedly, this is in part a function of the electoral systems used in such countries, and more proportional systems typically avoid this specific problem, though it is not obvious that those voting endorse the specific constellation of parties that end up wielding power. But more substantively, it is not clear that allowing a majority to decide such an issue does in fact result in the desired degree of democratic legitimacy, quite aside from whether we think it has the practical effect of ensuring that

---

[8] J Waldron, 'Rights and Majorities: Rousseau Revisited' (1990) 32 *Nomos* 44.

individual rights are upheld, given that they represent some, but not all, of the people. This is the key element of the puzzle: majority rule is a necessary but not sufficient condition of democratic legitimacy.

It is not that majorities do not matter. There is an inescapable truth about the role of majorities in democratic theory: when a decision has to be taken, giving each affected person the same say satisfies a principle of political equality that is generally located at the very heart of the modern-day polity, however unequal its workings may be in practice.[9] There is something profoundly unsettling, from a democratic point of view, in the idea that the rule of the state might rest upon the will of less than half of the citizenry. Numbers matter in a democracy. The ultimate democratic sanction against a regime is revolution: the massed people on the streets reclaiming popular sovereignty from its rulers. Ultimately no constitutional order can stand against such a force. So majority rule is necessary for democratic legitimacy, but it is not sufficient. The majority cannot simply do anything it wants. The obvious problem with majority rule is the minority which does not get to have its way on the matter in question. The challenge faced by any theory of legitimacy is how to deal with this issue: how to ensure that the laws that bind do not have the character of chains, imposed on the few by the many, without the latter's consent. Different theorists have responded with more or less demanding accounts of democracy, that place varying degrees of limitations upon the actions of majorities. Less demanding accounts focus on the fairness of democratic procedures, maintaining that so long as minorities have the opportunity to put their case to the public, an appropriate respect for political equality requires that they respect the outcome of the decision-making process. More demanding accounts, often associated with the republican tradition, are more avowedly counter-majoritarian, seeking to disperse political power across different institutions, allowing multiple access points to political decision-making, providing avenues for the contestation of political decisions by citizens, and, in some cases, seeking to entrench individual rights against majorities by some form of constitutional protection.[10] One the face of it, the former approach compromises on desideratum (1) of the judicial trilemma by leaving the determination of rights-based questions to elected majorities, whereas the latter will end up sacrificing either (3) the democratic legitimacy of the regime, if courts manage to stay independent of majoritarian institutions, or (2) judicial independence, if they do not. Yet the republican tradition has resources to seek the square the circle and satisfy all three desiderata. To see how this can, at least, in theory, be done, it is helpful to return to how Rousseau sought to answer this very question.

[9] J Waldron, 'The Constitutional Conception of Democracy' in *Law and Disagreement* (Oxford, Oxford University Press, 1999); P Jones, 'Political Equality and Majority Rule' in D Miller and L Siedentop (eds), *The Nature of Political Theory* (Oxford, Oxford University Press, 1983).

[10] P Pettit, 'Republican Freedom and Contestatory Democratization' in I Shapiro and C Hacker-Cordon (eds), *Democracy's Value* (Cambridge, Cambridge University Press, 1999).

III. FIRST- AND SECOND-ORDER LEGITIMACY

In *The Social Contract*, Rousseau argues that citizens can be both free and yet subject to law, even in cases where the law in question does not accord with their initial judgement as to how the polity should be governed. The work is primarily concerned with voluntary forms of political association, whereby each individual freely consents to join the society in question. Thus, he writes:

> There is but one law which, from its nature, needs unanimous consent. This is the social compact; for civil association is the most voluntary of all acts. Every man being born free and his own master, no one, under any pretext whatsoever, can make any man subject without his consent.[11]

So unanimity is needed in order to join the polity in the first place. Thereafter, however, Rousseau argues that it is possible to have majority rule and yet retain one's freedom. This in itself is not an unusual idea: Locke argues for a version of the claim in his *Second Treatise on Government*, arguing that the idea is entailed by the decision to join the polity in the first place: 'When any number of Men have so *consented to make one Community* or Government, they are thereby presently incorporated, and make *one Body Politick*, wherein the *Majority* have a Right to act and conclude the rest.'[12] Accepting that decisions will have to be taken by majority rule is necessary if the association is to be practicable: 'For if *the consent of the majority* shall not in reason, be received, *as the act of the whole*, and conclude every individual; nothing but the consent of every individual can make any thing to be the act of the whole: But such a consent is next impossible ever to be had.'[13] Whether a persistent minority in such a position may truly be said to have avoided the tyranny of the majority is evidently open to question. Rousseau's account, in any case, is more sophisticated. The thought is that a member of the minority in Rousseau's society does, in fact, consent to the law, even though they voted against it: 'The citizen gives his consent to all the laws, including those which are passed in spite of his opposition, and even those which punish him when he dares to break any of them.'[14] The key to understanding Rousseau's position is his concept of the 'general will', which represents, in some sense, the common good of society, though its precise meaning is much disputed. Thus he writes:

> When in the popular assembly a law is proposed, what the people is asked is not exactly whether it approves or rejects the proposal, but whether it is in conformity with the general will, which is their will. Each man, in giving his vote, states his opinion on that point; and the general will is found by counting votes. When therefore the

[11] Rousseau (n 4) 4.2, 93.
[12] J Locke, *Two Treatises of* Government, ed P Laslett (Cambridge, Cambridge University Press, 1988) s 95, 348.
[13] ibid s 98, 350.
[14] Rousseau (n 4) 4.2, 93.

opinion that is contrary to my own prevails, this proves neither more nor less than that I was mistaken, and that what I thought to be the general will was not so.[15]

There are two primary ways of understanding this passage. Both, however, make use of the same underlying idea – the thought that the consent of the people can be preserved even in circumstances of first-order disagreement if there is a second-order agreement that the decision of the majority is the right way to proceed. The minority, accordingly, now endorses the decision of the majority – either because they believe, as a result of the information about others' beliefs revealed by the vote, that they were wrong, or because they believe that given the fact that the majority feel as they do, the right thing for the polity to do is to implement the will of the majority.[16] In both cases, there is now consensus on how to proceed. This goes beyond the idea of 'agreeing to disagree' to a more substantive type of concord: one would expect, if the initial vote were to be re-run, that there would now be unanimity. Accordingly, Rousseau seems to have squared the legitimacy circle – the minority have been outvoted, but they endorse the outcome of the decision-making procedure in which they have been involved as representing the right course for society. As such, they can be meaningfully subject to the law, even a law they initially opposed, and yet as free as they were in the state of nature.

Rousseau's particular model is, as many have observed, a particularly demanding one, even for small city states in the eighteenth century, and undoubtedly for complex modern-day states. An approach to legitimacy that requires universal initial consent to the terms of association, at least some degree in active law-making for all citizens (though Rousseau excluded women), and some kind of unanimous and profound commitment to upholding the outcome of the legislative procedure is probably best seen as modelling an ideal type of legitimacy, rather than providing a readily replicable standard in the real world. (Indeed, Rousseau's own foray into constitution writing in Poland was rather less expansive in its ambitions.) But the underlying idea of the possibility of there being second-order agreement about what to do in a context of first-order disagreement points the way to a resolution of the judicial trilemma. The thought here is that judicial action, or other forms of counter-majoritarian intervention, could be legitimate if they had their own form of democratic support, of a majoritarian or even super-majoritarian nature. Put simply, if the people are in favour of judges acting to uphold the rights of minorities, then such action cannot be said to contravene the will of the people. This could be so even if a majority of the people were opposed to the specific decision that the courts were making in a given case. There is no logical contradiction in the idea that one is on one level in favour of course of action A, but believes that there is good reason to allow another body to make the decision, even if one knows that this will lead

---

[15] ibid 93–94.
[16] For discussion, see C Brooke, 'At the Limits of General Will: Silence, Exile, Ruse, and Disobedience in Rousseau's Political Thought' (2007) 4 *Les études philosophiques* 425.

to course of action B. (This is why Richard Wollheim's much discussed democratic paradox, whereby an outvoted minority that is committed to the rule of the majority seemingly wants two different things to happen at the same time, is not strictly speaking a paradox at all.)[17] Indeed, it was in the past commonplace in a US context to point out that the Supreme Court generally had a relatively high level of public support as measured through opinion polling, consistently outperforming both the US Congress and (often) the US president, though increasing political polarisation means that this is less true now than once it was.[18] It seems clear that it would be too much of a stretch to suggest that the judicial trilemma is resolved in the contemporary United Kingdom, as one could plausibly maintain that none of the three desiderata are met in a context where the powers of the courts are limited and receding, and where their exercise has recently nonetheless been the subject of considerable contemporary disquiet. But might one seek to appeal to the idea of second-order legitimacy and the long-accepted principle of judicial review to suggest that the judicial trilemma has been resolved in the United States? There are real problems with such a move.

The first issue concerns the emaciated idea of democratic legitimacy being deployed. Recall the three aspects of Rousseau's ideal type account of legitimacy: universal consent to the terms of association, active participation in the passage of legislation, and a high (indeed unanimous) degree of consensus over political outcomes. The contemporary United States falls short on all three. Consider, for example, the notion of universal, or even widespread, consent to the terms of association. The need for some kind of non-partisan, supermajority approval for the ratification of constitutions is well understood, and one could, if particularly charitably disposed, describe the process of the 1787 Constitutional Convention in such terms. The problem comes with the amendment procedure. Amendments to the US Constitution requires the approval of two-thirds of both houses of Congress and three-quarters of state legislatures.[19] Imagine (counterfactually) that the initial Constitution had been endorsed by the unanimous agreement of all US citizens. We could at that point cast the counter-majoritarian character of the amendment procedure in terms of second-order legitimacy: the demos, or more, precisely, all the individual members of the demos, would have agreed to constrain itself, in the manner of Ulysses ordering that he be bound to the mast so that he should not be driven to jump overboard

---

[17] R Wollheim, 'A Paradox in the Theory of Democracy' in P Laslett and WG Runciman (eds), *Philosophy, Politics and Society* (Oxford, Basil Blackwell, 1962).

[18] For current opinion polling data on the US Supreme Court, see https://news.gallup.com/poll/4732/supreme-court.aspx. For historical data, see JM Scheb, 'Public Holds US Supreme Court in High Regard' (1993) 77 *Judicature* 273; R Handberg, 'Public Opinion and the United States Supreme Court 1935–1981' (1984) 59 *International Social Science Review* 3.

[19] Although this is how all twenty-seven amendments to the Constitution have been passed to date, Article V of the Constitution also allows for two-thirds of state legislatures to require Congress to call a constitutional convention. Amendments which came out of such process would then need ratification by three-quarters of the states.

by the song of the Siren. But it is not clear that such a justification can hold once significant periods of time pass, and the people living in the polity are no longer the people who supported the passage of the constitution at its inception, or who (more realistically) were represented by the participants at the Convention. The best-case scenario is now one whereby there is still widespread support for the Constitution's counter-majoritarian measures, even though they were not the doing of anyone currently alive. Of course there is no guarantee that this will be the case, and it is also possible that what will ensue will be an unhappy majority constrained by anti-majoritarian institutions that prevent it enacting its will. (It seems likely that coming years may see difficult disputes about the fairness of the US electoral system of just this kind, in relation to both the role of the Electoral College in electing the president, and the composition and powers of the US Senate, which is premised on each state wielding the same degree of power regardless of its population size). Even the best-case scenario, however, leaves a great deal to be desired from a democratic perspective. It cannot be said that the people are authors of their own governmental institutions in any meaningful sense if these institutions have their origins in the eighteenth century and there is no practicable pathway to their reform. Popular support for these institutions in such a context may represent not so much a genuine endorsement of the system of government as a form of Stockholm Syndrome on the part of the electorate. Public approval, on this account, is not sufficient for legitimacy: on such a metric, any number of authoritarian, explicitly non-democratic governments would possess legitimacy, and indeed, would be more legitimate insofar as they were more successful in moulding their subjects to accept their rule. There needs to be a more meaningful link between political opinion and political outcome. Without it, second-order legitimacy looks to be second class.

The claim, then, is that regardless of its system of judicial review, the constitutional order of the contemporary United States falls short of desideratum (3), on democratic legitimacy. Yet it can also be contended that it fails in terms of desideratum (2), on independence and the protection of rights. This is because despite the significant degree of power which the US judiciary wields, it is far from clear that this power is in fact being used independently of established political parties in defence of individual liberties. This charge may be levelled in thinner or thicker ways, depending on whether one's theory of the appropriate role of the judiciary includes a substantive commitment to a particular, progressive understanding of individual rights. On a thin level, there is good evidence to demonstrate that the Supreme Court, for example, more typically acts in accordance with, rather than contrary to, public opinion, even though scholars disagree as to the precise mechanisms that seem to constrain its decision-making.[20] Michael J Klarman, for example, argues that, in practice,

[20] CJ Casillas, PK Enns and PC Wohlfarth, 'How Public Opinion Constrains the US Supreme Court' (2011) 55 *American Journal of Political Science* 74; MEK Hall, 'The Semiconstrained Court: Public Opinion, the Separation of Powers, and the US Supreme Court's Fear of Nonimplementation' (2014) 58 *American Journal of Political Science* 352.

constitutional interpretation 'almost inevitably reflects the broader social and political context of the times'.[21] Thus, he suggests, even seemingly progressive judicial interventions really represented the Supreme Court playing catch-up with wider society, only protecting women under the Equal Protections Clause after the hard running had been made by the women's movement, and invalidating racial desegregation only after a dramatic change in public opinion on race following the Second World War. Klarman argues that this means that judges are unlikely to be heroes or villains:

> Judges who generally reflect public opinion are unlikely to have the inclination, and they may well lack the capacity, to defend minority rights from majoritarian invasion. It is difficult to treat them as villains, because their rulings simply reflect the dominant opinion of their time and place. Yet neither are their interventions on behalf of minority rights likely to be particularly heroic, as such decisions will usually reflect the views held by a majority or a sizable minority of the population.[22]

A conclusion that the courts are doing little to impact public policy contrary to public opinion is problematic if we believe, as under desideratum (2), that they should be seeking to uphold individual rights against the majority, and if we hold that public opinion is at least sometimes hostile to these rights. It is not hard to find instances of judicial acquiescence in the face of political pressure: the initial timidity of the courts in protecting the rights of terrorist suspects in the aftermath of 9/11 being an obvious case in point. If one believes that the courts should be standing up to a hostile Congress and presidency, there is little to draw the eye since the shift to accept aspects of Roosevelt's New Deal in the 1930s, the likes of *Brown v Topeka Board of Education* and *Roe v Wade* notwithstanding. More substantively, if one believes that the Supreme Court should be playing a progressive role in protecting the rights and interests of the most vulnerable members of society, there is much in its decision-making in recent years, from voting rights to reproductive health and corporate personhood, that should give rise to considerable consternation.

It may seem as if the argument of the previous paragraphs asks too much – is it not unreasonable to accuse the Supreme Court both of lacking democratic legitimacy and of tracking too closely to public opinion? But there is no contradiction here: a successful resolution of the judicial trilemma would see a court that was willing and able to stand against majority public opinion in defence of individual rights, and which would have a mandate to so act which stemmed not from a historic constitution but from contemporary process of democratic authorisation. It is to the possibility of such a model, grounded in a richer account of second-order legitimacy, that we now turn.

---

[21] MJ Klarman, *From Jim Crow to Civil Rights: The Supreme Court and the Struggle for Racial Equality* (Oxford, Oxford University Press, 2006) 5–6.
[22] ibid 6.

IV. TRANSFORMATIVE CONSTITUTIONALISM AND THE COURTS

Suppose we accept the argument of the preceding section: that both the limited exercise of judicial power in the United Kingdon and the more expansive US model fail to resolve the judicial trilemma. Is there an alternative approach available, one that allows for the protection of individual rights by counter-majoritarian institutions without violating principles of democratic legitimacy? This section suggests that the blueprint for such a model – in theory, at least – can be found in the South African experience of transformative constitutionalism.

Recent years have seen burgeoning interest in the idea of transformative constitutionalism, with some identifying a judicial movement spreading from the Global South with the potential to revolutionise the political role of the courts around the world. In Karl Klare's influential description, the term refers to, 'a long-term project of constitutional enactment, interpretation, and enforce-ment committed ... to transforming a country's political and social institutions and power relationships in a democratic, participatory, and egalitarian direc-tion'. This is an enterprise aimed at bringing about large-scale social change through non-violent political processes grounded in law. 'In the background', he writes, 'is an idea of a highly egalitarian, caring, multicultural community, governed through participatory, democratic processes in both the polity and large portions of what we now call the "private sphere".'[23] Although it has often been associated with the justiciability of socioeconomic rights, Michaela Hailbronner argues that it should not be understood only in terms of enabling the courts to combat poverty in the South, writing:

> Transformative constitutions cherish a broader emancipatory project, which attributes a key role to the state in pursuing change. As a result, transformative constitutional-ism as a legal concept is not a distinctive feature of Southern societies, but part of a broader global trend toward more expansive constitutions which encompass positive and socioeconomic rights and which no longer view private relationships as outside constitutional bounds.[24]

Accordingly, authors have identified projects of transformative constitutionalism in a large number of diverse polities, including India, Hungary, Germany and a range of states in Africa and Latin America.[25] This section, however, focuses on the location where the term was coined and first implemented: South Africa,

---

[23] KE Klare, 'Legal Culture and Transformative Constitutionalism' (1998) 14 *South African Journal on Human Rights* 146.

[24] M Hailbronner, 'Transformative Constitutionalism: Not Only in the Global South' (2017) 65 *American Journal of Comparative Law* 527, 529.

[25] O Vilhena, U Baxi and F Viljoen, *Transformative Constitutionalism: Comparing the Apex Courts of Brazil, India and South Africa* (Pretoria, Pretoria University Law Press, 2013); A von Bogdandy et al (eds), *Transformative Constitutionalism in Latin America: The Emergence of a New Ius Commune* (Oxford, Oxford University Press, 2007); E Kibet and C Fombad, 'Transformative Constitutionalism and the Adjudication of Constitutional Rights in Africa' (2017) 17 *African Human Rights Law Journal* 340.

following the end of the apartheid era. Advocates of the approach in a South African context, such as Klare and Justice Pius Langa, an original member of the Constitutional Court of South Africa and later Chief Justice, outlined a central role for the judiciary in advancing a programme of social reform grounded in an expansive understanding of human rights, anchored in respect for the rule of law. Langa located the basis of the idea of transformative constitutionalism in the Epilogue to the interim Constitution of South Africa, which describes the Constitution as providing

> a historic bridge between the past of a deeply divided society characterised by strife, conflict, untold suffering and injustice, and a future founded on the recognition of human rights, democracy and peaceful co-existence and development opportunities for all South Africans, irrespective of colour, race, class, belief or sex.[26]

This is the essence of the desired transformation of South African society, which Langa filled out in terms of three overarching goals. The first is the achievement of substantive equality, going beyond the provision of basic socioeconomic rights to include 'also the provision of greater access to education and opportunities through various mechanisms, including affirmative action measures'.[27] This rests upon an unusually expansive understanding of minimal rights, framed not only in terms of ensuring the provision of a minimal degree of well-being up to a sufficientarian threshold, but also taking into account positional goods which have a bearing on individuals' ability to compete for desirable positions within society. The second is the transformation of legal culture. Citing Etienne Mureinik's claim that the transition from apartheid needed to be characterised by a shift from a 'culture of authority' to a 'culture of justification', he writes:

> The Constitution demands that all decisions be capable of being substantively defended in terms of the rights and values that it enshrines. It is no longer sufficient for judges to rely on the say-so of parliament or technical readings of legislation as providing justifications for their decisions. Under a transformative Constitution, judges bear the ultimate responsibility to justify their decisions not only by reference to authority, but by reference to ideas and values.[28]

Finally, the transformative aspect of the constitution is understood in terms of a never-ending work in progress. For Langa, the 'transformative' aspect of transformative constitutionalism does not refer solely to the transition from the apartheid era and the consolidation of a new democracy. Rather, he writes:

> [T]ransformation is not a temporary phenomenon that ends when we all have equal access to resources and basic services and when lawyers and judges embrace a culture of justification. Transformation is a permanent ideal, a way of looking at the world that creates a space in which dialogue and contestation are truly possible, in which

---

[26] P Langa, 'Transformative Constitutionalism' (2006) 17 *Stellenbosch Law Review* 351, 352.
[27] ibid.
[28] ibid 353.

new ways of being are constantly explored and created, accepted and rejected and in which change is unpredictable but the idea of change is constant.

One could also look in this regard at recent work supporting 'dialogic' courts that sees them as instigators of society-wide constitutional debate. Such a perspective does not see courts as possessing a monopoly on constitutional interpretation, but as working in partnership with other political institutions to produce answers to constitutional questions that both engage society and, in the face of 'pervasive yet reasonable disagreement about the meaning of rights', are 'satisfying to the citizenry as a whole'.[29]

This is undoubtedly an ambitious vision. The model described goes beyond the articulation of a procedure of constitutional endorsement: it is not sufficient, for example, that large numbers of the public be involved in the process of constitutional drafting; rather, it must be the case that they do so in such a way that they are willing to accept the upshot of the process as sufficiently reflective of the will of the people to warrant their assent. There is no guarantee that such a process will in fact lead to a good settlement in constitutional terms. Its focus on transformation means that the success of the project is to be judged not only by the public's initial enthusiasm, nor indeed their ongoing commitment, but also by the extent to which particular progressive outcomes are realised in practice. As will be seen, the extent to which such outcomes have actually come about in South Africa is very much open to question. The model of transformative constitutionalism does, however, provide the raw materials for a resolution of the judicial trilemma. The courts are explicitly mandated with the project of social transformation, understood not only in terms of basic rights, but the more demanding ideal of social equality. The laws are to be interpreted and implemented in the light of this ideal. The ideal does not come from parliamentary law-making, nor from some idea of the original meaning of an eighteenth-century constitution,[30] nor the judges' own 'moral reading' of the polity's constitutional tradition.[31] The people's second-order agreement to judicial authority, then, is not a passive acceptance of a fait accompli. It is a result of their own active involvement in the business of constitution-making; understood not as a one-off event, but an ongoing process. Speaking in Oxford in 2008, while still Chief Justice, Langa argued that the Constitution could be understood not in terms of the hypothetical social contracts beloved by contemporary political theorists, but as an actual historical contract between the people of South Africa, at least in relation to the current generation:

> The Constitutional Assembly directly responsible for the drafting and adoption of the final Constitution took public participation to a new level. A host of public

---

[29] C Bateup, 'The Dialogic Promise – Assessing the Normative Potential of Theories of Constitutional Dialogue' (2005) 71 *Brooklyn Law Review* 1109, 1175–76.

[30] A Scalia, 'Originalism: The Lesser Evil' (1988) 57 *University of Cincinnati Law Review* 849.

[31] R Dworkin, *Freedom's Law: The Moral Reading of the American Constitution* (Oxford, Oxford University Press, 1999).

meetings and workshops were held around the country. It received over two million submissions from private individuals and organizations before the first draft was circulated for public comment. The unprecedented scale of public participation is evidence that the constitutional settlement is expressed in terms that many South Africans embrace.[32]

The explanatory memorandum attached to the beginning of the Constitution makes clear that the idea of popular agreement lay at the heart of the adoption process. It notes that the objective of the drafting process

> was to ensure that the final Constitution is legitimate, credible and accepted by all South Africans. To this extent, the process of drafting the Constitution involved many South Africans in the largest public participation programme ever carried out in South Africa. After nearly two years of intensive consultations, political parties represented in the Constitutional Assembly negotiated the formulations contained in this text, which are an integration of ideas from ordinary citizens, civil society and political parties represented in and outside of the Constitutional Assembly. This Constitution therefore represents the collective wisdom of the South African people and has been arrived at by general agreement.

Abrak Saati details the extensive iterative process of consultation and popular participation that led to the passage of the Constitution, including an extensive public education programme involving a newsletter, television and radio programmes, a website, and talkline as well as public hearings, public meetings and participatory workshops. Thus during the first stage of the process 'a total of 20,549 people and representatives from 717 civil society organizations attended the public meetings. By the end, two million submissions had been written by the South African public and sent to the Assembly'.[33] Following the production of a working draft, a second stage of consultations was launched: 'Two hundred fifty thousand submissions were collected during this second stage. Once the submissions were reviewed, the Assembly prepared a revised edition of the draft. A copy of the revised draft was subsequently sent to each person who had made a submission.'[34] Admittedly, Saati draws attention to 'the somewhat idealized story that has developed around the South African process', noting that 'it is often "forgotten," or at least not mentioned – that the participatory elements of the process were preceded by elite negotiations on the highest political level'. The public was only invited to participate once a degree of consensus had been reached at an elite level, and then final decision-making on the contents of the Constitution rested with the directly elected

---

[32] D Butt, 'Transformative Constitutionalism and Socio-economic Rights: Report of a Lecture by the Chief Justice of South Africa' (The Foundation for Law, Justice and Society, 2008) www.fljs.org/sites/www.fljs.org/files/publications/ChiefJusticeLanga_report.pdf.

[33] A Saati, 'Participatory Constitution-making as a Transnational Legal Norm: Why Does it "Stick" in Some Contexts and Not in Others?' (2017) 2 *UC Irvine Journal of International, Transnational, and Comparative Law* 113, 133–34.

[34] ibid 134.

constitutional assembly and the Constitutional Court. As such, the sense in which this might be genuinely described as representing the 'collective wisdom' of the South African people is open to question. Nonetheless, she maintains that there is 'no denying the fact' that the South African case 'was impressive in terms of the many avenues through which people were able to get involved in the process'.[35] This is not quite the Rousseauian model outlined above: there is no pretence that involvement or agreement was universal, and questions naturally arise as to how the passage of time has affected and will affect the initial popular grounding of the constitutional order.[36] One would not wish to overstate the degree of persisting constitutional consensus in contemporary South Africa, nor to deny the presence of deep social and economic inequalities in the present day.[37] But the project has had some real achievements in practice,[38] and in theory it provides the basis for a form of judicial policy-making extensive in scope, progressive in outcomes, with a significant degree of independence of other political actors and which possesses a much more plausible claim to democratic legitimacy than is the case in the United States or United Kingdom. Could it provide a blueprint for judicial reform in these polities? One could answer this question in an optimistic or pessimistic fashion.

The pessimistic answer is not hard to articulate. Both the United Kingdom and the United States are currently experiencing a high degree of political division and polarisation, typified by the Brexit divide in the former, and attitudes to the Trump presidency in the latter. The project of transformative constitutionalism seems to require some high degree of initial consensus if it is to attain its goal of empowering the judiciary to act in a democratically legitimate fashion, and indeed of ongoing second-order consensus given the potential for acute conflict between different branches of government. But consensus seems hard to

---

[35] ibid.

[36] For more on the recent workings of transformative constitutionalism in South Africa, see M Rapatsa, 'Transformative Constitutionalism in South Africa: 20 Years of Democracy' (2014) 5 *Mediterranean Journal of Social Sciences* 887; Kibet and Fombad (n 25).

[37] Statistics South Africa, 'Inequality Trends in South Africa: A Multidimensional Diagnostic of Inequality' (2019) available at www.statssa.gov.za/publications/Report-03-10-19/Report-03-10-192017.pdf.

[38] For example, Kibet and Fombad (n 25) argue: 'There is little doubt that the present South Africa is better off than in the apartheid era as far as the protection of human rights, the rule of law and constitutionalism are concerned. The landmark decisions of the South African Constitutional Court in *National Coalition for Gay and Lesbian Equality & Another v Minister of Justice & Others* (striking down laws criminalising sex between consenting males); *Minister of Home Affairs & Another v Fourie & Another* (validating same-sex marriages); *Du Toit & Another v Minister of Welfare and Population Development & Others* (affirming the rights of a lesbian couple to jointly adopt a child); *S v Makwanyane & Another* (striking down the death penalty); *Government of the Republic of South Africa & Others v Grootboom & Others* (affirming the right to adequate housing for the most vulnerable in the society); and *Economic Freedom Fighters v Speaker of the National Assembly & Others; Democratic Alliance v Speaker of the National Assembly & Others* (ordering President Jacob Zuma to refund public funds used to improve his private Nkandla home in violation of the Constitution) and others, are outstanding, and illustrate this point' (354–35).

find in either polity at present. It is not that these states have never experienced such moments: one might look, for example, to the immediate aftermath of the Second World War in the United Kingdom, and the subsequent foundation of the welfare state and National Health Service, for evidence of the possibility of mass determination to make meaningful changes to the political order, inspired by concern for the least advantaged and, to at least some degree, a belief in the value of social justice and equality. But it is admittedly hard to imagine such a coming together across partisan divides in the present day. The context of South Africa in the 1990s was obviously particular and unusual, not least on account of the dominance of a single political party, the African National Congress, following the end of apartheid. From the pessimistic vantage point, even if one is willing to accept that transformative constitutionalism has made the jump from theory to practice in South Africa (which may, of course, be disputed), it does not follow that the model is applicable elsewhere, and perhaps especially not in consolidated, as opposed to transitional, democracies with, for good or ill, well-established and entrenched political institutions. One could point, for example, to the condemnation that has recently been visited upon European and British courts given their role in upholding the European Convention on Human Rights and the Human Rights Act, and suggest that the implementation of some version of transformative constitutionalism would lead to an even greater degree of conflict and vilification, as familiar political divides were reopened in the judicial branch. On this account there is no way to resolve the judicial trilemma in states such as the United States or the United Kingdom, and we will simply have to decide which of scope, independence or democratic legitimacy it is best to compromise in the name of the best all-things-considered course of action.

The optimistic perspective denies that things are as set in stone as this would appear. It points to a resurgence of interest in questions of constitutional design in both countries, even if it acknowledges that such issues have come to the fore at least in part as a result of dissatisfaction with the current order of things. Aside from the aforementioned political divisions, many feel that current systems of government have proved unable to act appropriately in relation to serious present-day and near-future threats, most obviously in relation to the COVID-19 pandemic and the prospect of the devastating impact of climate change. The United Kingdom will necessarily need to reflect on its constitutional arrangements once the final nature of its withdrawal from the European Union becomes apparent, and there is increasing discussion of the idea of some kind of a constitutional convention to consider such issues, as well burgeoning interest in alternative forms of government such as mini-publics and citizens' juries.[39] As previously stated, dissatisfaction with many aspects of the constitutional order in the United States is becoming readily apparent, and there is good

---

[39] See eg S White, 'Parliaments, Constitutional Conventions, and Popular Sovereignty' (2017) 19 *British Journal of Politics and International Relations* 320.

reason to think that pressure will increase at least for reform of the Electoral College in presidential elections, the make-up and powers of the Senate, and the make-up and powers of the Supreme Court, whatever the outcome of the 2020 presidential and congressional elections. So serious constitutional change will plausibly at least be on the agenda in both countries. But constitutional debate, even significant constitutional reform, is not sufficient to resolve the trilemma, in the absence of genuinely widespread consensus as to the appropriate role of the judiciary and the values which it should be seeking to reflect and implement in its rulings. Could such a consensus come about?

It is not impossible to think that it could. One could envisage various types of constitutional reform process that would seek to address the judicial trilemma. One approach would aim at identifying areas of genuine widespread agreement, such as on schedules of basic rights, and seeking popular endorsement for assigning a role to the judiciary in the protection of these rights. Quite how 'transformative' such a model would be might be open to question: a minimal approach might simply seek public inputs and look for areas of overlap between the submissions, a more ambitious programme would see popular participation as being more deliberative in character, and so would wait to see what schedule of rights came out of the relevant consultative processes before placing the final results before the public for ratification. Such a process could seek to mirror certain types of aspects of the South African model, in terms of encouraging widespread public participation and debate. But the South African example is also suggestive of a potentially much more radical approach. Scholars who write on transformative constitutionalism in the aftermath of apartheid often stress the role of the Truth and Reconciliation Commission in paving the way for the subsequent widespread acceptance of the rule of law and of the role of the judiciary in promoting the values of the Constitution. Mashele Rapatsa, for example, writes

> The establishment of this commission paved a way for a genuine reconstruction and development, particularly with regards to soliciting a societal acceptance of democracy as a tool to heal the nation. It bred tolerance and forgiveness among the people, while also inculcating respect for the established justice serving institutions of the Constitution.[40]

The United Kingdom and the United States are not facing the same kind of political challenges as South Africa in 1994. But they are both states, like South Africa, with complicated and problematic histories of imperialism and racial malfeasance. Recent years have seen what may prove to be deeply significant stirrings of public consciousness, as a younger generation becomes interested in the persisting effects of historic wrongdoing. The model of the South African Truth and Reconciliation Commission has proved influential in a number of

---

[40] Rapatsa (n 36) 894.

other states, including, for example, the work of the Truth and Reconciliation Commission of Canada in relation to Native Peoples. Transformative constitutionalism in South Africa is explicitly grounded in the particular circumstances of South African history – a link is drawn between the egregious racist wrongdoing of the apartheid era and the Constitution's present-day commitment to social equality. One could imagine an equivalent process in the United States or the United Kingdom which would represent a genuine coming to terms with the country's past, and which would result in handing the courts a role in seeking to rectify deep-rooted structural injustice, in pursuit of a shared vision of societal redress.[41] Admittedly, for so long as questions relating to reparative justice are seen through the prism of culture wars and partisan politics it is hard to see such a project coming to fruition. But perhaps the seeds have been sown for a truly progressive resolution to the judicial trilemma, whereby the people affirm an active role for the courts not only with reference to basic rights, but to the full-blooded pursuit of social justice.

[41] For related thoughts in a British context, see S White, *A New Kind of Dreaming: Democratic English Patriotism* (London, Compass, forthcoming).

5

Self-fulfilling Prophecies: 'Populism' and 'Judicial Independence' in Europe

BOGDAN IANCU

I. COURTS UNDER ATTACK: WHERE, WHICH, IN WHAT WAYS, AND FOR WHAT REASONS

THE 2019 DEBATES from which this chapter originated seized upon wider, well-timed concerns about the impact of 'populism' upon 'courts'.[1] In the wider context, both terms need a great deal of fine-tuning and tweaking. Populism, an exacerbated form of democracy regarded as unfettered majority rule, is itself an umbrella notion. This label has been affixed in recent years to a congeries of phenomena, ranging – among others – from the Brexit referendum or the vagaries of the Trump presidency to the Polish (2015–), Hungarian (2011–) or Romanian (2012, 2017–19) crises. To be sure, if the driving force of populism is perceived to lie in the aversion towards certain kinds of elites,[2] courts are an obvious target, insofar as the judiciary is the prototypical, classic type of counter-majoritarian structure. The judiciary, as a corporate profession and as an institution, is undoubtedly, necessarily elitist. But, at the level of phenomena, the reference to 'courts' in the public and academic discourses is also a generous synecdoche. In the various jurisdictions used in recent debates to illustrate this trend, political attacks on 'courts' (or reforms perceived or presented as such) concern a variety of judicial, quasi-judicial and even administrative bodies, ranging from constitutional tribunals (not formally parts of the third branch), courts proper or only apex courts, public prosecutors and judicial councils. Thus, using the same formulas to describe derailments in the yellow press, such as the infamous 'Enemies of the People' front page published by the

---

[1] www.putneydebates2019.co.uk (all websites last visited on 29 June 2019).
[2] Paradoxically, politicians are also 'elitist', by definition. For the argument that representative democracy is an inherently 'aristocratic' form of selection (as opposed to drawing lots, the archetypical democratic modality of selection), see B Manin, *The Principles of Representative Government* (New York, Cambridge University Press, 1997).

Daily Mail in the aftermath of the *Miller* judgment,[3] *and* the ongoing Polish constitutional crisis is arguably imprecise, if not misleading.

This contribution seeks to do justice to a sliver of the phenomenon, namely to analyse the implications of relevant recent conflicts in two newer EU Member States: Romania and Poland. In both cases, political majorities sought to overhaul organic legislation, using as primary justifications the alleged unaccountability of the judiciary and the need to make it more responsive. These reforms encountered strong opposition and disapproval from internal political factions and civil society actors, parts of the national judiciaries and international institutions. In the case of Poland, 'the lack of an independent and legitimate constitutional review' and various judicial reforms generated a reasoned proposal by the EU Commission under Article 7(1) TEU, asking the Council to determine 'the existence of a clear risk of a serious breach of the rule of law'.[4] Romanian amendments to the organic laws of the judiciary elicited a cascade of reproofs on the part of the EU Commission and its counterparts in the Council of Europe (Venice Commission, the Consultative Council of European Judges, GRECO).[5] Although in the Romanian case formal Article 7 proceedings were not triggered (unlike in Poland or Hungary), credible threats to this effect were made by EU officials, notably by socialist *Spitzenkandidat* (and then-incumbent EU Commission Vice-President) Frans Timmermans,[6] whereas the European Parliament issued a resolution to express dissatisfaction and worry with the effects of said changes on 'the independence of the Romanian judicial system'.[7]

The argument I make in this chapter is that clashes between the majoritarian branches and the judiciary in the new Eastern European EU Member States do not result only from political instrumentalism ('populism'). Conflicts are also fomented by an understanding of judicial independence that transcends both the accepted meaning of this notion in comparative constitutional law and the received wisdom of constitutionalism, namely that all changes must be incremental and adapted to context. More precisely, the current orthodoxy at the level of international organisations is that the concept of judicial independence dictates institutional blueprints that exclude, to the utmost extent possible, political (and by implication democratic) mechanisms of judicial accountability. This orthodoxy, which pervades international judicial organs, advisory bodies

---

[3] www.dailymail.co.uk/news/article-3903436/Enemies-people-Fury-touch-judges-defied-17-4m-Brexit-voters-trigger-constitutional-crisis.html.

[4] https://eur-lex.europa.eu/legal-content/EN/TXT/HTML/?uri=CELEX:52017PC0835&from=EN.

[5] Cooperation between the EU Commission and Council of Europe institutions is well documented and up to a point justified but the fact that all too often the interacting bodies speak univocally where place for disagreement and diversity of views exists may give rise to justified procedural concerns.

[6] https://reconnect-europe.eu/blog/grabowska-moroz-rule-of-law-romania-timmermans/.

[7] www.europarl.europa.eu/doceo/document/TA-8-2018-0446_EN.html.

and political entities, has crystallised by virtue of 'conditionalities' into structures that generate their own set of problems. Describing this credo by reference
to traditional constitutional law concepts such as the rule of law and judicial
independence is – I will argue – inaccurate. The consensus at the supranational
level creates or reinforces patterns of counter-majoritarian instrumentalism that
collide with populist representations, generating complex pathologies. These
pathologies are then oversimplified in the cosmopolitan institutional and political discourses monochromatically, as attacks by the 'populists' (bad, vicious,
illiberal) on 'independent courts' and 'independent judicial systems' (good,
virtuous, liberal), or, in apotheosis, on 'the rule of law' itself. This exercise in
conceptual fast and loose invites equally partial, knee-jerk reactions, for which
the term 'constitutional democracy' is a misnomer: the rudimentary populist
narrative is that of a 'democratic' fight against 'corrupt' judicial elites. Yet the
boomerang effects of these polemics have resulted in the consequence that both
descriptions are becoming increasingly spitting images of each other: sloganised,
simplistic accounts that reduce complex phenomena to Manichaean caricatures
and by implication reinforce existing deficiencies.

Moreover, due to the synergies of cooperation within the Union, evolving conformities of discourse have the capacity to set in motion sophisticated
boomerang and ratchet effect patterns, by virtue of which certain institutional
models initially intended for use in the liminal parts of Europe have the capacity to influence institutional designs and patterns of justification in older, more
stable European systems. As I have argued elsewhere,[8] the fact that 'garbage'
(cognitive, institutional, political) initially generated or 'dumped' at the periphery will be recirculated at the centre is inevitable in the case of the European
Union, where the difference between centre and periphery is legally blurred by
design.[9] Thus newer uniformities and wider paradoxes are generated, whose
peril lies in an emerging incapacity to use juridical concepts in a rational, normative way, with attendant consequences in terms of the conditions of possibility
for meaningful collective action.

In what follows, I will first present a conceptual layout of the principle of
judicial independence, arguing that this notion, albeit by no means open-ended,
dictates only a very limited common denominator at the level of practices.
This 'ecumenical modesty' has resulted in traditional acceptance of a wide
degree of institutional (constitutional and legislative) variation across stable,
paradigmatic constitutional systems. A second part of my argument analyses,
using recent Romanian and Polish developments, the interactions between the
fledgling European constitutionalism (meaning the Council of Europe and

---

[8] B Iancu, 'Status Quo Hegemony? Conflicting Narratives about the "Rule of Law"' *VerfBlog*,
6 October 2020, https://verfassungsblog.de/status-quo-hegemony/.

[9] M Neves, 'Die Staaten im Zentrum und die Staaten an der Peripherie: Einige Probleme
mit Niklas Luhmanns Auffassung von den Staaten der Weltgesellschaft' (2006) 12(2) *Soziale
Systeme* 247.

the European Union) and the two former communist Member States, in the context of international reactions to domestic legislative changes. Out of a treasure trove of multilayer interactions that could easily yield substance for a book, I selected a couple of examples that are emblematic for the wider trends identified here and best illustrate the general argument.[10] The contribution ends with a tentative conclusion.

II. JUDICIAL INDEPENDENCE: THE VIRTUES OF ECUMENICAL MINIMALISM

In the theoretical and historical logic of separation of powers, the judiciary has always occupied an idiosyncratic place. Montesquieu's foundational theoretical argument is emblematic in this respect. The power of judging is paradoxically defined by the former *président* of the Bordeaux 'parliament' as both 'terrible among men' and as 'amounting to nothing'. Some of the ambiguity resides in the peculiar sociological-analytical methodology of the author, straddling the poles of empirical, inductive observations about idiosyncratic eighteenth-century English practices and deductive, normative appraisals of the 'essential' functions of the three branches. In the former, contingent sense, adjudication could be considered to 'amount to nothing' by reference to the jury system. In this logic, since the jury is not crystallised institutionally, it has no political existence and could therefore pose no danger to the constitutional 'spirit' of freedom. In the latter meaning, the author notes, with a formulation that has become a boilerplate of judicial descriptions and self-depictions, that judges are 'only the mouthpiece of the law, inanimate beings that can moderate neither its force nor its rigors'. Montesquieu, a judge himself, surely understood what all authoritative interpreters know, namely that interpretation implies a measure of discretion inherent in the –often-intended – indeterminacy of the text or applicable customs and precedents, in the time-lag between promulgation and adjudication and ensuing needs for adaptation to new realities, in the inevitable distance between norms of all types and facts. Neutrality is essentially also the argument of Alexander Hamilton in 'Federalist 78' ('The Judiciary Department'). Leaning on 'the celebrated Montesquieu', Hamilton defends the constitutional protections of the judicial office by insisting on the 'passive virtues' of judges as defendants of individual rights and constitutional boundaries:

> The judiciary, on the contrary, has no influence over either the sword or the purse; no direction either of the strength or of the wealth of the society; and can take no active resolution whatever. It may truly be said to have neither FORCE nor WILL,

---

[10] The chapter was written and submitted in 2019, with minor revisions in 2020. Since the argument uses (also) positive law *to exemplify discourses*, I did not consider it necessary in all instances to address black-letter law updates in the formally, doctrinally 'orthodox' manner (eg a judgment instead of an AG opinion or the latest relevant CJEU judgments).

but merely judgment; and must ultimately depend upon the aid of the executive arm even for the efficacy of its judgments.[11]

Nuances and caveats aside, in both Montesquieu and the gloss by Hamilton, the place of the judiciary in the state is defended along the line of neutrality and reason versus will. This is a trope that has dominated in different renditions mainstream accounts of adjudication ever since, from 'inanimate being' and 'mouthpiece' down to the Weberian 'paragraph automaton'.[12] To wit, one of the most authoritative recent restatements of the neutrality thesis, Lon Fuller's article on the forms and limits of adjudication,[13] focuses on the systemic needs for rationality embedded in the structure of the third branch and the relative strengths and weaknesses deriving from this paradigm. Many other examples could be provided to substantiate the claim that the privileged position of the judiciary in the classical triad, namely insulation from the vagaries of majoritarian politics, is highly dependent on the belief that the function of adjudication is rational and neutral. Judges are independent in order to ensure impartiality from the parties but their guarantees of independence are also predicated upon the belief that the function they exercise is essentially bounded, fettered. It is true that questioning the neutrality of the judicial function has been a recurrent theme of fringe currents in Western jurisprudence (*Freirechtsbewegung*, legal realism of the American or Scandinavian varieties, critical legal studies). Such questioning has, however, always opened a Pandora's box, inviting a radical structural overhaul. To put it bluntly: if adjudication is discretionary, an exercise in counting heads as it were, why not appoint judges for shorter terms or perhaps elect/remove them at regular intervals?

From a historical point of view, the independence of the judiciary, undoubtedly a keystone of modern constitutionalism, has traditionally been understood to encompass very few 'hard law' elements. By implication, provided that the minimal threshold of impartiality guarantees was reached, the value of judicial independence was accommodated across liberal-constitutional systems by a broad palette of institutional solutions. In English constitutional history, which bequeathed to all constitutional systems the achievement of judicial independence, independence was understood as tenure during good behaviour of each individual judge of the Crown. The Act of Settlement of 1701 stated in positive law what had already been accepted in fact as of 1690, once the struggles between the Crown and parliament were in effect concluded, namely that judges

---

[11] https://avalon.law.yale.edu/18th_century/fed78.asp.

[12] M Weber, *Economy and Society* (Berkeley, University of California Press, 1978) vol II, 979: 'The conception of the modern judge as an automaton into which legal documents and fees are stuffed at the top in order that it may spill forth the verdict at the bottom along with the reasons, read mechanically from codified paragraphs – this conception is angrily rejected, perhaps because a certain approximation to this type would precisely be implied by a consistent bureaucratization of justice.'

[13] LL Fuller, 'The Forms and Limits of Adjudication' (1978) 92 *Harvard Law Review* 353.

were to be appointed *quamdiu se bene gesserint*, for life tenures ('during good behaviour') and would no longer serve at will (*durante bene placito*, removable at the pleasure of the monarch). During the reign of Queen Anne, it was also established that judicial salaries would be paid from general revenues, a principle extended to Scottish judges after the Union of 1707. Paying judicial salaries out of public revenues drawn from customs and excise taxes (as opposed to royal grants) was undoubtedly a security of office and thus a guarantee of impartiality of equal importance to that of irremovability. In the US Constitution of 1787, both rules are entrenched against the legislative branch itself, by virtue of the two-pronged guarantee of Article III, which provides that federal judges have tenure during good behaviour – in effect, life tenure – and prohibits the diminishment of judicial revenues.[14]

At the same time, it should be noted that both of these archetypal liberal-constitutional systems preserved essentially political instruments of control. In the United Kingdom, higher judges can be removed using the instrument of a joint address of both Houses to the Queen (Article 11(3), Supreme Court Act (now Senior Courts Act) 1981). In the United States, impeachment applies to all federal judges, including those sitting on the US Supreme Court. Moreover, as the US Supreme Court itself stated in *Nixon v United States*,[15] the judgment of the Senate in an impeachment process is non-justiciable, ie final and not susceptible to be judicially second-guessed on either form or substance. As the English and American examples show, even tenure during good behaviour does not mean that removals must be limited to clear violations of disciplinary rules or follow a definitive criminal conviction. In practice, both the resignation of Abe Fortas from the Supreme Court bench, under the credible threat of an impeachment (stopped short only by his stepping-down voluntarily) and the threat of impeachment that hovered over Justice William O Douglas were underpinned by much vaguer charges. Although not used (UK) or very sparsely used (US), such procedures are constant reminders of the fact that judicial accountability triggered by political (democratic) means is always a possibility. Conversely, the difficulties inherent in the impeachment procedures make it in practice extremely difficult to remove judges except in the case of the most egregious infringements. At the intersection of democratic checks and judicial life tenure, a fragile constitutional balance between the rule of law and democratic accountability has been created and subsequently reinforced.

Until very recently, the meaning of judicial independence has not transcended, in paradigmatic liberal systems, a limited consensus at the level of the lowest common denominator, that of a credible guarantee of tenure during

---

[14] 'The judges, both of the supreme and inferior Courts, shall hold their office during good Behavior and shall, at stated Times, receive for their Services, a Compensation, which shall not be diminished during their Continuation in Office.'
[15] *Nixon v United States* 506 US 224 (1993).

good behaviour, the core instrument that serves the main purpose underlying the institution (ensuring impartiality). Even tenure during good behaviour does not necessarily mean life tenure, as shown by the examples of judicial elections in US states or the automatic retention referendum applicable to Supreme Court judges in Japan. Consequently, judicial selection models and judicial organisation systems have traditionally differed considerably across liberal constitutional jurisdictions, along a spectrum covering the 'democratic' judiciaries of US states, with the myriad forms of electoral accountability mechanisms applicable to the third branch,[16] the 'recognition' judiciaries prevalent in common law jurisdictions (including the federal US judiciary), and the numerous judicial organisation systems patterned on the 'career judiciary' typology dominant across continental Europe.[17] This high degree of variation, especially if we compare it to the relatively simpler structural templates of the other two branches, also indicates a tension between the crucial need of ensuring neutrality as impartiality vis-a-vis parties and the strength of the actual belief in the neutrality of judicial interpretations of the law (the 'mouthpiece' thesis). The third branch is essential in the architecture of the constitutional state. But the need to ensure impartial interpretation of the law in the resolution by the courts of discrete cases must not result in full isolation of the judiciary as such from the other branches and thus in insulation from accountability triggered by majoritarian, democratic means.

Most debates on the proper place of the judiciary in the Western systems have been skirmishes about methodology and interpretation, in effect variations on the validity of the 'mouthpiece' hypothesis. The attack on the UK Supreme Court in the aftermath of its decision in the *Miller* case started from what was in purely legal terms a technical decision on the reach of royal prerogative: can the executive trigger the procedure under Article 50 TEU relying solely on the residual powers of the Crown in the field of foreign affairs or does parliamentary sovereignty dictate that formal authorisation is needed in this case (in the event, Notification of Withdrawal Act 2017). The finer points of law inevitably elude the people and the possibilities of the populists to translate them in political vernacular, but the broader context and a well-known, consistent tradition

---

[16] The models differ from state to state, on a range encompassing partisan elections, non-partisan elections, combinations of merit selections and gubernatorial appointments (the so-called Missouri Plan) with unopposed or opposed retention elections, recall procedures, etc. About 90 percent of state judges of general jurisdictions and a fair number of appellate judges are either elected or retained by the electorate, in one way or another; see DE Pozen, 'The Irony of Judicial Elections' (2008) 108 *Columbia Law Review* 265. The decision of the Supreme Court in *Republican Party of Minnesota v White* 536 US 675 (2002) equated in practice judicial elections with electoral politics (striking down a Minnesota Supreme Court rule of conduct prohibiting candidates for a judicial office from announcing their views on contested political or legal issues).

[17] D Kosař, *Perils of Judicial Self-government in Transitional Societies* (New York, Cambridge University Press, 2016); C Guarnieri and P Pederzoli, *The Power of Judges* (Oxford, Oxford University Press, 2002).

of judicial deferentialism in grand design, high-stakes constitutional questions partly explain the adverse reactions to this judgment. In the United States, where the stakes of interpretative choices are widely known and where the Supreme Court has traditionally been far from deferential, attacks on particular judges/courts are always attacks on what doctrinally may be termed the methodology of interpretation. For instance, since liberal choices are always fused at the hip with dynamic interpretative techniques, including the use of foreign law to substantiate particular solutions, the Feeney–Goodlatte Resolution attempted to counter the cross-referencing of comparative constitutional law in US constitutional adjudication. The tendency towards comparativism is shared by a handful of Supreme Court liberal judges and strenuously opposed by conservative justices, who are as a rule 'originalists' (US sources alone matter in the interpretation of the US Constitution, in accordance with the original meaning of legal concepts and institutions).[18] In the full title of this resolution, a reference to Zimbabwe is an implicit attack on Justice Breyer, who, perhaps ill-advisedly, cited a Supreme Court of Zimbabwe judgment in his dissent from a denial of certiorari.[19]

In sum, such tensions and occasional political skirmishes in courts in standard Western jurisdictions have not yet determined radical reassessments of the institutional settings.[20] In the newer democracies of Eastern Europe, the conflict is essentially different, relating to a paradigm shift in what concerns the constitutional design of the judiciary and its interactions with the political branches.

III. 'JUDICIAL INDEPENDENCE' AND JUDICIAL POLITICS: THE PARADOXES OF MAXIMALISM

The migration of constitutional forms hearkens back to the beginnings of normative constitutionalism. Günter Frankenberg, who coined the term 'Ikea constitutionalism' to designate both the phenomenon as such and the relatively limited number of prepackaged norms and ideas with which constitution-making operates in practice, traces back Ikea-style engineering to the early

---

[18] www.congress.gov/bill/110th-congress/house-resolution/372/actions.

[19] *Knight v Florida* (98-9741); *Moore v Nebraska* (99-5291) decided 8 November 1999 (Breyer J, dissenting).

[20] Such influences do exist, notably, the Constitutional Reform Act of 2005. The Constitutional Reform Act *partly* shifted the functioning paradigm of the British judiciary towards the newly prevalent logic of 'judicial independence', by severing political/democratic interfaces (the rethinking of the Lord Chancellor's position and role) and enhancing, continental-style, elements of 'merit-based' selection/promotion (Judicial Appointments Commission). On the English judiciary, see Shimon Shetreet's classic (as rewritten with Sophie Turenne in 2013, to take stock of these changes), *Judges on Trial: The Independence and Accountability of the English Judiciary* (Cambridge, Cambridge University Press, 2013).

nineteenth century.[21] Yet, although the practice of transplanting constitutional norms and institutions is by no means new, the nature of the transfers in recent decades differs. Transplants are in many cases no longer resulting from the willing reception and adaptation to the local context of reputationally successful models at the centre by domestic entrepreneurs at the periphery. Ikea constitutionalism now often reflects the imposition of certain reforms by international conditionalities or 'nudging' towards certain preferred solutions by way of multilayer interactions and transnational good practice advocacy. This metamorphosis of the migration and interaction pathways has further standardised the Ikea toolbox but, as a flip-side, induced new distortions and a degree of oversimplification in the conceptual apparatus of justifications.

In the field of judicial reforms, the dominant model is the judicial council, meaning the entrusting of all crucial decisions concerning the judiciary to the judges, in essence judicial self-government (according to the good-practice model, at least half of the council members should be elected by their peers).[22] Consequently, a dense network of primarily soft law instruments has generated a conformity at the level of international organisations, to the point where, for example, all but one of the new EU Member States have reformed their judiciaries to this effect. Under the sway of anticorruption conditionalities, other blueprints (autonomous prosecutor's offices) further reinforce and modify this emerging orthodoxy. Such reforms have been forcefully advocated or downright required by the EU Commission, with the backing of its international partners in the Council of Europe.[23] In some states, not only judges but also prosecutors are organised according to the council model. In Romania, for example, the convergence of the judicial council conditionality and the anticorruption conditionality has resulted in a complex overlap of autonomous judicial structures, namely a highly autonomous council which takes decisions in two sections (for prosecutors and for judges, respectively) and in plenary formation and a fully autonomous anticorruption prosecutor's office within the Public Ministry, itself an autonomous institution within the 'judicial authority'. In the same vein (judicial innovations), the International Monetary Fund, seconded by the EU and the Venice Commission, successfully campaigned for the creation of an independent anticorruption court in Ukraine.[24]

There are various reasons for this insistence on somewhat Procrustean, one-size-fits-all reform patterns, in spite of the paradoxical fact that the

---

[21] G Frankenberg, 'Constitutional Transfers and Experiments in the Nineteenth Century' in G Frankenberg (ed), *Order from Transfer: Comparative Constitutional Design and Legal Culture* (Cheltenham, Edward Elgar, 2013) 279–305.

[22] Recommendation CM/Rec (2010) 12 of the Committee of Ministers of the Council of Europe on *Judges: Independence, Efficiency and Responsibility*.

[23] Kosař (n 14).

[24] B Iancu, '*Quod licet Jovi non licet bovi?* The Venice Commission as Norm Entrepreneur' (2019) 11(1) *Hague Journal on the Rule of Law (Special Issue: Rule of Law Decay)* 189.

presumably universalisable 'good practice' – in what concerns councils – reflects the judicial organisation model of only one older Member State of the European Union/Council of Europe, namely Italy.[25] Prudential considerations may partly explain the constraints of choice. For example, in the case of recent EU Member States or current candidates, the master of the conditionalities is the EU Commission. Faced with the staggering diversity of models in stable systems, the multiplicity of contexts in the former communist states that had to be monitored by it prior to the accession, and the value imponderables inherent in constitutional engineering, the Commission took a shortcut. It reduced complexity by reference to common, thus more easily administrable, vade mecums.[26] In part and related, these choices also reflect the structure of the Commission as such. The Commission is a bureaucracy. As an autonomous, bureaucratic structure, the Commission has its own institutional limitations, generating tunnel vision predilections towards isomorphism. Its preferred reform solutions usually tilt towards the promotion of politically autonomous bodies.[27] A more disconcerting explanation for extreme counter-majoritarian preferences lies in a wider 'distrust in politicians and discomfort with the idea of democracy in general'.[28] The normative bandwagon is drawn not only by the EU Commission but also by consultative and monitoring bodies of the Council of Europe (the Consultative Council of European Judges (CCJE), the European Commission for Democracy through Law (Venice Commission) and the Group of States Against Corruption (GRECO)). More recently, the European Court of Justice and the European Court of Human Rights have joined in, adjusting their jurisprudence to the emerging good-governance consensus and the consensus over the unfolding anti-populist crusade.

In what follows, I shall exemplify my thesis using a variety of both soft and hard law instruments, namely EU Commission, Venice Commission, CCJE and GRECO reports, recent ECJ case law, and a recent opinion of the Advocate General. These are, to be sure, formally distinct instruments. Nonetheless, the methodological syncretism is warranted, since at the discursive level all the sources display an unsettling degree of uniformity. The fact that distinct

[25] S Benvenuti and D Paris, 'Judicial Self-government in Italy: Merits, Limits and the Reality of an Export Model' (2018) 19(7) *German Law Journal* 1641.

[26] D Smilov, 'EU Enlargement and the Constitutional Principle of Judicial Independence' in W Sadurski, A Czarnota and M Krygier (eds), *Spreading Democracy and the Rule of Law? The Impact of EU Enlargement on the Rule of Law, Democracy and Constitutionalism in Post-Communist Legal Orders* (Dordrecht, Springer, 2006) 313.

[27] B Iancu, 'Changed Vocabularies: A Few Semantic Ambiguities of Network Constitutionalism' in I Motoc, K Wojtyczek and P Pinto de Albuquerque (eds), *New Developments in Constitutional Law: Essays in Honour of András Sajó* (The Hague, Eleven International Publishing, 2018) 191–212. On Europeanisation and politically autonomous bodies, see the contributions by M Mendelski, SE Tănăsescu and J Ziller in B Iancu and E Simina Tănăsescu (eds), *Governance and Constitutionalism: Law, Politics and Institutional Neutrality* (London and New York, Routledge, 2018).

[28] D Kosař, *Perils of Judicial Self-government in Transitional Societies* (Cambridge, Cambridge University Press, 2016) 130.

institutions, of different typologies, speak with one voice results from cross-hybridisation and the crystallisation of consensus around a limited number of conformities. In the recent, 'populist' context, the perceived need to respond momentarily to domestic developments leads to often contradictory instrumental reactions that further distort the frameworks of reference. International institutions, in order both to 'put out the populist fire' and find a common normative language, often swing the pendulum in the opposite extreme, fetishising counter-majoritarian solutions when and where these are not warranted or taking irreconcilable positions across time or across jurisdictions.

There are reasons for distrusting politicians, especially in flawed, fledgling constitutional states, such as Poland, but there is, conversely, no justification for blind trust in the judiciary and in the ensuing belief, that, if left to its own devices, a judicial system will function optimally. Likewise, the need to peg 'democratisation' reforms on a simpler, unifying explanation such as corruption as the root of all evils in backward jurisdictions is bureaucratically understandable. But the belief in 'robust' anticorruption as a shortcut to modernity in, say, Romania, is simplistic in historical terms and anathema to any form of normative constitutional thinking. Liberal constitutionalism is not only built on distrust towards unfettered democracy but rather on generalised yet pragmatic foundational scepticism. Otherwise put, the liberal-constitutional anthropological profession of faith abhors not democracy and politics as such but rather all miracle solutions (majoritarian, counter-majoritarian and non-majoritarian), especially when predicated upon leaps of faith.

1. *Celmer* and the Paradoxes of Constitutional (Anti-)Politics

Poland has in recent years become a standard example of 'populist backsliding', this term being used to describe the erosion of democracy of a Member State after EU accession.[29] Once the 2015 parliamentary and presidential elections in Poland had entrenched the Law and Justice Party (PiS) in all democratic branches (parliament/government and the presidency), this new majority sought to overhaul the non-majoritarian institutions (Constitutional Court and the judiciary) through sweeping legislative reforms. A number of controversial political decisions were also carried through, for example the refusal to accept all appointments to the Constitutional Court made by the previous majority and the entrenchment in the court of five PiS counter-appointees.

In the discourse of the international (Venice Commission) and supranational institutions (EU Commission), all the measures adopted by the new

---

[29] See W Sadurski, 'How Democracy Dies (in Poland): A Case Study of Anti-constitutional Populist Backsliding' (17 January 2018) Sydney Law School Research Paper No 18/01; available at SSRN: https://ssrn.com/abstract=3103491 or http://dx.doi.org/10.2139/ssrn.3103491.

government were presented indiscriminately as populist attacks on the rule of law. It is certainly true that many actions have been highly questionable in any framework of reference, for example a Hungarian-style attempt to vet the judiciary by reducing the retirement age. Nonetheless, the penchant on representing the divisions in a melodramatic key, as a heroic fight against populism and for judicial independence and the rule of law, has not always been helpful. In contexts where the concept of the rule of law describes political and judicial practices in an imperfect, approximate way, such stark dichotomies are inaccurate. To wit, the Constitutional Court crisis started with an attempt by the outgoing parliamentary majority to pack the court with its appointees and thus cripple the winner of the latest elections, an instrumental action which generated an equally unprincipled response. Thus, whereas discrete measures call for condemnation and also, where applicable, legal action,[30] international activism under the guise of an all-out 'war on populism' serves no normative purpose and may only reinforce domestic pathologies. In this sense, the condemnation by the Venice Commission of Polish public prosecutor reforms bordered on frivolity, inasmuch as the main argument advanced by the Commission was that such reforms would be backtracking on a Polish tradition of prosecutorial autonomy from the executive hearkening back to communist times.[31]

The *Celmer* judgment,[32] which is emblematic of the international antipopulist consensus, originated in a preliminary reference by the Irish High Court, asking the Court of Justice whether a request for the execution of a European Arrest Warrant issuing from Poland could be denied based on the reasoning that (i) the changes to the judiciary laws undertaken by the Polish parliamentary majority had undermined the independence of the judiciary; and (ii) in so doing, had affected by implication the right to a fair trial of the person whose surrender to Poland is requested, a right protected under Article 47 of the EU Charter of Fundamental Rights. The ECJ, diverging from a more carefully drawn opinion by the Advocate General, decided in essence that refusing to execute the warrant would be possible, insofar as a two-step analysis was followed. The executing court would need to determine, first, whether the reform endangers systemic independence to the point where a real risk would exist that the fundamental right to a fair trial would be breached; and second, whether in the circumstances of the case an individualised assessment would result in the conclusion that the

---

[30] Judgment of 24 June 2019, Case C-619/18 *Commission v Poland* (Independence of the Supreme Court). The ECJ found incompatible with EU law a Polish statute that, lowering the retirement age for Supreme Court judges from 70 to 65, made continuation in office of those wishing to serve after the age of 65 conditional upon a certificate of good health and a request to that effect made to the president of the Republic, who has to consent.

[31] I discuss this in Iancu (n 24).

[32] ECJ (Grand Chamber) 25 July 2018, Case C-216/18 PPU *Minister for Justice and Equality v LM* ECLI:EU:C:2018:586.

person would be subjected to an unfair trial if surrendered.[33] The term 'real risk' is a clear reference to the preventive procedure under Article 7 TEU, by virtue of which the Council may determine that a clear risk of a serious breach of EU values is revealed by developments in a Member State. The sanctioning mechanism is a distinct procedure,[34] whereby the European Council determines by unanimous decision that a serious and persistent breach of Article 2 values has already taken place. Following this latter determination, the Council of Ministers may apply, by a reinforced majority vote, specific sanctions, including that of suspending the execution of all European Arrest Warrants issuing from that state.

Many jurisprudential perplexities attach to the general context of the *Celmer/LM* case. The judgment relied, for example, on a previous ruling on essential guarantees of judicial independence[35] and on the *Aranyosi and Căldăraru* judgment. The first precedential prop (*Associação Sindical dos Juízes Portugueses*) referred, however, to a non-problematic hypothesis: reducing judicial salaries by measures targeting the judiciary has always been considered an attack on judicial independence (as would, arguably, changing the retirement age in order to vet the profession and free the bench for one's own appointees). Conversely, how the balance between accountability and independence must be struck systemically, outside the limited case of long-standing court impartiality guarantees, is a much more difficult question, to be pondered rule by rule, from jurisdiction to jurisdiction. Likewise, the judgment in the *Aranyosi and Căldăraru* cases constituted a limited departure from the prior jurisprudence of the Luxemburg court, denying the possibility to refuse surrender under the European Arrest Warrant Framework Decision on fundamental rights grounds. This judgment is, however, also of limited use in the *Celmer* context. *Căldăraru* referred to an absolute right, the prohibition of torture, which, in the context of prison overcrowding, has already been interpreted in a predictable, consistent manner by the European Court of Human Rights (hygiene, possibility to exercise or work, number of square metres per inmate, and the like). The Luxemburg Court could in this limited case piggyback on European Convention on Human Rights case law. But judicial interpretation as to whether conditions in Romanian and

---

[33] Para 68. If, having regard to the requirements noted in paras 62 to 67 of the present judgment, the executing judicial authority finds that there is, in the issuing Member State, a real risk of breach of the essence of the fundamental right to a fair trial on account of systemic or generalised deficiencies concerning the judiciary of that Member State, such as to compromise the independence of that state's courts, that authority must, as a second step, assess specifically and precisely whether, in the particular circumstances of the case, there are substantial grounds for believing that, following his surrender to the issuing Member State, the requested person will run that risk (see, by analogy, in the context of Art 4 of the Charter, judgment of 5 April 2016, *Aranyosi and Căldăraru* C-404/15 and C-659/15 PPU EU:C:2016:198, paras 92 and 94).

[34] Judgment of 27 February 2018, *Associação Sindical dos Juízes Portugueses* C-64/16 EU:C:2018:117.

[35] Judgment of 5 April 2016, *Aranyosi and Căldăraru* C-404/15 and C-659/15 PPU EU:C:2016:198.

Hungarian prisons are of such a dismal nature as to preclude the surrender of specific individuals, since rendition would amount to a form of complicity in torture, is unproblematic if compared to the assessment of complex, context-laden judicial selection and organisation systems.

More striking still are the unstated assumptions of the *Celmer* judgment. The Irish Court relied on the 2017 reasoned proposal by the EU Commission, asking the Council to determine the existence of a risk (*clear risk of a serious breach*; preventive mechanism) and on Venice Commission findings. The ECJ, paraphrasing the language of the preventive procedure under Article 7 (*real risk of breach*), enables any court to reach *sua sponte*, albeit piecemeal, a result that under the Treaty could only be attained under the sanctioning mechanism, at the end of a painstaking political process, implying significant procedural hurdles. Furthermore, if populism is an excessive outgrowth of democratic politics, the remedy fashioned by the CJEU against populism veers towards the other end of the spectrum. A court far removed from the concerned legal culture, with all its idiosyncratic heuristics and complexities, is encouraged to assess the fitness of a judicial and political-constitutional system. For guidance, in the case at hand, the Irish High Court was encouraged to use the nineteen pages of the EU Commission's Reasoned Opinion and the responses provided by the Polish court, under the benevolent hermeneutic supervision of the pithily reasoned CJEU judgment. Not only are the standpoints of the national majoritarian branches incidental in this procedural chain but the democratic points of ascription at the EU level as such (Council, European Council) are side-stepped and elided. In other words, if populism extolls (its own simplistic definitions of) democracy, the ethos animating the *Celmer* reasoning abhors it. Both poles are arguably in antithesis to liberal constitutionalism, whose historical and philosophical tenets caution against extremes, striving to strike a delicate balance between rule by majority and counter-majoritarian or non-majoritarian constraints.

That *Celmer* was not an isolated incident can be gleaned from a recent opinion by the Advocate General Tanchev, regarding the Disciplinary Chamber of the Polish Supreme Court.[36] The preliminary reference raises the question whether a newly created Disciplinary Chamber would satisfy requirements of judicial independence under EU law. In essence, Advocate General Tanchev answers in the negative. The nutshell argument is that (i) the selection to the new section is made by the fifteen-member National Council of the Judiciary (NCJ), and (ii) since the Polish NCJ is itself elected by the parliament rather than by judges, political pressures bear on the NCJ, so that (iii) the Supreme Court judges appointed to this new chamber are 'persons beholden to political authorities'. According to the opinion, 'judicial councils should in principle be composed of at least a majority of judges to prevent manipulation and undue pressure'.[37]

---

[36] Advocate General's Opinion in Joined Cases C-585/18, C-624/18 and C-625/18 A.K. and Others v. *Krajowa Rada Sądownictwa and Others* (delivered on 27 June 2019), ECLI:EU:C:2019:551.
[37] Para 126.

This is a standard restatement of a generalised preference at the international level for advocating Italian-style councils in the context of constitution-building. The preference, however, albeit couched in the language of EU law, reflects neither common European traditions (a standard) nor care for the normative concerns that ought to inform institutional designs. Furthermore, this resilient conformity ignores the complexities embedded in the evolution of the archetypal systems that generated the standard. In terms of common European practices, even if one frames the comparison within the limited confines of the judicial council systems, all the members of the Spanish Council (Consejo General del Poder Judicial) are elected almost identically as under current Polish legislation, by three-fifths majorities in parliament,[38] as are the non-judicial members of the Italian Consiglio Superiore della Magistratura. In a normative key, the predilection for the elected, corporatist council format reflects a belief that external independence (independence from parties and the executive) is the major determinant of an optimal structure. This is, however, a rudimentary understanding of the necessary trade-offs between checks and balances and functional separation, between internal and external independence, between independence and accountability. Last but not least, the compulsive insistence on advocating for Italian-style councils flies in the face of reams of studies showing that the model, presumably a panacea for new democracies, functions far from optimally in the jurisdiction of origin[39] or in the newer settings in which it was transplanted.[40] Indeed, the blueprint to which Advocate General Tanchev dedicates his EU law dithyramb used to be referred to as the French–Italian model. But, following long-standing dissatisfaction with 'judicial endogamy'[41] and the gross miscarriages of justice revealed by the 2004–05 'Outreau' scandal,[42] 2008 amendments entrenched a different configuration of the French CSM. In the French context, stress is placed now on accountability, achieved by hierarchy, plurality of stakeholders in the sections (bar association, Council of State) and a large number of political appointees. In both sections and the plenary formation, elected judges are now a minority.

[38] I am not arguing that the Spanish system functions optimally. See, for sharp criticism of the Spanish Council, accusing it primarily of the overpoliticisation ('capture') of its appointment, A Torez Pérez, 'Judicial Self-government and Judicial Independence: the Political Capture of the General Council of the Judiciary in Spain' (2018) 19(7) *German Law Journal* 1769.

[39] Benvenuti and Paris (n 25).

[40] There is a wealth of literature on the manipulation (sloganisation) of the principle of judicial independence by corporatist elites in Central and Eastern Europe. See M Bobek, 'The Fortress of Judicial Independence and the Mental Transitions of the Central European Judiciaries' (2008) 14(1) *European Public Law* 99; A Czarnota, 'Rule of Lawyers or Rule of Law? On Constitutional Crisis and Rule of Law in Poland' in Iancu and Tănăsescu (n 27) 51–63.

[41] 'Le CSM et la démocratie' *Le Monde*, 9 Novembre 1998, 12.

[42] In effect, judicial self-government in France spans two brief intervals, from 1946 to 1958 (the Fourth Republic) and from the reforms of 1993 to the counter-reform of 2008. For a nuanced analysis, revealing continuities (the prevailing power of a 'duopole' formed of judicial elites and the Chancellerie in the Ministry of Justice) straddling institutional changes, see A Vauchez, 'The Strange Non-death of Statism: Tracing the Ever Protracted Rise of Judicial Self-government in France' (2018) 19(7) *German Law Journal* 1613.

Hence, whereas attempts by the current majority in Poland to subordinate politically the local judiciary are to be condemned, standing this position right on its head is equally unjustifiable, either prima facie or contextually.

2. Romania: Judicial Independence from Judicial Independence

Romania has in recent years often been compared to Poland and Hungary, in the context of crises related to a 2012 attempt to impeach the sitting president and, more recently (2016–18), in the trail of attempts by the Social Democratic majority in power to significantly amend both judicial organisation laws and criminal legislation. The country was a laboratory of major institutional reforms, deriving from EU reform requirements concerning the transplantation of the 'Judicial Council Euro-model.' Furthermore, local judicial reforms were implemented with an original, anticorruption-derived twist, anticorruption having become the driving EU conditionality by the time Romania and Bulgaria prepared for pre-accession negotiations.[43] In effect, the imperative of combating high- and medium-level corruption by repressive means constituted the main impetus for all changes, including judicial organisation reforms.[44]

To be sure, the negotiation process is partly symbiotic; external conditionalities resulted in a particular institutional setting since they were in sync with local political interests. To be sure, judicial independence and anticorruption are in the abstract and prima facie apolitical concepts. In practice, both terms have been sloganised as shibboleths of the local political right, also as the result of domestic peculiarities. The Romanian political system is semi-presidential and the appointment powers of the president have meant, until recently, that high-level judicial and prosecutorial appointments and demotions depended on the presidential pen; the presidency also has the technical upper hand in terms of defence, foreign affairs and intelligence. The nature of the local political system has over the past fifteen years generated centre-right presidents and centre-left parliaments (and governments). Moreover, institutional conflicts reflect social cleavages between left-leaning small town and rural Romania, on the one hand,

---

[43] P Szarek-Mason, *The European Union's Fight Against Corruption – The Evolving Policy Towards Member States and Candidate Countries* (Cambridge, Cambridge University Press, 2010).

[44] On the Judicial Council Euro-model and its shortcomings (the authors also coined the term), see D Kosař and Michal Bobek, 'Global Solutions, Local Problems: A Critical Study in Judicial Council in Central and Eastern Europe' (2007) 15(7) *German Law Journal* 1257. On the distinctiveness of its Romanian avatar, see (critical) B Iancu, 'Perils of Sloganised Constitutional Concepts, Notably that of "Judicial Independence" (Review Essay on Kosař, *Perils of Judicial Self-Government in Transitional Societies*)' (2017) 13(3) *European Constitutional Law Review* 582 and a more favourable study by B Selejan-Guțan, 'Romania: Perils of a "Perfect Euro-Model" of Judicial Council' (2018) 19(7) *German Law Journal* 1707. Selejan-Guțan attributes the idiosyncratic features to the need to combat corruption, in line with my own remarks above, and believes that rampant political corruption justifies the peculiar institutional setting (and its shortcomings).

and the right-voting, more affluent bigger cities, on the other. The anticorruption and rule-of-law jargons used on the right of the political spectrum provide an easily falsifiable veneer of normativity to these searing tensions, with superadded ('European'!) respectability provided by international requirements and accolades.

The judicial council (Consiliul Superior al Magistraturii, CSM) entrenched by constitutional revision in 2003 has in its composition an overwhelming majority of 'magistrates', both elected by their peers (nine judges and five prosecutors) and ex officio (General Prosecutor, President of the High Court), compared to three 'political' members (Minister of Justice, two civil society representatives elected by the Senate). In 2005, an anticorruption watchdog, initially (2002) set up as a fully autonomous institution, was grafted onto the structure of the General Prosecutor's Office (Parchetul de pe lângă Înalta Curte de Casație și Justiție, PÎCCJ), in order to deflect constitutionality problems and also render it efficient.[45] In reality, even though the National Anticorruption Directorate (Direcția Națională Anticorupție, DNA) is nominally a division within the PÎCCJ, it is in practice fully autonomous from the latter, since the General Prosecutor has no leverage over the Chief Prosecutor of the DNA. Both officials are appointed and removed according to the law for the same terms, in the same way (for three-year terms, renewable once, by the president, at the proposal of the MJ. The DNA has exclusive competence to prosecute high-level graft, defined according to the value of the bribe, the value of the damage or the quality of the defendant. In a visual show of power, in 2016, the DNA has in fact prosecuted a General Prosecutor, the nominal head of the Public Ministry. The latter was accused of using illegally a police escort car, while commuting to Bucharest from a nearby city. Hounded by the cameras, the General Prosecutor resigned in shame and was promptly replaced, only to be cleared in court by an acquittal two years later. The higher the number and profile of officials the DNA indicted, the higher the praises sung by the European Commission or the monitoring body of the Council of Europe (GRECO). Due to the public stigma attached to even the opening of a file, the external eulogies to the DNA, the intricacies of judicial process and the extreme autonomy (meaning also opaqueness) of all concerned institutions, the fight against corruption has been overwhelmingly perceived by the Romanian political centre-right and by international bodies as an unqualified public good.

Yet, more recently, a number of problematic features have cast a growing shadow over Romanian anticorruption, among which the timing of certain investigations, a troublesome piling up of acquittals in high-profile cases, a spike in surveillance justified by the professed need to combat corruption and sedulous

---

[45] The Public Ministry is constitutionally defined as hierarchical, Art 132(1). Furthermore, a fully autonomous structure would not have had the power to investigate precisely the high officials it had been created to prosecute (deputies and senators, who can only be indicted by the General Prosecutor's Office, according to Art 72(2)).

collaboration of the prosecutors with the Romanian Intelligence Service by means of classified protocols with the General Prosecutor's Office (and thus with the DNA). Protocols were also concluded with the Judicial Inspection, the High Court of Cassation and Justice and the judicial council. Cooperation with internal intelligence was rendered possible by declaring corruption a threat to national security, by means of an also classified decision of the National Security Council. This facet of the fight against corruption is particularly problematic, in view of the large resources of the service and of its nature. The Constitutional Court has recently declared two such protocols unconstitutional, reasoning that these paralegal instruments have fostered a distortion of the justice system, to the detriment of the accused.[46]

Problems of accountability clearly exist. One way of making a judicial system more accountable, in the logic of the council system, is to broaden the spectrum of stakeholders represented in the council, especially through the input of political appointees. Parliamentary selection of the judicial members, possibly with reinforced majority voting, from lists submitted or supported by judicial associations, is also a possibility (eg Spain). Some degree of external oversight in the nature of checks and balances is at any rate needed, since judicial council systems marked by a significant degree of corporatism are notoriously reluctant to use accountability tools efficiently. For instance, the five prosecutors in the respective section of the Romanian Council, a majority of whom represent the lower tiers, can hardly be expected to decide in a disciplinary procedure against the upper rungs of the Public Ministry officialdom (and, in practice, they virtually never do). Amending the constitution to achieve systemic responsibility by rethinking the institutional design is an option foreclosed by virtue of the fact that the essential features of the Romanian judicial system are constitutionalised, whereas the constitution is rigid and therefore difficult to amend, especially in the context of a fragmented political environment.

Recent amendments to the organic laws sought therefore to change the sub-constitutional rules,[47] by stressing the liability for miscarriages of justice (judicial error resulting from bad faith and gross negligence), by reinstating a recall procedure, through which the judicial and prosecutorial constituencies represented in the Council may revoke their representatives before the end of their six-year terms, and by creating a prosecutor's section, within the General Prosecutor's Office. This new entity (Secția Pentru Investigarea Infracțiunilor din

---

[46] DCC No 26/16.01.2019.

[47] The argument here is neither that these legislative changes were necessarily the proper or ideal solutions to the various problems nor that the amendments were necessarily driven by public interest considerations. My claim is only that they have been routinely impugned by international institutions in an unreflective polemical manner, i.e., by denying implicitly or explicitly that any problems existed. This course of action (rote reinforcement of a consensus/preferred status quo ante) is suboptimal. It foments factionalism, thus polarisation and by implication what one claims to be combating (i.e., populism).

Justiție, SIIJ[48]) has by law exclusive competence to prosecute crimes committed by magistrates. The Romanian innovation is, as one may notice, roughly similar to the Polish Disciplinary Section, from which it differs in two important respects. First, unlike the Polish Supreme Court section, the Romanian institution is a specialised, autonomous prosecutor's office, which means that redress against all its solution is available in court. Second, the appointment of the head of this section is made, following initial vetting by a commission, by the plenary of the Romanian CSM, a council which enjoys almost complete independence from visible, formalised political influence. The procedure of appointing the section chief differs from other appointments to high positions in the Public Ministry, which are political. All other prosecutorial high positions are appointed by the president, at the proposal of the minister of justice, with the council having only the right to be heard. The reasons for making these changes were in and of themselves not innocuous. A number of officials in the left-dominated coalition that passed the amendments have been under investigation by the DNA, most notably former Social Democratic Party president Liviu Dragnea, currently serving time for corruption. Yet, unlike the case of attempts to change criminal legislation and criminal procedure law to the putative benefit of specific politicians, the amendments to the judiciary laws do not benefit any particular individual, have passed constitutional scrutiny and have been favourably received by a part of the professional spectrum. Left- or progressive-leaning judicial associations, such as the National Union of Romanian Judges (UNJR), saluted the creation of the SIIJ.[49] In this configuration, it is surprising that all international reports on the matter have taken the one-sided view that the recent amendments imperil judicial independence, the rule of law and anticorruption (and should therefore be undone).

This is essentially the position of the Venice Commission,[50] which, in a recent report, opines, somewhat contradictorily, that the creation of the new section is not warranted, either because the need is not apparent or because anticorruption prosecutors would be better suited to the task. Yet, the structure was created precisely because of fears that anticorruption prosecutors could use the threat of indictments in order to coax reluctant judges to adopt particular solutions (eg conviction of high-profile defendants, approval of pretrial arrest, authorisation of surveillance warrants). Such fears were not fully unfounded, with a large number of files, some of them kept dormant for years, transferred from

---

[48] In the Romanian centre-right press, the acronym 'SS' (from special section) is used to denote the institution, for obvious polemic reasons. For instance, www.dw.com/ro/refeudalizarea-româniei-reîngenuncherea-europei/a-49360216.

[49] Romanian professional associations are ideologically polarised, some (the UNJR and the Association of Romanian Magistrates, AMR) increasingly sceptical towards anti-corruption and overall favourable towards the recent changes, some, most notably the Judges' Forum (Forumul Judecătorilor) enthusiastically supporting the fight against corruption with all its trappings (and, consequently, rejecting any alteration of the status quo).

[50] Opinion No 924/20 October 2018, CDL-AD (2018) 017.

the DNA to the new watchdog.[51] Many international reports are riddled with inaccuracies and logical faux pas, as, for example, the 2019 opinion of another consultative body of the Council of Europe, the CCJE.[52] Following a request by an internal professional association, the 'Judges' Forum', this opinion recirculates the position of this (*one*) professional representative body, without however addressing the diametrically opposed stands of the other analogous entities. In essence, the CCJE advocates reversing all changes and returning to the status quo ante. The creation of the section, in particular, is considered detrimental because it would allegedly induce a deleterious belief that magistrates would be prone to criminality and thus severely damage public confidence in the judiciary. Citing symmetric language in a CVM report by the European Commission,[53] the CCJE recommends the abandonment of this institution, lest the capacity of the DNA and its anticorruption work be imperilled. In order to feign a concern for accountability, the CCJE suggests that political appointees should participate in the judicial council section meetings and castigates the government for not permitting this, oblivious to the fact that the readily available text of the Constitution specifies otherwise.[54] The most recent international position on the issue, a GRECO follow-up report published in July 2019, declares the section an 'anomaly in the existing institutional setting'.[55] Needless to say, GRECO recommends that it be abolished forthwith. In reply, one could easily argue that the Romanian setting as such is anomalous, with an extreme understanding of external 'magistrate' independence, coupled with intractable dependencies. GRECO experts also deplore the placement of the section 'outside the hierarchical structure of the Romanian prosecution'.[56] This statement conveniently blots out the fact that the DNA is functionally even more autonomous from Public Ministry hierarchy, constituting in essence a fully contained integrity agency, grafted nominally on the General Prosecutor's Office frame. The opinion cross-cites and echoes the fears, already expressed by the Venice Commission, that 'the new structure would serve as an (additional) instrument to put pressure on judges and prosecutors'. The glaring contradiction, as in the other reports, concerns the fact that, unlike the other prosecutorial bodies, especially the DNA, whose heads are politically appointed and can be politically removed,

---

[51] A recent scandal resulted in the termination of secondment of a high-profile DNA prosecutor who, in leaked recordings of conversations with his colleagues, intimated that unpliable judges should be coerced into cooperating with the prosecution.

[52] https://rm.coe.int/ccje-bu-2019-4-en-opinion-romania-2019-final-25-april-2019/168094556c.

[53] Report from the Commission to the European Parliament and the Council on Progress in Romania under the Cooperation and Verification Mechanism (Strasbourg, 13 November 2018 COM(2018) 851 final).

[54] According to the Romanian Constitution (Art 133(2(b)), the two civil society representatives take part only in plenary meetings. The Venice Commission also recommends an increase in the number of civil society representatives, in spite of the fact that the current configuration, a product of 2003 amendments, has been long known to the Commission and had been favourably received by the Commission when entrenched.

[55] GRECO, Ad Hoc Report (2019) 1, para 25.

[56] Ibid para 29.

this newer structure is selected by the high council itself. This, in turn, begs the question as to the nature of the fears concerning pressures. It is judges and prosecutors in the council who select the head of this section and vet the entire membership. If a judicial council composed of as many elected members of the profession as possible is the best embodiment of judicial independence (which seems to be the orthodoxy at the international level), what better reflection of independence than creating a mechanism of accountability that is fully 'internalised', ensconced in the judicial system itself?

Particularly problematic, if we compare the Romanian and Polish cases, are the normative dissonances. One remembers that the Venice and EU Commissions defended the judiciary in Poland by opposing excessive politicisation, meaning a politically selected judicial council. If the politically elected judicial council would select a disciplinary section of the Supreme Court, the argument ran, judicial independence would be imperilled by 'persons beholden to political authorities'. Contrariwise, in Romania, an overwhelmingly judicially selected, hence highly autonomous ('independent'), judicial council is deemed to endanger judicial independence by means of its selection of a special prosecutorial unit, whose remit is the investigation of judicial criminal infractions. In other words, judicial independence must be protected from politicians in Poland and from judges in Romania.[57]

Pun aside, the international crusade described in this section of the article both reflects and reinforces divisions within the Romanian CSM, where the five prosecutors and some of the judges have boycotted the process of selecting the new head of this section by not attending the plenary meetings in order to sabotage the quorum. The argument of this minority council faction was that Venice Commission and GRECO reports prevail over binding Romanian law. The boycott is underpinned by the international validation and, at the same time, may itself offer arguments for future GRECO reports, in an overlap of local and international intermingling power-plays.[58] These interactions appositely

---

[57] In AG Tanchev's opinion in Joined Cases C-585/18, C-624/18 and C-625/18, a submission by the EFTA Surveillance Authority is referred to, at para. 69, invoking a newfangled 'principle of non-regression of judicial independence'. This novelty, if incorporated in international standards and EU law, would make it possible not only to freeze in perpetuity judicial legislation and relevant constitutional provisions but also to square the circle of logical consistency and make all these contradictions fit well together. Any change perceived as inconvenient could be labelled a regression (recommendation: reverse immediately to status quo ante), any convenient change would be a progression (result: green light to domestic changes).

[58] At the time of revising this chapter, the provisional version of AG Bobek's opinion in Joined Cases C-83/19, C-127/19 and C-195/19 was published (ECLI:EU:C:2020:746). The three preliminary references challenge inter alia the conformity of the Section for the Investigations on Offences Committed within the Judiciary (SIOJ) with the second paragraph of Art 19(1) TEU ('Member States shall provide remedies sufficient to ensure effective legal protection in the fields covered by Union law') and Art 47 of the Charter (the right to a fair trial provision). AG Bobek's position reproduces some of the standard biases, insofar as it emphasises possible objections to the SIOJ, some of which are legitimate and reasonable, but also goes beyond the call of duty to downplay the deeper causes that resulted in the creation of this structure. For instance, one of the main justifications, as

exemplify the logical limits of instrumentalising constitutional language and the contradictions embedded in current patterns of multilayer constitutionalism.

IV. CONCLUSION: JUDICIAL INDEPENDENCE AND POST-TRUTH CONSTITUTIONALISM

This chapter has made the argument that, even though the institutional structure of the third branch revolves around the principle of judicial independence, the meaning of this principle has a rich and layered texture, whose complexities preclude 'one size fits all' practical solutions. The common denominator at the level of comparative constitutional law is too thin to allow for wholesale transposition of institutional recipes from one country to another. In Europe, as a result of intense cross-hybridisation of reform packages preferred and proffered by international bodies in the context of conditionalities, a consensus has crystallised in the sense of favouring external over internal independence and independence as autonomy from politics over accountability mechanisms. This newly minted orthodoxy does significant violence to the complex trade-offs between conflicting values (independence and accountability, rule of law and democracy) and concerns that have traditionally informed constitutionalist tradition(s). Insistence over ready-made patterns of reform at the periphery of Europe has already 'ricocheted' in the sense of inducing a need for similar conformities in central constitutional jurisdictions. A recent ECJ judgment denied, for example, to German prosecutors, who are formally subordinated to the executive, the authority to issue European Arrest Warrants, in a reverse harmonisation frenzy unsupported by any real need, in the setting of a system that has been functioning tolerably well for many decades.[59]

Such tendencies are not without risk. A trend towards depoliticisation (as opposed to achieving the proper balance) produces or reinforces violent backlashes in the inevitable attempt to repoliticise the contested spheres. The backlash is currently called 'populism', in order to stress – correctly – that it denotes a perverted understanding of constitutional democracy. But the Rousseauian–Jacobin fetishism of majority rule masquerading as 'the people's sovereignty' and the Orwellian–Huxleyan fantasies of 'technocratic constitutionalism' bereft of any recognisable form of democratic choice and input are equally dangerous expressions of a wider pathology.

---

discussed above, was that the DNA, the anticorruption watchdog, had (kept) open files on members of the judiciary as a potential intimidation instrument. According to Bobek's reasoning (para 299 in the Opinion), this justification is invalid, since the official report of the Judicial Inspection substantiating such apprehensions, which were a matter of public record, with hard facts was published after the law creating the SIOJ had been published.

[59] Judgments in Joined Cases C-508/18 OG (*Public Prosecutor's office of Lübeck*) and C-82/19 PPU PI (*Public Prosecutor's office of Zwickau*) and in Case C-509/18 PF (*Prosecutor General of Lithuania*).

6

Judicial Independence –
The View from Israel

AMIR PAZ-FUCHS

T HE ISRAELI SITUATION offers an interesting case study for inquiring
whether courts are 'friend or foe'. This is not to say that the Israeli
experience, in this regard or more generally, is unique. Indeed, in the
US context, for example, similar concerns were voiced over forty years ago.[1]
And yet, the challenges that arrive at the doorsteps of Israeli courts, ranging
from corruption through religious protection, free speech and, of course, a
wide range of issues emanating from the prolonged Israeli–Palestinian conflict,
place it at the very centre of political debate on a regular basis. It is not only
a court seeking to preserve constitutional foundations such as due process and
human rights in the context of a military conflict. In addition, from a legal
perspective, it has done so against the background of a 'state of emergency' in
place since Israel was established in 1948; and burdened further by the decision
to hear petitions against the military commander of the Occupied Palestinian
Territories (OPT) brought by residents of the OPT.[2]

Internationally, the Israeli courts, and the Supreme Court in particular, are
held in high regard, sometimes viewed as the last defence for Israeli democracy. Domestically, however, the picture is a mixed one, with both sides either
routinely 'disappointed' in the court, or resigned to see it as an antagonistic
force whose powers should be limited.

To an extent, the intense public debate concerning judicial independence in
Israel suffers from similar misunderstandings and conceptual confusions that
plague similar debates elsewhere. Therefore, this chapter will, at times, refer
to the theoretical issues that are apparent. Chief among them is the confusion

---

[1] I Kaufman, 'Chilling Judicial Independence' (1979) 88 *Yale Law Journal* 681, 689–90.

[2] A Reichman, 'Judicial Independence in Times of War: Prolonged Armed Conflict and Judicial
Review of Military Actions in Israel' (2011) *Utah Law Review* 63, 74; D Kretzmer, *The Occupation
of Justice: The Supreme Court of Israel and the Occupied Territories* (Albany, State University of
New York Press, 2002) 1–16; HCJ 302/72 *Abu-Hilu v Gov't of Israel* 27(2) PD 169, 176 [1973] (Isr).

between limiting judicial power and encroaching on judicial independence, which is the focus of section I. This discussion leads into the efforts to distinguish between legitimate and illegitimate limits placed on the courts by the political branches, which are analysed in section II. Section III will then show why this conflation between power and judicial independence, and between legitimate and illegitimate political initiatives, are particularly dangerous for advocates of those who wish to preserve judicial independence, and for a democratic ethos more generally. Section IV then brings the various strands together by attempting to answer the question: 'are the Israeli courts friend or foe?' and how the answer to this question should impact the construction of judicial independence in the Israeli context.

I. BETWEEN POWER AND JUDICIAL INDEPENDENCE

In May 2018, the President of the Israeli Supreme Court, Esther Hayut, delivered a remarkable speech, declaring that 'Israel's judicial branch is under an unprecedented attack that threatens to damage its independence irreparably'.[3] The background to this claim was a ministerial initiative to curtail the courts' power to strike down laws that have an adverse, and disproportionate, impact on human rights. Speaking after President Hayut, the justice minister at the time, Ayelet Shaked, declared that it is within parliament's power and duty to map the mutual relationship between the branches of government.[4]

The urgency apparent in President's Hayut approach is understandable. Over twenty years ago, a prominent Israeli constitutional scholar observed that: 'The increased public interest in the courts in general and the involvement of the courts in cases with intense political implications have made public comment on judges and judicial decisions more frequent and more violent.'[5] When reflecting on the current atmosphere, in which a member of parliament called to send a bulldozer to raze the Supreme Court (following a decision to demolish a number of dwellings which had been built illegally in the Jewish settlement of Beit El),[6] the heated deliberations on the role of the court from the turn of the century seem timid and quaint in comparison.

In the highly contentious context of Israeli politics it is worth clarifying that the argument that proceeds below is not intended to offer support to the politics of those who made and make it their mission to target the courts in

---

[3] R Hovel, 'Israel's Chief Justice Warns Government in Landmark Speech: Judicial Branch "Under Unprecedented Attack"' *Ha'aretz*, 7 May 2018, www.haaretz.com/israel-news/israel-s-chief-justice-judicial-branch-under-attack-1.6062718 (accessed 2 April 2020).

[4] ibid.

[5] S Shetreet, 'Judicial Independence and Accountability in Israel' (1984) 33 *ICLQ* 979, 1005.

[6] HCJ 794/17 *Ziyada v The Military Commander in the West Bank* (2017); Hezki Baruch, 'MK: Raze the High Court' *Arutz Sheva*, 29 July 2015, www.israelnationalnews.com/News/News.aspx/198771 (accessed 10 April 2020).

a highly politicised fashion. Quite the opposite, in fact. However, is it wrong to maintain, as the former minister of justice did, that it is parliament's duty to map the relationship between the branches of government? After all, the nature of this relationship is the ultimate political question, in the true sense of the word. These are the questions that troubled Aristotle, Montesquieu and Madison. Why should they not be the subject of open debate within the most political of branches? The answer is that the theoretical debate has very practical implications insofar as parliament is concerned. Thus, one may ask: how can parliament decide the extent of its own power, vis-a-vis other branches, in a manner that is intellectually honest? This is a fair objection, but it is not the one advanced by judges and their supporters. That is, the objection is not that parliament has no role in debating the powers and limits of judicial authority, because it is in an inherent conflict of interest. That is: here parliamentarians are debating the extent to which their decisions will be 'checked and balanced' by the judicial branch. Whether cynically or not, institutions would understandably opt to have the outcome of their deliberations – in the form of statutes – withstand scrutiny; and they would clearly prefer to have the 'final say' in the matter. However, there is no obvious way to avoid this parliamentary conflict of interests. Like any public authority, judicial power stems, in the main, from parliamentary legislation.

Indeed, every judiciary in the world owes at least some of its power to parliament. Parliamentary acts tend to establish the courts, regulate their jurisdiction, set the procedure through which court budgets are allocated, and determine the terms and conditions of the employment of the judges.[7] So the argument is, to be precise, that a change to the status quo, which changes the balance of power in a manner that is detrimental to the courts, is inherently threatening to judicial independence. But it will be argued below that this approach is not only misguided. In being misguided, it also serves opponents of the courts with ammunition.

One final preliminary observation: the matter of judicial independence covers a wide range of issues, but those can mostly be categorised as either 'institutional' judicial independence or 'personal' judicial independence.[8] Many scholars have described, analysed and criticised threats to the latter, which relates to matters such as tenure, job and pay security, and other forms of protection for judges who do not toe the line.[9] For present purposes, suffice to say that judicial tenure is inherently related to judicial independence because a

---

[7] L Kornhauser, 'Is Judicial Independence a Useful Concept?' in S Burbank and B Friedman (eds), *Judicial Independence at a Crossroads: An Interdisciplinary Approach* (Thousand Oaks, CA, Sage, 2002) 45.

[8] M Agmon-Gonnen, 'Judicial Independence: The Threat from Within' (2005) 38 *Israel Law Review* 120, 122; Shetreet (n 3) 992; Kornhauser (n 3).

[9] Shetreet (n 3); Agmon-Gonen (n 7); Kaufman (n 5); A Winkler and J Zabel, 'The Independence of Judges' (1995) 46 *Mercer Law Review* 795.

judge should not find an argument to be more 'persuasive' simply because she fears that she will lose her position if she decides otherwise. For this reason, this value is arguably endangered by the fact that judges that face elections tend to impose longer sentences on criminals convicted of serious felonies closer to an election.[10] The latter phenomenon, ironically justified through reference to democracy and accountability,[11] seems antithetical to judicial independence. If it is to be considered of any value, judicial independence should allow judges to reach decisions that are unpopular in the eye of the public or other branches of government, including reaching decisions that find against parliament or the government of the day, without fear or favour.

Before turning to the institutional facet of judicial independence, some background to the Israeli constitutional context is necessary. As is well known, Israel is one a few countries without a codified constitution. Instead, over the years, the Israeli parliament – the Knesset – enacted a series of sixteen 'Basic Laws', the first of which, Basic Law: The Knesset, was promulgated in 1958; and the most recent one, Basic Law: Israel, the Nation State of the Jewish People, passed in July 2018. The lack of a constitution means that, problematically, a simple majority in parliament can pass, amend or abolish a 'constitutional' law, which holds a higher place in the legal order.

Arguably, the most important moment in Israeli constitutional history is located in the early 1990s, for two complementary reasons, one doctrinal, the other realist. From a doctrinal perspective, the Knesset passed the first – and to date, the only – two Basic Laws devoted to human rights: Basic Law: Human Dignity and Liberty; and Basic Law: Freedom of Occupation. Although these laws do not mention a wide range of rights (eg freedom of speech, religion, equality or any social, economic or cultural right), they refer to the Israeli Declaration of Independence from 1948. That Declaration was viewed, until then, as solely … declaratory and having no legal, let alone constitutional, status. The Supreme Court placed high value on the reference to the Declaration and, in particular, its preamble, which states, inter alia, that the State of Israel

> will uphold the full social and political equality of all its citizens, without distinction of race, creed, or sex; will guarantee full freedom of conscience, worship, education, and culture; will safeguard the sanctity and inviolability of the shrines and Holy Places of all religions; and will dedicate itself to the principles of the Charter of the United Nations.

---

[10] K Berry, 'How Judicial Elections Impact Criminal Cases' (Brennan Center for Justice, 2015) www.brennancenter.org/sites/default/files/publications/How_Judicial_Elections_Impact_Criminal_Cases.pdf (accessed 2 April 2020).

[11] C Geyh, 'Customary Independence' in Burbank and Friedman (n 3) 160l; *cf* Shetreet (n 3) 997–98.

The realist perspective, or explanation, places much emphasis on the identity of the Israeli President of the Supreme Court during the time, Aharon Barak. Formerly a legal academic and Israel's Attorney General, Barak became, in 1978, the youngest ever judicial appointment to the Supreme Court, and its President in 1995. Until his retirement, in 2006, he was the most recognisable and authoritative voice, judicially and extra-judicially,[12] promoting the judicial agenda and legacy according to which 'everything is justiciable'. This position combined with the doctrinal structure that, putatively at least (and notwithstanding a number of prominent judicial and scholarly[13] opinions to the contrary) found that the 1992 Basic Laws constituted a 'constitutional revolution', moving Israel from a British constitutional paradigm of absolute parliamentary sovereignty to an American-style system under which the powers of the legislature are checked by the judiciary to see if they have a disproportionately harmful effect on human rights.[14] Together, the wide breadth of powers, covering vast realms of society and the economy, and the ability of the courts to review statutory instruments that were, previously, beyond judicial authority, raised the profile and stature of the court to one that is at least on equal footing to that of the other two branches. Finally, with respect to an important subset of the matter at hand, Barak ruled, in accepting a petition to publish the name of the head of the Mossad, that:

> Judges can and should review the reasonableness of discretion in security matters as much as they can and should review administrative discretion in any other field. Hence, there are no special limits on the scope of judicial review in security matters.[15]

But to what extent did that extension and enhancement of judicial powers change the manner in which courts should be perceived as independent? It appears that, notwithstanding dramatic pronouncements concerning a 'constitutional revolution' executed by the judiciary in the 1990s,[16] Israel was following

---

[12] See eg A Barak 'The Constitutional Revolution: Protected Human Rights' (1992) 1 *Mishpat u'Mimshal – Law and Government in Israel* 9; A Barak, *Interpretation in Law* (Jerusalem, Nevo, 1994) vol 3, 37–38; *Bank Hamizrachi v Migdal* 49(4) PD 221, 352.

[13] eg H Sommer 'The Non-enumerated Rights: On the Scope of the Constitutional Revolution" (1997) 28 *Mishpatim* 341; R Gavison, 'The Constitutional Revolution: A Reality or Self-fulfilling Prophecy?' (1997) 28 *Mishpatim* 21.

[14] M Hofnung, 'The Unintended Consequences of Unplanned Constitutional Reform: Constitutional Politics in Israel' (1996) 44 *American Journal of Comparative Law* 585; A Harel, 'The Rule of Law and Judicial Review: Reflections on the Israeli Constitutional Revolution' in David Dyzenhaus (ed), *Recrafting the Rule of Law: Recrafting the Legal Order* (Oxford, Hart Publishing, 1999) 143, 146.

[15] HCJ 680/88 *Shnitzer v Military Censor* (1988) 639–40. For a critique of Barak's legacy, see N Sultany, 'The Legacy of Aharon Barak: A Critical Review' (2007) 48 *Harvard International Law Journal Online* 83.

[16] Aharon Barak stated that 'In 1992, a constitutional revolution took place in Israel': 'Human Rights in Israel' 39 *Israel Law Review* (2006) 12, 18; also R Hirschl, 'The "Constitutional Revolution" and the Emergence of a New Economic Order in Israel' (1997) 2 *Israel Studies* 136.

an existing path. Thus, a brief comparative observation could be useful at this stage.

Canada and the United Kingdom provide the most relevant examples of courts that found their powers extended following an act of parliament. The 1982 Canadian Charter of Rights and Freedom granted the court the power of judicial review;[17] whereas in the UK, the 1998 Human Rights Act gave the courts power to declare a law incompatible with the European Convention on Human Rights. In other countries, the courts were even more adventurous, and yet, the similarities to the Israeli Supreme Court's innovation are clear.

In 1971, the French Constitutional Council declared that the Preamble to the 1958 Constitution is a legally enforceable provision.[18] This was followed by a decision to allow any sixty members of either house of the French parliament to refer a law for review by the Council. And this power was quickly put into effect: opposition parties referred nearly one-third of all legislation to the Council, and since 1981, this has resulted in the annulment of at least parts of the laws.[19] Similarly, the Indian Supreme Court declared that the Preamble to the Indian Constitution created a basic structure upon which the court may rely to strike down not only legislation, but also unconstitutional constitutional amendments.[20] In Hungary, the Constitutional Court developed a legal doctrine that expanded its powers and legitimacy significantly, enabling it to strike down one out of three laws that came under its review, and even to instruct the Hungarian parliament when it is at fault for acting 'unconstitutionally by omission'. These extensive powers have led one of the most prominent scholars of post-Soviet legal regimes, Kim Lane Scheppele, to refer to the Hungarian regime of the time as a 'courtocracy'.[21]

In all of these examples, the powers of the courts have increased in relation to the government and the legislature. And yet, I would argue, this did not increase their independence. To offer just one comparison, the Israeli courts currently have far more powers than their British counterparts, even *following* the enactment of the Human Rights Act 1998. So much so, that the most 'extreme' version of the current proposals debated to constrain the reach of the Israeli courts is to adopt the British model, and allow the courts only to declare the unconstitutionality of a law. This proposal is perceived, by its opponents, as a death knell to ... judicial independence. But does that mean that British courts

---

[17] ER Alexander 'The Supreme Court of Canada and the Canadian Charter of Rights and Freedoms' (1990) 40 *University of Toronto Law Journal* 1; *Law Society of Upper Canada v Skapinker* (1984) 9 DLR (4th) 161.

[18] P Lindseth, 'Law, History and Memory: "Republican Moments" and the Legitimacy of Constitutional Review in France' (1997) *Columbia Journal of European Law* 3.

[19] A Stone Sweet, *Governing with judges: Constitutional Politics in Europe* (Oxford, Oxford University Press, 2000).

[20] *Kesavananda Bharati v State of Kerala* (1973).

[21] KL Scheppele, 'Declarations of Independence: Judicial Reactions to Political Pressure' in Burbank and Friedman (n 3) 227.

do not enjoy judicial independence? That obviously is not the case. The conclusion must be, therefore, that if Israeli courts were to lose their existing powers to strike down laws, they would not lose judicial independence, but rather lose some judicial power. A clear distinction must be maintained, in academic and public discourse, between judicial power and judicial independence.

Winkler and Zagel thus rightly identify that whilst this issue of parliament's power to limit the courts' jurisdiction is often discussed as integral to judicial independence,[22] its relevance to the matter at hand is 'considerably less' pronounced than it is perceived to be.[23] 'Independence to the judge', they note, 'turns on the amount of discretion she has in deciding a particular issue before her and not on whether she can hear the issue in the first place.'[24] Judges are not allowed to hear cases that are brought before them after the applicable statute of limitations, or cases that belong in another forum, or another jurisdiction; and they will not respond positively to requests to make declaratory rulings or on matters that have become hypothetical. These limits have no bearing on judicial independence.

II. LEGITIMATE AND ILLEGITIMATE POLITICAL INCURSIONS

However, notwithstanding the analytical distinction, we should not be so naïve as to suggest that the source of this conflation, between judicial independence and judicial power, is simply a matter of confusion. Where the powers of the judiciary are concerned, parliamentarians and government representatives become excited and tend to hyperbole not as an abstract, theoretical matter; nor with regards to particular areas of private law (eg the power to impose punitive remedies in tort). Such a dialogue exists between branches of government, but is usually confined to specialists, and does not attract much public attention. This issue becomes far more contentious when the power in question involves a tug of war between two (or more) branches of government, and is perceived as a zero-sum game. Such debates bring to the fore concepts such as 'separation of powers', 'checks and balances' and the 'rule of law'. In this particular case, parliament and government feel unduly constrained by the dictates of the judiciary, and seek to limit its powers; whereas the judiciary senses that it is being constrained in its role, and duty, to ensure that the executive and legislative branches adhere to the rule of law.

Interestingly, the United Kingdom and Israel recently offered two strikingly similar case studies in that regard, in which each respective Supreme Court found that parliamentary practices were executed in a manner that was unlawful.

---

[22] See eg Lawrence Sager, 'Foreword: Constitutional Limitations on Congress' Authority to Regulate the Jurisdiction of Federal Courts' (1981) 95 *Harvard Law Review* 17.
[23] Winkler and Zagel (n 9) 819.
[24] ibid.

In the United Kingdom, this occurred when the Supreme Court found that the prime minister's decision to prorogue parliament (or, technically, to advise the Queen to do so), against the background of the Brexit debate, was 'unlawful, void and of no effect'.[25] In Israel in March 2020, following the general election, the (at the time interim) Speaker of the House refused to allow a vote to put in place a new, permanent Speaker.[26] The similarity between the cases was not lost on the Israeli Supreme Court which found justification for intervening in the Speaker's decision, inter alia, by reference to the British case.

These were highly contentious cases, which will probably be studied by future generations of students as touchstones in the debate over separation of powers. But they tell us very little about 'judicial independence'. The phrase is not mentioned in either decision, nor by decisions of the British lower courts, two of which reached a different decision. Those courts rejected the challenge, categorising the prime minister's decision as 'inherently political in nature' and determining that there were 'no legal standards' against which to assess its legitimacy.[27] In other words, this was a clear example of different positions regarding normative theories of adjudication and separation of powers. However, one can envisage, as has happened in the past, that if a few politicians decided to speak out against the decision, and to 'promise' to revisit the powers of the (unelected) court to act in a manner that is 'undemocratic', members of the judiciary and their advocates would cry out against the danger to judicial independence. That, again, would be a mistake.

So, if judicial independence is distinct from power, separation of powers and the rule of law, what is it about? One answer suggests that judicial independence is concerned with the type of influence that can sway judicial decisions. In particular, it seeks to distinguish between 'appropriate' and 'inappropriate' influences.[28] A judge may be influenced, or persuaded, by arguments made by one of the parties in open court; but she may not be influenced by a party who makes her case when meeting in a bar, after hours, or by a lawyer who offers a bribe if she wins the case. She should decide a case, then, according to the law and free from inappropriate pressure.[29]

Kim Lane Scheppele suggests a slightly different distinction, one that focuses on the difference between external (political) intervention at the level of the rule, and external (political) intervention at the level of the case. Particularly in cases in which the political branches have a clear interest, she asks: what is the

---

[25] *R (Miller) v the Prime Minister* [2019] UKSC 41.

[26] HCJ 2144/20 *The Movement for Quality in Government et al v the Speaker of the Knesset et al* (23 March 2020).

[27] *Miller v the Prime Minister* [2019] EWHC 2381 (QB); *Cherry v the Advocate General* [2019] CSIH 49.

[28] Kornhauser (n 3).

[29] G Gee et al, *The Politics of Judicial Independence in the UK's Changing Constitution* (Cambridge, Cambridge University Press, 2015) 3.

difference between a political 'intervention' in the form of ministerial regulation that would instruct judges to decide cases in a particular way (eg that remedies in tort cases should be capped at a given amount; or that some forms of evidence may be admissible); and the type exemplified by the Soviet 'telephone justice' cases (or, for that matter, in *Miracle on 34th Street*[30]), where political officials called judges to instruct them how to decide the case?[31] Political intervention is, we understand, legitimate if it appears at the level of a rule, even if it pre-empts a particular family of cases. Indeed, at that level, per Scheppele, a judge is *expected* to follow the political edict, which is embodied in the form of a regulation, for example.[32] In contrast, political intervention is suspect, and endangers judicial independence, when it appears at the level of a case.

This position, she suggests, should be questioned. Political intervention of any sort (ie both at the level of the case and at the level of the rule) is suspect. As Scheppele explains:

> If judges have to take a positivist attitude toward law and simply follow the rules laid down by the political branches, then they are not really independent of politics but … completely subservient to it. … If there is no struggle between the political branches and the judicial branch over the meaning of the law and the way that it is to be applied in concrete cases, then there is not only no meaningful separation of powers but also no meaningful distinction between law and politics.[33]

In other words, Scheppele takes the realist intuition to its logical extreme, by suggesting that not only does politics impact law in familiar ways, but that *conceptually* there is no distinction between a political rationale and a legal one. This conclusion, paradoxically, is the result of the positivist paradigm according to which judges should, and do, follow rules laid down by the legislature and by government ministers. The peculiar consequence (for this author, but perhaps not for Scheppele) is that '[o]nly when judges are empowered to resist direct commands through invoking the power to make law themselves can they be truly independent within a broader legal order'.[34]

As such, Scheppele's position is clearly an outlier, but it is intellectually stimulating, offering as it does what may be viewed as a 'political' approach to judicial independence, as opposed to a 'jurisprudential' approach. Whilst the latter takes into account basic jurisprudential principles, such as the courts' duty to follow the law as articulated by the political branches, the political approach suggests that 'true' independence is made manifest precisely when the courts

---

[30] In the classic Christmas film from 1947, a judge presiding over a case in which he must determine if the defendant is *truly* Santa Claus is instructed by his political sponsor to determine that such is the case if he wishes to retain his judgeship, and indeed decides accordingly.

[31] Scheppele (n 10).

[32] For such a position, see eg C Franklin 'Behavioral Factors Affecting Judicial Independence' in Burbank and Friedman (n 3) 148, 149.

[33] Scheppele (n 10) 279.

[34] ibid.

ignore those directives and 'make law themselves'. Extreme as this position may seem, it clarifies that our expectations for 'what qualifies as judicial independence?' is on a spectrum, and that criteria for answering this question need to be established before we can answer if judicial independence is in danger.

III. JUDICIAL INDEPENDENCE IN ISRAEL

I suggested that it is important to distinguish between the range of powers held by a court and the degree of independence we attribute to it. I turn now to clarify that danger of this conflation in the Israeli context.

We can start this part of the inquiry by returning to President Hayut's rebuke of the recent initiatives. Responding to the claim that the court is too powerful, she indicated that since 1992, the US Supreme Court had voided fifty federal laws, while the Israeli court reached the same decision only on eighteen occasions, making it one of the least 'activist' courts in the world. To paraphrase the president's argument, perhaps unfairly, she is saying: we're playing nice, so why be so hostile? Even more unfairly, one may even find a normative element in her argument: if the court promises to continue to 'respect' the decisions made by other branches of government, will you preserve our 'judicial independence'? This is a dangerous path to follow. It is also somewhat paradoxical: for if the court has voided only eighteen laws in twenty-seven years, five of which involved two issues which reached the court on different occasions, why is it so important to maintain that power and, moreover, to leverage the threat to judicial independence in the process?

The reason that this is a dangerous path to follow is because judicial independence *is* important, and is particularly important in a country such as Israel, where the issues at stake could hardly be more dramatic. In Israel, a number of justifiably celebrated decisions by the Supreme Court established the rule of law, and fundamental ideas of administrative law, such as due process and ultra vires, in a very difficult context. Among them, we can note the following: in 1950, a mere two years after the war of independence, the Supreme Court overruled a decision by the prime minister, the powerful David Ben Gurion, to dismiss a (Jewish) teacher who was considered a right-wing terrorist by the establishment.[35] Three years later, the court struck down the minister of interior's decision to shut down a communist paper which was published both in Hebrew and Arabic.[36]

Following the war of 1967, the control over Palestinian land and population engaged the Supreme Court in issues with which it was not previously familiar. In 1979, the court ruled for the first (and last, prior to the Beit-El decision, noted

---

[35] HCJ 144/50 *Schweib v Minister of Defense* 2 PD 5 (1950).
[36] HCJ 73/53 *Kol Ha'am v Minister of Interior* 7 PD 871 (1953).

in the opening[37]) time that the order to confiscate private land for the purpose of building the Elon Moreh settlement was ultra vires and void, as it lacked a security rationale.[38] In the present context, the reaction of the Israeli prime minister at the time, Menachem Begin, to the decision, is noteworthy: 'There are judges in Jerusalem.'[39] As Begin was the leader of the conservative, Likud, party, and a vocal advocate of the historical and religious ties between the Jewish people and the land, this pronouncement was perceived as a clear endorsement of the importance of the rule of law.

In 1999, the Supreme Court found that, without explicit legal authorisation, the General Security Service (comparable to MI5 or the FBI) is not empowered to use force against suspects when conducting inquiries. The decision was understandably lauded by the international community (the decision was immediately translated and distributed) and rebuked by the security forces.

In 2004 and 2005, the Supreme Court heard a number of cases concerning the 'Separation Barrier', and ordered the government to dismantle 40 km of the barrier north of Jerusalem,[40] and about 100 km of the barrier that enclosed the settlement of Alfei Menashe, along with five Palestinian villages.[41] The latter case led the Israeli government to withdraw its objection to yet another petition, on a further segment of barrier.[42] The court reached these decisions after carefully scrutinising the evidence placed before it and, predominantly, questioning whether there was *any* security reason for the route of the barrier, which led to a disproportionately harmful effect on the lives of Palestinians in its vicinity. And yet, this careful approach notwithstanding, the court's decisions were followed by an outcry by right-wing members of parliament to 'circumvent the Supreme Court' by passing legislation which would deny the court the power to question security justifications.[43] This legislation, it should be noted, was never passed, and its proposal could be viewed, in retrospect, as mere sabre rattling.

---

[37] Text to n 4.

[38] HCJ 390/79 *Dawikat v Gov't of Israel* 34(1) PD 1 [1979]; M Kremnitzer and R Segev, 'The Legality of Interrogational Torture: A Question of Proper Authorization or a Substantive Moral Issue?' (2000) 34 *Israel Law* 509, 540.

[39] Reichman (n 6) 77.

[40] *Beit Sourik Village Council v the Government of Israel* PD 58(5) 807 (2004).

[41] HCJ 7957/04 *Hamoked – Centre for the Defence of the Individual v The Prime Minister of Israel* (2004).

[42] HCJ 2732/05 *Hamoked – Centre for the Defence of the Individual v The Prime Minister of Israel* (2005); D Barak-Erez, 'Israel: The Security Barrier – Between International Law, Constitutional Law and Domestic Judicial Review' (2006) 4 *International Journal of Constitutional Law* 540; A Bendor, 'Justiciability of the Israeli Fight Against Terrorism' (2007) 39 *George Washington International Law Review* 149, 159–63; A Gross, 'The Construction of a Wall Between the Hague and Jerusalem: The Enforcement and Limits of Humanitarian Law and the Structure of Occupation' (2006) 19 *Leiden Journal of International Law* 393.

[43] G Alon, 'Decision Draws Fire from the Right, Praise from the Left' *Ha'aretz*, 1 July 2004, www.haaretz.com/1.4746667 (accessed 14 April 2020).

This list of cases (to which others may be added) may suggest that Israeli courts have been the rear-guard in preserving the rule of law and democratic principles in an extreme situation, in which those principles are tested routinely. Some scholars, however, are more sceptical. Ronen Shamir and Aeyal Gross, for example, suggest that such landmark cases allow courts in general,[44] and the Israeli courts in particular, to navigate the treacherous waters of public approval, siding with the government in the vast majority of cases (to retain the necessary political capital vis-a-vis other branches of government and the mainstream media) whilst finding against the government on a number of isolated cases, to retain credibility with the liberal elites and the international community.[45]

In fact, during the period under review (1967–86), Shamir found that of the 557 petitions submitted by Palestinians to the Supreme Court, only five (of which one concerned Elon Moreh) were successful.[46] Moreover, he notes that each of these cases had a particular set of characterisations which barred it from being perceived as a general precedent. To return, by way of example, to the Elon Moreh case, he notes that whilst in past (and future) cases the settlers and the military establishment highlighted the security necessity for the settlement, in this case the settlers insisted that no such security considerations existed. Rather, they proclaimed that the settlement was 'a Godly commandment to inherit the land promised by our ancestors ... *not inspired* by security considerations'.[47] In his discussion, Shamir reviews the overwhelming consensus from the media, from academic scholars and human rights groups, praising the court for these decisions.[48] However, he notes:

> None of the decisions had any significant effect on later policies, save the growing sophistication of the authorities in their implementation of legal procedures. Yet the significance of the cases was exaggerated, allowing them to appear as symbols of justice.[49]

Gross maintains, with reference to the occupation, that the success in a few cases creates 'the myth of a "benign occupation" that protects human rights even though they are mostly denied'.[50]

---

[44] S Scheingold, *The Politics of Rights* (New Haven, CT, Yale University Press, 1974).

[45] R Shamir, '"Landmark Cases" and the Reproduction of Legitimacy: The Case of Israel's High Court of Justice' (1990) 24 *Law and Society Review* 781; A Gross, 'Human Proportions: Are Human Rights the Emperor's New Clothes of the International Law of Occupation?' (2007) 18 *European Journal of International Law* 1.

[46] The others are *El-Asad v Minister of Interior* (1979) [requiring the Minister of Interior to issue a permit to an East Jerusalem publisher to publish a newspaper]; *Kawasme v Minister of Defense* (1980) [revoking a decision to deport three Palestinian leaders without due process]; *Samara v Military Commander of Judea and Samaria* (1979) [allowing a Palestinian to return from Germany to join his family in the OPT]; *Jerusalem District Electric Company v Minister of Energy* (1981) [striking down the military takeover of a Palestinian electricity company in East Jerusalem].

[47] Cited in Shamir (n 42) 788 (emphasis added).

[48] ibid 795–96.

[49] ibid 797.

[50] Gross (n 43) 9.

As Gross's argument indicates, Shamir's analysis has been proven prescient, time and again, since it was written. Thus, in 1993, the Supreme Court approved, per curiam, the midnight deportation, without due process (including the right to a fair hearing) of 415 putative Hamas 'members' to Lebanon.[51] As Reichman notes:

> [T]he political and military pressure appears to have been too strong for the Court: the judges found that the right to a hearing can also be granted after the deportation to Lebanon. Needless to say, the legal community met this decision with disbelief.[52]

In the *Targeted Killings* case,[53] the court assessed the practice which, at the time, led to the killing of 338 Palestinians, of whom 128 were innocent bystanders, including 29 children. The court denied the government's preliminary argument of justiciability. However, as a matter of substance, it created a category of 'unlawful combatants' who 'are not entitled either to the privileges of combatants or to the immunities of civilians'.[54]

Similarly, in cases concerning the demolition of houses of Palestinian families where one member, who lived in the house, committed a suicide attack, the court granted the family a right to challenge the decision, but then routinely accepted the military's position, and allowed the collective punishment.[55] David Kretzmer, for example, found that the High Court of Justice (HCJ)[56] intervened in only three of 150 house-demolishing orders until the 1990s.[57] Data collected by scholars and human rights organisations suggest that over 2,000 houses have been demolished or sealed through these measures.[58] Guy Harpaz finds that, when challenged, the Supreme Court has adopted 'a deferential attitude towards the security authorities, manifested in and facilitated by a very low burden of proof. [House demolition] judgments are in most instances unanimous, jurisprudentially brief, abstract, formalistic and unrefined, displaying almost

---

[51] HCJ 5973/92 *Association for Civil Rights in Israel v Minister of Defense* 47 PD 267 [1993].

[52] Reichman (n 6) 82.

[53] HCJ 769/02 *Public Committee against Torture in Israel v Government of Israel*.

[54] O Ben-Naftali and K Michaeli, 'Public Committee against Torture in Israel v Government of Israel, Case No HCJ 769/02' (2007) 101 *American Journal of International Law* 459, 465. See also A Cohen and Y Shany, 'A Development of Modest Proportions: The Application of the Principle of Proportionality in the Targeted Killings Case' (2007) 5 *Journal of International Criminal Justice* 310; D Kretzmer, 'Targeted Killing of Suspected Terrorists: Extra-judicial Executions or Legitimate Means of Defence?' (2005) 16 *European Journal of International Law* 171, 205.

[55] M Hofnung and K Weinshall-Margel, 'Judicial Setbacks, Material Gains: Terror Litigation at the Israeli High Court of Justice' (2010) 7 *Journal of Empirical Legal Studies* 664.

[56] In Israel, the Supreme Court sits as a High Court of Justice when reviewing petitions against public authorities.

[57] D Kretzmer, 'Judicial Review Over Demolition and Sealing of Houses in the Occupied Territories' in I Zamir (ed), *Klinghoffer Book on Public Law* (Jerusalem, Harry Sacher Institute, 1993) (in Hebrew).

[58] U Halabi, 'Demolition and Sealing of Houses in the Israeli Occupied Territories: A Critical Legal Analysis' (1992) 5 *Temple Journal of International and Comparative Law* 251.

uniform support of the practice'.[59] In doing so, he asserts, the court has 'virtually granted [the authorities] a *carte blanche*',[60] whilst simultaneously ignoring well-established administrative and constitutional standards.

The final category of cases which suggests a reluctance of the courts to intervene is that which concerns the administrative detention of individuals; that is, the deprivation of liberty for an indeterminate period without a criminal charge or trial. According to the human rights organisation B'Tselem, Israel has held up to 1,800 Palestinians at a given time, and since 2002, 'not a single month has gone by without Israel holding at least 1,000 Palestinians in administrative detention'.[61] Administrative detention in the West Bank is authorised under a military order, which empowers the military commander in the area to detain an individual for up to six months if they have 'reasonable grounds to believe that a certain person must be held in detention for reasons to do with regional security or public security'.[62] At the end of the six months, a subsequent order can be (and frequently is) issued, leading to dozens of detainees being held for over a year, without trial. An empirical study of Supreme Court decisions concerning the OPT has revealed that, at 35 per cent, administrative detention cases constitute the largest portion of the five categories (the others are: house demolitions, separation barrier, closures and curfews, and military actions).[63] At the same time, the court is most reluctant to intervene in such cases, finding for the petitioner less than 5 per cent of the time.[64]

In summary, the decisions discussed in this section advance the inquiry into whether Israeli courts may be considered 'friends or foes' by further demarcating judicial powers and judicial independence. Whether granting or denying the petition, Israeli courts refrained from engaging in controversial political territory, such as the legality of a prolonged occupation; and did not take the opportunity to enhance human rights discourse in this context. Instead, they relied on principles of procedural due process, evidentiary requirements and standards of reasonableness and proportionality. Needless to say, these decisions, of which there are several thousand, impact the rights and livelihood of millions, whilst rarely engaging with the controversial question of the court's

---

[59] G Harpaz, 'When Does a Court Systematically Deviate from its Own Principles: The Adjudication by the Israeli Supreme Court in the Occupied Palestinian Territories' (2015) 28(1) *Leiden Journal of International Law* 31, 34.

[60] ibid 42.

[61] B'Tselem, *Administrative Detention* (November 2017) www.btselem.org/administrative_detention (accessed 17 April 2020).

[62] Military Order 1651, Art 285(A); P Langford and T Mariniello, *Israel's Administrative Detention in the Occupied Palestinian Territories: An Assessment of the Applicable norms of International Law and Possibilities of Enforcement* (Edgehill, 2019) https://research.edgehill.ac.uk/ws/files/22096758/Report_Administrative_Detention.pdf (accessed 17 April 2020).

[63] M Hofnung and K Weinshall Margel, 'Judicial Setbacks, Material Gains: Terror Litigation at the Israeli High Court of Justice' (2010) 7 *Journal of Empirical Legal Studies* 664, 673 fn 12.

[64] ibid 680.

powers to strike down legislation. The judicial powers were traditional, as were the judicial principles relied upon. Judicial independence is under threat, then, not because of the application of nuclear powers, such as striking down laws. The threat becomes apparent when government agencies are given '"room to manoeuvre" to act in ways which otherwise should have been curtailed *under a straightforward application of the substantive law*',[65] and when judges refrain from using the full amplitude of their existing powers.[66]

IV. FRIEND OR FOE – A NUANCED VIEW

There seems to be a consensus that judicial independence is important for the courts for instrumental reasons. In particular, judges demand judicial independence so they can maintain their role as 'friends' to democratic principles and the rule of law. This position is particularly popular amongst judges themselves. Thus, California Superior Court Judge Terry Friedman maintained that attacks on judicial independence 'imperil ... our fundamental rights and freedoms as Americans, especially free speech and equal opportunity, which historically the courts have protected, sometimes even when contrary to majority will'.[67] And in a recent visit to Israel, Justice Rosalie Abella Silberman, of the Canadian Supreme Court, addressed this very issue, saying that:

> Independent judges who are not politically compliant are not anti-democratic, they are doing their job; those critics, on the other hand, who think patriotism means doing only what politicians want, are the biggest threat to Israel's values, because they misconceive democracy as majoritarian rule.[68]

The causal link between judicial independence and democratic principles is more often declared than explained. Clearly, when supporting such a link, the narrow understanding of democracy as majority rule is rejected, since courts often work as counter-majoritarian institutions. Instead, courts may be uniquely important and successful in protecting 'potential or unorganised interests or values which are *un*likely to be represented elsewhere in government'.[69] Alternatively, they may be supporting democracy in the narrower, process-based

---

[65] G Davidov and A Reichman, Prolonged Armed Conflict and Diminished Deference to the Military: Lessons from Israel' (2010) 35 *Law and Social Inquiry* 919, 922.

[66] J King, 'Institutional Approaches to Judicial Restraint' (2008) 28 *OJLS* 409.

[67] T Peretti, 'Does Judicial Independence Exist? The Lessons of Social Science Research' in Burbank and Friedman (n 3) 103, 120.

[68] RA Silberman, 'Without an Independent Judiciary, Israel's Cherished Democracy will be at risk' *The Times of Israel*, 19 April 2018, www.timesofisrael.com/without-an-independent-judiciary-israels-cherished-democracy-will-be-at-risk/ (accessed 17 April 2020).

[69] Martin Shapiro, 'Judicial Modesty, Political Reality and Preferred Position' (1962) 47 *Cornell Law Quarterly* 175, 199.

sense, by reinforcing democratic government where its representatives have failed to uphold their own ground rules.[70]

If judicial independence is a means to an end – to ensure the protection of democracy, the rule of law, and right and liberties – how should we rate courts in general, and the Israeli courts in particular, in this regard? First, it is not at all clear that the intuitive link between strong courts and protection of rights withstands scrutiny. Thus, Peretti concludes that there is a common claim 'that independent judges can ensure the certain protection of our rights and liberties, particularly those of powerless minorities, even when doing so arouses the opposition of majorities or powerful politicians. The empirical evidence … does not support these expectations'.[71]

The discussion up to this point seems to suggest two conclusions: that the narrative, in general, but prominently in Israel, which conflates judicial powers and judicial independence misses the mark. In addition, that the court is a 'friend' of advocates of liberalism, human rights and tolerance on a number of landmark cases, but in the vast majority of cases, quietly prefers to side with the government, preserving its own institutional legitimacy.

In this section I would like to muddle the waters somewhat, on both counts.

First, we noted above the differentiation between the personal and institutional versions of judicial independence.[72] It is now worth adding that that the two categories are not wholly distinct. Thus, due to their fidelity to the judiciary as an institution, judges may well view any harm to it as sufficiently worrisome as to constrain themselves in their decision-making. This, in its own right, could raise their concern that judicial independence is under threat.[73] Similarly, judges may be concerned with the perception of their legitimacy, also referred to in terms of public trust. Idealistically, judges repeatedly note that their ability to preserve the rule of law is reliant on their perception as impartial arbiters who are not concerned with their own powers. Thus, President Barak has stated that 'The need for public trust is not the need for popularity. … The meaning is the awareness that the judge is not a party to the legal fight, and that he is not fighting for his own power, but for the power of the law.'[74] If judges perceive that a political 'fight' with the executive or legislature would lead them to lose political capital, they may choose their battles more carefully. Davidov and Reichman note that the 'price' that may be exacted from the judiciary may be far more

---

[70] J Hart Ely, *Democracy and Distrust: A Theory of Judicial Review* (Cambridge, MA and London Harvard University Press, 1980) 102–04; but *cf* the persuasive critique by D Galligan, 'Judicial Review and Democratic Principles: Two Theories' in M Tushnet, *Bills of Rights* (Aldershot, Ashgate, 2007) 37.

[71] Peretti (n 64) 120.

[72] Text to n 8.

[73] T Peretti, 'Does Judicial Independence Exist? The Lessons of Social Science Research' in Burbank and Friedman (n 3) 103, 110.

[74] HCJ 732/84 *MK Yair Tzaban v Minister of Religions* 40 PD 141, 147–48.

mundane, and yet far more exacting, than that of limiting judicial powers. Thus, agencies may be reluctant to implement a judicial decision, citing delays and lack of resources; they may join forces with other agencies to frustrate judicial policies in other areas; and government may be inclined to redraft the law, thus entrenching and clarifying its (unwelcome) position.[75]

On the other hand, categorising court decisions as 'pro-petitioner' or 'pro-state' may not be wholly reflected in the court's decision. Hofnung and Weinshall, for example, find that in a substantial number of cases, 'in the course of deliberations and under the HCJ's questioning, the security establishment changes its initial stand and moves toward a position that accepts some or most of the petitioner's demands'.[76] They refer to this strategy as one that is 'latent, and is discernible only to those participants actively engaged in the legal process'[77] because, in many of these cases, the petition is formally rejected, simply because the state has withdrawn its objections. In such situations, they conclude, 'the HCJ's political power and influence is manifested without having to actually activate its powers, and thus helps preserve it'.[78] A similar conclusion is reached by Dotan, who suggests that 'while, in general, Palestinian petitions to the Court during this period enjoyed a low rate of success, Palestinians were far more successful in achieving their goals in out-of-court settlements and other informal arrangements with legal authorities within the government'.[79]

V. CONCLUSION

I conclude this chapter with a recent example that highlights the political tensions concerning judicial powers, judicial independence and the importance of a clear analysis. The example covers three separate Supreme Court decisions to strike down laws that allowed the administrative detention of asylum seekers ('infiltrators', in Israeli government parlance) for three years, in the original version, and up to one year, in the watered-down version.[80]

As is the case elsewhere, there are few constituencies in Israel with less political backing than asylum seekers and refugees. Therefore, targeting the court for protecting their interests carries, relatively, few political risks. Thus, it may be unsurprising that, following these decisions, a coalition of nationalist forces

---

[75] Davidov and Reichman (n 62) 926.

[76] Hofnung and Weinshall (n 53) 677.

[77] ibid 678.

[78] ibid.

[79] Y Dotan, 'Judicial Rhetoric, Government Lawyers, and Human Rights: The Case of the Israeli High Court of Justice During the Intifada' (1999) 33 *Law and Society Review* 319, 322.

[80] That is, the Supreme Court struck down the harsher version (HCJ 7146/12 *Adam v The Knesset* (2013)), the Israeli Parliament amended it, and the Supreme Court struck it down again (HCJ 7385/13 *Gavrisilasi v The Knesset* (2014)), and again (HCJ 8665/14 *Desta v The Knesset* (2015)).

materialised, aiming to limit the court's ability to safeguard the rights of asylum seekers. Realising that such a targeted approach may be politically feasible but legally difficult, this coalition broadened its ambition by introducing, as recently as November 2018, an amendment to the Basic Law: Human Dignity and Freedom, limiting the courts' ability to hold a law as unconstitutional, through a variety of 'override clause' versions. In addition, they managed to make the appointment process of judges to the Supreme Court a highly political affair, by reducing the power of judges in the selection committee and by forcing through the appointment of first one judge and then a second who live in a settlement in the OPT.

These factions advocating reform care very little about theories of separation of powers or judicial independence. They are not bothered, and are probably not aware, of the cases that concern property rights, social security or taxation in which the court has struck down primary legislation. They want to send the court a political message: to preserve your existing, traditional, administrative and constitutional powers, you must align with our political agenda.

A country that is steeped in an ongoing national and ethnic conflict since its existence, and for over fifty years in prolonged occupation, has an uphill battle to maintain respect for the rule of law and for human rights, particularly for Palestinian citizens and non-citizens, but also for others. Those constituencies depend on judicial independence to stand guard against calls that seek to portray them as 'power grabbing', 'authoritarian' and, indeed, enemies of the people.

If the Supreme Court is dragged into the political theatre, forced to fight for its own limited power to strike down laws by leveraging the argument of judicial independence, it will lose the battle for its powers; but more importantly, it will lose the war for its own independence.

The powers of the court are numerous. Its administrative reach, which includes an overview of home office regulations, security measures, health and education guidance, and a variety of government dictates, are far more important and effective in Israel's daily struggle to maintain what is left of a core of democratic and constitutional values than the power to strike down laws.[81]

---

[81] Winkler and Zagel (n 9) 802.

7

The Nature of Judicial Review in America

JOHN W ADAMS

I. INTRODUCTION

T HE CONSTANT UNEASE and tension within the US constitutional order was created deliberately by the delegates to the Constitutional Convention in 1787. Attached to the ideological grounding of the British Constitution, yet mindful of the arbitrary power exercised by king and parliament, they set out to establish a 'more perfect union' by creating a strong executive, an active legislature and the further, unique measure of an independent judiciary headed by a Supreme Court. Sovereignty was diffused among these three branches, designed to be separate and equal, as well as in balance or tension with each other. Each branch was expected, in its own way, to represent the interests of the people.

The concept of an unelected judiciary, its members appointed for life and having the ability to check the other, more representative branches of government, raised from the very beginning the concern that the Supreme Court might settle issues of wide-ranging effect while ignoring any direct accountability. By and large, however, over the past 230 years the court has tended to elicit public concurrence by carefully rooting its decisions in generally established constitutional principles, rather than political expediency. It has neither, for long, lagged too far behind public opinion, nor pushed too far ahead. Even today, to do otherwise might well undermine the perceived legitimacy of the court.

* * *

Over the summer of 1787, four years after the United States won its independence from England, fifty-five state representatives met in Philadelphia, with the intention of revising the existing agreement among the then thirteen states of America approved in 1781 by the Articles of Confederation. The Articles, retaining political power in the individual states, had created a weak federal government, and the representatives struggled, on a number of levels, with the nature of sovereignty for their new government. One concern was to rebalance the influence between the individual states and the federal government. Another issue, learned through experience as a British colony, was the intent to resolve the classic dilemma of democracy, creating a strong central government incorporating the benefits of democracy, whilst building in measures to mitigate the risk of it succumbing to either mob rule or tyranny of the aristocrats.

Front and centre in the minds of the Convention participants was repudiation of the power exercised by George III and the English parliament over the American colonies. The resulting disputes with the British led to rebellion and, ultimately, independence; yet the experience also left a profound imprint on the American psyche and its approach to government and the Constitution. They believed in the fundamental ideal of the British Constitution and a representative government, but one deriving its power from the people, a principle which the king and parliament had singularly failed to respect in dealings with the colonies. In a notably Burkean moment, the founders of the US Constitution sought to adopt much of the structure of the English government, yet address those problems which vexed the colonists. The result proved monumental.

After some months of debate, the Convention proposed a unique, indeed radical, proposal. The new Constitution diffused the sovereignty of the government by establishing three separate branches. Two branches comprised the legislature, consisting of the House of Representatives (chosen directly by the people) and the Senate (a legislature to be chosen by the states), and the president (the executive chosen by electors appointed by each state). The expectation was that these two branches would deal with political matters, especially concerning current issues.

The unique feature presented by the drafters was the creation of a third branch of government independent from the legislative and executive branches. It was to be a value-based institution of a federal judiciary, comprising judges chosen not by the people, but by the president with consent of the Senate, and these judges would serve for life. The intention of this third branch was to separate law from politics, removing judges from participation in partisan political issues of the day.

The drafters had adapted a concept proposed by Montesquieu to create a mixed government of checks and balances, three separate and equal branches, but with interlocking duties. A government structure which caste the judiciary in a branch independent from the executive and legislature yet somehow equal in authority fundamentally altered the nature of the judiciary and significantly affected its role in government. Sovereignty, the ultimate source of authority in the government, was intended to lie in no single branch. The Constitution was drafted to provide a form of popular sovereignty, each branch of the federal government, in its way, representing the people. 'Representation of the people' in this chapter is understood to mean representing the attitudes and opinions of the American community, their principles and ideals. 'The people' refers to those persons who are part of the American community.[1]

In the United States prior to the adoption of the Constitution in 1789, the administration of justice was considered a part of the executive branch of government. While in general, judges assumed it to be their 'duty' to void laws as appropriate, courts were nonetheless often identified with the political and magisterial role of the executive. The separation of powers reflected in the new Constitution would unequivocally separate the judiciary from the executive and legislature. The increased authority granted to the federal government proposed by the 1787 Constitutional Convention, and especially the establishment of an independent judiciary, responsible to neither the executive nor the legislature, did not sit well with the anti-federalists, that faction of Convention representatives concerned with maintaining substantial political power in the states.

As the late American constitutional scholar Robert G McCloskey observed in his mid-twentieth-century writings, from the moment of ratification of the Constitution in 1788, the political hearts of Americans were inextricably bifurcated between the will of the people and the rule of law. 'Rule of law' is an elusive concept, but McCloskey is referring to the reliance on fundamental law, monitored by an independent judiciary, as a restraint to the will of popular sovereignty. This chapter will use 'rule of law' in that context.

In McCloskey's view, the founders effectively had in mind two sovereigns: the politically representative institutions of the legislature and the executive, and the value-based institution reflected in the judiciary. The 'hard' question, as it has turned out, is one of the degrees of separation appropriate among the branches, and the likely conflation of the political and the juridical nature of courts. Will the judiciary limit its role to remedies traditionally fit for judicial determination, or will it extend its remit to intervene in affairs normally left to the other branches? Ultimately, expansion of its participation in government affairs, especially in the area of the court's review of legislation, proved inevitable. Judicial review by the court evolved rapidly to include interpreting the Constitution, evaluating the constitutionality of statutes, and even opining on the validity of the action of other government officials. The ultimate issue, necessarily, was when did such activity by the judiciary undermine the legitimacy of the court; that is, did the court maintain sufficient credibility to render effective constitutional adjudication?[2]

The nature of judicial review as it evolved in the United States was the product, not of deliberate mandate, but of institutional development, and has, over the past 220 years, seemingly retained its credibility with those it is expected to represent – the people. Yet, since the Second World War in particular, there has

---

[1] See eg (2013) 126 *Harvard Law Review* 1078.

[2] RG McCloskey, *The American Supreme Court*, 6th edn, rev S Levinson (Chicago, University of Chicago Press, 2016).

been a significant increase in the judicial involvement in the making not only of law itself, but, as well, in determining public policy. The Supreme Court, in the opinion of most constitutional scholars, has operated, with some exceptions, within the band of public opinion sufficiently narrow to maintain public credibility and institutional judicial legitimacy.

The Constitution reflects the supreme law of the land. Yet, over time, values, politics and society evolve. The court has struggled to manage the tension between being faithful to the written constitution and adapting to changing circumstances. It has needed to provide stability and change in the midst of pressures of the moment. The court has been required to neatly balance power of the government, while recognising the rights of minorities. The tension between law and politics has been persistent, and the court's legitimacy as an institution in the American governmental structure has been dependent on the judiciary's effective use of its authority, and the history of the court has been one of constant controversy.

The past four decades have been especially challenging for the Supreme Court. The liberal tendencies reflected in the decisions of the mid-1950s by the court of Chief Justice Earl Warren led to challenges by conservative political activists. Enabled by the establishment of the Federalist Society in 1982, and in an effort to reverse the liberal nature of the court, political conservatives have employed their criteria to the appointment of federal judges, including those of the Supreme Court. The appointment process and the judgments of the court have attracted bitter controversy in Congress. The sheer number of acts of Congress invalidated by the Supreme Court over this period is telling. For instance, between 1995 and 2004, more than three dozen federal enactments were overturned by the Supreme Court, a record number in the nation's history. Many of these decisions were by a five–four split among the justices.

The implications of this troubling tendency are well stated by Linda Greenhouse in a 21 June 2018 commentary appearing in the *New York Times*. Recognising that the Supreme Court need not obtain public concurrence in all cases, she does consider that it skates on thin ice when it serves its agenda rather than that of the public, and especially when decisions are consistently by a five–four vote.[3]

She draws the distinction between 'legal legitimacy' and 'social legitimacy'. It is one thing for the court to justify a decision; it's another for public opinion to accept it. Her point is that, in a constitutional regime such as the United States, a judicial decision possesses legitimacy only insofar as the public regards it as justified, appropriate or otherwise deserving of support. The number and nature of recent decisions of the Supreme Court overturning Congress may well reflect the thinness of the ice.

---

[3] L Greenhouse, 'A Question of Legitimacy Looms for the Supreme Court' *New York Times*, 21 June 2018, www.nytimes.com/2018/06/21/opinion/supreme-court-janus-unions.html.

II. EARLY AMERICAN EXPERIENCE WITH JUDICIAL AUTHORITY

From the beginning of their country's colonial history, Americans had a complicated relationship with the judiciary. The ultimate review of colonial statutes was conducted by privy councillors and colonial judges who had specialised jurisdictions and who were politically accountable. But it was the king, and at critical times, the parliament who, Americans believed, disregarded their rights as British citizens. The irregular practices of the Privy Council left judges in the states to rely on their sense of judicial duty to test the constitutionality of state legislation.

In 1610, the Chief Justice of England's Court of Common Pleas, Sir Edward Coke, declared in a case before his court, famously known as *Bonham's case*, that the common law will control, and the court has the duty to hold an act of parliament unlawful when the act 'is against the common right or reason, or repugnant or impossible to be performed'. Whatever favour this ruling had during the early seventeenth century, it was clearly disregarded in England by the time of the Glorious Revolution in 1688–89. In America, by contrast, it was conveniently revived to suggest that an act of parliament might be unlawful, or at least subject to equitable interpretation of statutes. More importantly, though, the argument gave weight to American judges to render void state statutes for reasons of a common law test of 'law and reason'. The ideal of judicial duty had currency when dealing with state statutes that lacked the sovereignty of parliament.[4]

The concept of a judiciary independent from the executive was also evolving in political thought in America. In 1776, John Adams, later to become the second president of the United States, was an early proponent of an independent judiciary. His concern was that the judges were considered part of the executive, being appointed and paid by that office. In his 'Thoughts on Government', a pamphlet published in 1776, he suggested that, in any government dedicated to the preservation of liberty, judges need to be independent of both the legislature and the executive, to act as a necessary check on the other two branches. It was an idea that was subsequently incorporated in early state constitutions.

The sentiment expressed by Adams gained the general acceptance of judicial review by the time of the Constitutional Convention in 1787. Indeed, by the summer of 1787, when the Convention delegates met to consider a new governmental structure, it was widely accepted that the judiciary had the power to interpret a written constitution and to set aside an act of the legislature.

Judicial review had staked a hold in the colonies. It was in the very essence of 'judicial duty', courts held, to find, interpret and apply statutes in cases being adjudicated, and the judiciary asserted its authority to review the legality of legislative acts. The parallel evolution of the legislature and the courts in

---

[4] See, generally, P Hamburger, *Law and Judicial Duty* (Cambridge, MA, Harvard University Press, 2008).

America reflected the inherent competing fundamental beliefs that Americans held, as viewed by McCloskey: the will of the people and the rule of law.

All that said, no single case in America decisively established judicial review until *Marbury v Madison* in 1803. But a series of precedence had the cumulative effect, and Chief Justice John Marshall's opinion in *Marbury* was not unfounded. A case of particular note, in that regard, is the *Case of the Prisoners*, which took place in Virginia in 1782. It is considered one of the most important early cases in which an American court, with the responsibility of judicial review, directly considered the issue of whether it could declare an act of the legislature unconstitutional. Three condemned men claimed before an appellate court that Virginia's Treason Statute violated the Virginia Constitution. The case is notable both for the explicit discussion by the judges on the court as to whether the statute was void because it violated the Constitution, and the discussion of the issue that subsequently ensued. Included in the discussions regarding judicial review were two judges on the appellate court who later were delegates from Virginia to the 1787 Constitution Convention, an attorney who argued as an amicus in the case who was also a delegate to the Convention from Maryland, and James Madison, a principal architect of the Constitution.[5]

St George Tucker, a lawyer and professor of law at the College of William and Mary, edited the popular American edition of Blackstone's, *Commentaries on the Laws of England*. In it, Tucker, acknowledging that Blackstone was the best treatise to use for learning the common law, thought it nonetheless demonstrated fundamental weaknesses in its exposition of certain legal principles. Among other things, Tucker claimed, Blackstone was too sympathetic to the power of the crown. Citing the *Case of the Prisoners*, for example, Tucker claimed that Backstone failed to recognise in America the right of courts to judicial review, and that this right was based on the separation-of-powers doctrine.[6]

The concept of judicial review as a check on Congress was much discussed during the ratification process. James Wilson, for one, a major force in the drafting of the new Constitution, reaffirmed the general sense of the participants that it was within the duty of a court to pronounce a federal law void when inconsistent with the Constitution.[7]

And in ratification discussions in Connecticut, Oliver Ellsworth, also a contributor to constitution-drafting and third Chief Justice of the Supreme Court, explained:

> [I]f the United States [that is, the individual states] go beyond their powers, if they make a law which the Constitution does not authorize, it is void; and the judicial

[5] See WM Treanor, 'Case of the Prisoners and the Origins of Judicial Review' (1994) 143 *University of Pennsylvania Law Review* 491, available at: https://scholarship.law.upenn.edu/penn_law_review/vol143/iss2/3.

[6] W Blackstone, *Blackstone's Commentaries*, ed St George Tucker (Philadelphia, PA, Birch & Small, 1803) 2:162.

[7] J Elliot (ed), *The Debates in the Several State Conventions on the Adoption of the Federal Constitution* (Washington, DC, Jonathan Elliot, 1836) 3:553.

power, the national judges, who, to secure their impartiality, are to be made independent, will declare it to be void.[8]

The anti-federalists, that group of representatives intent on retaining political power in the states, were increasingly concerned with the proposed establishment of an independent judiciary. Their objections were expressed well in the pseudonymous writings of 'Brutus', published in a series of political essays during the ratification debates between 1787 and 1789. Brutus argued that the federal courts would make broad interpretations of the Constitution, expanding greatly the courts' jurisdiction and influence – unfettered by the constraints of Congress or the president:

> The opinions of the Supreme Court, whatever they may be, will have the force of law; because there is no power provided in the constitution that can correct their error, or control their adjudication. From this court there is no appeal.[9]

The objections of the anti-federalists were addressed in *The Federalist Papers*, a collection of eighty-five essays by James Madison, Alexander Hamilton and John Jay. Written principally to influence the ratification process in New York, the essays were studied throughout America. Both Madison and Hamilton wrote in support of the need for a separate judiciary.

Madison, in 'Federalist No 47', asserted that under the proposed constitution, judges can exercise no executive or legislative action, and further asserted that there can be no liberty if the powers of judging are not separated from the legislative and executive powers.

Hamilton, in 'Federalist No 78', rejected the charge that the power of the judges would be superior to legislators.

> It only supposes that the power of the people superior to both; and that where the will of the legislature declared in its statutes, stands in opposition to that of the people declared in the constitution, the judges ought to be governed by the latter, rather than the former.

The judiciary, he pointed out, have neither force nor will, and must rely on its judgement.

Clearly, the degree of judicial authority to void laws of the legislature was well established in America by the time Chief Justice Marshall exercised that authority in *Marbury v Madison*. But this is not to deny that a fundamental existential problem arises from this recognition of the authority of the federal courts, not merely to declare unconstitutional legislative laws, but to do so from a position of an independent branch of the government, from which there is no appeal. It raises the concern, as expressed by former Yale law professor Alexander Bickel,

---

[8] ibid, 2:196.

[9] 'Brutus' is widely thought to be the pseudonym of New York Supreme Court Judge Robert Yates. Brutus Essays excerpt taken from the *New York Journal*, 31 January–7 February 1788.

that the court was acting in a counter-majoritian fashion, thwarting the will of the representative branches.[10]

The political institutions established by the 1789 Constitution implicitly recognised the belief of Americans both in a representative government and in the rule of law. With this, it had created a tension between power and liberty that exists to this day, wherein the judicial branch of the government plays an ever-increasing role.

III. THE FOUNDATION OF JUDICIAL REVIEW IN AMERICA

The American Constitution of 1789 established a government of three horizontal branches: executive, legislative and judicial. Left unexpressed was the extent of jurisdiction the Constitution conferred on the federal courts, and especially the Supreme Court. There exists no deliberate mandate of the constitutional framers. The Constitution provides no written word, no express intent, nor legitimate scope of constitutional adjudication by the federal courts.

The jurisdictional reach and authority of the federal judiciary, at best, is reflected in the Constitution by implication alone. The most that can be said is that neither language nor apparent intent *precludes* exercise of judicial review of laws of Congress or acts of the executive. The assumption of judicial power of review, on the other hand, was consistent with the temperament and tradition of early American judicial experience. Specifically, it reflects the reliance of the rule of law and distrust of unchecked political majorities.

This lapse, or indeterminacy, regarding the intended role of the judiciary broadly conceived is consistent with the general character of the Constitution itself. The Constitution is the product of uneasy compromise between those delegates favouring a strong federal government, and those intent on preserving strong state rights. As a result of the stand-off that emerged between the parties, several issues, including the nature of the jurisdiction of the judiciary, were left unaddressed, to be resolved at a future date. It was that compromise that made possible ratification of the proposed Constitution.

The concept of a government of three separate branches, including an independent judiciary, had been controversial throughout the drafting Convention, as well as during the debates for ratification of the Constitution. Anti-federalists had denounced the judicial power, established as an independent branch, as a potential instrument of national tyranny. Ultimately, the success of judicial independence was due in large measure to the political ascendency of the federalists in the decade following ratification of the Constitution, principally under the leadership of George Washington, John Adams and Alexander Hamilton.

---

[10] AM Bickel, *The Least Dangerous Branch: The Supreme Court and the Bar of Politics* (New Haven, CT, Yale University Press, 1962) 16.

The federal court was further strengthened by the enactment by the new Congress of the Judiciary Act of 1789, which created a system of federal courts with broad jurisdiction, and gave rise to a process for enforcement of national laws within each state. Thus was born a federal court system capable of engaging in judicial review and expanding on its constitutional decision-making.

But it was not until the appointment in 1801 of John Marshall as Chief Justice of the US Supreme Court that the nature of judicial review under the new American Constitution was fully articulated.

Chief Justice Marshall wrote the 1803 opinion of *Marbury v Madison*, which conclusively established the judicial power of review over laws of Congress and acts of the executive. The authority of the legislature, he stated, was constitutionally limited, it was the judiciaries' duty to say what the law is, and any act of the legislature repugnant to the written Constitution is void.

Although until this point, there had been no constitutional mandate for judicial supremacy, Marshall drew support for his position evident from the evolution of the American judicial tradition, and in the debates during the Constitutional Convention. *Marbury v Madison* was the convergence point for all contemporary ideas about the fundamental nature of law in America, that the moral restraint on government was legally enforceable.

IV. THE MODERN COURT 1937–82

The practice of judicial review has evolved over many years and through the decisions of many courts. The relatively modest power that judges asserted in the early years of the Constitution continued to grow as an important component of the American constitutional system. It was Congress, during much of the nineteenth century, that struggled to settle disputes regarding the proper exercise of authority of the federal government, especially relative to rights retained by the states. But as America entered the twentieth century, the courts became ever more involved with disputes with both Congress and the president, and there grew a more evident reflection of the tension between the judiciary, legislature and the executive.

The controversial nature of the influence of the court over the legislature and the executive is illustrated in the often-cited Supreme Court case of *Lochner v New York* in 1905.[11] The court struck down state legislation which limited, for health reasons, the numbers of hours bakers could work. The law, the court stated, violated the right of contract protected by the Fourteenth Amendment.

Justice Oliver Wendell Holmes dissented, stating that the court needs to account for the force of public opinion, especially when recognised in legislation. The court should not strike down legislation merely because it offends the

---

[11] *Lochner v New York*, 198 US 45 (1905).

justices' sense of reason or justice, but only if it can be shown to be a violation of principles that are long-standing and deeply held.

The mandates of the court, Holmes was saying, must be shaped with an eye not only on legal right and wrong, but also with an eye to what popular opinion will tolerate. Otherwise, the court's legitimacy as an institution charged with representing the expressed interest of the people will be undermined. The court was charged with balancing the responsibility of the government to advance the public good against the rights of individuals, in ever-changing circumstances.

The social progressives early in the twentieth century had advocated programmes of social welfare, intended to protect workers from unfair and unsafe labour. Large-scale manufacturing economy in the new century was fundamentally different from the economy of the nineteenth century based on agriculture and trade. The legislature, in the face of a changing economic and social environment, reacted against the philosophy embodied in the majority opinion in *Lochner*, especially when it came to the realities of the Great Depression of the early 1930s.

Franklyn Roosevelt, upon becoming president in 1932, understood that the people had given him the mandate to address social sufferings caused by the Depression. He pushed economic policies well beyond then existing regulatory authority, striking at perceived core property rights, and concentrated greater power in the federal government, especially the president. The Supreme Court, then still reactionary, time and gain struck down Roosevelt's legislation, alleging that it exceeded Congress's power under the commerce clause of the Constitution.

Roosevelt overwhelmingly won re-election in 1936 and, assessing that the people agreed with his economic programmes, undertook to deal with the recalcitrant court. The strategy he chose was to increase the number of members of the court, effectively putting control of the majority in the hands of those friendly to the president. While Roosevelt could rightfully insist that the court was standing in the way of duly enacted legislation, the public reacted against his proposed remedy. The people, it turned out, still believed fundamentally in the legitimacy of the institution; it became clear that Congress politically could not support Roosevelt's 'court-packing' plan.

The court had taken notice, though, of the public outcry that it was obstructing programmes intended to relieve the harsh realities of the Depression. In the first significant case brought before the court in 1936 (even before the president had withdrawn his court-packing plan), a case turning on the constitutionality of minimum-wage law, a member of the conservative majority of the court switched his vote, upholding the important social legislation.

Further indication of the court's about-turn on social legislation came a year later, in the case of *United States v Carolene Products Company*, 304 US 144 (1938). The Supreme Court, in an opinion by Justice Stone, upheld Congress's exercise of broad power to regulate interstate commerce, in this case to prohibit the shipment of 'filled' milk. The court took the further step of setting the standard the court would assume when reviewing legislation of Congress, the self-imposed exercise of judicial restraint, and to assume presumptively constitutional, economic and social welfare legislation.

The *Carolene Products* case is further noteworthy for what is understood to be perhaps the most important footnote in constitutional law. Justice Stone, in footnote four of his opinion, indicated that the court was not going to embrace judicial restraint unequivocally. He distinguished between statutes dealing with economic and social welfare legislation, and those that discriminate against 'discrete and insular' minorities, paying particular attention to the rights of individuals. Laws dealing with 'the very essence of ordered liberty' would call for the higher standard of judicial review, that of 'strict scrutiny'.

The Court's struggle to find balance between 'judicial restraint' and 'strict scrutiny' came not long afterwards in cases early in the 1940s involving Jehovah's Witnesses and their religious prohibition on saluting the American flag. This expression of religious freedom became an issue when public schools required all children to salute the flag during the school day. Jehovah's Witness siblings Lillian and William Gobitis refused to salute the flag and were subsequently expelled from school. They challenged the expulsion in court, maintaining that it violated their First Amendment rights. A federal court agreed, and ordered the West Virginia State Board of Education to eliminate the mandatory nature of the flag salute. On appeal, the Supreme Court disagreed.

Justice Frankfurter, writing for an eight–one court majority, stated that the law requiring the flag salute dealt with an interest, national unity and security, inferior to none in the hierarchy of legal values. The legislature should not be denied the right to pursue that responsibility.[12]

Just three years later an appeal came before the Supreme Court based on almost identical facts. But circumstances had changed, and so did the Supreme Court. Jehovah's Witnesses had become ostracised by their communities for the expression of their religious beliefs. Their children were expelled from school, their families' property was vandalised and they were the victims of mob violence. The United States was now at war with Germany, a country whose policies suppressed religious minorities, and the American salute at the time was strikingly similar to the Nazi straight-arm salute. Public opinion, in light of Germany's civil transgressions, had developed tolerance of individual exercise of rights and liberties.

The court reversed *Gobitis*, six–three, with Justice Jackson, newly appointed to the court, writing for the majority that in cases such as the one at hand, when the sole conflict is between state authority and the rights of the individual, those rights must be protected by the courts unless compelling reasons exist. For Jackson, free expression overrode the goal of national unity.

---

[12] *Minersville School District v Gobitis*, 310 US 586 (1940).

Frankfurter, now writing a dissent, held fast to the notion of judicial restraint: 'The only opinion of our own ... that is material is our opinion whether legislators could in reason have enacted such a law.'[13]

In essence, Frankfurter was rejecting the rational basis of the above-mentioned 'strict scrutiny' test laid out in footnote four of *Carolene Products*, instead expressing his belief that no provisions within the Constitution occupied a 'preferred position'. He was urging the court not to look to the consequences of the law, but to understand what the legislature, those directly accountable to the people, was attempting to do. If legislation needs to be corrected, let it be done by the people, not the courts.

This tension between power and liberty was out in the open, between the political nature of the Constitution (leaving social dispute resolution to the elected branches of the government) and the juridical Constitution (encouraging courts to assert authority over such political and social issues). Frankfurter's pleas notwithstanding, the court had increased its involvement in the making not only of law itself, but also in determining public policy.

The appointment of Robert Jackson by Roosevelt to the court in 1941 represented a shift of the court's fundamental judicial philosophy. Jackson had a pragmatic view of the Constitution. Constitutional pragmatists such as Jackson, while constrained by precedent and what other courts have done, believe it both wise and appropriate to change constitutional norms to serve contemporary needs. Courts must be flexible, not dogmatic, in dealing with social change. Yet, to the pragmatist, balanced judgments must guide the court, with careful consideration of practical consequences of its decisions. Grand pronouncements, like a loaded gun, Jackson said, tend towards unknown consequences in future cases.[14]

The judicial limitations of Frankfurter's concern for judicial restraint and Jackson's reliance on constitutional pragmatism were put to the test in the great school desegregation case of *Brown v Board of Education*, 347 US 483 (1954). The decision in *Brown* ventures actively into social policy, articulating so-called legal realism, the judicial philosophy of a 'living constitution', which adapts to the evolving nature of community values. The concept of the living constitution goes well beyond any sense of the restraint of Frankfurter and concern for practical consequences of Jackson. The court must act when the legislature fails, and broaden where necessary the ideals of liberty and equal protection. Yet both Frankfurter and Jackson joined with the rest of the court in its decision.

While the Fourteenth Amendment guaranteed all US citizens equal treatment under the law, American public schools remained segregated well into the middle of the twentieth century. A majority of the country in 1954 considered this treatment of blacks was fundamentally wrong; moreover, that the cost of segregation was hurting America's reputation and interests abroad.

---

[13] *West Virginia Board of Education v Barnette* 319 US (1943).
[14] See Jackson's dissent in *Korematsu v US* 323 US 214 (1944).

President Truman had in 1948 issued an executive order committing the military to integration, but Congress, controlled by a southern-dominant Congress, resisted addressing the issue in public education. The belief in much of the country was that the Fourteenth Amendment did not outlaw segregation. Indeed, the public schools in Washington DC, the capital of the country and under the jurisdiction of Congress, remained segregated.

Segregation and the Fourteenth Amendment had been addressed in 1896 by the Supreme Court opinion in *Plessy v Ferguson* 163 US 537 (1896) which held that, although the Fourteenth Amendment established the legal equality of white and black Americans, it did not and could not require the elimination of all other 'distinctions based upon color'. Facilities available to the public could remain segregated, provided similar facilities offered to blacks were equal to those available to whites.

Brown v Board of Education was the culmination of a long, and largely successful, litigation campaign aimed at overturning the ruling of *Plessy*. The culmination of the campaign came in an appeal to the Supreme Court in 1952 and involved the barring of a young black girl from attending an all-white public school which was located closer to her family than the all-black school she was otherwise required to attend.

The court was unable to reach agreement among the justices after the initial arguments, and scheduled a second hearing. It instructed the parties to focus their arguments particularly on the meaning of the Fourteenth Amendment regarding racially segregated schools. The key to ultimate consensus by the court, indeed unanimity, was the death in the interim of the then chief justice and the appointment of Earl Warren as his successor. Warren was both politically adroit and intent on delivering justice to oppressed minorities. He pushed the justices to go beyond their individual judicial philosophies to work toward a unanimous opinion, written by Warren himself, declaring segregation in public schools unconstitutional.

Liberal and results-driven, the opinion articulated the full sense of a living constitution, reflecting a constitution that evolves and adapts to changed circumstances, without the need of formal amendment:

> In approaching this problem, we cannot turn the clock back to 1868 when the Amendment was adopted, or even to 1896 when *Plessy v Ferguson* was written. We must consider public education in the light of its full development and it present place in American life throughout the Nation. Only in this way can it be determined if segregation in public schools deprives these plaintiffs of the equal protection of the laws. …
>
> Whatever may have been the extent of psychological knowledge at the time of *Plessy v Ferguson*, this finding [that to separate students based solely on race generates a feeling of inferiority] is amply supported by modern authority. Any language in *Plessy v Ferguson* contrary to this finding is rejected.[15]

---

[15] *Brown v Board of Education* 347 US 483 (1954).

If there is credence to Justice Oliver Wendell Holmes's belief that the benefit of the common law is that judges tend to first decide the case, and only then to look for law to support the decision, then *Brown* is a model of good common law jurisprudence. It isn't that Justice Jackson did not know well the likely resistance to the decision, and even non-compliance in much of the country. It took the president's use of the national guard to enforce integration in the south. And, Frankfurter, who personally believed that segregation was unjust and must be abolished, knew well that his affirmance reflected anything but judicial restraint.

Noah Feldman, professor of constitutional law at Harvard, argues that in the unanimity of *Brown* also lay its greatest flaw: that it was a compromise by the justices of their deeply held constitutional visions, and, in that sense, incoherent as a statement of constitutional law. The failure of the Warren court to cast the law in a recognised constitutional interpretation undercut the legitimacy of the court's activism, and drove the Rehnquist court's 'confused and incomplete turn to originalism'.[16]

There were many and varied responses to the *Brown* decision from academia.

Robert A Dahl, a political theorist then at Yale, published a canonical article about the Supreme Court's position in American democracy. Cases such as *Brown* raise difficult questions, he opined, as the court's decisions gain legitimacy by resting on the fiction that the court is a legal, and not political, institution. Decisions turning on vague or ambiguous wording of the Constitution undermine that understanding.[17] In general, though, he concluded that the court did not deviate from general public opinion, either in the *Brown* case or over the long term.

Alexander M Bickel, then professor of law at Yale University, had a different point. (Not-so-coincidently, Frankfurter's law clerk at the time of the court's discussion of *Brown* and, at the time the court was deliberating the case, drafted an opinion for Frankfurter proposing a contrary argument to his final position.) Bickel did not object to the merit of the decision of the court; rather, that a 'greater measure of pragmatism would have produced more caution, and less speedy development of doctrine'. His concern was that it should have been the legislature, and not the court, which mandated segregation of the schools. Judicial review, when articulating social policy, in that sense is undemocratic as counter-majoritarian.[18] The Court in *Brown*, though, clearly felt that it was upholding its role as representative of the people, as envisioned by Hamilton in his 'Federalist No 78'.

Historian Robert McCloskey also assessed the position of the court in *Brown*, in his highly respected *The American Supreme Court*. McCloskey

---

[16] N Feldman, *Scorpions: The Battles and Triumphs of FDR's Great Supreme Court Justices* (New York, Twelve, 2010) 407–08.

[17] RA Dahl, 'Decision-making in a Democracy: The Supreme Court as a National Policy Maker' (1957) 6 *Journal of Public Law* 279; reprinted in (2001) 50 *Emory Law Journal* 563, 570.

[18] AM Bickel, *The Supreme Court and the Idea of Progress* (New York, Harper & Row, 1970).

observed that, after 1937, there had grown a generation of jurists and scholars who were convinced that judges are shapers of policy, and that the Constitution left open many questions, including that of the Supreme Court's proper role.[19] He cautioned, though, that what the court cannot do is to thwart the will of national majorities for very long, and that the court, ultimately, is constrained by public opinion.

The desegregation case of *Brown v Board of Education*, McCloskey observed, set in train an interruption in the prevailing spirit of judicial decision-making – which has from time to time enlivened the history of the court – the clamour over which has provoked much scrutiny and analysis. After *Brown*, no longer was it possible, McCloskey said, for judges and their supporters to take refuge from criticism behind that old adage that the court was merely the passive mouthpiece of an unambiguous Constitution. To put it another way, the court had learned to become a political institution, and to behave accordingly.

Eleven years later, in *Griswold v Connecticut*, 381 US 479 (1965), the Supreme Court ventured further into the political thicket, declaring unconstitutional a state statute which prohibited married couples from buying and using any drug for the purpose of preventing conception. Justice Douglas's majority opinion found that the law violated the defendants' right of privacy:

> Although 'privacy' is not mentioned in the Bill of Rights, it is found in the 'penumbras.' [S]pecific guarantees in the Bill of Rights have penumbras, formed by emanations from those guarantees that help give them life and substance. ... Various guarantees create zones of privacy.[20]

Relying on the 'penumbra' of the Constitution was, to Justice Black, taking the active judicial role too far. In his dissenting opinion, Black stated that nowhere in the Constitution could he find 'right of privacy' as an emanation from and of its provisions.[21]

The concept of inferring privacy from the body of the Constitution also offended the judicial philosophy of the 'originalists', who maintained that a court must limit its analysis to the original understandings of the Constitution at the time it was drafted. There is no evidence, they argue, that the right of privacy, either by intent or text, can be found in the Constitution.

Griswold was followed by a case, *Roe v Wade*, 410 US 113 (1973), which further widened the scope of privacy to include striking down bans on abortion which existed in forty-six states. It accelerated a growing cultural divide and the political struggles over gender roles, the sexual revolution and morality-based legislation that had emerged in the late 1960s. In retrospect, the decision violated the pragmatist standard in that it greatly underestimated the reaction

---

[19] McCloskey (n 2) 290.
[20] *Griswold v Connecticut* 381 US 479 (1965).
[21] ibid 508.

of competing constitutional views of Congress and the moral standards of large segments of the community. The consequences were far reaching.

Over time, the Republicans, sensitive to the cultural divide engendered by the liberal decisions of the Supreme Court, had become committed to a 'pro-life' agenda, and responded to *Roe* by adopting as part of their 1976 platform the intent to seek enactment of a constitutional amendment to restore protection of the right to life for unborn children.

New conservative interest groups emerged to reshape constitutionally acceptable understandings and the role of courts in the constitutional order. They pursued reinstating judicial restraint in determining social policy. In 1982, two years following conservative Republican Ronald Reagan's election to the presidency, the Federalist Society was formed. Consisting principally of conservative and libertarian academics, judges and practising lawyers, it set out to reform the American legal system in accordance with a textualist and originalist interpretation of the US Constitution, to promote the principle 'that it is emphatically the province and duty of the judiciary to say what the law is, not what it should be'.[22]

McCloskey had said that it was hard to find a single historical instance when the Supreme Court had stood firm for very long against a clear wave of public demand. The court, he said, has seldom lagged far behind or forged ahead of American opinion.

The Federalist Society has been extraordinarily successful in attaining a refocus of the judiciary to a more conservative approach to constitutional restraint. The organisation attracted influential members, including Supreme Court Justice Antonin Scalia, who infused in his Supreme Court decisions a firm sense of 'originalism'. Members of the Federalist Society now comprise a clear majority of the court, all avowed originalists, including Chief Justice John Roberts.

Republican presidencies, from Ronald Reagan to Donald Trump, benefited from a preponderance of appointments to federal judgeships, with the predictable result that those courts have become more conservative. Between 1968 and 2020, Republican presidents selected fifteen new justices for the Supreme Court, while Democratic presidents filled only four seats. In 1980, 57 per cent of Federal Appellate Judges had been appointed by Democratic presidents; by 2004, only 34 per cent were Democratic appointees. The current composition of the federal courts will have a strong effect on the likely outcome of judicial decisions for a significant time.[23] The 'judicial activism' of the liberal Warren court has now been replaced with the 'judicial activism' of a conservative Chief Justice Roberts court.

The conservative movement had caught off-guard those proponents of legal philosophies such as the so-called 'living constitution', those whose legal

---

[22] See https://fedsoc.org/about-us.

[23] See C Sunstein, D Schkade, L Ellman and A Sawicki, *Are Judges Political? An Empirical Analysis of the Federal Judiciary* (Washington, DC, Brookings Institute, 2006).

activism resulted in *Griswold* and *Roe*. The courts had miscalculated the consequences of pushing into policies beyond the opinion of other powerful political groups. They had offended the morality of large and vocal segments of the community. It was a mistake on both a judicial and a political level.

V. CONCLUSION

In those rare cases, such as *Roe v Wade*, when the courts have acted unilaterally, trying to impose a constitutional vision contrary to other powerful forces of the community, there develops a backlash that tends to undermine the very causes the judges are attempting to advance. That the Supreme Court plays partly a political role and that it guides, and sometimes makes, public policy under the doctrine of judicial review is no longer in debate. The difficult question is one of degree: how large a political role should the court play, how far should the court venture into the affairs of the other branches and what criteria should the court exercise in pursuing social policy?

To the extent that a court reaches too far into the political realm, as the progressive court did in *Roe*, is it simply attempting to adapt to the evolved needs of the country, or has it lost its legitimacy as an instrument of policy, and should it more properly confine itself to traditional constitutional adjudication?

Keith Whittington, a professor of politics at Princeton, suggests that, in general, the court to date has not pushed too far into politics; nor has it lost its legitimacy as a political institution operating in a political environment to advance controversial principles, often with the encouragement of other political leaders.

Whittington, in his 2019 work *Repugnant Laws*,[24] demonstrates that the principal role assumed by the Supreme Court over the course of its history has been to legitimate rather than strike down federal legislation. While the court has been a defender of minority interests against majoritarian political leaders, that has been ultimately a much smaller function than its role as an arm of the national state. The justices of the Supreme Court are part of the national political environment; they pursue their own priorities with the lens of the rule of law, but within the bounds set by the larger political context in which they operate. The court has played an important part in the constitutional system of checks and balances, neither subordinate to nor above legislature or executive.

Whittington's conclusions are based on his analysis of the 1,308 cases decided by the Supreme Court between 1789 and 2018 that involve constitutional challenges to federal legislation. Over that period, the court upheld the constitutionality of congressional law in 963 cases, and struck down or constitutionally

---

[24] K Whittington, *Repugnant Laws: Judicial Review of Acts of Congress from the Founding to the Present* (Lawrence, University Press of Kansas, 2019).

narrowed a statutory provision in only 345 cases. Even during periods of relative activism during which the court struck down a large number of laws of Congress, Whittington found, it was still more likely to uphold a law than to strike it down.

Concluding from his examination of the history of the court's decisions, Whittington disputes the counter-majoritarian difficulty surrounding judicial review, as espoused most prominently by Alexander Bickel. Bickel's premise is that, when the judiciary uses its power to strike down laws as unconstitutional, its action is undemocratic. In the first place, Whittington argues, the judicial process has in general not been too principle-bound nor too remote from the opinions and attitudes of the community. But further to Whittington, judicial review has operated within the clear political context of fractious political coalitions.

It may well be that the history of American constitutionalism, and the unique role of the American judiciary, reflect a balancing of the tensions as McCloskey presented them, between the two sovereigns embedded in the Constitution – a representative government subject to the rule of law; the tension between law and politics. This dualism has meant that fundamental law, meant to restrain popular will, nevertheless must reckon with it. The Supreme Court, while sometimes modifying the popular will, is in turn checked or modified by it.

The current conservative composition of the Supreme Court offers yet another challenge to the fragile balance between the judicial philosophy of the court and the demands of popular opinion. Six of the nine members of the court espouse allegiance to the judicial philosophies of 'textualism' and 'originalism', which assume social views that a majority of the public might not tolerate if pursued in the Court's decision-making.

The Supreme Court's 2019–20 term consisted of many controversial and deeply partisan cases. It also was the first full year with a clear majority of conservative justices. In the end, the court's term was less conservative that anyone had expected. In many of its most prominent cases, one or more conservative justices joined their liberal colleagues in rendering politically centrist decisions, which surveys would suggest are aligned with majority public opinion.

The Senate, dominated by conservative Republicans, has in October 2020 approved, over the bitter opposition of liberal Democrats, President Trump's nomination of yet another conservative jurist to the Supreme Court, many of whose views are not, according to political polls, shared by a large section of the public. While Chief Justice John Roberts seemingly has worked hard to maintain some measure of balance in the decisions of his court, his often-deciding vote will lose its leverage when six of the nine justices are committed to their conservative, originalist philosophy. Democrats have vowed to address the imbalance of the court; they have indicated that they would consider, among other remedies, packing the court.

If the court follows the historical trend of its decision-making, it will not for long pursue an agenda against a clear wave of public demand. It will not, as McCloskey believed, lag far behind or push far ahead of the will of national majorities. To do otherwise, to pursue decisions in the name of a constitutional principle contrary to the views of the majority of the American people, will undermine its institutional legitimacy. The establishment of the judiciary as an independent branch of the government, after all, was with the implicit responsibility of representing the people.

8

Under Pressure: Building Judicial Resistance to Political Interferences

KATARÍNA ŠIPULOVÁ[1]

I. INTRODUCTION

THE TREND OF the judicialisation and empowerment of courts after the Second World War has become an axiom of legal scholarship.[2] We have witnessed courts becoming more visible, more powerful and, eventually, also more political.[3] As a result, courts significantly constrain executives and function as checks against illiberal policies. The empowerment of courts has also led to substantial changes in the scope of executives' powers, removing certain areas from their political control.

It therefore hardly comes as a surprise that periods of judicialisation were followed by waves of political backlash against courts and judges world-wide.[4] While attacks on courts are not a new phenomenon and we can trace tendencies to remove non-conforming judges back to previous centuries, the court-curbing techniques employed in the last decade stand out as more frequent and more sophisticated.[5] Moreover, episodes from Central Europe demonstrate that these attacks are not isolated to non-democratic regimes. Many populist leaders[6]

[1] The research leading to this chapter has received funding from the European Research Council (ERC) under the European Union's Horizon 2020 research and innovation program (grant no 678375- JUDI-ARCH-ERC-2015-STG).
[2] G Helmke, *Judicial Manipulation in Latin America*, available at www.gretchenhelmke.com/uploads/7/0/3/2/70329843/judicial_manipulation_helmke.pdf.

[3] S Rosenbaum. 'Courts as Political Players' (2019) 8 *Israel Journal of Health Policy Research* 32; MM Taylor. 'Beyond Judicial Reform: Courts as Political Actors in Latin America' (2006) 41(2) *Latin American Research Review* 269; RB Chavez. *The Rule of Law in Nascent Democracies: Judicial Politics in Argentina* (Standford, CA, Stanford University Press, 2004); S Gloppen and R Gargarella and E Skaar. *Democratization and the Judiciary: The Accountability Function of Courts in New Democracies* (London, Frank Cass, 2004); B Bugaric and M Tushnet, 'Court-packing, Judicial Independence, and Populism. Why Poland and the United States Are Different' *Verfassungsblog*, 11 July 2020, https://verfassungsblog.de/court-packing-judicial-independence-and-populism/.

[4] Helmke (n 2).

[5] D Kosař and K Šipulová, 'How to Fight Court-packing?' (2020) 6 *Constitutional Studies* 133.

[6] There are different types of populism. For the purposes of this chapter, I am using Bugaric's and Mudde and Kaltwasser's definition tying populism to anti-pluralist and illiberal politics.

do not shy away from blatant political interferences, packing the courts with loyal nominees, hijacking selection procedures[7] or attempting to discredit and delegitimise the courts in the eyes of the public.

Some of the most striking examples of the crusades against the courts come from Poland, owing to the skilful use of media by the leading party, Law and Justice (PiS). In summer 2019, the Polish news portal Onet.pl exposed the Ministry of Justice's online campaign designed to discredit a specific group of judges. In February 2020, PiS went even further, funding a new documentary series on Polish state television (also fully controlled by the government) called *Kasta*[8] (*The Caste*), which depicted judges as corrupt and incompetent. The goal of the series did not leave any room for confusion. Daily episodes broadcast for over a month picked out the most controversial judgments and episodes of judicial conduct, labelling them as hurtful, corrupt and unjust.[9] What is even more worrying, the programme received an enormous $2 million from the government and featured on billboards and in television spots with black-and-white photographs accompanied by slogans such as 'a judge stole a sausage from a shop', or 'a drunk judge found fighting in a bar'. While some of the portrayed stories were truthful, the majority were simply exaggerated.

The vibrant examples of political interference naturally spurred a lot of academic interest, exploring strategies by which political leaders rig, pack and dismantle the courts,[10] and what formal and informal safeguards can prevent them from doing so.[11] Nevertheless, very little attention has been paid so far to how courts react and what tools they have to protect themselves from imminent political attacks. The existing evidence is mostly anecdotal.[12]

This chapter bridges this gap and steps into the field with a unique study of judicial reactions to court-curbing attacks. Based on examples from Poland, Hungary, Czechia and Slovakia, it offers a systemisation of judicial resistance strategies which domestic courts have at their disposal when facing an imminent political attack, and discusses their effectiveness.

See B Bugaric, 'The Two Faces of Populism: Between Authoritarian and Democratic Populism' (2019) 20 *German Law Journal* 390; C Mudde and CR Kaltwasser, 'Studying Populism in Comparative Perspective: Reflections on Contemporary and Future Research Agenda' (2018) 51 *Comparative Political Studies* 1667; or JW Müller, *What is Populism?* (Philadelphia, University of Pennsylvania Press, 2016).

[7] Kosař and Šipulová (n 5).

[8] The derogatory title actually comes from the unfortunate occasion when Polish judges called themselves the upper caste of Polish population.

[9] See www.tvp.info/46255229/kasta, also www.theatlantic.com/ideas/archive/2020/01/disturbing-campaign-against-polish-judges/605623/ and https://polandin.com/46515871/analysis-judging-the-judges-takes-political-centre-stage.

[10] Kosař and Šipulová (n 5).

[11] G Helmke and J Staton, 'The Puzzling Judicial Politics of Latin America: A Theory of Litigation, Judicial Decisions, and Interbranch Conflict' in G Helmke and J Ríos-Figueroa (eds), *Courts in Latin America* (New York, Cambridge University Press, 2011).

[12] For a rare exception, see Trochev and Ellet, who however focus exclusively on off-bench alliances of judges. A Trochev and R Ellett. 'Judges and Their Allies: Rethinking Judicial Autonomy through the Prism of Off-Bench Resistance' (2014) 2 *Journal of Law and Courts* 67.

The chapter proceeds as follows. Section II offers a bird's-eye view on court-curbing practices implemented in four Central European countries: Hungary, Poland, Slovakia and Czechia. Section III defines judicial reactions and proposes their categorisation, discussing various examples of individual strategies applied around the world. Section IV concludes with a suggestion that most common judicial reactions, involving invalidation of an interference, are effective only in regimes that abide by the rule of law. If executives stop respecting the principles of judicial independence, judges have to rely on more informal strategies, among which accumulation of public trust plays a vital role.

II. POLITICAL ATTACKS AND COURT-CURBING PRACTICES

Attacks on the judiciary may come from many directions, with the quality and independence of courts being scrutinised by the media or the wider public. Nevertheless, the most dangerous types of attack are those coming from the executives, who can use these attacks to get rid of an important veto player, alienate courts from citizens, dismantle courts or, at the very worst, turn courts into a weapon against their enemies. This chapter therefore concentrates on judicial reactions to political attacks.

Depending on their aim, political attacks against courts take various forms (Table 8.1). One of the most common attacks, attractive to both democratic and non-democratic executives, is court-packing.[13] Court-packing strategies aim to change the composition of the existing court by enlarging, emptying or swapping its judges, leaving the executive power with a new, loyal majority on the bench. A similar effect can be achieved by a monopolisation of judicial selection (ie absolute control and removal of veto players involved in the selection of new judges).

Another court-rigging strategy aimed at controlling the courts is delegated governance. This strategy allows political actors to keep up a pretence of judicial independence by controlling a small number of judges in top managerial positions. The low-cost technique was particularly popular in Eastern Europe during communist rule, where it secured the communist parties a high level of loyalty among judicial ranks.[14]

Some political attacks interfere with courts' decision-making more openly (politicisation), exerting direct pressure on judges in order to achieve a favourable result in high-profile cases. An example of such a politicisation strategy is 'telephone law', ie unsolicited calls in which politicians urge judges or court presidents to resolve a given case in a particular way.[15] The most recent evidence of

---

[13] Kosař and Šipulová (n 5).

[14] D Kosař, 'Politics of Judicial Independence and Judicial Accountability in Czechia: Bargaining in the Shadow of the Law between Court Presidents and the Ministry of Justice' (2017) 13 *European Constitutional Law Review* 96.

[15] K Hendley '"Telephone Law" and the "Rule of Law": The Russian Case' (2009) 1 *Hague Journal on the Rule of Law* 241. See also M Popova, *Politicized Justice in Emerging Democracies: A Study of*

telephone law comes from Slovakia, which revealed a group of judges exchanging thousands of text messages with an influential oligarch currently charged with murder, corruption and tax offences.[16]

A more far-seeing invasive strategy, jurisdiction stripping, seeks completely to incapacitate and remove the courts from the decision-making process. Executives typically opt for this step if the office-stripping, ie removal of rebellious judges, is too costly or otherwise impossible.[17] An example of jurisdiction stripping may be found in the exception of any fiscal legislation from the scope of the constitutional review in the 2011 Hungarian constitution,[18] or the removal of administrative jurisdiction from the existing courts into a completely new branch of the judiciary.[19]

Finally, attacks pressuring the courts can also be implemented by other informal means, be it limiting the career options of judges after they leave the bench,[20] or steering the media against the courts with the aim of denting public confidence and trust in the courts.

Table 8.1 Types of political interference

Court-packing[21]	Expanding, lowering the number of judges or swapping judges on board
Contained selection	Monopolising the selection and appointment process
Delegated governance	Control of courts via court presidents
Jurisdiction stripping	Removal of policy arenas, restricting guidelines for review and legal interpretation, limitation of access to courts
Politicisation	Exerting pressure on the result of decisions (telephone justice, street protests, rhetorical signalling)
Other pressure	Disregarding the decision, limiting career options of judges after leaving the bench

Source: author.

Courts in Russia and Ukraine (New York, Cambridge University Press, 2012), and A Ledeneva, 'Telephone Justice in Russia' (2008) 24 *Post Soviet Affairs* 324.

[16] M Ovádek, 'Deep Rot in Slovakia' *Verfassungsblog*, 15 October 2019, https://verfassungsblog.de/deep-rot-in-slovakia/.

[17] MM Taylor, 'The Limits of Judicial Independence: A Model with Illustration from Venezuela under Chávez' (2014) 46 *Journal of Latin America Studies*. See also L Hilbink, 'The Origins of Positive Judicial Independence' (2012) 64 *World Politics* 587.

[18] R Uitz, 'Can You Tell when an Illiberal Democracy Is in the Making? An Appeal to Comparative Constitutional Scholarship from Hungary' (2015) 13 *International Journal of Constitutional Law* 279.

[19] The Law on the Administrative Courts – T/3353; K Than, 'Hungary to Set Up Courts Overseen Directly by Government' *Reuters*, 12 December 2018, https://perma.cc/NT9M-WZXC; ICJ, 'Hungary: ICJ Calls for Reconsideration of the Law on the Administrative Courts' (20 December 2018) https://perma.cc/U5SZ-WWAX.

[20] E Ramseyer, 'The Puzzling (In)Dependence of Courts. A Comparative Approach' (1994) 23 *Journal of Legal Studies* 721.

[21] Kosař and Šipulová (n 5).

Constitutional crises in Central Europe have brought into being all the afore-mentioned forms of attacks. Populist leaders such as Kaczyński and Orbán have instigated crusades against the courts, striving to strip them of powers and fill them with loyal judges, or at least to incapacitate the non-aligned ones.

Hungarian Prime Minister Victor Orbán introduced his first court-curbing proposals immediately after his overwhelming electoral win in 2010. He first monopolised the selection of constitutional justices, removing the requirement of a joint decision by the government and the opposition.[22] He then increased the number of Constitutional Court justices from eleven to fifteen, gaining a major-ity. The aim of his reforms was, however, not only to have a loyal Constitutional Court, but also to weaken it. The new constitution therefore stripped the Constitutional Court of the power to review any law related to fiscal policies.[23]

His next target was the Supreme Court (Kúria), whose former leader, András Baka, was a vociferous critic of Orbán. The reconstruction of the Supreme Court, although presented as a merely formal matter, cost Baka his post as court president, as the amending law presumed the renomination of all court func-tionaries, while simultaneously altering the conditions applying to candidates in a way that Baka, a former judge of the European Court of Human Rights, (ECtHR) clearly did not meet.[24] General courts were next in line. Through a series of smaller technical laws (such as the lowering of the retirement age of judges), he effectively packed the most senior positions with his own nominees. Finally, in 2019, he completed his assault by stripping the existing courts of a part of their agenda and creating a new branch of administrative courts.[25]

In Poland, Jaroslaw Kaczyński, the leader of the PiS, approached court-curbing in a similar fashion. Although not enjoying a constitutional majority in parliament (Sejm), he orchestrated a set of smaller reforms, monopolising the selection processes, stripping some courts of their jurisdictions, and silencing them with the threat of disciplinary proceedings.[26]

Kaczyński's arch enemy was the Constitutional Tribunal, whose jurispru-dence, in his view, imposed 'blocks on government policies aimed at creating a fairer economy'.[27] The animosity between Kaczyński and the Tribunal goes back to the PiS's first government of 2006–07, when the Tribunal quashed all the legislative proposals adopted under Kaczyński's rule. In 2017, in a controversial

---

[22] Uitz (n 18).

[23] ibid.

[24] D Kosař and K Šipulová, 'The Strasbourg Court Meets Abusive Constitutionalism: Baka v Hungary and the Rule of Law' (2018) 10 *Hague Journal on the Rule of Law* 83.

[25] Act T/8016 resurrected the attempt to install a separate branch of administrative courts from 2018, which the government originally dropped under the pressure of international organisations. For more, see R Uitz, 'EU Rule of Law Dialogues: Risks – in Context' (2020) *Verfassungsblog*, 22 January 2020, available at https://verfassungsblog.de/eu-rule-of-law-dialogues-risks-in-context/.

[26] F Zoll and L Wortham, 'Judicial Independence and Accountability: Withstanding Political Stress in Poland' (2019) 42 *Fordham International Law Journal* 875.

[27] B Bugaric and Tushnet (n 3).

and highly contested step, the PiS decided not to appoint three new constitu-tional justices legitimately selected by the previous Sejm.[28] The government subsequently paralysed the Tribunal and rendered it harmless by a combination of jurisdiction-stripping and court-packing.[29]

Kaczyński's toughest stick to beat the courts with, however, was the ques-tionable use of accountability mechanisms. Kaczyński's minister of justice frequently initiated disciplinary proceedings against judges who opposed his policies. Moreover, the government adopted a controversial 'muzzle law', which forbade judges from reviewing the judicial independence of their newly appointed peers.[30]

The Slovak and Czech judiciaries faced a different, more informal type of court-curbing. After the division of Czechoslovakia in 1993, Slovakia fell under the semi-authoritarian rule of Vladimír Mečiar. Non-democratic tendencies targeted the courts as Mečiar attempted to control the judiciary through the Ministry of Justice and to punish any rebelling judges through disciplinary measures and financial penalties. The most flagrant example of interference happened around the 1994 dispute in which Mečiar's party attempted to annul the election of fifteen opposition deputies (which would, if successful, have left the government with the three-fifths ruling majority needed for the implementa-tion of any constitutional change). When the Constitutional Court blocked the attempt, the government reciprocated with a set of 'saving measures', ridding the Chief Justice of the Constitutional Court of, among others, a personal driver and security.[31]

In 2003, five years after the fall of Mečiar's regime, Slovakia introduced the Judicial Council, transferring considerable powers to the judiciary.[32] However, the transition from a government-controlled judiciary to an independent one was not smooth. The old elites managed to hijack the Judicial Council and use it to capture the judiciary from the inside, staffing the most senior positions with subservient and obedient judges. The level of corruption was revealed only recently, during the investigation of the shocking assassination of a young journalist, Ján Kuciak, and his fiancée, Martina Kušnírová. The investigation pointed to an informal network between judges, high governmental functionar-ies and oligarchs, securing favourable judgments in proceedings relating to their economic interests.[33]

---

[28] The decision was in part a retaliation for illegitimate and premature selection of two more constitutional justices by the previous government. Zoll and Wortham (n 25).

[29] W Sadurski, *Poland's Constitutional Breakdown* (Oxford, Oxford University Press, 2020).

[30] THEMIS, 'Close to the Point of No Return' (2020) http://themis-sedziowie.eu/materials-in-english/close-to-the-point-of-no-return-current-situation-of-polish-judiciary/.

[31] H Schwartz, *The Struggle for Constitutional Justice in Post-Communist Europe* (Chicago, University of Chicago Press, 2004).

[32] S Spáč, K Šipulová and M Urbániková, 'Capturing the Judiciary from Inside: The Story of Judicial Self-governance in Slovakia' (2018) 19 *German Law Journal*.

[33] Ovádek (n 16).

Czechia has so far enjoyed top scores for judicial independence, with a relatively strong and influential Constitutional Court. There were, however, also a couple of episodes in which political groups attempted to interfere with courts' decision-making or to staff the apex court with aligned judges.[34] At the beginning of 2019, the former chief justice of the Supreme Administrative Court, Josef Baxa, and a constitutional justice, Vojtěch Šimíček, testified to the media that they had repeatedly been approached by a political advisor to President Miloš Zeman, attempting to influence their decisions in high-profile cases related to the office of the president or the selection of new judges for the Supreme Administrative Court.[35]

This mix of court-curbing techniques makes the Central European region an excellent choice for a probing study of judicial reactions to political interferences and tinkering with judicial independence. All four countries started off as young transitioning democracies. They all enjoyed some level of judicial independence. However, they also faced different forms of political attacks upon judicial independence at different stages of their regime consolidation. The exploration of judicial reactions to these political interferences therefore allows us an interesting analysis of the effectiveness of judicial resistance, depending on the type and motive of political attack.

III. CATEGORIES OF JUDICIAL RESISTANCE

Although notoriously called 'the least dangerous branch',[36] courts do have a set of tools they can use to resist political attacks. For the purposes of this chapter, I address these as 'judicial resistance', which I understand as a set of *techniques, tools* and *practices* which *courts or individual judges* can use to *prevent, avert, stay* or *punish imminent* political attacks on judicial independence.

Judicial resistance analysed in this chapter addresses only those responses that can be instigated by courts or judges. It does not include changes to the institutional set-up aimed at raising the level of judicial independence, or preventive measures such as tenures or judicial salaries which typically aim to shield judges from corruption or patronage. Judicial resistance can be implemented both by courts as a part of their decision-making authority, and by individual judges acting in their personal capacity. This means that judicial resistance includes both techniques and tools implemented *on* and *off the judicial bench* (Table 8.2).

---

[34] The most controversial example was a repeated attempt by President Klaus to remove Chief Justice of the Supreme Court Iva Brožová from office. See Kosař (n 14).

[35] O Kundra and A Procházková, 'Pozor, volá Mynář' *Respekt*, 5 January 2019, www.respekt.cz/tydenik/2019/2/vola-mynar.

[36] A Bickel, *The Least Dangerous Branch: The Supreme Court at the Bar of Politics* (Indianapolis, IN, Bobbs-Merrill, 1962).

Table 8.2 Categorisation of judicial resistance

On bench: Strategic judicial decision-making		Off-bench: Extra-judicial pressure	
Averting	Timing of decisions important to public Pivoting Delaying decisions important to government Pushback against government	**Off-bench pressure**	Organised judicial action (JU) High-risk individual judicial activism
Invalidating	(Constitutional) review of legislation *embedded competence* *derived competence* Petition to an international court for a review	**Allied pressure**	Transnational judicial networks Political opposition pressure Media pressure Academic pressure Public riots

Source: author.

On-bench resistance translates into *strategic judicial decision-making*, with which judges attempt either to *avert* the imminent looming attack by raising its costs for the political actor, or to *invalidate* it by legally quashing a political decision and proclaiming it illegal or unconstitutional.

Off-bench resistance, or *extra-judicial pressure*, refers to a set of strategies by which judges themselves engage in high-risk individual activism outside the courtroom – individually acting *off-bench*, or by *allying* with public, opposition or media.

1. Invalidation as Strategic Decision-making

The majority of judicial reactions to constitutional crises in Central Europe have occurred on a formal level, with courts using various jurisdictional tools to invalidate the political interferences of domestic governments. The great reliance on formal tools is understandable. First, it is the most direct way in which courts can make use of their decision-making competence and address assaults upon judicial independence. Second, the common characteristic of court-curbing practices implemented in Central Europe was their legal character and a pretence of constitutionality.[37]

The use of invalidation techniques depends to a large extent on the given constitutional design and the competences wielded by respective courts. All four Central European countries recognise a constitutional review of

---

[37] Kosař and Šipulová (n 5).

legislation vested in constitutional courts. Moreover, they all also commit to principles of judicial independence in their domestic constitutions and in international law. This opened two major forms of invalidation techniques for their judges: invalidation through domestic *(constitutional) legislative review* and *petition to a supranational court*.

An example of a judge successfully using constitutional review to protect her function is the repeated attempt by Czech President Václav Klaus to remove the Chief Justice of the Supreme Court, Iva Brožová, and replace her with his own candidate, closely linked to his former conservative party.[38] In a set of three cases initiated by Brožová[39] the Czech Constitutional Court significantly limited the competence of the president and minister of justice to interfere in 'court high politics' and arbitrarily influence and change the personal composition of the judiciary.

Courts are in more difficult situation if the executive has enough power to pass court-rigging legislation via constitutional amendments,[40] as their review requires that the principle of judicial independence is formally *embedded* in the constitution as an eternity clause. Nevertheless, many courts were recently able to *derive* unwritten eternity clauses on their own, adopting the doctrine of 'unconstitutional constitutional amendment'[41] even without an explicit textual provision.[42] For example, the Slovak Constitutional Court in 2019, amidst rising public criticism of corruption and patronage in the judiciary, struck down the constitutional amendment seeking to introduce security clearances for Slovak judges, claiming that judicial independence is the main component of the unamendable core of the Slovak Constitution.[43]

The second type of invalidation technique is available to courts in countries which locked-in the core principles of judicial independence via commitments to various international human rights treaties.[44] Favourable rulings of international courts may serve as an important signal for overly creative political leaders, impose sanctions on court-curbers and give domestic judges another layer of legitimacy.

In the European setting, the European Convention on Human Rights ('Convention') and the ECtHR in particular have long represented an important

---

[38] The attempts were motivated by a wish to select his own candidate, Bureš, into the position.

[39] Czech Constitutional Court, judgments no II ÚS 53/06, Pl ÚS 17/06 and Pl ÚS 87/06.

[40] As was the case in Hungary; see G Lengyel and G Ilonszki, 'Simulated Democracy in Pseudo-transformational Leadership in Hungary' (2012) 1 *Historical Social Research* 107, 108.

[41] D Landau, R Dixon and Y Roznai, 'From an Unconstitutional Amendment to an Unconstitutional Constitution? Lessons from Honduras' (2019) 8 *Global Constitutionalism* 40.

[42] Y Roznai, *Unconstitutional Constitutional Amendments: The Limits of Amendment Powers* (New York, Oxford University Press 2017); R Albert, 'Constitutional Amendment and Dismemberment' (2018) 43 *Yale Journal of International Law* 1.

[43] For more detail, see Slovak Constitutional Court, judgment no Pl ÚS 21/2014 of January 30, 2019, or M Domin, 'A Part of the Constitution Is Unconstitutional, the Slovak Constitutional Court Has Ruled' *Verfassungsblog*, 8 February 2019, https://verfassungsblog.de/a-part-of-theconstitution-is-unconstitutional-the-slovak-constitutional-court-has-ruled/.

[44] On explanation of the locking-in strategy, see A Moravcsik, 'The Origins of Human Rights Regimes: Democratic Delegation in Postwar Europe' (2000) 54 *International Organization* 217.

obstacle to violations of democratic standards, including attempts to capture the courts.[45] *Individual complaints* coming from domestic judges led to a string of rulings and pilot judgments which determined clear rules on how to structure domestic judiciaries in order to comply with the Convention.[46] The best-known example of judges seeking redress in the ECtHR is the case *Baka v Hungary*,[47] a petition of the aforementioned former Hungarian Chief Justice of the Supreme Court, András Baka, who successfully argued that the premature termination of his mandate was a retaliation for his criticism of governmental reforms. An even more interesting example is the latest ECtHR judgment *Xero Flor*, which was brought to Strasbourg by a private company arguing that one of the Polish Constitutional Tribunal justices hearing its case has not been elected in accordance with the domestic law.[48]

The Strasbourg court, however, played a less well-known role in the case of Slovak judicial independence and the attempts of the Iveta Radičová government in 2011 to break down a patronage network inside the Supreme Court. In 1997, Prime Minister Mečiar chose Štefan Harabin, the former Chief Justice of the Supreme Court, as his minister of justice. Not only did Harabin manage swiftly to polarise the judiciary, but he also vastly utilised his power to appoint close allies and friends to important positions.[49] In 2009, Harabin managed to secure his election as chairman of the newly established Judicial Council and as Chief Justice of the Supreme Court. Since then, he has purposefully used his combined functions to oversee selection processes and to threaten opposing judges.

In 2011, the new government repeatedly attempted to end Harabin's rule by the initiation of disciplinary proceedings. Nevertheless, Harabin successfully challenged the disciplinary proceedings before the ECtHR on procedural grounds, arguing that his guarantees of independence had been violated. Not only did he win the case, but he also presented the government's repeated attempts to dismiss him from the position of Chief Justice as blatant interferences with his independence in various international fora.[50] The government's efforts to dismiss Harabin were, without doubt, politically motivated. Irrespective of the moral of the story, Harabin managed to successfully use the ECtHR as a shield to protect his mandate.

A second international forum that courts can use to counter political interference is the *preliminary ruling procedure* at the Court of Justice of the European Union (CJEU). This procedure allows national judges to ask the CJEU to interpret the compatibility of new legislation with EU law. Compared to infringement proceedings initiated by the European Commission, preliminary rulings also

---

[45] D Kosař and L Lixinski, 'Domestic Judicial Design by International Human Rights Courts' (2015) 109 *American Journal of International Law* 713.

[46] S Trechsel, *Human Rights in Criminal Proceedings* (Oxford, Oxford University Press, 2005).

[47] ECtHR, GC judgment *Baka v Hungary* 23 June 2016.

[48] ECtHR, *Zero Flor v Poland*, 4907/18, judgment of 7 May 2021.

[49] Spáč, Šipulová and Urbániková (n 31).

[50] ECtHR, *Harabin v Slovakia* judgment, 20 November 2012.

have a time benefit: they allow domestic judges to stay existing proceedings until the CJEU has decided. This advantage was demonstrated by Orbán and Kaczyński's court-packing statutes lowering the retirement age of judges.

In 2012, Orbán proposed lowering the retirement age of judges from seventy to sixty-two years, arguing that the step would make the courts more efficient, open up positions to younger unemployed judges and cleanse the judiciary of the communist burden.[51] In effect, Orbán got rid of 274, mostly senior, higher court judges.[52] The controversial step spurred the European Commission to instigate infringement proceedings against the Hungarian government, in which the CJEU found the reviewed legislation in violation of EU law.[53] Yet, the judgment came far too late, only after targeted judges had already had to leave their posts.

In 2017, following the Hungarian example, Kaczyński also announced legislation lowering the retirement age of judges from seventy to sixty-five years.[54] The European Commission turned to the CJEU once again; nevertheless, a case was also brought before the CJEU by the national judges.[55] The CJEU swiftly issued a preliminary order[56] staying the domestic proceedings and subsequently found a violation of EU law,[57] stopping the wholesale removal of at least some of the most senior Polish judges.[58]

A downside to invalidation strategies is that compliance with the invalidation ruling still lies in the hands of the relevant government. While we can expect democratic regimes to submit to the voice of the judiciary, less can be expected from non-democratic countries, dictatorships or even populist leaders leaning towards semi-authoritarianism, as was recently demonstrated in Poland. The CJEU's finding that the change in the National Council of the Judiciary and its role in the selection of judges violates principles of judicial independence[59] provoked a rebellious answer from PiS, unheard of in the EU setting. Not only did the government openly condemn the judgment, but it also immediately issued another express law explicitly forbidding the courts from following the CJEU's ruling,[60] and eventually started disciplining domestic

---

[51] Kosař and Šipulová (n 5); U Belavusau, 'On Age Discrimination and Beating Dead Dogs: Commission v Hungary' (2013) 4 *CML Rev* 1145.

[52] G Halmai, 'The Early Retirement Age of the Hungarian Judges' in F Nicola and B Davies (eds), *EU Law Stories: Contextual and Critical Histories of European Jurisprudence* (Cambridge, Cambridge University Press, 2017).

[53] CJEU, *European Commission v Hungary*, C-286/12, judgment of 6 November 2012.

[54] Zoll and Wortham (n 25).

[55] CJEU, *European Commission v Poland*, C-619/18, judgment of 26 June 2019.

[56] CJEU, *European Commission v Poland*, C-619/18 R, decision of 17 December 2018.

[57] CJEU (n 52) (in relation to the Supreme Court) and *European Commission v Poland*, C-192/18, judgment of 5 November 2019 (in relation to lower courts' judges).

[58] P Bogdanowicz and M Taborowski, 'Why the EU Commission and the Polish Supreme Court Should Not Withdraw their Cases from Luxembourg' *Verfassungsblog*, 3 December 2018.

[59] CJEU, *Krajowa Rada Sądownictwa*, Joined cases C-585/18, C-624/18 and C-625/18, *A.K., CP and DO*, judgment of 19 November 2019 and CJEU, *A.B*, C-824/18, judgment of 2 March 2021.

[60] CJEU, *Commission v Poland*, C-791/19, order of 8 April 2020.

judges for further asking the CJEU to interpret the independence of their newly appointed peers.[61]

2. Averting Strategies

A second type of strategic decision-making courts can adopt is *averting* a looming political attack. If a government is threatening courts with plans for jurisdiction stripping, containing of the selection process or court-packing, courts might seek to *avert* the threat by raising the costs or lowering the benefits for the political authority, hence forcing it to backtrack. Generally speaking, courts can achieve this either by demonstrating their loyalty (*pivoting*) or by strategically *timing* their decisions and *pushback* against the government.

While we have seen many examples of *pivoting* or *strategic timing* of decisions in Latin America[62] and the United States,[63] Central European courts typically opt for much less dramatic departures from their case law and instead rely on heavy technical language.[64] This was, for example, a common practice in the Slovak Constitutional Court under Mečiar's rule. The Constitutional Court played an important balancing role, stopping the prime minister from taking a number of controversial steps and concentrating too much power in the hands of government-controlled bodies. Nevertheless, apart from a couple of instances such as the financial cuts mentioned above, it managed to slip mostly under Mečiar's radar. One of the common interpretations is that lengthy reasonings devoid of direct references to democracy or backsliding, paired with a highly technical textual interpretation, helped the court to retain the image of a relatively harmless opponent.

A different scenario played out in Czechia. Considering its power and normative influence, the Czech Constitutional Court has remained politically almost uncontested. The most invasive attempt of political power to contain it took place in 2012 when the retiring president of the country, Klaus, repeatedly refused to appoint new constitutional judges after the upper chamber of the parliament rejected his candidates.[65] Although the Constitutional Court has never shied away from vociferous statements and normative evaluations,

---

[61] THEMIS (n 29); L Pech, P Wachowiec, D Mazur, '1825 Days Later: The End of the Rule of Law in Poland (Part I)' (2021) *Verfassungsblog*, 13 January 2021, available at https://verfassungsblog.de/1825-days-later-the-end-of-the-rule-of-law-in-poland-part-i/.

[62] Helmke (n 2).

[63] The most famous being the reaction of the US Supreme Court to FD Roosevelt's 1937 court-packing plan. See GA Caldeira, 'Public Opinon and the US Supreme Court: FDR's Court-Packing Plan' (1987) 81 *American Political Science Review* 1139.

[64] Note that this practice occurred also outside of Central Europe; see, for example, the famous remark of Shapiro, who called British courts a marvellously impenetrable lump: M Shapiro, *Courts: A Comparative and Political Analysis* (Chicago, University of Chicago Press 2013); Taylor (n 17) and J Staton, *Judicial Power and Strategic Communication in Mexico* (Cambridge, Cambridge University Press, 2010).

[65] D Kosař and L Vyhnánek, 'The Constitutional Court of Czechia' (2019) *The Max Planck Handbooks in European Public Law*, vol III: *Constitutional Adjudication: Institutions*.

a careful comparison of its case law with that of other European constitutional courts also suggests that it only rarely significantly constrained the legislator in its choices of how to amend disputed legal norms. In other words, it mostly left the discretion to create new rules to parliament.[66] It would be worth exploring whether this version of the self-contained approach helped the Constitutional Court to dodge the populist rhetoric of majoritarian difficulty.

3. Off-bench Pressure

Judicial resistance can also be used by judges in their individual capacity, without relying on their formal decision-making competence.

Organised judicial action, most often carried out through judicial unions, can often be an effective voice in advocating judicial independence. Judicial unions typically enjoy some level of official competence. They also have an access to important political networks, which allow them to issue statements and communicate more easily with the media or political opposition.[67] Examples of judicial unions actively protecting judicial independence have been seen in all Central European countries. The most striking example, however, comes from Poland. In January 2020, in a March of Thousand Robes, judges took to the streets, supported by colleagues who travelled to Warsaw from France, Norway and the Czech Republic, to protest against the PiS's policies dismantling Polish judicial independence.[68] Similarly, when the CJEU held a hearing in one of the latest ongoing cases against Poland, that hearing was attended by Dutch, Belgian and Turkish judges as a gesture of support for their Polish colleagues.[69]

Judicial activism can also take *individual* form. Judges can act on their own, depending on the practices in a given country, issuing public statements, communicating with other political actors or even marching in the streets. Public or political statements are often exerted by court presidents, as they, given their authority, have better channels for reaching the media and often enjoy a specific competence to comment officially on new legislation targeting the judiciary. This was the case with the former Hungarian Supreme Court Chief Justice András Baka, who was removed from office in retaliation for his parliamentary speeches criticising reforms proposed by Orbán.[70]

Similar professional assertiveness outside the courtroom is of particular importance in cases where political actors have limited formal avenues for

---

[66] K Šipulová, 'The Czech Constitutional Court' in K Pocza (ed), *Constitutional Politics and the Judiciary* (Abingdon, Routledge, 2019).

[67] D Beers, 'A Tale of Two Transitions: Exploring the Origins of Post-Communist Judicial Culture in Romania and the Czech Republic' (2010) 18 *Demokratizatsiya* 28.

[68] C Davies, 'Judges Join Silent Rally to Defend Polish Justice' *The Guardian*, 12 January 2020, www.theguardian.com/world/2020/jan/12/poland-march-judges-europe-protest-lawyers.

[69] J Morijn, 'Commission v Poland: What Happened, What it Means, and What it Will Take' *Verfassungsblog*, 18 March 2020, https://verfassungsblog.de/commission-v-poland-what-happened-what-it-means-what-it-will-take/.

[70] Kosař and Šipulová (n 24); *Baka v Hungary* (n 45).

asserting their authority over the judges. Nevertheless, as suggested in the case of Chief Justice Baka, off-bench pressure rather often leads to a political backlash, especially in regimes backsliding from democracy. The Polish PiS, for example, reacted to protests organised and held by unions of judges with a specific provision in the 'muzzle law' requiring judges to disclose their membership of any association, their functions in the NGO sector and their membership of any political parties before they became judges.

Similarly, the government retaliated against individual judges. A Janus-faced symbol of governmental harassment and defiance of Polish judges is the case of judge Waldemar Żurek (former spokesperson of the previous National Council of the Judiciary). While still in office at the Council, he was subjected to an eighteen-month investigation by the Central Anti-Corruption Bureau (on a fraud charge), received numerous telephone and email threats, and became a target of public harassment, which included the PiS-controlled press publishing headlines about his personal life and divorce. Professionally, Żurek was transferred against his will to a different division at the court as a punishment for alleged failures to execute his duties promptly. His appeal to the Supreme Court languished for several months until it was picked up and swiftly dismissed by a new Extraordinary Control Chamber.[71]

4. Allied Resistance

Finally, *allied resistance* comprises a set of practices and resistance techniques which can only be implemented by an alliance of the courts with their peers or other political or civil actors.

Recent court-curbing attacks in Poland and Hungary prompted large-scale activity in *transnational judicial networks*.[72] Many of the CJEU preliminary rulings targeting judicial independence in Poland and Hungary actually arrived from the courts of other Member States. The Network of Presidents of Supreme Courts of the European Union played a particularly important role. In 2012, the Network initiated a questionnaire among its members, inquiring whether it was possible to use the principle of mutual trust as a vehicle for stopping the free movement of judgments and exerting pressure on the rebelling Hungarian government. The infamous Irish preliminary question[73] was also first discussed in this forum during the Irish presidency of the Network. The Network also actively sought the help of Viviane Reding, the European Commissioner for

---

[71] E Siedlecka, 'To Shoot Down a Judge' *Verfassungsblog*, 8 June 2020, https://verfassungsblog.de/to-shoot-down-a-judge/.

[72] E Holmøyvik, 'For Norway it's Official: The Rule of Law Is No More in Poland' *Verfassungsblog*, 29 February 2020, https://verfassungsblog.de/for-norway-its-official-the-rule-of-law-is-no-more-in-poland/.

[73] CJEU, C-216/18 PPU, *Celmer*, judgment of 25 July 2018.

Justice, Fundamental Rights and Citizenship from 2010 to 2014, adding to the pressure on the European Commission to act against Hungary.[74]

Similarly, in the aftermath of the controversial Polish 'muzzle law', the German District Court of Appeal in Karlsruhe refused to extradite a person sought by the Polish authorities. The District Court reasoned that Polish courts could no longer be considered independent, as Polish judges could at any point be subjected to arbitrary disciplinary proceedings and sanctions.[75]

Apart from their international judicial peers, judges can also ally with *political opposition, supranational institutions, NGOs, media* or *the public*. On the supranational level, the European Commission in particular is an important ally of domestic judges, having the competence to initiate both *infringement proceedings* before the CJEU and (together with the European Parliament) the sanctioning process under Article 7 TEU. The infringement proceedings allow the CJEU to review the compatibility of domestic legislation with existing EU law obligations. The European Commission initiated three infringement proceedings against Hungary and four against Poland. The latest development, however, raises many doubts related to the effectiveness of infringement proceedings. The Polish government seems no longer to bother to comply with CJEU rulings, adopting instead a very nationalistic rhetoric. It therefore seems that while the CJEU can give domestic judges new ammunition, it can no longer on its own exert its dominance over rebelling populist governments.

Another important ally of judges is the *media*. They can report on court cases with their own independent agenda or on behalf of other actors. The investigation into the murder of Ján Kuciak in February 2018 stirred up Slovak society and eventually helped to uncover a convoluted corruption network including the mafia, entrepreneurs, politicians and very senior judges.

Coincidentally, in that very same year the Constitutional Court faced a large-scale personnel change, with nine out of thirteen justices coming to the end of their terms. The government –fearful it would lose the next parliamentary election – first tried to use the opportunity to pack the court with loyal people and secure some posts for its own party members. Public pressure and frequent media coverage, however, prevented it from doing so. In an unprecedented move, a local NGO organised a three-day-long live streaming of candidate interviews by a selection committee in Košice's main square.[76]

Independent media also played their role in the alleged attempts by the Czech president and his advisors to influence apex courts. The decision of former Chief Justice Baxa and constitutional justice Šimíček to publicise the pressure exerted by a presidential advisor gained high coverage and provoked much public

---

[74] Network of Presidents of Supreme Courts of the European Union, Newsletter 26/2014.

[75] T Wahl, 'Refusal of European Arrest warrants Due to Fair Trial Infringements' (2020) 4 *EUCRIM – The European Criminal Law Association's Forum* 321.

[76] M Steuer, 'The First Live-Broadcast Hearings of Candidates for Constitutional Judges in Slovakia: Five Lessons' *Verfassungsblog*, 5 February 2019, https://verfassungsblog.de/the-first-live-broadcast-hearings-of-candidates-for-constitutional-judges-in-slovakia-five-lessons/.

interest, making it very difficult for political actors to continue their activities without ramifications.[77]

As much as politicians may use public protests to pressurise the courts,[78] high public confidence may also protect judges against political interference with their independence. Frontal assaults on courts often trigger antipathy to executive power.[79] *Public riots* therefore increase the costs of political interference and may force the executive to reconsider its plan.[80] Nevertheless, the readiness of the public to riot in the streets depends to a large extent on social legitimacy, public confidence and trust in courts. This was clearly demonstrated by the Polish case, where the government benefited from overall low prestige and public antipathies towards judges for the crucial months in which it managed to sufficiently weaken the courts. Riots in the streets followed only once the PiS had interfered with rule-of-law principles in a very obvious way.

IV. CONCLUSION: CAN COURTS PREVENT POLITICAL INTERFERENCE?

This chapter has been built on an understanding that courts can prevent, avert or punish political interference by raising the costs and lowering the benefits of attacks for the executive. However, examples from Central European countries have demonstrated that they have done so with different levels of success. The study of four cases is certainly not enough to aspire to a general theory about the effectiveness of judicial resistance. It is limited to the experience of post-transitional democratic regimes partly backsliding from democracy, with at least some level of judicial independence. It also reports on the European legal and cultural setting, where supranational commitments play a much stronger role than in the rest of the world.

Nevertheless, certain patterns appearing in Poland, Hungary, Czechia and Slovakia force us to think more broadly about the potential link between forms of political interference and effective retaliation of domestic judges, which would allow the courts to move from simple incidental reactions to forming systemic judicial resistance strategies.

We have seen that neither populist nor democratic politicians shy away from court-curbing practices. However, judicial reactions and their effectiveness differ with the intensity of interference and aims followed by executives.

The Czech case, involving a democratic regime with fully independent courts, demonstrated examples of both formal and informal political attacks. These attacks did not aim to incapacitate the courts, nor did they aim to make the judiciary dependent. Instead, political actors occasionally tried to influence the

---

[77] Supra (n 34).
[78] Taylor (n 17).
[79] ibid.
[80] G Vanberg, 'Establishing Judicial Independence in West Germany' (2000) 32 *Comparative Politics* 333.

result of particular high-profile cases (via pressure exerted by President Zeman), award their loyal allies with prestigious positions at apex courts (via attempts to remove Chief Justice Brožová) or to slightly shift the ideological stance of the court (via attempts to influence the composition of the Supreme Administrative Court). So far, Czech courts have been able to protect their independence, either quashing problematic proposals in a constitutional review, or using the media to stir the public debate and push the executive power into a corner. In other words, judicial reactions followed the character of a political attack: formal legislative interferences met with an *invalidating strategy* before the Constitutional Court, while informal attempts at politicisation were countered by informal individual activity on the part judges and the media (*allied strategy*).

A case worthy of particular attention is the Slovak struggle to remove the former Chief Justice Harabin from his position and break down his informal network. Harabin managed to twist the principle of judicial independence and use the ECtHR as a shield against accountability. Yet, the government, aware that reform of the judiciary was conditional on Harabin's removal, backtracked after the ECtHR ruling, making his *invalidation strategy* successful. This case suggests that a democratic regime committed to rule-of-law principles can be willing to comply with international pressure even if convinced that its court-packing is for a legitimate end.

The Polish and Hungarian cases, on the contrary, show that *invalidation strategies* have little effect in countries which lack sincere commitments to the principles of judicial independence and the rule of law. Resistance in backsliding or non-democratic regimes can be costly for judges and lead to a backlash. Just think of Orbán reorganising the Supreme Court to strip his Chief Justice and biggest critic, András Baka, of his function. Or the case of Polish judge Waldemar Żurek; or scholar Wojciech Sadurski, who is being prosecuted for tweets in which he described the PiS as 'an organised criminal group'.[81]

Even supranational courts, including ECtHR and CJEU, can do little against rebelling governments. The CJEU is limited in addressing questions of judicial independence by its jurisdiction related to the application of EU law. This lack of jurisdiction has already resulted in procedural refusals of several preliminary questions of Polish judges.[82] The CJEU, however, did bite in a couple of infringement proceedings, invalidating Hungarian and Polish court-packing early-retirement laws and ordering the suspension of the new Polish Disciplinary Chamber.[83] While blatant disobedience was for decades a topic of only academic interest among European legal scholars, Kaczyński's attitude shows that times are changing and populist politicians, especially those who built their popularity around nationalism and the direct democracy narrative, do not feel threatened

---

[81] J Morijn and B Grabowska-Moroz, 'Supporting Wojciech Sadurski in a Warsaw Courtroom' *Verfassungsblog*, 28 November 2019, https://verfassungsblog.de/supporting-wojciech-sadurski-in-a-warsaw-courtroom/.

[82] For more on this complex problem, see CJEU cases C-558/18 and C-563/18.

[83] CJEU, case C-79/19.

by possible exclusion from the EU club – all the more so now that the United Kingdom has voluntarily left the EU.

The ECtHR is technically better equipped to hear and decide cases of judges whose independence has been violated by executive power. On the other hand, the decision-making process in Strasbourg is notoriously slow and lacks enforcement powers – even more so than the CJEU, which can, to an extent, rely on the European Commission. The question therefore is whether it can do more than to hinder partial court-curbing steps and delay the capture of the judiciary.

Despite this gloomy picture, it is important to note that both supranational courts are not completely toothless. The informal pressure which the ECtHR and the CJEU can exert on governments by organising hearings and publicly debating the problems and their repercussions should not be underestimated. More generally speaking, this suggests that *invalidation strategies* can be effective even in regimes that do not abide by the rule of law when paired with *allied* strategies, and leverage courts can find help from various judicial and non-judicial actors. Allied strategies typically have an informal character and function as an *auxiliary* measure to formal judicial resistance. A promising example is the financial pressure successfully applied to Orbán in 2012, when the International Monetary Fund made loans for Hungary conditional on its compliance with CJEU and European Commission demands, as well as the February 2020 decision of Norway's Administrative Court to withdraw from cooperation under the EEA Grants and to stop funding any justice-related issues in Poland.[84]

The examples discussed above therefore suggest that two factors are essential for the efficiency of judicial resistance. First, timely reaction of the court is absolutely crucial. Any *preventive* and *averting strategies* require vigilant courts to act before governments can actually take their steps – or at least, before they completely dismantle the rule of law. Second, *alliances* are vital for effective judicial retaliation, as courts cannot execute their own rulings and, if silenced by court-curbing legislation, need other actors to pressurise the government. *Allied strategies* are mostly of informal character and function as auxiliary measures to more formal invalidation techniques.

Nevertheless, alliances between judges and the media or public depend to a large extent on the ability of courts to garner sufficient public trust and prestige. This finding also suggests the importance of preventive strategies that courts should implement to build their relationship with the public. Although not omnipotent, public confidence can significantly raise the stakes for politicians seeking to dismantle principles of judicial independence. It could therefore be argued that long-term *preventive strategies*, aimed at increasing public confidence and public trust, should be considered a part of judicial resistance, allowing the courts to shift from incidental reactions to curbing political interferences, to meticulously planned judicial resistance strategies.

---

[84] Holmøyvik (n 68).

9

Transparency in the 'Fairyland Duchy of Luxembourg'

CATHERINE BARNARD*

I. INTRODUCTION

IT IS A truth universally acknowledged among Brexiters that the Court of Justice, even if in possession of a good reputation, should have no jurisdiction over the United Kingdom. As Mark Francois MP put it in his letter to Michel Barnier on 26 June 2020:

> In the spirit of honesty between friends, and for the avoidance of doubt, there can be no way that the European Court of Justice (ECJ) can be allowed to have a role in UK national life after the end of this year.

The question, then, is why is it that a court which expounds fundamental Western values – democracy,[1] the rule of law[2] and the protection of fundamental rights[3] – should have become such an object of loathing for the Brexiters. I think there are three explanations.[4]

The first concerns control by an external (unelected) body. This feeds into the broader 'take back control' mantra so powerfully advocated by the Leave campaign.[5] Returning to Francois's letter: '[A]ll I and my colleagues in the ERG[6] have ever really wanted is to live in a free country which elects its own government and makes its own laws and then lives under them in peace.' For them

---

* I am grateful to Hugh Whelan for his research assistance in the preparation of this chapter and Dennis Galligan and Eleanor Sharpston for their very helpful comments.

[1] See eg Case 294/83 *Parti écologiste "Les Verts" v European Parliament* EU:C:1986:166.

[2] See eg Case C-619/18 *Commission v Poland* (retirement age of judges) EU:C:2019:531.

[3] See eg *Opinion 2/13* EU:C:2014:2454.

[4] See also www.politico.eu/article/brexit-ecj-european-court-of-justice-9-reasons-why-some-brits-hate-europes-highest-court/.

[5] For a discussion as to what this might mean, see M Elliott, 'The UK–EU Brexit Agreements and "Sovereignty": Having One's Cake and Eating It?', https://publiclawforeveryone.com/2020/12/31/the-uk-eu-brexit-agreements-and-sovereignty-having-ones-cake-and-eating-it/.

[6] European Research Group, the Leave 'party' within the Conservative Party.

the decision in *Factortame*[7] brought to the fore what had long been clear to insiders since the European Communities Act 1972: that EU law did indeed take precedence over UK law (and, of course, the laws of all other Member States[8]). However, it was a decision of the *Court* of Justice that confirmed this. For Brexiters, the supremacy of EU law (as enunciated by the court) posed a direct challenge to the doctrine of parliamentary sovereignty,[9] a principle which has become increasingly deified for some in this group.

The second explanation concerns the constitution-building, integrationist agenda pursued by the Court of Justice. I have written about this elsewhere.[10]

The third concerns a lack of understanding about what the Court of Justice actually does and why it does it, and this, I think, is an issue for the court – indeed all courts – about transparency and legitimacy and, most fundamentally, about why there is a need for courts in a democratic society. Specifically, in respect of the Court of Justice, it is about being clearer to the public about its decision-making process, about who the judges are, about why it decides cases as it does. The Brexit debate has shown that simply being the highest court in Europe is not enough for it to be legitimate. In an increasingly populist age, driven in part by social media, where respect for institutions is subject to constant challenge and contestation, all courts, but the supranational Court of Justice in particular, have to work hard(er) to demonstrate their importance and relevance. I will argue that transparency in the thickest sense is an important way to deliver this.

The chapter is structured as follows. First, I will examine the wider context to demonstrate why the Court of Justice needs to be transparent and more broadly accountable (section II). I then consider why transparency is important, and what transparency means in the judicial context (section III). I next look at whether and how the Court of Justice lives up to the stated aspiration of transparency. I argue that while it satisfies the formal indicators of transparency, this is no longer sufficient. I argue for a broader approach to transparency and suggest what more can be done (section IV). This is all the more important in a populist age (section V). Section VI concludes.

---

[7] *R v Secretary of State for Transport, ex parte Factortame (No 2)* [1991] 1 AC 603.

[8] See, for example, the fight for supremacy of EU law in Italy in the *Simmenthal* litigation, already well documented in the UK legal literature: D Freestone, 'The Supremacy of Community Law in National Courts' (1979) 42 *MLR* 220.

[9] For a helpful summary of how different constitutional lawyers view parliamentary sovereignty, see the Written Evidence from Professor Adam Tomkins, John Millar Professor of Public Law, University of Glasgow to the European Scrutiny Committee https://publications.parliament.uk/pa/cm201011/cmselect/cmeuleg/633ii/633we02.htm#:~:text=Factortame%20was%20a%20case%20in,law%3A%20only%20of%20English%20law.

[10] C Barnard and E Leinarte, 'From Constitutional Adjudication to Trade Arbitration: Enforcing Mobility Rights Post Brexit' (2020) 25 *European Foreign Affairs Review* 589. See also M Blauberger and D Sindbjerg Martinsen, 'The Court of Justice in Times of Politicisation: "Law as a Mask and Shield" Revisited' (2020) 27 *Journal of European Public Policy* 382.

II. THE CONTEXT

In 1981 Eric Stein famously described the work of the Court of Justice as follows:

> Tucked away in the fairyland Duchy of Luxembourg and blessed, until recently, with benign neglect by the powers that be and the mass media, the Court of Justice of the European Communities has fashioned a constitutional framework for a federal-type structure in Europe. From its inception a mere quarter of a century ago, the Court has construed the European Community Treaties in a constitutional mode rather than employing the traditional international law methodology.[11]

With these eloquent words, Stein identified the core of our problem: a court with such power and influence had largely avoided the public gaze. It deliberated in the 'fairyland Duchy of Luxembourg', on the plateau of Kirchberg,[12] crafting a constitutional framework for the European Union. In 2014 the Court of Justice catalogued the 'the specific characteristics of EU law'[13] in Opinion 2/13 (accession to the ECHR):[14] the conferral of powers, supremacy of EU law, direct effect and the protection of fundamental rights as recognised in the Charter. These were constitutional doctrines which it, itself, had crafted out of (or despite of?[15]) the skeletal framework of the Treaty of Rome.[16]

The work of the Court of Justice was rarely scrutinised, let alone challenged, by a hostile audience. Indeed, for many years most of its interlocutors were largely its supporters, mainly from the European institutions[17] and supportive academia,[18] who recognised and valued the role of law and, with it, the centrality of the court,[19] as instrumental in building a successful European Union.[20]

---

[11] E Stein, 'Lawyers, Judges, and the Making of a Transnational Constitution' (1981) 75(1) *American Journal of International Law* 1, 1.

[12] A criticism that is still thrown at it today – see eg P Anderson, 'Ever Closer Union', *London Review of Books*, 7 January 2021.

[13] Para 200.

[14] EU:C:2014:2454, paras 165–69.

[15] T Horsley, *The Court of Justice of the European Union as an Institutional Actor: Judicial Law Making and its Limits* (Cambridge, Cambridge University Press, 2018).

[16] See eg Phelan (n 17).

[17] See eg J Bailleux, 'Michel Gaudet a Law Entrepreneur: The Role of the Legal Service of the European Executives in the Invention of EC Law and of the Common Market Law Review' (2013) 50 *CML Rev* 359; W Phelan, *Great Judgments of the Court of Justice: Rethinking the Landmark Decisions of the Foundational Period* (Cambridge, Cambridge University Press, 2019), focusing on the role of Robert Lecourt.

[18] As Anderson notes (n 12), in 1961 Gaudet created an umbrella group, FIDE, 'with the explicit aim of facilitating exchanges across political, bureaucratic and scholarly boundaries'. Citing the words of its first president, 'FIDE acted as "a private army of the European communities". "In Europe around 1950", a member of its German branch recalled, "the idea of European unification was capable of evoking almost religious enthusiasm among young lawyers."'

[19] For detailed analysis, see A Arnull, *The European Union and Its Court of Justice*, 2nd edn (Oxford, Oxford University Press, 2006).

[20] See eg B Leucht, 'The *Cassis de Dijon* Judgment and the European Commission' in A Albors-Llorens, C Barnard and B Leucht (eds), *Cassis de Dijon: Forty Years On* (Oxford, Hart Publishing, 2020). See also M Rasmussen, 'The Origins of a Legal Revolution – The Early History of the European Court of Justice' (2008) 14 *Journal of European Integration History* 77.

The court did become subject to more academic critical scrutiny (see, for an early prominent example, Rasmussen's 1986 study *On Law and Policy in the European Court of Justice*,[21] one of the first comprehensive critiques of the court's judicial activism; later, cases such as *Viking* and *Laval*[22] were subject to a tsunami of criticism[23]). Some of the national constitutional courts followed suit.[24] However, the court's response was muted. Even when those criticisms reached a crescendo, as was the case with the German Bundeverfassungsgericht in the *PSPP* case,[25] the court adopted the mantra of the British royal family – 'never complain, never explain'[26] – as its laconic press release on *PSPP* demonstrates:

> The departments of the institution never comment on a judgment of a national court. ... Divergences between courts of the Member States as to the validity of such acts would indeed be liable to place in jeopardy the unity of the EU legal order and to detract from legal certainty. Like other authorities of the Member States, national courts are required to ensure that EU law takes full effect. That is the only way of ensuring the equality of Member States in the Union they created.[27]

Crucially, it concludes 'The institution will refrain from communicating further on the matter.'

The Court of Justice's understated, almost technocratic approach[28] served it well in the early years. However, as Brexit has shown, in the longer term, the court's reluctance to engage with a wider, non-specialist audience has had damaging effects. In certain parts of Europe – notably but not exclusively the United Kingdom[29] – large parts of the public have not been brought along too. This points to the need for the court to be more transparent and to explain what it is doing and why (sections III and IV). However, even that may not be enough in this age of populism (section V).

---

[21] H Rassmussen, *On Law and Policy of the European Court of Justice* (Leiden, Brill, 1986).

[22] Case C-438/05 *Viking Line* EU:C2007:772 and Case C-341/05 *Laval* [2005] ECR I-11767.

[23] For a summary, see C Barnard, 'The Calm after the Storm. Time to Reflect on EU Scholarship after *Viking* and *Laval*' in A Bogg, C Costello and A Davies (eds), *Research Handbook on EU Labour Law* (Cheltenham, Edward Elgar, 2016) 337.

[24] For a brief summary, see P Craig and G De Búrca, *EU Law: Texts, Cases and Materials* (Oxford, Oxford University Press, 2020) 328–39 and the references cited therein.

[25] 2 BvR 859/15, 2 BvR 980/16, 2 BvR 2006/15, 2 BvR 1651/15. See T Violante, 'Bring Back the Politics: The *PSPP* Ruling in its Institutional Context (2020) 21 *German Law Journal* 1045.

[26] The criticism it has been subject to about the replacement of the British Advocate General has also resulted in silence: eg www.google.com/search?q=blog+flynn+sharpston+court&rlz=1C1CHBF_en-GBGB902GB902&oq=blog+flynn+sharpston+court&aqs=chrome.69i57j33.5691j0j15&sourceid=chrome&ie=UTF-8.

[27] https://curia.europa.eu/jcms/upload/docs/application/pdf/2020-05/cp200058en.pdf. Although see hints in K Lenaerts, 'No Member State is More Equal than Others: The Primacy of EU law and the Principle of the Equality of the Member States before the Treaties' *Verfassungsblog*, 8 October 2020, https://verfassungsblog.de/no-member-state-is-more-equal-than-others/.

[28] As Anderson (n 12) wrote of Lecourt, appointed president of the court in 1967, 'Lecourt's strategy had always been to move gradually, avoiding any blatant provocation of national governments, deflecting their attention from momentous juridical pronouncements by attaching them to matters of seemingly minimal commercial importance.'

[29] See generally, S Wall, *Reluctant European* (Oxford, Oxford University Press, 2019).

III. TRANSPARENCY AND THE COURTS

1. Transparency in the Judicial Context?

a. What Transparency Means

Transparency is a core principle in any democratic society. As Advocate General Sharpston put it in *Volker*:

> [The purpose of transparency] is to further openness in a democratic society. Transparency may help to protect the citizen against arbitrary abuse of power. More generally, granting wide access to information so as to achieve an informed public and democratic debate enables citizens to exercise effective supervision over how public authorities make use of the power that those very citizens have conferred on them. Thus, transparency is about public control over public institutions.[30]

Transparency is also a key component of the rule of law, itself a fundamental value of any liberal democracy.[31] In his seminal work,[32] Lord Bingham said that the rule of law meant that 'all persons and authorities within the state, whether public or private, should be bound by and entitled to the benefit of laws publicly and prospectively promulgated and *publicly administered* in the courts'.[33]

At the broadest level, transparency means 'openness, communication, and accountability'.[34] In a review of *judicial* transparency, or 'open justice', in Australia, Frank Vincent, a former Supreme Court of Appeal judge, identified three components of transparency: (1) open courts, (2) open information and (3) free publication.[35] We shall look at these in turn.

The necessity of *open courts* can be traced to Bayley J's comments in *Daubney v Cooper*:

> [W]e are all of opinion, that it is one of the essential qualities of a court of justice that its proceedings should be public, and that all parties who may be desirous of hearing what is going on, if there be room in the place for that purpose ... have a right to be present for the purpose of hearing what is going on.[36]

The existence of open courts is also a spur to other actors, such as witnesses, to be open and honest

> first, by stimulating the instinctive responsibility to public opinion, symbolised in the audience, and ready to scorn a demonstrated liar; and next, by inducing the fear of

---

[30] Joined Cases C-92/09 and C-93/09 *Volker und Schecke* EU:C:2010:662, para 68. However, in that case she was, in fact, talking about publication of information relating to who gets CAP money and the proper *limits* to transparency in the interests of protecting the privacy of data subjects.

[31] For a summary of the vast debates on this topic, see the paper by Professor Paul Craig, 'The Rule of Law', appended to the Select Committee on the Constitution's Report: https://publications.parliament.uk/pa/ld200607/ldselect/ldconst/151/15115.htm.

[32] Lord Bingham, *The Rule of Law* (London, Penguin, 2010).

[33] ibid ch 1 (emphasis added).

[34] H Addink, *Good Governance: Concept and Context* (Oxford, Oxford University Press 2019) 94.

[35] F Vincent, 'Open Courts Act Review' (2017) https://apo.org.au/node/195236.

[36] *Daubney v Cooper* (1829) 10 B & C 237, 240.

exposure of subsequent falsities through disclosure by informed persons who may chance to be present or to hear of the testimony from others present.[37]

The leading case on the necessity of *open information* is *Scott v Scott*[38] where Viscount Haldane LC said:

> [U]nless it be strictly necessary for the attainment of justice, there can be no power in the Court to hear in camera either a matrimonial cause or any other where there is no contest between parties. He who maintains that by no other means than by such a hearing can justice be done may apply for an unusual procedure.[39]

Finally, in respect of *free publication* of judicial proceedings, Lord Diplock in *AG v Leveller Magazine Ltd*[40] said: 'If the way that courts behave cannot be hidden from the public ear and eye this provides a safeguard against judicial arbitrariness or idiosyncrasy and maintains the public confidence in the administration of justice.' He continued that the application of this principle of open justice has two aspects: it requires (i) that proceedings should be held in open court (see above) and (ii) the publication to a wider public of fair and accurate reports of proceedings.

b. The Justification for Judicial Transparency

Having looked at what transparency means in the judicial context, we turn to examine why it is so important. There are two justifications for judicial transparency. The *intrinsic view* sees judicial transparency as valuable in its own right and does not need to be justified to any further degree. The *instrumental view* sees judicial transparency as valuable because it provides a means of working towards greater goals: '[B]ecause openness to the public is a fundamental feature of a democracy, open justice should be seen not merely as a legal principle, but as a broader democratic ideal.'[41]

Transparency is also about engagement between the rule-makers and the ruled, and thus accountability. Heald refers to 'inwards transparency', where administrative insiders are transparent to outsiders, and 'outwards transparency', where organisational insiders can gain an accurate perception of those outside the organisation, ie the public.[42] For the Australian High Court, outward transparency is key. Speaking in the context of criminal law, the High Court of Australia in *Markarian v The Queen*[43] said that a judge's sentence and reasons

---

[37] Wigmore (n 2) 436.
[38] *Scott v Scott* [1913] AC 417.
[39] ibid 438.
[40] *AG v Leveller Magazine Ltd* [1979] AC 440, 450.
[41] Vincent (n 4).
[42] D Heald, 'Varieties of Transparency' in *Transparency: The Key to Better Governance?* (Oxford, Oxford University Press 2006).
[43] *Markarian v The Queen* (2005) 215 ALR 215, 236 [82].

are usually exposed to public scrutiny through publication or media reporting. It continued:

> Public responses to sentencing, although not entitled to influence any particular case, have a legitimate impact on the democratic legislative process. Judges are aware that, if they consistently impose sentences that are too lenient or too severe, they risk undermining public confidence in the administration of justice and invite legislative interference in the exercise of judicial discretion.

We shall return to the question of accountability below. First, we shall look at the EU's approach to transparency both generally and in the judicial context.

2. The EU's Approach to Transparency

The EU legal order places considerable value upon the transparency of administration, stemming from the value of 'openness' in Article 1 of the Treaty on European Union (TEU).[44] An early example can be found in Declaration No 17 of the Maastricht Treaty, which said that 'transparency of the decision-making process strengthens the democratic nature of the institutions and the public's confidence in the administration'. In *Hautala*,[45] the court noted the 'importance of the public's right of access to documents held by public authorities' and recognised that 'Declaration No 17 links that right with the democratic nature of the institutions'. For the court in *Kuijer*[46] transparency is about not only democracy but also efficiency: '[T]he principle of transparency is intended ... to ensure that the administration acts with greater propriety, efficiency and responsibility vis-à-vis the citizens in a democratic system. It helps to strengthen the principle of democracy and respect for fundamental rights.'

In respect of the Court of Justice, Advocate-General Bobek, in his Opinion in *Commission v Patrick Breyer*,[47] sees publication as a precursor to public engagement and the kind of inward and outward transparency identified by Heald:

> 96. When conceiving of the *means* to enhance courts' legitimacy in constitutional democracies, openness appears to be the natural candidate. Openness strengthens the overall legitimacy of courts. On the one hand, it enhances their democratic credentials by rendering courts somewhat more responsive to the citizens .... On the other hand, it improves the quality of justice by creating incentives to improve judicial work and output.

---

[44] See eg www.europarl.europa.eu/RegData/etudes/IDAN/2016/556973/IPOL_IDA(2016)556973_EN.pdf. See also Art 11(3) TEU; Art 15(3) TFEU.
[45] Case C-353/99 P *Hautala* EU:C:2001:661, para 24.
[46] Case T-211/00 *Kuijer v Council* EU:T:2002:30, para 52.
[47] C-213/15P *Commission v Patrick Breyer* EU:C:2017:563.

The need for transparency has also been recognised by Koen Lenaerts, the President of the Court of Justice. Writing extra-judicially,[48] he said the question whether courts enjoy (internal) legitimacy amounts to examining whether the rationale for a particular judgment is

> sufficiently transparent and easy to understand or whether it is cryptic; whether the grounds of judgment are strong enough to be convincing and adequately meet the arguments put forward by the parties; whether the court's rulings are coherent with the existing case-law and based on impartial criteria known in advance or whether they are simply unpredictable and arbitrary.

In conclusion, transparency is a key component of the legitimacy of any process of decision-making, whether administrative or judicial. As Jeremy Bentham put it, 'Publicity is the very soul of justice, it is the keenest spur to exertion, and the surest of all guards against probity. It keeps the judge himself, while trying, under trial.'[49]

So how does the Court of Justice, in fact, measure up to these standards?

IV. TRANSPARENCY AND THE COURT OF JUSTICE

1. A Thin Notion of Transparency

a. How Does the Court of Justice Measure Up in Law ... ?

The Court of Justice would answer that it satisfies the formal requirement of transparency: its Statutes[50] and Rules of Procedure are published;[51] its hearings are in public;[52] where appropriate, witnesses, including the Commission, are asked questions;[53] it has a website; its reasoned[54] judgments are read in open court;[55] and published in the EU languages;[56] and are available for free. Press releases are issued on the most important cases. There is a twitter feed. Some of the judgments are even explained in lay terms in videos (but these are rarely viewed).[57] The judges and advocates general also give public speeches and attend

---

[48] K Lenaerts, 'How the ECJ Thinks: A Study on Judicial Legitimacy' (2013) 36 *Fordham International Law Journal* 1302, 1306.

[49] J Bentham, *A Treatise on Judicial Evidence* (London, JW Paget, 1825) 67.

[50] https://curia.europa.eu/jcms/upload/docs/application/pdf/2016-08/tra-doc-en-div-c-0000-2016-201606984-05_00.pdf.

[51] For the Court of Justice, see https://curia.europa.eu/jcms/upload/docs/application/pdf/2012-10/rp_en.pdf.

[52] Art 31 of the Statutes of the Court of Justice and Arts 78 and 79 of the Rules of Procedure.

[53] See eg Art 67 of the Rules of Procedure of the Court of Justice.

[54] Art 36 of the Statutes of the Court of Justice.

[55] Art 37 of the Statutes of the Court of Justice.

[56] Art 40 of the Rules of Procedure of the Court of Justice.

[57] See eg The Court of Justice of the EU and Sport (www.youtube.com/watch?v=Dhxpe3_H5GU) which has had about 1,500 views.

conferences. They have regular engagement with the national judiciary,[58] as well as with judiciary in other major jurisdictions such as the US Supreme Court and the European Court of Human Rights. At the formal level, the court satisfies Vincent's three criteria for transparency: (1) open courts, (2) open information and (3) free publication.

b. … And in Practice?

But let's dig a little deeper. First, who is deciding the case – a three- or five-judge chamber or the Grand Chamber or even (very occasionally) the full court? Who decides which formation? What are the criteria? What difference does this make?[59] Common sense would suggest that a chamber of three judges is unlikely, intentionally, to depart radically from well-established jurisprudence of the court, especially a Grand Chamber decision.[60] But which cases get a three-judge chamber and which the treatment of the full court?

The Court's Rules of Procedure (RP), read in conjunction with the Statute of the Court,[61] provide limited information on the question of the criteria according to which cases are allocated to particular formations. Article 59 RP says that the Judge-Rapporteur shall present a 'preliminary report' to the general meeting of the court which 'shall contain proposals as to whether particular measures of organisation of procedure, measures of inquiry or, if appropriate, requests to the referring court or tribunal for clarification should be undertaken, and as to the formation to which the case should be assigned'. It shall also contain the 'Judge-Rapporteur's proposals, if any, as to whether to dispense with a hearing and as to whether to dispense with an Opinion of the Advocate General …' and that, 'The Court shall decide, after hearing the Advocate General, what action to take on the proposals of the Judge-Rapporteur.'

Article 60 RP provides a bit more detail: cases are assigned to chambers of five and three judges (but where is the dividing line between the two?) 'in so far as the difficulty or importance of the case or *particular circumstances* are not such as to require that it should be assigned to the Grand Chamber' (emphasis added). Article 60 also provides that under Article 16(3) of the Statute a Member State or an EU institution can effectively insist that the case be heard by the Grand Chamber. The Statute also governs attribution of a case to the full court,

---

[58] See Anderson (n 12), who noted that Lecourt 'wooed national judges with regular invitations to learn from Luxembourg. … Lecourt, with long experience of journalism and politics, also encouraged his colleagues to give lectures and write articles.' However, for Anderson these outreach activities were aimed at the 'cognoscenti to spread the glad word of the court'.

[59] See further M Bobek, 'More Heads, More Reason? A Comparative Reflection on the Role of Enlarged Judicial Formations in Apex Jurisdictions', talk, Centre for European Legal Studies, 11 November 2020.

[60] I am grateful to Eleanor Sharpston for the elaboration of this point.

[61] Protocol (No 3) on the Statute to the Court of Justice of the European Union, annexed to the Treaties.

either because that is required by specific Treaty provisions,[62] or because the court 'considers that the case is of exceptional importance'.[63] At any stage of the procedure, the chamber hearing a case may request the court to allocate it to a larger formation.[64] However, in reality, the criteria applied every week by the court in deciding which formation is to hear a case, a case which is so important to a particular claimant, remains obscure. What is meant by the phrase 'particular circumstances' in Article 60 RP? True transparency would imply that the court would formulate, publish and apply clearer criteria governing such an important case-management decision.

Secondly, what about the objective of a clearly reasoned judgment, a criteria pushed by Judge Lenaerts? For the Court of Justice a single judgment, where compromises must be reached to ensure that all judges can agree to it, already provides some limits on its ability to reason clearly. It has long been said that a working rule of the court is that if a paragraph or phrase is causing trouble, it is removed. In some judgments it is almost possible to see the scissor cuts.[65] The judgment in *Keck*,[66] one of the most discussed in the court's canon, was subject to severe criticism for its lack of clarity in providing the very clarification it espoused.[67]

Some judgments are simply bad. Take, for example, *Parkwood v Alemo Herron*,[68] a decision that prompted Weatherill to say:

> On occasion a decision of the Court of Justice of the European Union is so down right odd that it deserves to be locked into a secure container, plunged in the icy waters of a deep lake and forgotten about … sadly, we are not allowed simply to consign maverick rulings of the Court to oblivion.[69]

The Court of Justice is not alone in delivering poorly reasoned judgments and, of course, scholars tend to focus on the bad judgments rather than on the good. We also know that the court is under tremendous pressure to deliver judgments in a reasonable period of time, that most judges are not working in their mother tongue, meaning they have to rely on tried and tested (French) formula which may (or may not) quite say what they think they say. And the legacy of the parsimonious, French Conseil d'État-style of judgment drafting stills lives on.

---

[62] See Art 16(4) of the Statute.

[63] Art 16(5) of the Statute.

[64] Art 60(3) RP.

[65] Case C-376/98 *Germany v Council and EP (Tobacco Advertising)* EU:C:2000:544, between paras 79 and 80.

[66] Joined Cases C-267/91 and C-268/91 EU:C:1993:905.

[67] S Weatherill, 'After Keck: Some Thoughts on How to Clarify the Clarification' (1996) 33 *CML Rev* 885.

[68] Case C-426/11 *Alemo-Herron and Others v Parkwood Leisure Ltd* ECLI:EU:C:2013:521, paras 31–35. See J Prassl, 'Business Freedoms and Employment Rights in the European Union' (2015) 17 *Cambridge Yearbook of European Legal Studies* 189.

[69] S Weatherill, 'Use and Abuse of the EU's Charter of Fundamental Rights: On the Improper Veneration of "Freedom of Contract"' (2014) 10 *European Review of Contract Law* 167.

All of this points to more time being spent on fewer cases to ensure the quality of the debate, the quality of the language and the quality of the reasoning. That raises the vexed question of a more effective system of docket control.

The absence of dissents in the Court of Justice, done to protect the judiciary and the authority of the court,[70] is an old chestnut. Those from common law systems tend to be much in favour of dissents: Entrikin claims that the US judicial system is 'generally understand globally as among the most transparent of judicial systems', crediting the US practice of individualised (and dissenting) opinions as facilitating this transparency.[71] However, Entrikin notes that the practice of publishing separate opinions is entirely determined 'by custom and tradition'.[72] And, even in the common law world, dissents are losing some of their appeal, given the confusion they can generate. In the UK Supreme Court they are now somewhat discouraged. In the Supreme Court's most important judgment this century, *Cherry/Miller*[73] (considered below), there were no dissents from the eleven-judge panel.

It is also true that the Advocate General's Opinion is a significant resource for the court. Eleanor Sharpston, a former Advocate General, explained the AG's Opinion to me in these terms:

> A good AG crawls all over each case in which he's writing an opinion – doing detailed further research, combing the national file deposited with the Registry (in the case is a reference for a preliminary ruling); standing back and setting the case in its wider context; lining up the possible options available to the Court and then explaining what is right/wrong with each of them before making a carefully reasoned 'pitch' for a particular solution which he formally proposes to the Court. The investment – in terms of time, depth of analysis and intellectual effort – is utterly different [to a first instance decision].[74]

As a result, Advocate Generals' Opinions may be clearer than those of the Court of Justice since they speak with a single, named voice. Yet, many observers do not understand who or what the Advocate General is, and how far the court is prepared to go in following the Advocate General's Opinion. Where the court says, 'As the Advocate General said at para 25 ...', does that mean the court agrees only with the reasoning in paragraph 25 but not the rest? Or is it an

---

[70] M Erb, 'Dissent Aversion at the Court of Justice of the European Union', https://scholarship. law.duke.edu/cgi/viewcontent.cgi?article=1010&context=mjs; R Raffaelli, Dissenting opinions in the Supreme Courts of the Member States, www.europarl.europa.eu/document/activities/cont/2013 04/20130423ATT64963/20130423ATT64963EN.pdf.

[71] JL Entrikin, 'Global Judicial Transparency Norms: A Peek behind the Robes in a Whole New World – A Look at Global Democratizing Trends in Judicial Opinion-issuing Practices' (2019) 18 *Washington University Global Studies Law Review* https://heinonline.org/HOL/Page?handle=hein. journals/wasglo18&id=61&div=5&collection=journals (accessed 19 August 2020).

[72] ibid.

[73] *R (on the application of Miller) (Appellant) v The Prime Minister (Respondent) Cherry and others (Respondents) v Advocate General for Scotland (Appellant) (Scotland)* [2019] UKSC 41.

[74] Correspondence on file with the author.

implicit assertion that the rest is good too? What if paragraph 25 is merely a fairly uncontentious statement of law? Does this mean that it is the only part the court can agree with? This further adds to the obscurity.

Thirdly, the majority of cases come to the Court of Justice as a result of Article 267 references on interpretation. Many observers do not realise that this means that it is the national court, not the Court of Justice, that will have the final say on the outcome of the case. The division of responsibilities means that the court has to be very careful in the language it deploys to avoid overstepping the jurisdictional limits. But this also means that its language can be obscure. Take, for example, *Akrich*,[75] where the Court said:

> That said, where the marriage is genuine and where, on the return of the citizen of the Union to the Member State of which *he* is a national, *his* spouse, who is a national of a non-Member State and with whom *he* was living in the Member State which *he* is leaving, is not lawfully resident on the territory of a Member State, regard must be had to respect for family life under Article 8 [ECHR].[76]

Yet, on the facts, the wife was the EU citizen and the husband the third-country national. The use of the male pronoun and the male possessive pronoun add confusion not clarity.

In conclusion, these criticisms, many of which are well known and long discussed, are part structural and part about poor communication. The structural ones (eg the outcome of cases may be unclear as a result of the Article 267 reference mechanism) are harder to address. But the failure to clarify how cases are allocated to different formations of the court, and the lack of clarity around the role of the Advocate General could be addressed through better communication.

Yet even making these changes would not address the visceral anti-court reaction found in Francois's letter referred to in the introduction. So what then is the problem? I would argue that while formal transparency requirements remain essential, a more substantive approach to transparency is becoming more important. This relates to questions of accountability and responsiveness which themselves raise serious issues for the courts.

2. A Thicker Notion of Transparency

Judges, are of course, independent but nevertheless their judgments must live and breathe in a broader social and political context. Friedman points out that: 'The available empirical evidence suggests one way that courts can, and sometimes successfully do, bolster their institutional strength' is 'by enhancing the public's perception of their legitimacy through decisions that track the

---

[75] Case C-109/01 *Secretary of State for the Home Department v Akrich* ECLI:EU:C:2003:491.
[76] ibid para 58 (emphasis added).

public's prevailing political mood over time'.[77] Citing various studies, including Robert Dahl's well-known statistical analysis of the US Supreme Court's decisions,[78] Friedman suggests that the Supreme Court was, over time, 'typically in sync with public opinion about national policy'. He concludes that the mechanism by which the Supreme Court achieves consistency between its decisions and prevailing political attitudes is unknown. He suggests it may be a case of correlation: 'whatever factors cause public opinion to shift in one direction may be the very factors causing the Justices' political opinions to shift in that same direction'. However, he also argues that another 'plausible explanation is the so-called "strategic behaviour hypothesis", which posits that the Court is actively cultivating its legitimacy by consciously pinning its colours to the mast of public opinion over time'. He concludes that: 'The Court's democratic deficit and relative institutional weakness certainly give it very strong incentives to do this. Some recent studies suggest that judges are acting on just these incentives.'

In the absence of any such empirical studies in the European Union, how has the Court of Justice fared in enhancing the public's perception of its legitimacy through decisions that track the public's prevailing political mood? We have already seen the visceral reaction by the Union's detractors to the decision in *Factortame (No 1)*. For them, any incursion into parliamentary sovereignty would be too much and totally unjustifiable. Yet, for the Court's supporters, supremacy is no more than a rule on conflicts of law[79] and a necessary one to enable a quasi-federal EU to operate, a proposition to which all Member States signed up.

However, there are other areas where the court has gone far and fast, and its decisions have not always coincided with the public mood, or at least the public mood in some northern countries. Take the citizenship case law. In *Grzelczyk*[80] the Court of Justice pronounced that EU citizenship was destined to be the 'fundamental status' of nationals of the Member States, enabling those who find themselves in the same situation to enjoy the same treatment as nationals of another Member State.[81] This paved the way for the court to rule that Member States had to afford equal treatment with respect to social advantages to all EU citizens, not only workers. The profound effect of this analysis took a while to filter through the national systems but, when combined with the dramatic increase in free movement of people after the 2004 enlargement, the consequence for national welfare systems became serious and the backlash against the European Union and the Court of Justice grew ever louder, at least in northern

---

[77] N Friedman, *The Impact of Populism on Courts: Institutional Legitimacy and the Popular Will* (Oxford, The Foundation for Law, Justice and Society, 2019).

[78] R Dahl, 'Decision-making in a Democracy: The Role of the Supreme Court as a National Policy-Maker' (1957) 6 *Journal of Public Law* 279.

[79] C Joerges, 'Conflicts-Law Constitutionalism: Ambitions and Problems' (28 November, 2012) ZenTra Working Paper in Transnational Studies no 10/2012, available at SSRN: https://ssrn.com/abstract=2182092 or http://dx.doi.org/10.2139/ssrn.2182092.

[80] C-184/99 *Grzelczyk v Centre Public d'Aide Sociale d'Ottignes-Louvain-la-Neuve* [2001] ECR I-6193.

[81] ibid para 31 of the judgment.

European states, particularly the United Kingdom.[82] Yes, it is true that 'ECJ Judges read the morning papers'[83] and the decision in *Dano*[84] and *Alimanovic*[85] was the eventual response. But it was too little, too late, for the United Kingdom at least.

So this is really about what Heald terms 'outward transparency'. How does the Court of Justice find a way to really understand what a population of 450 million people think? Reading the newspapers is one way (although they may not truly reflect the views of their readers, let alone non-readers). But what Brexit has shown very clearly is that the elites tend to live in a like-minded bubble.[86] This raises the question of geography. Returning to Stein, the court is tucked away in Luxembourg. Why does it not sometimes hold the oral hearing in cases of major importance in the relevant country from which the reference originated? This is something the UK Supreme Court has experimented with. It sat in Belfast, not London, to hear the highly controversial, but significant, Northern Irish case of *Lee v Ashers Bakery*,[87] a case about discrimination on the grounds of sexual orientation. Why does the Court of Justice not relocate from time to time? Of course there are issues about translation, security and additional costs. There are also issues about judicial capture (it is a very good thing that the court is not in Brussels) and even judicial safety (an unpopular decision being taken on Poland?). But surely the value of being located for a while in the relevant country, talking to local judges about, for example, the problems they experience with applying EU law, being seen to be there and open and willing to listen, might be a significant step forward in substantive transparency.

And while the Court of Justice needs to listen to the public, the public also need to be able to listen to the court – literally. Yes, hearings are in public but they take place in Luxembourg, a country with a high cost of living, making it expensive for many people to visit (eg overnight stays, flights). Why is there no livestreaming of some cases so the public can actually see the judges at work?[88] Again, this has proved very effective in the UK Supreme Court. It is reported that the three-day hearing in *Miller/Cherry* attracted twelve million viewers on day one, seven million watched the footage on day two and five million on day three.[89]

---

[82] C Barnard and S Fraser Butlin, 'Free Movement vs Fair Movement: Brexit and Managed Migration' (2018) 55 *CML Rev* 203.

[83] M Blauberger et al, 'ECJ Judges Read the Morning Papers. Explaining the Turnaround of European Citizenship Jurisprudence' (2018) 25(10) *Journal of European Public Policy* 1422.

[84] Case C-333/13 *Dano* EU:C:2014:2358.

[85] Case C-67/14 *Jobcenter Berlin Neukölln v Nazifa Alimanovic and Others* EU:C:2015:597.

[86] J Fry and A Brint, 'Bubbles, Blind-Spots and Brexit', www.mdpi.com/2227-9091/5/3/37; www.timeshighereducation.com/cn/student/blogs/brexit-shows-uk-students-live-bubble.

[87] *Lee v Ashers Bakery* [2018] UKSC 49.

[88] www.supremecourt.uk/live/court-01.html.

[89] Although, the Supreme Court concedes, this figure would have been higher, but due to unprecedented demand it was unable to capture all the requests. These figures do not include viewings via television broadcasters Sky and the BBC: www.legalcheek.com/2019/10/parliament-prorogation-case-racked-up-30-million-views-supreme-court-confirms/.

There are issues with interpretation but the European Court of Human Rights manages to overcome this, albeit with only two languages (English and French).[90] One way would be for the Court of Justice to livestream in the language(s) of the cases (plus English?). In a case of considerable importance, interpretation could also be made into, say, the main 'pivot' languages: English, French, German, Spanish, Italian and Polish. This would be the twenty-first century's reinterpretation of genuine open justice. Drawing on *Wigmore on Evidence*, the leading US text on evidence law, through open justice, '[n]ot only is respect for the law increased and intelligent acquaintance acquired with the methods of government, but a strong confidence in judicial remedies is secured which could never be inspired by a system of secrecy'.[91]

But it is not about the rulings themselves but also about the judges. As Richard Posner (US Court of Appeal for the 7th Circuit) said, judicial transparency is 'not a matter of airing dirty laundry; it's about the public having a realistic understanding of the strengths and weaknesses of the judiciary'.[92] The Article 255 procedure clearly has improved the quality and integrity of the EU judiciary. The regular reports of the Article 255 committee are published on the website. They show that 22 per cent of proposed judges in 2019 received unfavourable opinions.[93]

But who are the judges? One comes from each Member State, selected by that state. This brings regional diversity but the gender and age balance is not good and there is not a single judge from a minority ethnic background.[94] This, of course, is not an issue unique to the Court of Justice; national judiciaries struggle with this too; and the court must accept those judges who are sent to it and who get through the Article 255 committee. But where are the calls for diversity and a judiciary which reflects the diverse population over which the Court of Justice has jurisdiction? What is the court doing to promote this? A diverse judiciary might bring in a diversity of views. It would enable people of real talent, irrespective of colour, ethnic origin or gender, to get into the top jobs at the court and make their contribution. In so doing, they would also serve as role models for the next generation.

In conclusion, a thicker form of transparency would help deliver a more legitimate Court of Justice. But even if the court adopted these measures, would this make any difference to the challenges from the Brexiters and their equivalents elsewhere in Europe?

---

[90] https://echr.coe.int/Pages/home.aspx?p=hearings&c=.

[91] JH Wigmore, *Evidence in Trials at Common Law ('Wigmore on Evidence')*, rev JH Chadbourn (Boston, MA, Little Brown, 1976) 335.

[92] E Figueroa, 'Transparency in Administrative Courts: From the Outside Looking In' (2015) 35(1) *Journal of the National Association of Administrative Law Judiciary*.

[93] https://curia.europa.eu/jcms/upload/docs/application/pdf/2020-01/qcar19002enn_002_-_public.pdf.

[94] https://curia.europa.eu/jcms/jcms/Jo2_7026/en/.

V. THE COURTS IN THE FACE OF THE POPULIST CHALLENGE

Transparency, even in its thickest form, only goes so far to address scepticism about courts in a populist world. Even in the US system, where the written constitution (like the EU's) expressly recognises the role of the courts, the courts are seen as the weakest branch of government: they possess 'neither purse nor sword'.[95] The problem is more acute in the British system where there is no written constitution. Parliament's legitimacy comes through direct election; in a first-past-the-post system, the executive has legitimacy through commanding the confidence of the largest party in parliament. So where do the courts fit? In the United States, the argument is that, in a liberal democracy, courts provide an important counterweight to excessive majoritarianism. They ensure that the rights of all, including those in the minority, are protected from, inter alia, an overbearing executive. The United Kingdom is different. The constitutional foundation of the courts is separate to the elective-parliamentary process. The courts have their own long history and justification.[96] As the Supreme Court powerfully put it in *Cherry/Miller II*:

> [T]*he courts have the responsibility of upholding the values and principles of our constitution and making them effective. It is their particular responsibility to determine the legal limits of the powers conferred on each branch of government*, and to decide whether any exercise of power has transgressed those limits. The courts cannot shirk that responsibility merely on the ground that the question raised is political in tone or context.[97]

In the European Union, the role of the Court of Justice is enshrined in the Treaty and it protects the individual, polices the division of powers between the other institutions, interprets the Treaty and determines its limits. The European Parliament, while now directly elected, does not inspire the same degree of loyalty as a domestic parliament. The balance between the institutions is different. Yet to populists this is just noise. Courts are suspect.

The UK Supreme Court has gone some way towards trying to achieve a thicker form of transparency. In addition to the formal indicia of transparency (hearings in public, judgments published and available online, press releases summarising the judgments), as we have seen it also livestreams its hearings, it is proactive on twitter, it offers educational materials[98] and it publishes adverts for new members of the Supreme Court. Yet despite its attempts to reach out

---

[95] K Mitchell, 'Neither Purse nor Sword: Lessons Europe Can Learn from American Courts' Struggle for Democratic Legitimacy' (2007) 38 *Case Western Reserve Journal of International Law* 653.

[96] I am grateful to the editor for this point.

[97] para 39 (emphasis added).

[98] www.supremecourt.uk/news/online-educational-resources.html.

and make itself more open, this has not protected it from the ire of populists. As Bagehot put it in *The Economist*:

> [T]hey use feelings of patriotism and resentment rather than facts about trade flows. ... They turned on the nation's core institutions – Parliament, the civil service, the Supreme Court – when they suspected attempts to frustrate their wishes. They succeeded in defeating the establishment ... by claiming to stand for emotion rather than reason and the people rather than the elite.[99]

This does not augur well for the Court of Justice, which is already well behind the Supreme Court in terms of transparency, at least in the thicker sense. It maybe that the European Union's polity is currently more stable than that of the United Kingdom and, with the departure of President Trump from the White House, the populist challenge may start to wane. This may help to protect national courts and the Court of Justice from a significant populist challenge. Yet the causes of populism have not waned and the legacy of COVID-19 may serve to aggravate the divide between the haves and have-nots. Courts may still yet get caught up in any ensuing backlash. They need to be on their guard. They need to continue reaching out and explaining. They need to be substantively transparent.

VI. CONCLUSION

The Consultative Council of European Judges, a working group within the Council of Europe, issued an Opinion regarding the purpose of judicial transparency on the European level:

> Integrating justice into society requires the judicial system to open up and learn to make itself known. The idea is not to turn the courts into a media circus but to contribute to the transparency of the judicial process. Admittedly, full transparency is impossible, particularly on account of the need to protect the effectiveness of investigations and the interests of the persons involved, but an understanding of how the judicial system works is undoubtedly of educational value and should help to boost public confidence in the functioning of the courts.[100]

I have argued that the Court of Justice scores well on the formal indicia of transparency but less well on its more substantive dimension. There is more the court could do to make itself more open to the public (outward transparency) and more responsive to the public (inward transparency).

---

[99] *The Economist*, 14 November 2020, 30.
[100] Opinion No 7 (2005) of the Consultative Council of European Judges to Committee of Ministers on 'justice and society', para 9.

This is important for a court of such significance to the EU – and ultimately global – legal order.[101] Transparency, in the fullest sense, will help improve the court's legitimacy. It will not protect it from full-blooded challenges by populists nor from its critics like Mark Francois, but transparency will at least give it some protection from some of the fairer accusations that it remains 'tucked away in the fairyland Duchy of Luxembourg' and not doing enough to engage with a less deferential public.

---

[101] See A Bradford, *The Brussels Effect* (Oxford, Oxford University Press, 2020).

10

From Mystery to Transparency: How Judges Promote Public Understanding of the Judicial Role

PAUL MAGRATH

I. INTRODUCTION

WHEN, IN THAT seismic moment in 2016, three High Court judges were accused by a tabloid newspaper of being 'Enemies of the People', the reaction of many in the legal profession was that it was for the Lord Chancellor to stand up and defend judicial independence and the rule of law. But the Lord Chancellor herself, Liz Truss MP, commenting on the fallout of this incident in an interview on BBC Radio 4's *Law in Action*, said she thought 'the way we build judicial morale and judicial value is by the judiciary themselves talking about what they do'.

The current Lord Chief Justice has since said much the same thing at his end-of-year press conference, when he spoke of the 'benefits of promoting a better understanding of the work of the judiciary and the rule of law'. Lord Burnett of Maldon CJ highlighted a number of ways in which the judiciary have become more engaged in that process. But perhaps they could do more.

This chapter looks at the four main ways in which judges can promote public understanding of their role, and of the rule of law more generally, namely:

1. By the way they give judgments;
2. By giving speeches and lectures;
3. By engaging directly with the media;
4. Through social media and other forms of direct public engagement.

One might begin, though, by making two general observations.

A. Accessibility

First, there has been a major change in the relationship between the judiciary and the general public in recent decades. In 1955, the then Lord Chancellor (who until recently occupied a senior judicial as well as ministerial role) offered the following explanation of what might be called the Doctrine of Judicial Reticence:

> So long as a Judge keeps silent his reputation for wisdom and impartiality remains unassailable: but every utterance which he makes in public, except in the course of the actual performance of his judicial duties, must necessarily bring him within the focus of criticism.[1]

That statement by Lord Kilmuir belongs firmly to what one might think of as the Age of Deference, when as far as the general public was concerned the judicial function was largely a closed book – much of it in Latin – and shrouded in mystique. Judges spoke publicly almost exclusively through their judgments. Any other form of engagement with the public would have been the exception rather than the rule.

We have come a long way since then, and what the judiciary have lost in deference and mystery they have gained in public awareness and transparency. That is a good thing. The respect in which the judiciary are held, if deserved, should be based on knowledge, not mystique. (Likewise, any lack of respect should be based on facts, rather than assumption and prejudice.)

B. Open Justice and the Rule of Law

My second preliminary observation concerns the importance, regardless of how accessible the judiciary themselves might be, of the principle of open justice. This goes to the very heart of the idea of the rule of law, and means that only in the most exceptional circumstances should the work of the judiciary be concealed from public view and the possibility of public scrutiny. Access to justice is not confined to litigants; it includes everyone who needs or wants to find out about the law and how it is being applied in the courts.

Although the principle is much older, its classic expression appears in the foundational case of *Scott v Scott* [1913] AC 417 (HL) where Lord Atkinson emphasised, that 'in public trial is to found, on the whole, the best security for the pure, impartial, and efficient administration of justice, the best means for winning for it public confidence and respect' (463).

As Lord Chief Justice Hewart famously observed, in *R v Sussex Justices, Ex p McCarthy* [1924] 1 KB 256 (DC), it 'is of fundamental importance that justice should not only be done, but should manifestly and undoubtedly be seen to be done' (259).

---

[1] Letter from Lord Kilmuir to Sir Ian Jacob KBE of 12 December 1955, reprinted in AW Barnett, 'Judges and the Media – The Kilmuir Rules' [1986] *PL* 383, 384–85.

More recently, in *R (Guardian News and Media Ltd) v City of Westminster Magistrates' Court* [2012] EWCA Civ 420; [2013] QB 618 (CA), Lord Justice Toulson said:

> How is the rule of law itself to be policed? It is an age old question. *Quis custodiet ipsos custodes* – who will guard the guards themselves? In a democracy, where power depends on the consent of the people governed, the answer must lie in the transparency of the legal process. Open justice lets in the light and allows the public to scrutinise the workings of the law, for better or for worse. (para 1)

To understand why it is so dependent on transparency, it may be helpful to clarify what we mean by 'the rule of law'. In his book on the subject, Lord Bingham of Cornhill, having discussed both the long history of the concept and the variety of its previous definitions, suggested the following formulation:

> The core of the existing principle is, I suggest, that all persons and authorities within the state, whether public or private, should be bound by and entitled to the benefit of laws publicly made, taking effect (generally) in the future and publicly administered in the courts.[2]

He went on to explain that the law must be 'accessible and so far as possible intelligible, clear and predictable'. All of that depends on its being made and applied in an open and transparent way.

With that introduction, I now come to the four main ways in which the judiciary can promote public understanding of their role and of the rule of law more generally.

II. GIVING JUDGMENTS

This is the core function of judging. No one can be a judge who cannot make up his or her mind about the issues in a case and come to a decision. But in the context of open justice and in a common law system where judges not only decide individual cases but, in doing so, apply, interpret and develop the law, it is crucial that they explain their reasons clearly. As Lord Neuberger observed in a lecture in 2012, soon after he became President of the Supreme Court, legal professionals are 'only part of the audience' for judgments, whose real audience is the public:

> Judgments must speak as clearly as possible to the public. This is not to suggest that judgments could, or even should, aim to be bestsellers. Chance would be a fine thing. But every judgment should be sufficiently well-written to enable interested and reasonably intelligent non-lawyers to understand who the parties were, what the case was about, what the disputed issues were, what decision the judge reached, and why that decision was reached.[3]

---

[2] Lord Bingham, *The Rule of Law* (London, Allen Lane, 2010) 8.
[3] First annual BAILII lecture, 'No Judgment, No Justice', www.bailii.org/bailii/lecture/01.html.

In speaking of the public as the real audience for judgments, Lord Neuberger was making clear the public nature of the performance of justice, and emphasising the need for judgments to be accessible in terms both of style and of openness to public scrutiny. That the public do, in fact, read judgments is clear from the user statistics for the free website of the British and Irish Legal Information Institute (BAILII), which in 2019 reported over 12 million visits, totalling 75.2 million page views.[4] A large proportion of its users are non-lawyers, including many journalists (who are, in turn, a further channel for distribution of the content of judgments to the public).

Paradoxically, perhaps, the result of an increasing awareness of the need to give clear and comprehensive reasons for their judgments has been a tendency for judges to write much longer judgments, which may make these less amenable to public consumption. Another reason for their increasing length is that the technology permits it. In the days before computers (or what were quaintly called word processors), it was comparatively rare for judgments to be given in writing. An oral judgment, given extempore (at the end of the hearing) was the norm, and would be recorded for posterity by the official shorthand-writer to the court. Nowadays judgments in the senior courts are far more likely to be reserved, even if only overnight, and delivered in written form. There are still cases where judgment is given extempore, but for any case above a certain level of complexity there is now the expectation of a written judgment; and while it may be tempting for judges to dispose of a case on the day, their anxiety to ensure they have not omitted anything important and to make the case, so far as possible, 'appeal proof' means they will generally prefer to think about it overnight, if not for longer, before delivering their judgment. All this has added enormously to judicial workloads, and it is not unusual for some judges to write twenty or thirty thousand words in a week. This is an astonishing volume of output, particularly in view of judges' additional administrative and case management duties.

A. Judgments Promoting Transparency

Although an increasing number of judgments are, indeed, freely accessible to the public via BAILII and elsewhere, many still are not. It was to boost the availability of judgments from family courts and the Court of Protection that the then President of the Family Division, Sir James Munby, issued his *Practice Guidance on Transparency* in 2014.[5] His intention was that, even where cases were heard in private to protect the parties, a suitably anonymised judgment could and should

---

[4] New BAILII Briefing Paper (May 2020) www.bailii.org/bailii/BAILII%20Update%20May%20 2020.pdf.
[5] [2014] EWHC B3 (Fam); [2014] 1 WLR 230.

still be published. This would enable the public to gain a better understanding of the exercise of draconian public law powers sometimes exercised by the courts, such as permanently removing children from their parents or approving the withdrawal of artificial life support for terminally ill patients, as well as more routine matters relating to divorce and the lives of children. The guidance came not long after a speech in the latter part of 2013 when he had said: 'I am determined that the new Family Court should not be saddled, as the family courts are at present, with the charge that we are a system of secret and unaccountable justice.'

Although the idea of 'secret courts' has persisted, the president's agenda for transparency has resulted in vastly more judgments being published and has generated an expectation that publication should be the normal practice, rather than the exception. However, the numbers have fallen off in recent years, and compliance among judges was patchy from the start, as a study by three members of the Transparency Project found in 2017.[6] In part, this has been attributable to the lack of additional resources to manage the burden of preparing anonymised judgments for publication, particularly at county court level, and the not inconsiderable risks of 'jigsaw identification' of anonymised parties through the piecing together of unredacted information remaining in the published judgment with other information already in the public domain. As a way of promoting public legal education and transparency, therefore, the president's guidance has not yet achieved its full potential.

III. SPEECHES AND LECTURES

Speeches, lectures and other public appearances give judges the opportunity to explain their role, and to increase public understanding of what they do, without compromising their independence. The fact that speeches are often published online and may be reported in the media means that the benefit of what they say can be spread far wider than the particular audience to whom they were addressed.

'Amongst the qualities a candidate for the Supreme Court must show is "a willingness to participate in the wider representational role of a Supreme Court Justice, for example, delivering lectures", and our justices have certainly taken that quality to their hearts', noted Lord Justice Moses (while giving a lecture himself) in 2014.[7] He went on to list some of the recent lectures, some of them

---

[6] J Doughty, A Twaite and P Magrath, 'Transparency Through Publication of Family Court Judgments: An Evaluation of the Responses to, and Effects of, Judicial Guidance on Publishing Family Court Judgments Involving Children and Young People' (Cardiff University, 2017) http://orca.cf.ac.uk/view/cardiffauthors/A0406408.html.

[7] 'Hitting the Balls out of Court: Are Judges Stepping Over the Line?', The Creaney Memorial Lecture, 26 February 2014, www.judiciary.uk/wp-content/uploads/JCO/Documents/Speeches/moses-lj-speech-creaney-lecture-2014.pdf.

in exotic locations, given by Supreme Court Justices, and observed that 'unauthoritative though they may be', such lectures, like case law, 'can be cited for any proposition you may care to advance'.

That is a rhetorical exaggeration. Nevertheless, one of the advantages of speeches is that they enable the judicial mind to focus its energies on general themes or matters of principle, unconstrained by the scope of a particular *lis* or point in dispute between litigants. But they can also provide ammunition for intellectual rivalries or controversies. A practising lawyer or academic can speak freely enough about what they really think about the law or how it should change; but once on the bench, they should be careful not to suggest either that they regard the law which they are bound to apply as wrong, or that they might be tempted to bend that law, under the guise of adapting it to a new situation. They should certainly avoid discussing matters of political controversy or pronouncing on issues on which they may later be called on to decide judicially – as Lord Neuberger warned in a lecture rather pointedly entitled 'Where Angels Fear to Tread'.[8] Nevertheless, law reform is a fairly popular subject for judicial speech-making, along with human rights, the interplay of law and morality, the domestic courts' relationship with Strasbourg or Luxembourg jurisprudence, the independence of the judiciary, recruitment and diversity, and (about which more below) the relationship between the law and the press.

Speeches necessarily involve making a public appearance and this in itself needs to be considered carefully. The latest edition of the *Guide to Judicial Conduct* (March 2020)[9] warns that judges, when participating in public debate, 'should be careful to ensure that the occasion does not create a public perception of partiality towards a particular organisation (including a set of chambers or firm of solicitors), group or cause or to a lack of even handedness'.

Opportunities for giving speeches tend to be more plentiful at a senior level, to judges in leadership or managerial roles. Supreme Court Justices, especially the President of the Supreme Court, will continually be asked to speak. From the court's website, where they are published, it appears that in 2019 the members of the Supreme Court gave thirty speeches, just over half of which (sixteen) were given by its President, Lady Hale. Speeches by other judges are published on the Courts and Tribunals Judiciary website. From this, it appears that out of thirty-two speeches published in 2019, five were given by the Lord Chief Justice, Lord Burnett, nine by the Chancellor of the High Court, Sir Geoffrey Vos, four by the President of the Queen's Bench Division, Sir Brian Leveson, two by the Master of the Rolls, Sir Terence Etherton, and two by the President of the Family Division, Sir Andrew McFarlane. But those figures may be misleading, because they only

---

[8] Holdsworth Club 2012 Presidential Address, 2 March 2012, www.judiciary.uk/wp-content/uploads/JCO/Documents/Speeches/mr-speech-holdsworth-lecture-2012.pdf.

[9] www.judiciary.uk/wp-content/uploads/2018/03/Amended-Guide-to-Judicial-Conduct-revision-Final-v002.-March-2020-pdf.pdf.

represent the speeches published on the Judiciary website. As with judgments and other material published on that site, they tend to focus on the content that is deemed to be of interest to the media and public, and perhaps what one might call prospective litigants, rather than offering a complete or permanent archive. It follows that while the site does also publish some speeches by less senior judges, it certainly does not publish them all. High Court judges, circuit judges and other members of the judiciary may not be prevented or discouraged from giving speeches and lectures, but they are perhaps less likely to be publicised by the Judicial Press Office.

A. Journals and Books

Few judges have the time to write books while serving on the bench, but a speech or lecture can be published as an article or the chapter of a book. In this way, the original thought may reach a wider audience, or at least enjoy a longer shelf-life. Writing journal articles or contributing a book chapter is also, of course, a way for judges to communicate their ideas to the public, albeit a more specialised public than might be reached via the mainstream media.

For 'judge spotters' and legal commentators, though, such writings add yet another category of raw material for their musings and predictions as to future judicial behaviour. This may be an underexploited seam for data mining. Those who look for activism on the one hand, or quietism on the other, tend to focus on previous judgments, the scope of which are necessarily limited to the facts and issues in the particular cases. Incompleteness of data may result in decidedly faulty extrapolation. Nor does rummaging about for evidence of a privileged education or a dubious or creditable client list whilst in practice necessarily result in accurate prediction of how a judge will rule from the bench. Whereas the thoughts of a judge when writing a speech or article, nurtured by their experience and intellect, can more accurately reflect their own views about the development and practice of law.

To take an example, the recent *UK Supreme Court Yearbook (2017–18)*[10] contains a number of essays not just by Supreme Court Justices but also by other judges and senior practitioners and academics. Among them is an essay by Sir Geoffrey Vos on 'Incremental Changes to the Common Law', which in view of Sir Geoffrey's subsequent promotion to Master of the Rolls might be a better place to begin any attempt to calculate the likely future development of civil justice in the next few years than by trawling through his old judgments.

---

[10] *The UK Supreme Court Yearbook*, vol 9: *2017–2018 Legal Year* (Barlaston, Appellate Press, 2019).

B. The International Aspect

The *Yearbook* also demonstrates the international aspect to the Supreme Court's public facing role. Not only do its justices also sit as the Judicial Committee of the Privy Council, hearing appeals from British, Commonwealth and former colonial jurisdictions overseas, but as an apex court it acknowledges and exchanges jurisprudential ideas with other apex courts. This exchange of ideas is not confined to the consideration of case law, though that is probably the largest part of it: it extends also to the giving of speeches, often in other jurisdictions, and the publication of essays and articles in foreign journals and anthologies.

By way of example, the 2017–18 *Yearbook* not only includes essays by Lord Mance and Lord Reed respectively celebrating 'dialogue and cooperation' with other top courts and pointing out that 'we have contact with a large number of jurisdictions in all parts of the world', but also an essay by the Chief Justice of the High Court of Australia, Susan Kiefel, on 'The Significance of Comparative Law to Common Law Judges – An Australian Perspective'. She notes that:

> [T]o the extent that Australian lawyers have regard to foreign sources of law and legal materials, the focus is generally on other jurisdictions within the common law tradition – principally, although not exclusively, Canada, England and Wales, and New Zealand.

Both Lord Reed's and Kiefel CJ's chapters were based on lectures given at international conferences, thus further underlining the international communication by and between judges.

IV. ENGAGING DIRECTLY WITH THE MEDIA

It is not a good idea for a judge to be too close to or friendly with the press, or too ready to supply a comment or quote on matters of popular interest or controversy. Such publicity risks harming the public's respect for the judiciary more generally. But, done carefully, judicial engagement with the media can undoubtedly be beneficial.

As with giving speeches, judges can write articles for the press, or give interviews (eg to BBC Radio 4's *Law in Action* programme). Some even hold press conferences, although usually that would only be done by senior 'managerial' judges such as the Lord Chief Justice, the President of the Supreme Court, or the heads of divisions. None of this should threaten the independence of the judiciary, and if done well it can do much to reinforce respect for the rule of law.

One of the problems which needs to be addressed is that judges are often portrayed in the media as being somewhat elitist and 'out of touch'. It does not help that the language used by judges in court and in their judgments is often archaic and obscure and may even be peppered with expressions in Latin or Law French.

If they are so at home in the past, how likely are they to be in touch with the present and its concerns? It also does not help that, from time to time, reports emerge of a judge asking a question betraying their apparent ignorance of some aspect of popular culture or modern technology and being duly ridiculed for it in the popular press. Although it may seem harmless enough, this mythology of comic remoteness undermines respect for the judiciary when news reports turn to more serious topics, such as criminal sentencing or child care orders, and the idea that judges are out of touch can be much more damaging to the public's respect for the rule of law. There is a risk of its being exploited by politicians and pundits who favour simplistic solutions, or by special agenda groups who sow distrust of the system. All of this speaks of the need for the judiciary, somehow, to engage in a more positive way with the media, if that can be done without threatening the very independence it should serve to reinforce. The question is not if, but how.

The *Guide to Judicial Conduct* (mentioned above) warns that 'Judges should refrain from answering public criticism of a judgment or decision, whether from the bench or otherwise.' Rather than responding directly, the more specialised guidance set out in the *Media Guidance for the Judiciary* (2012)[11] (cited in the 2020 *Guide*) suggests judges refer the matter to the Judicial Press Office. In the case of serious misreporting by the media, 'it is recommended that you immediately inform your Bench Chair, Chamber President, Presiding Judge, the Chief Magistrate or Head of Division and your court or tribunal manager'.

If a case is likely to be newsworthy, and particularly if the subject matter is controversial, the guidance suggests taking precautionary measures which could include putting the judgment or sentencing remarks in writing and supplying a copy to the Judicial Press Office to enable them to deal with media queries as soon as they arise. Better still, have copies available for the reporters and keep them informed. Where the case is complex and technical in nature, a separate press summary can be provided alongside the full judgment, to assist in the accurate reporting of the case. By and large, the media are not out to 'get' the judiciary; they just want a topical story. It is far better that they should get an accurate version from the court than a garbled and lopsided version from one of the parties, their PR agents or a pressure group with a particular agenda to pursue. If the media still get it wrong, 'the Judicial Press Office can phone news editors or media legal departments to try to correct inaccuracies'.

In some cases, the press can even be recruited to assist in the administration of justice. Thus from time to time the press will be encouraged to report a case where, for example, a runaway parent has absconded from justice with a child who is the subject of family court proceedings. In the case of one such 'missing mum', Rebecca Minnock, HHJ Stephen Wildblood QC gave a judgment

---

[11] www.whatdotheyknow.com/request/125047/response/307849/attach/8/mediaguide2012%201.pdf.

expressly thanking the press for their coverage of the case and the help it had given in locating Ethan, the child in the case.[12]

This approach demonstrates the best that can be achieved by working with, rather than in spite of or at cross-purposes to, the media. The effect is twofold. First, it harnesses the undoubted power of media publicity in securing the ends of justice. If the errant parent can be located or persuaded to return to the court, the case can be resolved in a way that avoids a more drastic, possibly punitive solution. Second, the media reporting of the case is itself a form of public legal education, reinforcing the public's awareness of the court's role and that of other parties (such as the local authority), and the legal framework under which it operates in resolving the case.

A. Cameras in Court

An obvious way of engaging with the media is to allow their cameras into the court. There has been a steady process of opening the courts up to public view in this way, but it has been slow and tentative.

The original ban on the use of cameras dates back to the Criminal Justice Act 1925, section 41 of which prohibited not only photography but also drawing, which explains why courtroom artists must repeatedly nip out of the court to execute hurried sketches of the participants for reproduction in newspaper reports. There is also a ban on sound recording under section 9 of the Contempt of Court Act 1981.

When the UK Supreme Court was opened in 2009, having been created anew under the Constitutional Reform Act 2005, it was not subject to these restrictions and one of its major innovations has been to livestream, via its own website, video footage of all its hearings. In this and other respects, the Supreme Court has been a beacon of court transparency, but perhaps it can afford to be. Cases which reach the court have been whittled down to the few that involve points of general public importance and long-term legal significance. It does not handle the same volume as the other senior courts, let alone those lower down the hierarchy.

An amendment made by section 32 of the Crime and Courts Act 2013 made it possible for filming to take place in the Court of Appeal, Criminal Division. Although announced as a major development in 2013, this has not resulted in a significant volume of material being made available to public view. The footage has been used in some news and documentary broadcasts, such as an ITV documentary, *Inside the Court of Appeal*, broadcast in the summer of 2018.

---

[12] *Williams v Minnock* (unreported), 12 June 2015, Bristol Crown Court. See also J Doughty, L Reed and P Magrath, *Transparency in the Family Courts: Publicity and Privacy in Practice* (London, Bloomsbury Professional, 2018) appendix 1, case study 2, 247–49.

(Whilst this gave some idea of what anyone could have seen if they had turned up and sat in the public gallery, the courtroom scenes were actually quite few and far between. Most of the programme was devoted to what the voiceover described as 'the human stories behind the courtroom drama'.)

More successful has been the livestreaming of some proceedings in the Court of Appeal, Civil Division, since November 2018, via the Judiciary's own YouTube channel, Court 71 (named after the Master of the Rolls' court). The Judiciary website has a video archive page which enables viewers to see earlier cases. However, the potential for open justice is huge, and the retention of archive recordings, whether by the National Archives (who store the older Supreme Court footage) or the Judiciary's own website (using YouTube), would be of huge benefit not just for educational purposes but also for legal and academic research. One can even imagine, in the future, multimedia law reports that incorporate not just a note of the argument, as the official series of the *Law Reports* published by ICLR have done since 1865, but also copies of the written ('skeleton') arguments and recorded footage of the oral presentation or extempore judgment.

Attractive as these potential developments might be, it took the international crisis of a coronavirus pandemic to force the next big boost to court video access. One of the main purposes of the Coronavirus Act 2020 (by section 55 and Schedule 25) was to relax still further the statutory ban on court photography in order to permit the use of livestreaming and video technology to facilitate the conduct of multiparty remote court hearings. This has enabled court hearings to accommodate not just the judge, parties, lawyers and witnesses engaging in a videoconference hearing from remote locations, but also the attendance of the press and public. Cases were listed for remote hearing with an email address or other details enabling those wishing to access the hearing to find out how to join. Efforts to involve journalists were praised by the *Press Gazette*,[13] but there was concern that access for the public – a virtual public gallery – was rather less consistently provided. Nevertheless, the possibility of being able to watch High Court or county court proceedings on a computer, either by joining a videoconference session or via a livestream on YouTube, represented a major advance in transparency, which open justice campaigners have seized upon as a blueprint for the future. It remains to be seen whether, when the lockdown has been sufficiently relaxed to reduce the urgent need for remote hearings, the gains in transparency will be reversed or, as with the efficiency gains to the administration of justice, retained for those cases where the need for a physical hearing is not made out.

---

[13] 'Journalists Praise Courts for Remote Open Justice During Coronavirus Crisis' *Press Gazette*, 26 March 2020, www.pressgazette.co.uk/journalists-praise-courts-for-open-justice-via-video-link-during-coronavirus-crisis/.

V. SOCIAL MEDIA AND DIRECT PUBLIC ENGAGEMENT

The idea that judges are 'out of touch' with modern life is closely allied to an assumption that they are generally not very adept at modern technology. But these days the judiciary use mobile phones and laptops as a matter of course, and the massive HMCTS reform court modernisation programme was already making them quite proficient in videoconferencing and digital case management, long before the coronavirus pandemic suddenly forced everyone to switch to remote hearings. Therefore the idea that they are not either culturally or technologically competent to use social media simply does not stand scrutiny. Yet for some reason, judges cannot blog, let alone tweet. They have effectively been banned from doing so. Why?

The ban stems from an internal direction issued in August 2012[14] and incorporated or referred to in subsequent editions of the official *Guide to Judicial Conduct* (mentioned above) on the subject of what it rather prissily calls 'web logs'. While not strictly prohibiting blogging (or tweeting) outright, it makes clear that judges cannot do so either under their judicial names or anonymously – which does not really leave much of an option:

> Blogging by members of the judiciary is not prohibited. However, judicial office-holders who blog ... must not identify themselves as members of the judiciary. ... The above guidance also applies to blogs which purport to be anonymous.

It adds that: 'For the purpose of this guidance blogging includes publishing material on micro-blogging sites such as Twitter.'

In fact a number of judges are on Twitter, but without identifying themselves as such. Nor, in many cases, do they engage in discussions about legal matters. But they see what's going on, and that's no bad thing.

The position in the United States is markedly different. Judges are active on twitter and many also have a Facebook account, which they see as a legitimate way of engaging with the public, *as judges* – no differently from giving speeches or interviews or writing articles in the newspapers or journals. But then judges in many states are elected rather than being appointed, and social media is just one more way to get their campaign message across.

An example is Chief Justice Stephen Dillard, Chief Judge of the Court of Appeals of the State of Georgia. A popular figure on legal twitter, he is followed by[15] (and follows) many British and Irish lawyers as well as those in the United States and Canada. Nor is he alone among the US judiciary in being active on twitter. Many belong to or engage with an online community of appellate

---

[14] 'Blogging by Judicial Office Holders' *Judiciary*, August 2012, www.judiciary.uk/wp-content/uploads/JCO/Documents/Guidance/blogging-guidance-august-2012.pdf.

[15] For a convenient explanation of the technical terminology of Twitter, including the effect of 'following' other users, see the appendix to the judgment of Warby J in *Monroe v Hopkins* [2017] EWHC 433 (QB); [2017] 4 WLR 68.

lawyers and judges (#AppellateTwitter) who discuss professional issues in much the same informal collegiate way as, say, members of the English Bench and Bar might do while socialising in the Inns of Court or over tea in chambers or on a weekend course at Cumberland Lodge.

I mention Dillard because he has written to explain his presence on social media. In an article in the journal *Judicature*, entitled '#Engage – It's Time for Judges to Tweet, Like & Share'[16] he said he thought judges had 'a duty to educate those we serve about the important role the judiciary plays in their daily lives'. Although judges must preserve their independence and not become embroiled in partisan politics, that should not require them to withdraw entirely from the public eye:

> The pernicious perception that a judge must remain cloistered in his or her chambers in order to foster or maintain judicial independence needs to change. I'll say it again: Judges are public servants. They are accountable to the people, and they need to be accessible to the people, so long as they do so in a manner that is consistent with their oath of office and the code of judicial conduct.

Obviously, there are risks. There have been cases of judges in some states being required to recuse themselves after connecting on Facebook with lawyers appearing in their court. Others have been censured for posting derogatory comments about witnesses or parties in part-heard cases. But the potential for some judges to embarrass themselves on social media is not a good reason to ban them all from the medium. A judge who is capable of behaving in an embarrassing fashion on social media may do so in other spheres of activity, and perhaps it is no bad thing that their unsuitability for the office is exposed rather than shielded from public view. But to isolate social media for such failings is to blame the medium for the message.

In a common law system where judges interpret, apply and in some cases extend old law to new circumstances, they need to be able to do so with an awareness of how social attitudes may have changed. They cannot do so in isolation from the community that they serve, and while they cannot divine or assume a universal set of moral values, they should at least be aware of the range of such values and attitudes. If used wisely, social media, as well as news media and other sources, can help them maintain that awareness.

Even if the ban on twitter is understandable (it is a rowdy and impatient forum that does not encourage nuance or discretion), the ban on blogging is much harder to fathom. It seems odd that judges should not be trusted in this respect, when we repose so much trust in their discretion and judgement in other respects, and that they should be allowed to discuss their work in a speech at a conference or in an article for a learned journal, but not in a post on their own

---

[16] S Dillard, '#Engage – It's Time for Judges to Tweet, Like & Share' (2017) 101(1) *Judicature*, https://judicialstudies.duke.edu/sites/default/files/centers/judicialstudies/judicature/judicature_101-1_dillard.pdf.

or someone else's blog. As Lucy Reed, a family barrister who is active on twitter (as @Familoo) and founded the influential Transparency Project charity with other legal bloggers encountered via the medium, commented on the original guidance:

> We select judges for being thoughtful, careful people and it follows that those who dip a toe in the waters of blogging are likely to do so with appropriate caution and forethought (and in my experience they do so). We pay them to think before they open their mouths. So why not trust their judgement?[17]

In the meantime, serving judges may publish what are effectively blogs under the guise of some other medium, such as Sir James Munby's series of bulletins described as 'Views from the President's Chambers',[18] or the Newsletter from HHJ Wildblood QC which appeared for a while on the local family court information website which he helped set up.[19] It might even be argued that some judgments are effectively blog posts by the judges who wrote them, so obiter are the dicta in which they comment tangentially on such matters as legal aid resources, problems with court bundles, or in the case of Mr Justice Peter Smith, in *Emerald Supplies Ltd v British Airways* [2015] EWHC 2201 (Ch) ... his lost luggage.

Perhaps it is only after retirement that judges can truly be themselves on social media; at any rate, that was the triumphant experience of Sir Henry Brooke, a pioneer of court IT and modernisation, a leading light in the Society for Computers and Law and founding chair of trustees of BAILII. After his retirement from the Court of Appeal, he set up a blog[20] on which he wrote about anything from legal tech (he helped judge hackathons) to legal aid (he continued to volunteer at a local law centre). He discussed his own life and work and anything that took his fancy. And he became a familiar figure on twitter (@HenryBrooke1), commenting in an informal but judicious way about all manner of legal developments. In many ways, he was a model of how a serving judge might (if they had the time) engage with the public and profession on social media.

A. Other Forms of Direct Engagement with the Public

As a medium, YouTube provides a combination of social media posting and more formal public broadcasting. We have already seen how it has been harnessed to enable livestreaming of senior court hearings. Another use to which it may be put is public legal education. One of the best developments in

---

[17] 'Judiciary silenced Out of Court' *The Guardian*, 14 August 2012, Www.Theguardian.Com/Law/2012/Aug/14/Judiciary-Banned-Blogging-Tweeting.

[18] See eg [2013] Fam Law 548.

[19] Newsletter From HHJ Wildblood QC, December 17 (Family Court Information) www.family-courtinfo.org.uk/news/newsletter-from-hhj-wildblood-qc-dec-17/.

[20] Henry Brooke, *Musings, Memories and Miscellanea*, https://sirhenrybrooke.me/.

judicial communication in recent years has been the amount of material put out in this way by the Judiciary website in the form of embedded video interviews and 'chats to camera' by judges explaining their roles to the public. It might be stretching a point to describe this as 'vlogging' (video blogging) but it is certainly less formal than an official television documentary type presentation.

The material includes segments on 'Why Apply to be a High Court Judge?', 'What Is a Typical Day for a Circuit Judge?' and 'What Are the Challenges for a District Judge?' Each segment features a number of the judges speaking to camera about their jobs. There is another section in which a number of judges at different levels each give an overview of their judicial careers.[21]

Another section of the website is entitled 'Judiciary in the Community', and here again there is a range of material by which judges are able to explain their role to the public. This includes articles on the 'Judiciary in Schools', 'Diversity and Community Relations Judges' and 'Magistrates in the Community'. The activities described include organising mock trials for school children, mentoring and work experience schemes for those wanting to know more about the justice system, and other forms of engagement with the wider community 'through outreach work ... to dispel the myths that surround the judiciary giving people a more accurate understanding of the role of the judge and the justice system'. As the name implies, one of the primary functions of Diversity and Community Relations judges is also to encourage greater diversity among those applying to become judges, helping to promote the role among underrepresented groups.

VI. CONCLUSION

What this chapter will have shown, I hope, is that the modern judiciary of England and Wales is not only very far from conforming to the intellectually remote and socially aloof model promoted by the traditional Doctrine of Judicial Reticence, but also that they engage with the public they serve in more ways, and more often, than might be appreciated. While they have always given reasons for their decisions, the judgments they deliver now are more comprehensive and explanatory; and their ready availability on the internet has massively boosted public access to primary legal source material. Judges may have given speeches and lectures in the past, or contributed to journals and books, but here again the internet has made possible much wider dissemination of their ideas in this form. While their engagement with the media is cautious and limited, and with social media still more so, the idea that judges are remote, stuffy and out of touch with the realities of modern life is more completely a myth now than it has ever been. In short, where we have open justice we also, to an increasing extent, have an open judiciary.

---

[21] 'Judicial Careers', *Judiciary* website, www.judiciary.uk/about-the-judiciary/judges-career-paths/.

11

Legal Elites, Lord Chancellors and Judicial Independence

GRAHAM GEE

I. INTRODUCTION

J
UDGES AND LAWYERS are rightly proud of the long and rich tradition of judicial independence in the United Kingdom. They are also rightly proud of their own role in promoting and protecting that tradition. Establishing and nurturing a tradition of judicial independence is, after all, a long, gradual and complex process. It requires judges and lawyers to work with politicians to cultivate the conditions in which judges are equipped, individually and institutionally, to decide legal disputes impartially, according to law and free from improper pressure.[1] Today, many legal elites worry that this tradition is fraying, with ministers in the UK government viewed as principally to blame due to a supposed failure to grasp what judicial independence and the rule of law requires of them. The office of the Lord Chancellor has become a particular flashpoint for concerns such as these, with many in the legal establishment arguing that Lord Chancellors no longer serve as effective guardians of judicial independence. In this chapter, I argue that these worries are overwrought, misunderstand the reformed role of the Lord Chancellor, and reflect common mistakes about both Lord Chancellors and judicial independence.

This chapter's focus is, therefore, on the office of Lord Chancellor. This reflects – and inevitably also to some extent reinforces – the tendency of Lord Chancellors to cast a long shadow over debates about judicial independence. A long shadow continues to be cast even though this office was remodelled in 2005 in ways designed, for better or worse, to distance Lord Chancellors from the culture of the legal system. Yet for many judges and lawyers, the role of Lord Chancellor retains a totemic significance: it exemplifies the need for a

---

[1] See S Shetreet, 'Creating a Culture of Judicial Independence: The Practical Challenge and the Conceptual and Conceptual Infrastructure' in S Shetreet and C Forsyth (eds), *The Culture of Judicial Independence: Conceptual Foundations and Practical Challenges* (Leiden, Nijhoff, 2012) 17, 17.

shared understanding to straddle both the political and legal domains of the nature, content and importance of judicial independence. Today, despite the 2005 reforms, many legal elites still regard the willingness of Lord Chancellors to defend judges as a critical barometer of judicial independence. It seems only a slight exaggeration to suggest that for many in the legal establishment debates about judicial independence begin and end with the Lord Chancellor. This outsized focus on this one office, along with the apolitical expectations that many legal elites project onto its occupants, is a large part of the problem that I aim to address in this chapter. For whilst the Lord Chancellor remains an important part of the arrangements that institutionalise judicial independence in the UK, it is only part of a much more complex web of institutions, rules and practices which secure the constitutional position of the judiciary. Differently put: an outsized focus on this single office mistakes a part for the whole in ways that distort how we understand judicial independence.

My aim, then, is to contest how the relationship between Lord Chancellors and judicial independence is generally understood by legal elites. For these purposes I take 'legal elites' to include serving and retired judges, leading practitioners, government lawyers, legal academics and legal entrepreneurs such as members of think tanks, legal journalists and bloggers for whom high-profile activity near the heart of political life is part of their roles.[2] Together these legal elites form what might be termed the legal establishment. There is of course a diversity of views amongst legal elites, but the premise of this chapter is that there is a dominant view shared by many (albeit not all) of those who comprise the legal establishment. I also focus only on the Lord Chancellor's functions in respect of judicial independence, and not on wider responsibilities that the office may have in respect of the rule law.[3] I begin in section II by mapping the judiciary-related responsibilities of the post-2005 office of Lord Chancellor along with the changed professional profiles of its occupants. In section III, I point to some mistakes that legal elites commonly make about this office, and I argue in section IV that each of these framed how the legal establishment assessed the performance of then Lord Chancellor, Liz Truss, in the frenzied fallout of the High Court's decision in the Article 50 litigation in 2016. Contrary to received opinion in the legal sphere, I suggest that events surrounding this litigation demonstrate not the precariousness of the political commitment to judicial independence in the United Kingdom, but rather its enduring strength.

---

[2] This is informed by D Kavanagh, 'Changes in the Political Class and its Culture' (1992) 45 *Parliamentary Affairs* 18, 27.

[3] The Lord Chancellor's duties in respect of the rule of law came into the spotlight at the time of writing in the context of the Internal Market Bill. The office's duties in respect of the rule of law are contested and ill-defined. Much of my analysis about the unrealistic apolitical expectations often projected onto Lord Chancellors in respect of judicial independence apply in respect of the rule of law, but I limit my focus to judicial independence. See the House of Lords Constitution Committee, *The Office of Lord Chancellor* (December 2014) HL 75 paras 43–51.

II. LORD CHANCELLORS

The modern form and function of the Lord Chancellor is regulated by the Constitutional Reform Act 2005, which refashioned this ancient office from a peculiar part of the historic constitution into a conventional ministerial job. Prior to 2005, the Lord Chancellor combined executive, legislative and judicial functions, with the officeholder the constitutional head of the judiciary in England and Wales, who enjoyed the right to sit in a judicial capacity in the United Kingdom's top court, which at that time was the Appellate Committee of the House of Lords. In its modern incarnation, the office has been stripped of its judicial functions and is now a midranking cabinet post with ministerial responsibility for the administration of justice. This ministerial portfolio includes five functions relating directly to judicial independence. First, the Lord Chancellor must ensure that the courts are efficient, effective and properly resourced.[4] Second, the Lord Chancellor determines the pay, pensions and conditions of judicial service.[5] Third, the Lord Chancellor is responsible for the judicial appointments system in England and Wales, and retains a limited residual role at the conclusion of the selection processes for senior judicial vacancies, including the UK Supreme Court.[6] Fourth, the Lord Chancellor shares responsibility (with the Lord Chief Justice) for judicial disciplinary proceedings, and must account to parliament for the working of the complaints system as a whole.[7] Finally, the Lord Chancellor has a statutory duty 'to have regard to the need to defend' judicial independence.[8] The requirement on the Lord Chancellor to uphold judicial independence is also reflected in a statutory oath that each new officeholder is required to swear upon appointment.[9] These responsibilities are the result of the 2005 reforms, but the office has continued to evolve in the intervening fifteen years. Notably, the post of Lord Chancellor has been combined since 2007 with the separate position of Secretary of State for Justice; in other words, these are separate but twinned roles to which the Prime Minister appoints the same person.

Today, the prime minister can in effect appoint whosoever he or she wishes as Lord Chancellor. True, unlike every other ministerial post, there is a statutory provision requiring the prime minister to be satisfied that the person selected for the job is 'qualified by experience'.[10] This was supposed to signal that appointments to this role should be treated differently than other ministerial

---

[4] Courts Act 2003, s 1; and Tribunals, Courts and Enforcement Act 2007, s 39.

[5] The Concordat, para 29.

[6] Constitutional Reform Act 2005, Part 4, as amended by the Crime and Courts Act 2013, Schedule 13.

[7] Constitutional Reform Act 2005, ss 109–19.

[8] ibid s 3(6)(a).

[9] ibid s 17.

[10] ibid s 2(1).

jobs, but the provision also permits prime ministers to take into account any experience that he or she deems relevant, and so in practice does not curb the prime minister's discretion.[11] This is a striking change, since prior to 2005 prime ministers would by convention always appoint a lawyer of 'first-class ability'[12] as Lord Chancellor. Typically, the Lord Chancellor was a politician with substantial experience in legal practice or a barrister (or occasionally a judge) with similar political sympathies as the government of the day. This requirement to select a respected lawyer reflected the fact that the pre-2005 office carried important judicial functions, including serving as the head of the judiciary. Today, there is no requirement for the Lord Chancellor to be a lawyer – and since 2005 only five of nine have been legally qualified. The political profiles of Lord Chancellors have also changed. Before 2005, the person selected was usually in the twilight of their careers, with their appointment as Lord Chancellor the ultimate profes-sional accolade, as well as their final role before retirement. If not already a peer, the appointee was elevated to the House of Lords and was thereby removed from much of the rough-and-tumble of political life. By contrast, the people appointed today are jobbing politicians with realistic ambitions for future advancement up the ministerial ladder, as reflected in the fact that six of the eight appointed between 2005 and 2019 subsequently served in at least one other front-bench position. In a similar vein, all of the Lord Chancellors since 2007 have been members of parliament. This has catapulted the role of Lord Chancellor into the hurly-burly of electoral politics, but also ensured that ministerial power is legitimised by the greater democratic accountability flow-ing from the office-holder's status as a member of parliament answerable to the House of Commons.

The result of the 2005 reforms is, then, that the Lord Chancellor is now a pared-down role in three overlapping respects. First, the position is now focused exclusively on executive responsibilities. Several of the responsibilities still relate to the judiciary, but many previously exercised by Lord Chancellors have been hived off to the Lord Chief Justice or arm's-length bodies such as the Judicial Appointments Commission. Second, in line with this focus on executive duties, there is no longer any requirement for prime ministers to appoint eminent lawyers at their end of their careers, with those appointed tending to resemble career politicians found in other cabinet jobs. Third, the officeholder no longer has an exclusive focus on the courts and judiciary, since the job is twinned with that of Secretary of State for Justice, which means that the former's policy portfolio competes in terms of time and resources alongside the latter's responsibility for prisons and probation. It is by design that the role is slimmed down in these ways. The office's executive responsibilities had grown in importance since the 1970s, but the Blair government felt that Lord Chancellors were insufficiently focused

---

[11] ibid s 2(2).
[12] RFV Heuston, *Lives of the Lord Chancellors: 1940–1970* (Oxford, Clarendon Press, 1987) 3.

on the delivery of government policy.[13] On this view, rather than immersion in the legal system, Lord Chancellors require a political grounding, with a similar set of skills as other ministers, such as the ability to manage both ministerial colleagues and external stakeholders, the political muscle to fight for resources, and the political agility to hold their own in fevered partisan debate.[14] Thus, the thrust of the reforms was to convert the Lord Chancellor into a conventional ministerial job detached from the culture of the legal system and aligned instead with governmental priorities.[15]

Care is required when drawing a distinction between pre-2005 and post-2005 Lord Chancellors for the office had been changing even prior to 2005, and in particular its executive responsibilities had expanded significantly since the 1970s, as noted above. There is a sense, in other words, that the 2005 reforms accelerated a transformation that was already well underway. It is also the case that care is required when drawing a line between the professional profiles of pre-2005 and post-2005 Lord Chancellors, since several officeholders have embraced elements of both the old and the new. Some post-2005 Lord Chancellors have been willing to pursue policies that disturb the entrenched interests of the judiciary and legal community in ways consistent with the logic of the 2005 reforms (Chris Grayling, for example), but there have also been sober and consensual figures who carefully fostered the confidence of legal elites in ways similar to pre-2005 Lord Chancellors (for example, David Gauke). Despite this, it remains clear that the Lord Chancellor is today a pared-down job, and it remains possible to talk meaningfully of pre-2005 and post-2005 configurations of the office. This leads many legal elites to worry that Lord Chancellors tend now to be deflated figures inside Whitehall who are unable and/or unwilling to defend judicial independence. It is against this background that I want to consider some common mistakes that legal elites make about Lord Chancellors.

III. COMMON MISTAKES ABOUT LORD CHANCELLORS

The Lord Chancellor occupies an outsized place in the constitutional imagination of legal elites. This is evident in the exaggerated importance that many in the legal community continue to attach to the reformed office together with the way in which they assess the performance of the politicians who occupy it. Underpinning this are three related mistakes that legal elites commonly make about the office of Lord Chancellor. The first mistake is that many in the legal establishment romanticise pre-2005 Lord Chancellors, usually by appealing to

---

[13] See T Blair, *The Journey* (London, Hutchinson, 2010) 632.

[14] See also J Rozenberg, 'Extinct? The Lawyer Lord Chancellor?' *Counsel*, October 2017.

[15] On the cultural changes to the department headed by the Lord Chancellor, see G Gee, R Hazell, K Malleson and P O'Brien, *The Politics of Judicial Independence in the UK's Changing Constitution* (Cambridge, Cambridge University Press, 2015) 43–45.

an idealised vision of the old-style officeholder as an infallible guardian of the constitutional position of the judiciary, which leads them in turn to harbour unrealistic expectations of the post-2005 officeholders. The starting point here is that prior to 2005 the Lord Chancellor was subject to a customary duty to protect judicial independence. In the words of a pre-2005 officeholder, effective performance of this duty was the Lord Chancellor's 'essential function'.[16] This duty was commonly assumed to entail ensuring that the courts received adequate resources, ensuring government policy did not encroach upon the constitutional function of the courts and cajoling ministerial colleagues to refrain from publicly criticising judicial decisions. This last limb traditionally featured prominently, given the constitutional convention that ministers avoid criticism that risks undermining judicial independence or eroding public confidence in the judiciary.[17]

Several factors were usually said to leave Lord Chancellors uniquely well placed to defend judicial independence.[18] The intertwining of executive and judicial functions meant that the old-style Lord Chancellors spent time with both ministerial and judicial colleagues, and in this way could foster the confidence of each group, which helped to ensure that judicial and government policy usually coincided.[19] If tensions arose between ministers and judges, Lord Chancellors could act as a private conduit to convey the concerns of one to the other, with the office's constitutional status as head of the judiciary widely assumed to lend a special weight when its occupants raised objections within cabinet to measures that might encroach upon judicial independence. Normally in the final stages of their eminent legal careers and insulated to some degree from short-term electoral pressures by virtue of sitting in the House of Lords, the Lord Chancellor was assumed to have little to fear from confronting colleagues, including the prime minister. Through this combination of attributes pre-2005 Lord Chancellors were assumed to be advocates inside government for judicial independence, functioning as bulwarks against executive interference with the judiciary.

There is clear evidence that the pre-2005 Lord Chancellors indeed took seriously their customary duty to defend judicial independence inside government and were frequently effective in ensuring that governmental priorities did not undermine the constitutional function of the courts. However, a reasoned assessment of the pre-2005 office would recognise its value in promoting a basic respect for judges and the judicial system within government, but whilst also

---

[16] Lord Hailsham, 'The Office of Lord Chancellor and the Separation of Powers' (1989) 8 *Civil Justice Quarterly* 308, 311.

[17] S Shetreet and S Turenne, *Judges on Trial: The Independence and Accountability of the English Judiciary*, 2nd edn (Cambridge, Cambrdige University Press, 2013) 400–05.

[18] See Gee et al (n 15) 32–54.

[19] See D Oliver, 'The Lord Chancellor as Head of the Judiciary' in L Blom-Cooper, B Dickson and G Drewry (eds), *The Judicial House of Lords 1876–2009* (Oxford, Oxford University Press, 2009) 97.

acknowledging that it was not entirely effective in containing inevitable tensions between judges and ministers. Many in the legal community do not engage in a reasoned assessment of the pre-2005 office-holders, but romanticise it by over-looking the extent to which by the 1980s and 1990s legal elites were invoking the rubric of judicial independence to criticise successive Lord Chancellors.[20] There were several occasions where senior judges and lawyers criticised Lord Chancellors for pursuing policies that many in the legal establishment viewed (rightly or wrongly) as imperilling judicial independence.[21] For example, many judges criticised the policies of two Lord Chancellors (Lord Mackay in 1989 and Lord Irvine in 1998) to reform the monopoly of barristers on rights of audience in court. Those policies were said to amount to ministerial interference with the legal profession, and by extension inappropriate ministerial interference with the judiciary itself. Further vocal criticism from serving and retired judges was directed at Lord Mackay in 1994 for what many legal elites viewed as an inappropriate attempt to pressure the president of the Employment Appeals Tribunal to adopt a new procedure in order to cut costs.[22] Many legal elites also forget that by the 1990s the Lord Chancellor was no longer wholly effective in preventing tensions between ministers and judges from bursting into public view. Successive home secretaries reacted aggressively to unfavourable judicial decisions,[23] without being rebuked publicly by Lord Chancellors, although it is of course possible that rebukes were delivered in private behind the veil of collective responsibility.

The point is that by the close of the twentieth century there was evidence that Lord Chancellors were not the unfailing guardians of judicial independence that many legal elites seem to imply. This is not to deny the role performed by Lord Chancellors in cultivating a basic respect for the judicial function inside government; rather, it is to recognise that Lord Chancellors were important but imperfect guardians. It is also to recognise that by the mid-1990s successive Lord Chancellors sometimes struggled to retain the confidence of judges whilst exercising effectively their executive responsibilities, especially given that efficiency and value for money acquired a higher salience for ministers in the administration of justice.[24] This is not always kept in mind when comparing office-holders. Whenever post-2005 office-holders fall short of the legal establishment's expectations, there is a tendency to lazily assume that pre-2005 Lord Chancellors would inevitably have risen to those expectations.

---

[20] See J Rozenberg, *Trial of Strength: The Battle between Ministers and Judges over Who Makes the Law* (London, Richard Cohen, 1997) 20–24.

[21] See R Stevens, *The Independence of the Judiciary: The View from the Lord Chancellor's Office* (Oxford, Oxford University Press, 1993) and D Woodhouse, *The Office of Lord Chancellor* (Oxford, Hart Publishing, 2001).

[22] See eg Sir Francis Purchas, 'What Is Happening to Judicial Independence?' (1994) 144 *New Law Journal* 6665, 1306.

[23] See A Le Sueur, 'The Judicial Review Debate: From Partnership to Friction' (1996) 31 *Government and Opposition* 8.

[24] See Lord Browne-Wilkinson, 'The Independence of the Judiciary in the 1980s' [1988] PL 44.

This is related to a second mistake that many legal elites commonly make, namely expecting post-2005 Lord Chancellors to behave in similar ways as their predecessors and, when they behave differently, to conclude that this means that new-style Lord Chancellors cannot effectively defend judicial independence. As we have seen, the Constitutional Reform Act stripped the office of Lord Chancellor of the attributes traditionally said to leave its occupants uniquely well placed to defend judicial independence. Lord Chancellors are no longer necessarily lawyers or required to sit in the House of Lords. There is no longer an expectation that they should be in their final role before retirement. Nor do they have the close day-to-day contact with senior judges that helps to nurture a mutual confidence and understanding. Instead, the post-2005 Lord Chancellors are first and foremost politicians, ensconced in the wider political culture and appointed to help the government to secure its policy objectives. Even post-2005 Lord Chancellors who have been legally qualified tend not to have the same immersion in legal practice as their predecessors, with their values and interests shaped more by Westminster and Whitehall than by Temple and the Inns of Court. In speeches, media interviews and evidence sessions before select committees, Lord Chancellors today sound like politicians grounded in the political realm, with their comments sometimes displaying only a limited appreciation of legal niceties and at other times displaying the rhetorical slipperiness familiar to political discourse.[25] They bring a different mindset and attributes to the job, viewing the role as not about protecting entrenched interests in the judicial system, but about implementing government policy in the public interest. In so doing, they will likely bring a more expansive notion of the public interest when weighing up judicial opposition to this or that government policy. They may be more keenly aware that the language of judicial independence has in the past been invoked by judges and lawyers to frustrate legitimate demands for greater openness and accountability in the justice system.[26] In brief, the post-2005 Lord Chancellors do not always sound like, or behave in ways similar to, their pre-2005 predecessors, but this does not mean that they cannot and will not defend judicial independence.

On the contrary, new-style post-2005 Lord Chancellors can and do protect judicial independence. Patrick O'Brien, Robert Hazell, Kate Malleson and I conducted 150 confidential interviews with many of those most closely involved in in the administration of justice between 2011 and 2015, including senior judges, politicians and officials. In those interviews a number of senior judges and officials commended post-2005 Lord Chancellors for taking seriously their

---

[25] For examples of post-2005 Lord Chancellors displaying a limited grasp of legal subtleties, consider Ken Clarke's inability to recall that there was one woman on the Supreme Court: House of Lords Constitution Committee, *Annual Meeting with the Lord Chancellor: Uncorrected Evidence* (19 January 2011) Q27.

[26] See eg R Brazier, 'Government and the Law: Ministerial Responsibility for Legal Affairs' [1989] *PL* 64, 74.

duty to protect judicial independence.[27] More recently, in a private seminar in 2020, a senior official who worked closely with five post-2005 Lord Chancellors suggested that each took seriously their oath to respect the independence of the judiciary,[28] whilst conceding that not all passed 'the oath test' with flying colours. The point is that Lord Chancellors will today defend judicial independence in a manner consistent with the fact that they are conventional politicians. They might thus be characterised as 'political guardians' of judicial independence, not only in the banal sense that they are ordinary politicians, but also in the more interesting sense that their willingness and capacity to defend the judiciary will be shaped by and responsive to the political process.[29] For example, they will tend to be reactive guardians, insofar as there will likely be more occasions where ministers propose policies that potentially interfere with the independent administration of justice, but where pressures inside the political system ultimately persuade Lord Chancellors to convince their ministerial colleagues to ditch the offending policies.[30] As a conventional politician, partisan considerations will inevitably weigh heavily in their decisions whether and how to defend judicial independence, with private rebukes of ministerial colleagues who criticise judicial decisions more likely than public rebukes. It may also sometimes seem as if Lord Chancellors do the right thing by defending the independence of the judiciary only after exhausting all other possibilities.[31]

Admittedly, this makes it difficult to know how rigorously any particular Lord Chancellor defends judicial independence. However, there is reason to believe that new-style Lord Chancellors have dissuaded colleagues from publicly criticising judicial decisions on occasion and, where colleagues have spoken out in public, rebuked them in private. A particular challenge arises if the offender is the prime minister, since it is difficult to admonish a political superior with the power to promote, demote and sack. Even here, there is an example where a post-2005 Lord Chancellor indirectly reprimanded the prime minister for intemperate criticism of the courts. In 2011, it was reported in the press that the then Lord Chancellor Ken Clarke wrote privately to the home secretary to remind her of ministers' duty to uphold judicial independence, copying the letter to the prime minister, after Theresa May (then home secretary) and David Cameron (then prime minister) were considered by many to have been excessively critical of the Supreme Court's decision in *R(F) v Secretary of State for the Home Department*.[32] To be clear, my argument is not that the post-2005

---

[27] Gee et al (n 15) 32–54.

[28] Private seminar, *Taking Stock of the Constitutional Reform Act 2005* (21 January 2020, Queen Mary).

[29] G Gee, 'What Are Lord Chancellors For?' [2014] PL 11, 25–26.

[30] One example concerns the Supreme Court's funding, where in 2009–10 the government initially refused to make up a shortfall after the court service failed to pay monies owed. Only a concerted effort by officials convinced the Lord Chancellor to make up the shortfall: G Gee, 'Guarding the Guardians: The Chief Executive of the UK Supreme Court' [2013] PL 538, 540–44.

[31] ibid 25.

[32] *R(F) v Secretary of State for the Home Department* [2010] UKSC 17.

Lord Chancellors are more effective than their predecessors. Nor do I claim that they always defend judicial independence as proactively as many legal elites desire. They are imperfect guardians, as were their predecessors. My contention is simply that, contrary to what some suggest, post-2005 Lord Chancellors can and do defend judicial independence inside government, but in ways which are consistent with the reformed nature of the office they occupy. It follows that it is wrong to suggest that there is no longer any value in retaining the role. There is value in having a minister tasked with the special responsibility for promoting judicial independence, who on their first day in the job receives a briefing from civil servants on that responsibility, and who attends cabinet briefed on policy questions potentially touching on it.[33]

A third common mistake is that many legal elites seem to cling to a 'saviour theory', whereby the importance of the Lord Chancellor for securing the constitutional position of the judiciary is vastly overstated. It almost seems, under the saviour theory, that the independence of the judiciary hangs on whether or not each Lord Chancellor visibly, energetically and proactively defends judges from each and every possible challenge, whether emanating from inside government or beyond. Today, the saviour theory is perversely strong: although the logic of the 2005 reforms was to dilute the role of the Lord Chancellor within the constitutional architecture, many legal elites now seem to pay even greater attention to Lord Chancellors and their role in promoting judicial independence. This obscures the fact that there have been always been other guardians of judicial independence and legal values inside the UK government beyond the Lord Chancellor alone. Others include the law officers (who advise the government on legal matters and help to ensure that minister act legally and in compliance with the rule of law); parliamentary counsel (in the principles they apply when drafting legislation); and lawyers in the Government Legal Service (who caution ministers where they risk transgressing the boundaries of the law and constitutional principle). Hidden from view behind the Whitehall curtain, their role in ensuring that the everyday work of government upholds judicial independence and legal values is largely invisible to outsiders, but vital nevertheless. Since 2005, an additional layer has been superimposed on this institutional landscape, with new public bodies such as the Judicial Appointments Commission having roles to play in upholding judicial independence. The saviour theory also obscures the role that judges have long played in defending their own independence, as illustrated by important interventions in policy debates through the years by senior judges such as the Lord Chief Justice. Senior judicial leaders such as the Lord Chief Justice and the President of the Supreme Court today have various tools available to them to seek to defend their independence, including the power to lay written representations before parliament on matters 'of importance

---

[33] *cf* P O'Brien, 'Does the Lord Chancellor Really Exist?' *UK Constitutional Law Blog*, 26 June 2012, https://ukconstitutionallaw.org/2013/06/26/patrick-obrien-does-the-lord-chancellor-really-exist/.

relating to the judiciary',[34] the ability to make an intervention in the media and the standing to request a meeting with the prime minister.[35]

IV. THE ARTICLE 50 LITIGATION

The combination of these common mistakes distorts how many legal elites understand the office of Lord Chancellor, and more particularly how they assess the performance of those who now occupy this reformed role, with this best illustrated by the furore surrounding the litigation on the Article 50 process for leaving the European Union. On 3 November 2016 the High Court held in *Miller v Secretary of State for Exiting the European Union* that the government could not rely on the prerogative to initiate the Article 50 process and instead required prior parliamentary authorisation via statute.[36] This complicated the government's plans for exiting the European Union at a time when the political atmosphere was charged and when passions were running high on all sides. The coverage in the Eurosceptic press on 4 November was predictably over the top, with the *Daily Mail* running a banner headline 'Enemies of the People' under photographs of the judges who handed down the decision.

On that same morning the then Lord Chancellor, Liz Truss, was reported to have written to her ministerial colleagues 'stressing that the judges were independent and urging them to desist from' intemperate criticism,[37] which was an appropriate intervention given that some members of parliament had been on the media criticising the High Court. But over the next twenty-four hours, Truss was criticised by retired judges, lawyers and legal academics for not issuing a statement defending the judges from what they regarded as a media attack not only 'on the judges who made the decision' but also on 'public confidence in the judiciary and the rule of law'.[38] For many legal elites, Truss's public silence was a serious failure to satisfy the statutory duty on Lord Chancellors to uphold judicial independence. According to one account, Truss was initially dissuaded by aides to the prime minister from responding to this criticism by issuing a press release. Around thirty-six hours after the judgment, and after much toing and froing inside Whitehall, Truss issued a press release affirming the importance of judicial independence and the rule of law and noting the government's intention to appeal to the Supreme Court. But for many in the legal community, this statement was mealy-mouthed in not explicitly condemning the *Daily Mail*'s headline. Emblematic was the reaction of the former Lord Chief Justice, Lord Judge, who said Truss may have acted unlawfully by failing to defend

---

[34] See Constitutional Reform Act 2005, s 5.

[35] On the latter, see Gee et al (n 15) 134.

[36] *Miller v Secretary of State for Exiting the European Union* [2016] EWHC 2768 (Admin).

[37] T Shipman, *Fall Out: A Year of Political Mayhem* (London, William Collins, 2017) 51.

[38] Lord Thomas, *The Judiciary Within the State – The Relationships between the Branches of the State* (Michael Ryle Memorial Lecture, 15 June 2017) para 49.

the judiciary more forcefully.[39] Several prominent lawyers also called on Truss to resign, including her political opponent the former Lord Chancellor, Lord Falconer.[40]

The dominant view in the legal establishment was clear that Truss spectacularly failed in her role as Lord Chancellor by not condemning the coverage and being too slow to publicly defend the judges. This view trades on six assumptions and echoing throughout each are the common mistakes about Lord Chancellors discussed above.[41] First, it is assumed that there was an indisputable need to defend judicial independence. Second, this need triggered the Lord Chancellor's statutory duty to uphold judicial independence. Third, it was only possible for the Lord Chancellor to vindicate this statutory duty by issuing a public statement. Fourth, this statement had to be issued within hours of the press coverage in order to satisfy the statutory duty. Fifth, only the Lord Chancellor was able to take effective action to defend the High Court, and in particular judges were unable to defend themselves. Sixth, pre-2005 Lord Chancellors would have instinctively recognised the need to publicly defend the judges and would have done so promptly and unambiguously. As I see it, each assumption is questionable.

First, for many legal elites, the press coverage constituted abuse of the judges and a serious attack on judicial independence, with particular ire reserved for the *Daily Mail*'s headline which relied on 'a phrase used by tyrants throughout history to justify the persecution and death of those who do not toe the line'.[42] The *Daily Mail*'s headline was ill-advised and excessive, as was some of the other coverage. Given the political temperature at the time it is both unsurprising and regrettable that the Lord Chief Justice felt it necessary for the first time in his career to liaise with the police to ensure appropriate security precautions were in place.[43] But it is not clear that the coverage was a serious challenge to judicial independence – and few of Truss's critics spelt out how the coverage posed such a challenge. Certainly, the coverage did not undermine the common indicia of judicial independence (security of tenure, a stable and reasonable remuneration, merit-based appointments and so forth). Nor was the coverage likely to influence

---

[39] 'Liz Truss May Have Broken Law in Failing to Defend Brexit Judges, Warns Former Lord Chief Justice' *The Independent*, 19 November 2016, www.independent.co.uk/news/uk/politics/liz-truss-broken-law-failing-defend-brexit-judges-warns-former-lord-chief-justice-igor-article-50-a7426511.html.

[40] 'Justice Secretary Must Quit for Failing Judges, Says Ex-Law Chief' *The Times*, 9 November 2016, www.thetimes.co.uk/article/justice-secretary-must-quit-for-failing-judges-says-ex-law-chief-lxdbrb2ll.

[41] See G Gee, 'A Tale of Two Constitutional Duties: Liz Truss, Lady Hale and *Miller*', Policy Exchange Judicial Power Project (28 November 2016) https://judicialpowerproject.org.uk/graham-gee-a-tale-of-two-constitutional-duties-liz-truss-lady-hale-and-miller/.

[42] Lord Burnett, *Becoming Stronger Together* (Commonwealth Judges and Magistrates' Association Annual Conference, 10 September 2018) para 30.

[43] House of Lords Constitution Committee, *Corrected Oral Evidence: Oral Evidence Session with the Lord Chief Justice* (22 March 2017) Q4.

individual judges. Truss was surely correct to note in a letter to *The Times* a few days later that the High Court was unlikely to be 'imperilled by the opinions of any newspaper'. Some legal elites assumed that the *Daily Mail*'s headline was an attempt to influence the Supreme Court, which would hear the appeal a few weeks later – but, if it was, this was ham-fisted, and more likely to produce the opposite outcome by emboldening the Supreme Court to be seen resisting media pressure. The headline was doubtless, above all, an attempt to sell newspapers using provocative language that would appeal to Brexit-supporting readers. Of course, it could be suggested that the headline risked eroding public confidence in judges at a time of more general volatility in public opinion. But with the benefit of hindsight there is no evidence that the headline and related coverage eroded public confidence, with the public's reaction to the Supreme Court's decision a couple of months later extremely muted.[44]

Second, even if it is accepted that the coverage risked eroding public confidence in the judiciary, it is not clear that this was sufficient to trigger the statutory duty on the Lord Chancellor to defend judicial independence beyond the steps that she took. Recall that on the morning after the decision, Truss was reported to have written to ministerial colleagues reminding them not to publicly criticise the High Court, which was an appropriate response. Truss could have reasonably concluded that she had thereby satisfied her duty. After all, this duty is best understood as applying to – and is also likely to be most effective in respect of – the Lord Chancellor's functions, which include encouraging ministerial colleagues to respect judicial independence. There is space for debate about how much wider this duty should apply, including for example whether it should apply to the behaviour of non-governmental actors such as a newspaper. Truss did not think her duty required condemnation of the press coverage, and indeed she viewed any such ministerial comment as improperly intruding upon press freedom. The Lord Chief Justice was critical of this a few months later, describing Truss's view as 'completely and utterly wrong',[45] presumably on the basis that the statutory duty does not make any exception for freedom of the press.[46] But it bears emphasis that section 3(6) of the Constitutional Reform Act only requires Lord Chancellors to 'have regard to the need to defend' judicial independence, while also requiring them to 'have regard to the need for the public interest' to be taken into account in matters relating to the judiciary.

---

[44] O'Brien argues that media criticism only rarely risks genuine harm to judicial independence but concludes that the *Miller* case and the febrile environment was an example because the coverage risked inciting hatred of particular judges or judges as a profession in ways that might lead judges to feel unable to decide impartially. True, some litigants in person were reported as calling judges 'enemies of the people'. But, beyond this, it is not clear what evidence leads O'Brien to conclude that *Miller* reached this level of risk. P O'Brien, '"Enemies of the People": Judges, the Media and the Mythic Lord Chancellor' [2017] *PL* 135, 143–44.

[45] House of Lords Constitution Committee, *Corrected Oral Evidence: Oral Evidence Session with the Lord Chief Justice* (22 March 2017) Q4.

[46] P Daly, 'Judicial Independence and Accountability in the British Constitution (2019) *European Journal of Constitutional Law* 141, 157.

It is plausible that a Lord Chancellor could conclude that her duty was met by ensuring ministers did not criticise the High Court and that consideration of the public interest in the open scrutiny of judicial rulings meant that it would be inappropriate to comment on what is acceptable for the press to print lest this chill future press comment on the judiciary.

Third, even if one accepts that the statutory duty was triggered by the coverage it does not follow that vindicating it required a public statement. In such circumstances the Lord Chancellor could reasonably conclude that the duty would be more effectively satisfied by speaking privately to the proprietors or editors of the newspapers to explain why the coverage was excessive, to remind them of the public interest in an independent judiciary, and to urge moderation in future coverage. Part of the price for making behind-the-scene entreaties may be to forgo public comment, and the Lord Chancellor may have to live with criticism for apparent inaction from political opponents and other commentators. In a similar vein, in the sort of circumstances surrounding the *Miller* litigation, a Lord Chancellor could reasonably conclude that a public statement might aggravate matters by giving more legs to the furore over the coverage than might otherwise be the case. Interestingly in a private seminar, in the context of a discussion about criticism of lower-level judges by local press, a senior judge acknowledged that it is sometimes counterproductive for the Lord Chief Justice to comment publicly on such criticism.[47] Similar reasoning could apply to a Lord Chancellor in the face of hostile national media coverage of a high-profile judicial decision.

Fourth, many legal elites criticised Truss for the time that it took her to issue a public statement, but at risk of being overlooked is that she did actually release a statement affirming the importance of judicial independence within thirty-six hours of the High Court's decision and also later wrote a letter to *The Times* in similar terms. True, her statement did not specifically condemn the coverage, but it reaffirmed the importance of an independent judiciary, prompting headlines in the national media that the Lord Chancellor had defended the judiciary. The former Lord Chief Justice Lord Judge was nevertheless quoted as describing the statement as 'a little too late ... and quite a lot too little'.[48] This is puzzling: if the concern is that the coverage risked undermining public confidence in the judiciary, this would presumably occur over the long term, with little hanging on whether the Lord Chancellor issued her statement within twelve or thirty-six hours of the decision.

Fifth, what drives much of the legal community's criticism of Truss is the belief that she should have acted more quickly and vigorously because judges cannot speak out on their own behalf. Yet, one consequence of the 2005 reforms is that senior judges today have a much greater responsibility to defend their

---

[47] See n 28.
[48] See n 39.

own independence. This includes considering whether and how to respond to press coverage that senior judges view as inaccurate or inappropriate. They now also have several means to do so, including arranging an intervention in the media by a senior judge such as a head of division (recognising that both the Lord Chief Justice and Master of Rolls sat on the *Miller* case, and thus could not themselves make any public comment) or arranging for a retired judge to do so as a proxy. The Judicial Office's Press Office can engage proactively with the media akin to the Supreme Court's Communication Team. The Lord Chief Justice can raise any concerns about press coverage in his occasional meetings with newspaper editors. Following the 2005 reforms, the Lord Chief Justice can also now lay written representations before parliament, which could have encouraged opposition member of parliament to seek to initiate a debate on the Lord Chancellor's duty. Of course just as Truss could reasonably conclude that her duty was not engaged, or that the duty was best discharged by taking action behind the scenes, or even that it was prudent to defer action to a later date once the heat of the moment had passed, so could senior judges reach similar decisions, and therefore I do not criticise them for not being seen to do more in the immediate aftermath of the High Court's decision.

Sixth, many legal elites seemed to assume that the pre-2005 Lord Chancellors would have swooped in to vigorously defend the judiciary in the immediate aftermath of negative press coverage.[49] This seems questionable. There were a number of occasions where press headlines savaged the judges without any public interventions by pre-2005 Lord Chancellors. More to the point, what many in the legal community often forget is that the post-2005 office is not the same as the pre-2005 office. The former Lord Chief Justice, Lord Judge, was flat-out wrong to suggest in the days following the High Court's decision that 'the whole point of the Lord Chancellor's job is that he or she is there to take an independent line'.[50] For better or worse, the point of the 2005 reforms was to standardise the job so that Lord Chancellors would take a governmental line on matters relating to the judicial system. The reforms sought to mould the role into one better able to deliver on government policy priorities, and so it was reconfigured into an ordinary ministerial job, albeit one with a special oath and statutory duty. Part and parcel of this was stripping the office of the attributes previously said to make its occupants well placed to defend judicial independence.

This does not mean that Lord Chancellors cannot defend judicial independence; they can and do. But there are limits on their ability to serve as effective guardians of judicial independence, and arguably we saw this in how Truss behaved following the High Court's ruling. She focused on her duty to promote

---

[49] J. Rozenberg, *Enemies of the People: How Judges Shape Society* (Bristol, Bristol University Press, 2020) 32.

[50] See n 39.

judicial independence inside government by advising ministers not to comment. She only took the further action of issuing a press statement in response to escalating pressure from the legal community and political opponents. She was a reactive political guardian, who weighed up political considerations alongside considerations of constitutional principle. This was not cost free for Truss. Her initial public silence upset many judges. By the time of the election in 2017 so low was the judiciary's confidence in Truss that her removal seemed a near certainty, and she was effectively demoted to a lower-ranking job. This underscores how retaining the confidence of judges will likely feature as one of the political considerations that future Lord Chancellors weigh up when deciding whether, when and how to vindicate judicial independence.

The fallout of the High Court's decision in the Article 50 litigation seems to have been traumatic for many in the legal establishment. The received view is that this episode confirms that Lord Chancellors 'lack the cultural background, constitutional authority and political incentive to defend judicial independence against a hostile media'.[51] But more than this, for many the episode demonstrates not only that the Lord Chancellor failed to fulfil her statutory duty, but also 'the potential frailty' of the constitutional arrangements for securing judicial independence'.[52] Contrary to received opinion in the legal sphere, I view events surrounding this litigation as demonstrating not the precariousness of the political commitment to judicial independence, but its enduring strength. In a febrile context, the Lord Chancellor took care in November 2016 to warn ministerial colleagues not to criticise the High Court, and indeed no minister did so.[53] This bears repeating: despite the High Court's decision potentially upending the government's plans for exiting the European Union, ministers were remarkably restrained. Truss also issued a statement reaffirming judicial independence, albeit in response to political pressure, and more slowly and less fulsomely than many legal elites might wish. When the Supreme Court delivered its decision in January 2017, Truss issued a public statement within minutes praising the impartiality and integrity of the Justices, and criticism of the court by members of parliament and by the press was subdued. No doubt Truss felt burned by the criticism of her in November 2016, and thus was keen to avoid a repeat, but this underscores how the political process can generate incentives for a politician Lord Chancellor to defend judicial independence.

---

[51] O'Brien (n 45) 136.

[52] Daly (n 47) 142.

[53] Sajid Javid made a clumsy comment, when he described the case as 'an attempt to frustrate the will of the British people and it is unacceptable'. This seemed to be directed towards those behind the litigation, and his characterisation of the litigation as politically motivated is hard to deny. See R Ekins and G Gee, '*Miller*, Constitutional Realism and the Politics of Brexit' in M Elliott, J Williams and A Young (eds), *The UK Constitution after Miller: Brexit and Beyond* (Oxford, Hart Publishing, 2018) 249, 257–60.

V. CONCLUSION

In one of his final set-piece speeches as Lord Chief Justice, Lord Thomas argued that in the United Kingdom's unwritten constitution 'it is of vital importance that the provisions of the [Constitutional Reform Act] relating to the office of Lord Chancellor are properly understood and effect is given to them'.[54] Encapsulating the dominant legal mindset, Lord Thomas had in mind that the Lord Chancellor is 'manifestly different from any other minister', and 'is not simply a Secretary of State with a separate title resonant of our long history'.[55] This is wishful thinking. The office is part of the arrangements for securing judicial independence, but its place in the constitutional firmament is much reduced since 2005. Whether or not legal elites like it, the Lord Chancellor is now a conventional ministerial office, albeit one carrying a statutory duty and oath to uphold judicial independence. Fifteen years on, it is time for legal elites to appreciate the office of Lord Chancellor for what it has now become: an ordinary ministerial role likely to be filled by a jobbing politician, but nevertheless still one that has attached to it functions relating to the courts, and one where its occupant can help to promote a culture inside government that respects judicial independence. The sooner legal elites accept this, the easier it will be to develop a shared set of realistic expectations for how Lord Chancellors should perform their important but much reduced role.

[54] Thomas (n 39) para 53.
[55] ibid.

12

Ally or Enemy, Friend or Foe

DJ GALLIGAN

I. INTRODUCTION

O**N FIRST IMPRESSIONS** the courts seem plainly to be allies and friends of the people. They settle disputes among them, protect rights and liberties against the excesses of agencies of government, and administer the unpleasant but necessary system of criminal justice. The judges are persons of maturity who are detached from the political process, have security of office, are amply provided for, and are experienced and learned in the law. They base their judgments on evidence tested in the courtroom, put aside extraneous factors and justify their decisions with reasons as to facts and law. They normally go quietly about their business, of small interest to anyone other than the parties to a case, then out of the blue hit the headlines. It is as if beneath the surface of calm and order, of gravity in deliberation and detachment from the boisterous world outside, the courts unleash a storm of feeling and high emotion usually suppressed. So why is it that courts, the natural allies of the people, the least dangerous branch of government and dispensers of justice, incite such sentiments? Is it the case that despite first appearances, dissatisfaction with the courts festers among the people and occasionally bursts to the surface? If so, does it mean that people caught up in the courts have a bad experience? Or is that the courts, instead of just applying the law, being the mere mouthpieces of the law as some judges still insist, have crossed into the political process, territory beyond their brief? Although these issues are much researched empirically and theoretically, there are still questions to ask and uncertainties to settle.

In this chapter I return to the seat of controversy, the relationship between the people and the courts. My aim is to sketch a model of the relationship based on experience and practice. By model I mean an idea, a construction of the mind, aimed at understanding a dimension of human endeavour, in this case relations between the people and the courts. It is not a generalisation from practice and experience, although both are useful guides in constructing the model. A model, once formulated, is of use in making sense of the relationship as it occurs in practice and is to be distinguished from an ideal as to how the world ought to be. The relationship has two aspects, one between the people engaged as litigants and the courts, the other between the people as a whole and the courts. The background history and practice is that of the United Kingdom but with an eye to general application. The focus in on the people and tries to capture their aims and purposes in daily endeavour, their reasons for entering into social relationships, their understanding of the constitutional order, and their expectations of government and the courts. The approach is pragmatic and pedestrian and slightly sceptical of the ideals, aspirations and fictions of official constitutional discourse.

II. THE CONSTITUTIONAL CONTEXT

The primary interest guiding the people's sentiments towards government is in being governed well. It used to be called the 'common good', which meant conserving the social, political and economic order in place. As the people freed themselves from forms of servitude and gained the liberty to move about, to assemble and to pursue their own ends, the common good was overtaken by other ways of stating the ends of government. The well-being of the people, of each person and hence of the aggregate of the people, perhaps best expresses the purpose of the constitutional order and government.[1] There are many ways of advancing well-being, some by persons acting alone, others by combining to coordinate efforts towards common goals. The agencies of government contribute in three ways, one a *protective* role to secure person and property, another a *welfare* role to provide social goods, and a third less noticed an *enabling* role to create the conditions under which the people are able to pursue and advance their own well-being. To be governed well is to have a system of government agencies that secures and advances the well-being of the people by performing each of the three roles.[2]

Good government we know from experience depends on many variables, many factors and influences. Agencies to govern need power, but power has to be contained and controlled. How to achieve both is the riddle of the constitution. The people have ways of guiding the use of power and holding it to the proper ends, including casting a vote, having a share in decisions and subjecting it to scrutiny. Constitutional history shows the long journey from the people's being on the margins of the political process, practically excluded from it, to securing

---

[1] For further analysis, see R Hardin, *Indeterminacy and Society* (Princeton, NJ, Princeton University Press, 2003).

[2] The source and most original and profound account of these ideas is Giambattista Vico, *The New Science* [1744] (Penguin Books, London, 1999). The ideas are central to but less developed in the writings of David Hume, *Essays, Moral, Political, and Literary* [1741], ed EF Miller (Indianapolis, IN, Liberty Fund, 1985) Essay IV, and in the lectures of Adam Smith, *Lectures on Jurisprudence* [1762–63], ed RL Meek, DD Raphael and PG Stein (Indianapolis, IN, Liberty Fund, 1978).

rights of engagement, at different levels and of variable influence. Such means, while precious, are occasional and scattered, the effects piecemeal, the bulk of Leviathan left unscathed. Since the role of the people is in practice limited, good government depends critically on each of its parts, from the high legislative to the low administrative, using its own power effectively for authorised ends. It depends on each agency restraining itself from going beyond such ends and each influencing the actions of other agencies. Roughly stated, parliament reins in the executive; the executive nudges and needles parliament, keeps an eye on the administration and oversees the civil service, which in turn disciplines the executive. While the courts keep a watching brief over the lot. Occasionally, even exceptionally, the tangle of ties between the people and agencies and among the agencies works well to produce good government.

How, then, does this pragmatic notion of good government grounded in the well-being of the people, the agencies of government instruments to that end, fit with ideas of democracy? According to democratic theory, good government consists not in setting an outcome and then working out the best way to reach it. Instead good government consists in attaining outcomes by certain procedures, the procedures by which the people are said to rule themselves, ranging from direct self-rule to rule through elected representatives with various positions in between. Outcomes reached by following the procedures are deemed to be justifiable. How, then, does this theory bear on and influence the attitudes and actions of the people? The sequence of social action shows the link. Interests valued give rise to sentiments; sentiments lead to dispositions to act; dispositions lead to actions. The people value democracy because it serves their interests in two ways. One is that self-rule, even in attenuated forms, is inherently valuable as a property of personhood and a mark of a free person. The other reason is outcome-based. The procedures of democracy are more likely than other forms of government to serve the well-being of the people. The procedures are imperfect and often lead to poor outcomes, but as history and experience show are over time probably the most reliable. In certain situations princely rule is most effective in restoring order and peace, in others a council of wise elders is the safest route to harmony and stability. The empirical case for rule by democratic procedures is strengthened by noting the fragmentation of society, the diversity of its members and the competition of interests. There is no independent standard by which to judge outcomes. Well-being by nature beyond a certain threshold is open to personal preference. What constitutes the well-being of the people and how it is reached have to be resolved in the political arena. How much value the people in fact place on the two dimensions of democracy is an empirical issue likely to vary among one people and across peoples.

However, it does not follow that the people's sense of good government is wholly absorbed into democratic procedures. Knowing the limits and defects of the democratic process, the people sensibly reserve the right to follow other routes to well-being. They accept that the political arena in which all are able to engage is generally the best way of settling policy and making law. At the same time, knowing its limitations, the unevenness of the process and the imbalance among groups and interests, the people have good reason to rely on other ways of protecting their interests, other means to good government. They know their own efforts to engage in the political arena can be productive but not enough to serve their ends. They know they have to rely on other agencies in both the public and private sectors to ensure good government. They share the common purpose of living well and strive to attain that end. The constitutional order, the agencies established and the social relationships entered are among the many means to that end. Their utility is judged by that end. An alternative image of constitutional order emerges. It has several features. One is the centrality of the elected legislature in settling major matters of policy and then delegating implementation to a host of agencies, executive, administrative and regulatory. Secondly, agencies once empowered, while answerable to the legislature, tend to acquire a sphere of autonomy in settling issues assigned to them. They become a site of political activity, of direct engagement with sectors of society. Thirdly and critically, the constitutional order includes and authorises, beside the legislature and its delegates, other institutions and practices, some in the private sphere, others in the public. All of which contribute to good government, the pursuit of common purposes, and hence the well-being of the people. The image is one of plurality of institutions rather than an organic unity with a single source. And into the plurality courts fit comfortably. Their jurisdiction is partly dependent on legislative delegation but their origins are more deeply grounded in constitutional history and in the understandings of the people.

Now that the constitutional gateway is open, let us enter to ask what part the courts play? The short answer is to administer justice. According to David Hume, peoples 'establish political authority, in order to administer justice'.[3] As a general claim about political authority, that is only half-true. The goals of protection, welfare and enablement are the substantive ends, in attaining which ideas of justice may have a guiding role. Whether ideas of justice enter into the contest over policy is contingent and variable. Once policies are decided and laws settled, justice comes into its own and Hume's claim is verified. Justice now means individualised justice, that each person be treated equally according to the law; that each receives what is due under law. Before the law, all are in principle equal, a legacy of the Roman law concept of juridical equality,[4] revised in modern terms in the legal theory of Ronald Dworkin as equal concern and respect.[5] Justice in the individualised sense casts a duty on all agencies of government, while for courts, administering individualised justice is their domain.

Yet the partnership of law and justice is not as plain and content as it looks, the edges uneven. First, the law has to be interpreted, uncertainties resolved,

---

[3] Hume (n 2).
[4] Vico (n 2).
[5] RM Dworkin, *Taking Rights Seriously* (London, Duckworth, 1978).

gaps filled, so justice reaches beyond the rules to ideas and values informing the rules. To view law as a system of rules is misleading because rules contain concepts of varying degrees of abstraction and generality. Even clear-line rules are a compressed expression of supporting ideas and values. Secondly, justice in deciding the case, ruling on rights and duties, demands a touch of creativity in interpreting rules, making exceptions, allowing modification, even outright departure. Thirdly, courts are expected to decide a case even if the law is stated in open and abstract standards. Declining to decide because the law is unsettled or the concepts abstract is not an option. The force of these factors is not to declare open season on the administration of justice. The courts are guided by understandings embedded in the constitutional order, a sense of their place in relation to the other agencies of government, and a sentiment of self-restraint, matters to which I return later. The point to note is that the distribution of functions between the courts and other agencies is marked not by lines precisely drawn but by concepts the content of which and the boundaries between which are a matter of interpretation. Adjudication in dispensing justice skirts around the political arena. The courts acknowledge and respect a border between the judicial and the political. Yet they know it is one of impressions rather than clear lines and cross over when the case so demands. Which means the power of the courts to do justice necessarily includes an element of policy, at times barely noticeable, at other times striking.

Tucked into this partnership of justice and power are two ideas about the constitutional order. One is that the legislative, executive and administrative bodies have primary responsibility for deciding policies and rendering them into law. They engage in, are guided by and respond to the political process. And so the policies of government at all levels are linked to the people. The people through democratic processes are deemed to consent to, to authorise or at least to acquiesce in the agencies' being responsible for settling policy. Reality tempers the image. The links between the people and government, sometimes clear and direct, are often blurred and broken, the people on the margins and their influence barely felt. That is an incentive for improving rather than abandoning the relationship. However, that the practice falls far short of the ideal even in decent constitutional systems is a reason for considering other routes to sound policy. Here the courts enter and proclaim their credentials. And rather than being damned as constitutional heresy, the courts' engaging with policy potentially contributes to good government.

The other idea of a constitutional character is that the courts' relations with the people are confined to those who appear before them. Between the courts and the people as a whole there is no direct relationship; judicial independence dictates there be none. The corollary is that the courts are not answerable to the people, nor to the other agencies. They are out on a constitutional limb of their own, an institution independent of the people and the other parts of government. This seems constitutionally dubious. The justification would be that to do their job the courts must stand apart from both. Guided by an inner integrity, a sense of responsibility and resolute self-restraint, judges know their constitutional role and cut their cloth accordingly. Here we detect an inkling of unease, a murmur of discontent. How is it that an institution holding power over both the people and agencies of government can be outside the line of constitutional relationships? When the courts are then seen to stray into the policy arena, the murmurs rise in pitch and suspicion of their being foes not friends confirmed. At this point the two ideas join force to produce the conclusion that policy is for the legislature and its delegate, while the courts, lacking a relationship with the people, have no business intruding. This seems to be wrong in principle and in practice and does not accurately describe the intricate relations between the people and the courts to which I now turn.

III. PARTIES AND COURTS

Let us return to that first impression of courts as friends of the people. Imagine an action between two people, or more tellingly against an arm of government, seeking redress for arbitrary treatment. Attempts at settlement having failed, the parties end up in court. They enter a temple of justice where rights and duties are settled by impartial judges learned in the law. The facts are established by tried methods of proof, guided by counsel, followed by judgment, reasoned with evidence, facts and law. A judgment binding on the parties, no matter how lowly or grand. Yet the parties often emerge from the encounter disappointed and resentful, feeling they have been treated unfairly and justice denied. How can such sentiments be explained? There are two main reasons, one the court setting, the other competing ideas of justice.

Instead of the parties entering a welcoming space with expectations of justice being done, the courtroom turns out to be alien territory. A social setting they struggle to understand and where they feel intruders. A setting with its own language, a discourse unfamiliar to them; puzzling procedures, rules restricting the recounting of events, standards remote from everyday experience. Add the mode of dress more suited to the theatre than the courtroom and the alienation is complete. The call of Jack Cade's rebellious butcher first to kill all the lawyers and then hang the clerk who could write his name, while grotesque, reflects the sense of exclusion and pent-up resentment of the common people.[6] The person who cannot read is unable to answer the charges, which anyhow are in French, which they do not speak. Documents are in Latin, which they cannot read, all contriving to hide from the commons knowledge of their rights and duties. Such practices are long gone but the sentiment lives on, well stated by the startled fisherman in *Pericles* who calls to his master: 'Here's a fish hangs in the net like a poor man's rights in law;' twill hardly come out.'[7]

---

[6] William Shakespeare, *Henry VI, The First Part of the Contention* (1592) Act 4:2:78.
[7] William Shakespeare, *Pericles Prince of Tyre* (1608) Scene 5:158.

A second and more fundamental reason for negative sentiments is the sense of justice. The responsibility of the courts is to do justice according to law, to decide the case according to the standards stated in law. Justice consists in applying the rules to the facts. Both ideas can be cause for the people's concern. The people are likely to have a sentiment of justice prior to law in which the law has its origins but from which over time it becomes detached. In a study of pre-modern England, Susan Reynolds captures the idea in three words: 'peoples precede nations'.[8] Communities form and networks of social relations are founded on understandings, expectations and practices that include ideas of justice. The justice embedded in social relations is formed prior to state authority and continues under it. It naturally adjusts but still retains its own roots from which to judge the official version of justice.

The English resented the yoke of the Normans because it imposed on a community notions of justice of foreign origin. In seventeenth-century England, the Levellers, disaffected with the justice of law and courts, set out to excavate ideas buried in pre-Norman communities, prior to and more fundamental than *Magna Charta*, itself a beggarly thing, a mess of pottage, a restatement of alien justice.[9] Even in more tolerable constitutional orders, notions of justice and fair treatment emerge within and are particular to the social relations of everyday experience. The ranchers of Shasta County, California, the yeomen and women farmers of Vacy Plains, the diamond traders of New York City, not least the London business community, show how ideas of justice are born and nurtured within social relationships. Common ideas mingle with official ideas although the two often diverge. Justice and fair treatment refer to the way one person treats another and so are common to practically any social relationship. Children acquire a sense of justice in their early years not by being instructed in law but by experience within the relationships through which they pass.[10] As a community becomes more culturally and ethnically diverse, as groups and identities previously denied gain recognition, new relationships form. New understandings and expectations are encouraged, ideas of justice ever variable adjust and change. The justice of law has its own origins and its own logic. It responds to shared understandings but is influenced by other factors. The power of sectors of society to have their interests protected, events forgotten and reasons of state far from the knowledge of the people, all influence the justice of law. A gap between the justice of law and the justice of communities is unavoidable, the size and seriousness variable.

---

[8] S Reynolds, *Kingdoms and Communities in Western Europe 900–1300*, 2nd edn (Oxford, Clarendon Press, 1997) 130.

[9] Explained more fully in DJ Galligan, 'The Levellers, the People, and the Constitution' in DJ Galligan (ed), *Constitutions and the Classics* (Oxford, Oxford University Press, 2014) 181–206 and '*Magna Carta*: A Mess of Pottage, A Beggarly Thing' (London, Meeting of the American Bar Association, 2015).

[10] J Piaget, *The Moral Judgement of the Child* (London, Kegan Paul, Trench, Trubner, 1932).

The other dimension of the justice of law stems from the need for rules, for reasonably clear and certain standards to guide action and to settle disputes. In order to serve the interests of the people, to provide security and welfare and assist each in achieving their own ends, the state has to coordinate social relations. Rules are the means of coordination. But rules are blunt instruments, flattening shades and smudging subtleties, blind to nuance, division and uncertainty. Rules force a division between doing justice in each case and the need for certainty, the two at times coinciding, at times separating. John Warr, a contemporary of the Levellers and troubled by the same issue, put the quest as substance over form, 'the reason and equity of the thing' over the narrowness of rules.[11] But there is no solution. Between form and substance, between rules and principles, each serving different purposes, tension is unavoidable. It can be softened and moderated but not removed. Citizens who reflect on the matter know the need for common rules and a common notion of justice, know that notions of justice indigenous to social relations are different, yet accept the need for compromise in reaching common standards. They know that in order to have the valued goods of order, protection and stability, common standards are necessary and justice trimmed to fit.

The image of the justice of law starkly presented is moderated by various measures. Measures to soften the law strictly applied and to allow other ideas of justice to seep in, to add to the canvas colour and contour. Some measures are institutional, others intellectual. Besides the image of courts earlier presented, the courts in formal dress, there are informal institutions of an adjudicative kind, among them tribunals, local courts, agencies to relieve grievances, to name a few. English history presents a tapestry of courts procedurally informal, easily accessible and licensed to take account of common notions of fairness and equity. Another is the jury which leaves to a panel of citizens the final decision not only on the facts but implicitly on the justice of the law. The intellectual route is through discretion, sometimes authorised by law, often informally assumed, as the entrance to a deeper sense of equity and fairness.[12] In John Warr's words all are ways of 'getting to the equity of the thing' while maintaining the justice of law and hence the constitutional order.[13] This does not rule out disappointment with a court's decision and a sense of justice not being done. Despite the disappointment, with the larger canvas in mind, the people might come to see the courts overall as allies not enemies.

---

[11] John Warr, *A Spark in the Ashes* [1648–49], ed S Sedley and L Kaplan (London, Verso Press, 1992).

[12] Discretion authorised and unauthorised is analysed in D J Galligan, *Discretionary Powers: A Legal Study of Official Discretion* (Oxford, Clarendon Press, 1987).

[13] Max Weber puts it in terms of formal and substantive rationality, decisions inevitably swinging between the two: M Weber: *Economy and Society*, ed G Roth and C Wittich (Berkeley, California University Press, 1968).

IV. THE PEOPLE AND COURTS

The relationship between the courts and the people as a whole is not so easy to define. On one view the need for independence in administering justice rules out any relationship. The model proposed here takes a different, more pragmatic view. The people have an interest with two parts, one in the administration of justice generally, the other in the court's engaging with matters of policy. As to the first, while the litigant has a direct and tangible interest in the administration of justice, the interest of the people is different. They value it as part of a humane and civilised order, the common purpose of which is the well-being of the people to which a system of justice is essential, an idea reinforced by the added interest in knowing that, if one were to end up in court, treatment would be just.

Plainly there is a relationship between the people and the courts, within which two factors intersect. The courts need the power to judge disputes free from interference, while the people have an interest in the courts doing their job properly. The common-sense case for autonomy and independence in deciding cases confronts the equally common-sense case that power poses risks and that power unpatrolled has no place in the constitutional order. There is no reason for exempting the courts, no reason why they should not be under the gaze of the people in the same way as other parts of government. A course then has to be found uniting the two factors, the courts' being able to administer justice and the people's being confident they do. One promotes independence, the other the rendering of account. Judicial independence, according to Jeremy Bentham, is 'tolerable only in a corrupt government; it is disastrous in a good one'. A court dependent on no one 'is dependent on its own passions and caprice', the only guarantee of probity and moral aptitude is 'judicial dependence upon, and full responsibility to, the people'.[14] Bentham did not mince his words or rein in his passions and went a bridge too far. For the people, perhaps sharing a milder scepticism, the solution is the partnership of independence and accountability along the following lines.

The central concept is agency: the agent is given space to do the job and then to account for it. The verb *to account* derives from the parent verb *to count* and has its origins in money transactions. Where one party acts on behalf of the other the equivalent is that the one answers to the other. The logic is as follows. The agencies of government, including courts, are *agents* charged to conduct certain actions on behalf of the *principal*, the people. The job of the courts as agents is to do justice in each case. Justice is done by following settled procedures to reach an accurate finding of fact and delivering an outcome justified according to the law, while respecting other relevant values. They do

---

[14] Bentham's ideas are well explained in G Postema, *Bentham and the Common Law Tradition* (Oxford, Clarendon Press, 1986) 363.

so without distraction, interference or obstruction by other agencies or by the people, the principal.[15] They must then be ready to render account to the principal, which means to explain their actions, to show they are justified, to be open to questions about them, and to correct mistakes and remedy defects. The conditions needed to discharge such duties relate to design, management and sentiments, some provided externally, others left to the courts internally.[16] Here we must be content with a sketch rather than a full account. Design includes procedures for appointment and dismissal, security of tenure, restrictions on holding other offices or positions, and immunity from outside interference.[17] Management includes the timely hearing of cases, giving reasons, and scope for appeal and review. Of special weight is the ability of courts to correct their own mistakes. Justice can be slow; for the Birmingham Six wrongly accused of bombing a pub dreadfully slow. But it came and it came from the courts. The processes of appeal and review are aimed at keeping each level of courts within the scope of its power and detecting and correcting errors. Even the highest court can review and reverse its own earlier decisions. The sentiments of judges and lawyers, critical in binding the system together, are cultivated by two factors. One is the social context, the sphere of normative, cognitive and regulatory dimensions suitable to the task of administering justice.[18] The other, equally essential to the constitutional order in all its parts, is a sentiment of self-restraint in the use of power.[19] Without these two qualities on the part of judges and lawyers, the edifice of justice, no matter how well designed, is a hollow space.

All agencies of government need independence in the sense of being able to perform their functions. It comes with a price, the duty to give account, to explain and justify one's actions to another. The courts are exemplary in giving reasons for their decisions. The manner and precision are beyond the norm of other agencies, especially the executive and administration. Their actions are rarely fully explained, and are laced with obscurities and clouded in secrecy. The courts now know the need better to explain their actions and to show how they match their constitutional duties, as Catherine Barnard and Paul Magrath ably show in their chapters.[20] The people's entitlement to scrutinise and criticise the reasons, the justifications and indeed the outcomes is grounded in constitutional

[15] For further analysis of what that means, see DJ Galligan, *Due Process and Fair Procedures* (Oxford, Oxford University Press, 1997).

[16] Discussed further in DJ Galligan, *Judging Judges*, Policy Brief (Foundation for Law Justice & Society, Oxford, 2008).

[17] See the analysis by R Sharpe, 'The Case for Independence in an Age of Populism' (chapter 1 of this book).

[18] Social spheres are analysed in DJ Galligan, *Law in Modern Society* (Oxford, Oxford University Press, 2007) ch 6.

[19] On self-restraint, ibid 278ff.

[20] P Magrath, 'From Mystery to Transparency: How Judges Promote Public Understanding of the Judicial Role' (chapter 10 of this book).

understandings. The people are not entitled to overturn a judicial ruling, just as they cannot reverse an executive decision; but they are entitled to subject a judgment to scrutiny and criticism, even condemnation. That is not to damn the courts as enemies but rather an expression of concern aimed at correcting and improving the administration of justice. It could be construed as a sign of common cause, an act aimed at sustaining healthy relations between allies. Miscarriages of justice, decisions defying common sense, wayward judges, all taint the courts and strain the alliance. The aim of scrutiny and criticism, whether of parliament, the executive or the courts, is to coax each to the better discharge of its constitutional duties. That comment occasionally should spill over into ridicule, the daily cartoon mocking the holders of high office, the front-page photograph of three gentlemen in bell-bottom wigs, are in the nature of things, tolerance of them a sign of maturity.

There was a time when courts were populated by the people: in republican Rome, Anglo-Saxon England and elsewhere, a practice still sometimes observed in local courts. Other signs of popular engagement remain as noted earlier. Over time the higher courts, in common with all organisations, tend to be formalised, professionalised and rendered remote from the people. They distance themselves from the people, cultivate an air of superiority and resist intrusion. The people are left struggling to know what is going on. What, then, are we to conclude about relations between the two? First, the people have an interest in having justice soundly administered. Secondly, in order to meet the standard, factors of design, management and sentiment have to combine. Thirdly, there are various ways of holding the courts to account without interfering in the adjudication of cases. There are ways of keeping them under scrutiny, monitoring their actions, exceptionally intervening. All are processes to which many institutions, public and private, contribute. Fourthly, the people themselves have only limited scope to contribute to the good functioning of the courts and depend on the efforts of others; efforts the people encourage. As long as the system works well, by whatever means, the people's interests are served.

V. AUTHORITY OF COURTS TO DECIDE POLICY

The other issue in the relationship is the power of the courts to decide policy in the course of judging. Several points to note. First, the courts confront policy issues only in the case before them and then only in applying the legal standards. Secondly, the case cannot be decided unless the point of policy is settled. Thirdly, applying a standard and deciding policy are not logically distinct; rather the one includes an element of the other. A famous example: no vehicles in the park; is a tricycle a vehicle?[21] Even in such a simple case the answer is found not

---

[21] HLA Hart's example, *The Concept of Law* (Oxford, Clarendon Press, 1961).

by logical deduction but by considering the setting, the purpose, the guiding standards and the contextual contingencies. The more open-textured the rule, the more reliance on context and the wider the scope for elements of policy.[22] Fourthly, settling a point of policy in the course of judging a case is an everyday matter and the higher up the court ladder the more everyday it is. When the context is clarified in this way, it is hard to see what objection the people could have. Courts are responsible bodies. They are staffed by mature persons enmeshed in social spheres to guide them to measured judgment in interpreting rules, filling in the gaps or updating the law. It could even be that judges more than politicians have the classic qualities, the virtues in republican discourse deemed essential in governing well. At least for the moderate task of resolving legal uncertainty judges are well equipped.

There are two potential objections: the one constitutional, the other competence. The constitutional case we have noted. Policy matters are for the political process, the legislative branch and its delegates. To this as a reason for judicial restraint is added the competence of institutions, the idea that each arm of government is designed to do certain jobs, and courts are unsuited to decide policy. The first is a matter of constitutional authority, the second of institutional design, and the two overlap. Here I concentrate on the constitutional issue with just a passing remark on competence. The constitutional case rests on the relationship between parliament and the people. The case for policy-making being the domain of the legislative branch relies on three grounds. One is the political process as an arena of ideas, opinions and interests; some combining, others competing. Another is that parliamentarians are elected by, representatives of, and accountable to the people. A third that representatives are able to distil from the arena the policies best serving the people. It is not a matter of the general will of the people emerging or consensus reached. Rather it is an arena in which legislators learn of and are guided by the interests, sentiments and dispositions of the people. The three grounds combine to make the case for entrusting matters of policy to parliament and its delegates. The contrast with courts is at first sight stark: parliament at the centre of the political arena, the court confined to the dispute before it; parliament directly connected to the people, the courts detached from the people, at best representatives only in a strained sense.

Under scrutiny the position of each is neither so clear nor so simple. Parliament and the people have a long and fraught history, some aspects of which bear on their contemporary relationship. One concerns the political process as an arena open to airing opinions and promoting interests. Members of the British parliament in the eighteenth century used brazenly to claim not just to be representatives of the people but their embodiment, their actions the actions of the people. The real people, the community of individual persons, are

---

[22] On applying rules and contextual contingencies, Galligan (n 18) chs 4 and 5.

left out in the constitutional cold. They have no status and no right to engage in the political process. In support came a barrage of invective asserting the incompetence of the common people not only to be engaged in governing but even to have their opinions considered.[23] The people over time found ways around, ways of expressing opinions and promoting interests, and eventually gaining entry to the political process.[24] But the irony remains and the memory retained that the supremacy of parliament, invented to keep the people out of the political process, now is enlisted to embrace them as its essence.

The burnished image of the political process as an open arena of ideas and interests loses its shine under scrutiny. The ability of any person or group to exert influence depends on many factors and varies widely. For most, the political process is neither easy to access nor readily responsive to their opinions nor alert to their interests. Imagine the process as part of Adam Smith's great scramble where all strive to improve their well-being. Yet the scramble is uneven, some win, some runners-up, some lose.[25] A few are well organised in groups, corporations and guilds, others are backed by economic power; some have inside influence due to class or status or wealth. For most, the political process is an arena they struggle to enter. When they do it is with caution and low expectations. This is not to condemn the political process for there is no alternative. The point is to be sceptical of the image of a bubbling cauldron from which comes the best-cooked version of the common good.

The shortfall in the people's direct engagement is meant to be made up for by electing representatives who advance the people's interests in the legislative process. The two combined, the people's own efforts and those of their representatives, justify the dominance of the political process. Parliamentarians are now content to represent the people rather than be them, but the sense of representation is still particular. Edmund Burke's account, declared to his electors in the eighteenth century, still stands. Parliamentarians, once elected, are under a duty to act in the public interest not at the direction of electors.[26] National constitutions generally, with a few exceptions, use representation in this sense.[27] The distinction is subtle but substantive. It means representatives are one step apart from electors, the direct line from electors to representatives to policy broken. Representatives act not as agents for the electors but as they think best. And thinking themselves a cut above the average voter, representatives have the qualities to form a measured view of the public interest.

---

[23] For further discussion, see DJ Galligan, 'The People, the Constitution, and the Idea of Representation' in DJ Galligan and M Versteeg (eds), *Social and Political Foundations of Constitutions* (New York, Cambridge University Press, 2015) 134–56.

[24] Mark Knights shows the ways open to the people and the restrictions on them: M Knights, *Representation and Misrepresentation* (Oxford, Oxford University Press, 2005).

[25] Smith (n 2).

[26] Edmund Burke, *The Writings and Speeches of Edmund Burke*, vol 2: *Party, Parliament, and the American War: 1766–1774* (Oxford, Oxford University Press, 1981) 442.

[27] Discussed in DJ Galligan, 'The Sovereignty Deficit of Modern Constitutions' (2013) 33 *OJLS* 345.

Having won admission to the political arena, the people find between them and action stand the representatives.

The blemishes are plain. First, the people's vote, far from affirming their being in charge of the political process, for which they appoint agents to act for them, is merely to nominate someone else to be in charge. The difference is subtle but critical. Law and policy are settled not by the people acting directly or through agents but by persons who, once elected, act independently of their electors. To think of them as representatives of the electors is to misunderstand the concept of representation. Secondly, the Burke principle tells only half the story. The elected official with one eye on the next election has to court enough constituents to stay in office, potentially compromising the priority of the national interest. Thirdly, representatives have to reckon with the political party system. We need not share AV Dicey's demonisation of political parties as a conspiracy against the people, yet note the dampening effect on the representative's freedom of action.[28] Fourthly, to such distractions from the representative's measured judgement must be added the pressure from special interests. There is a temptation to be recruited by special interests, financial, political and social. It is mostly resisted but common enough to warp judgement and deflect attention from the common good. Finally, the people notice that power drifts away from the elected branch to the executive, the administration and regulatory agencies. There it resides and accumulates without close supervision by the legislature.

So, knowing the imperfections, the unevenness, the contingent connections between their interests and the settling of policy, what do the people make of it? On the model proposed here they accept the political process with parliament at the centre as the seat of policy-making. They know that around parliament power moves to many sites, each acquiring a degree of autonomy, each charged with settling matters of policy. Two consequences follow: the diffusion of power among agencies, first, reduces the role of the elected body and spurs the growth of a political arena around each one; and secondly, contributes to good government but creates risks of excess and misuse. The way is then open for the courts to enter and impose restraints. And just as the agencies are a step removed from the democratic process, the need for judicial scrutiny increases and the case against it as a threat to democracy is weakened.

Turning now to relations between the people and the courts, we note similarities and differences. On the Burke principle that the critical faculty in governing well is independence of mind and judgement, the judge matches the parliamentarian. Indeed, not having to face electors, precluded from membership of a political party, and under strict rules to resist pressure from special interests, the judge not just equals but scores better than the politician. On other counts critical differences remain. First, the courts do not have the status or the

---

[28] AV Dicey, *Law of the Constitution* [1885] (Oxford, Oxford University Press, 2013).

responsibilities of elected representatives. Secondly, the courtroom can hardly be described as a marketplace of ideas and interests, rather more an auction-room with one item open to bids by the parties. Thirdly, there is the issue of competence.

Judges are not usually thought of as representatives of the people. They are spared having to face electors and are not directly answerable to them. That arguably augments their ability for measured judgement but marks a difference between them and politicians. Yet there is a sense of representation that fits the courts. A representative does not have to be appointed by or answerable to those represented. One can represent another in the sense of acting on behalf of the other, present the interests of the other, without reference to, permission of, or account to the other. Representation in that sense, ironically, prevailed for centuries between the people and politicians. The courts in administering justice present and preserve the interests of the people and in that way could be said to act as representatives.[29] If representation were considered a critical quality, the people could be said to authorise the courts to administer justice on their behalf in the same way as they authorise parliament to make law on their behalf. Representation is intelligible but whether relations between the people and courts are improved by its being better explained is questionable.

Perhaps the utility of reflecting on courts as representatives is in prompting further enquiry into the relationship as embedded in constitutional history. First, historically courts and legislatures united and intertwined with no strict division of functions. Parliament came into being as a court, the high court of parliament, to adjudicate matters touching on the state, while its legislative power grew only gradually.[30] The *freemen* of Anglo-Saxon society assembled to settle disputes and make law, the two functions hardly separate, the king as *mundbora*, the protector, charged with ensuring justice be done.[31] Gradually separating from parliament, the courts in the course of adjudicating disputes made the common law. Not by laying down rules but allowing them to form incrementally, guided by custom and tradition, a rigid separation of law and policy unheeded.[32] Secondly, while the people were excluded from the political process, had no voice or standing, the courts were accessible to them, their grievances heard. Justice was administered across an array of courts. From the local to the central, from the strictness of the common law courts to the equitable jurisdiction of chancery, to the prerogative, ecclesiastical and local courts, all varied in jurisdiction and approach. To take just two examples, the court of Star Chamber, the judicial arm of the Privy Council, 'was the last resort of poor

---

[29] Representation is sometimes used to mean judges should be drawn from the various groups in society, reflecting gender, ethnicity and class.

[30] JR Maddicott, *The Origins of the English Parliament, 924–1327* (Oxford, Oxford University Press, 2010).

[31] Explained in JEA Jolliffe, *The Constitutional History of Medieval England from the English Settlement to 1485* (London, Adam and Charles Black, 1961).

[32] See JH Baker, *An Introduction to English Legal History*, 4th edn (London, Butterworth, 2002).

men "who could not get what they considered justice elsewhere"'. In the later part of the sixteenth century and early years of the seventeenth, just under half of all plaintiffs in Star Chamber were not gentlemen but yeomen and women, husbandmen or labourers.[33] Star Chamber was controversial but 'also a popular resource'.[34] By the end of the sixteenth century the annual number of lawsuits across England was one million in a population of four million. The result was that 'almost everyone in the country had direct experience of the law whether as litigant, witness, juror, or curious observer'.[35] The Court of Requests was established by Henry VII expressly to provide justice to the poor.[36] Thirdly and critically, the courts of easiest access were alert to ideas of justice grounded in local communities. Alert and responsive to ideas formed in custom and tradition, ideas at the foundation of social relations, ideas from which the common law had sprung but over time had become separated.

The juridical constitution, so-called, now indicted as an intrusion of courts into territory not theirs, in fact precedes the political constitution. The people's sense of law and justice, formed in social relations, grounded in ideas of reason, equity and justice, precedes the political constitution; the political constitution of positive law-making by government agencies.[37] And just as the notion of a juridical constitution precedes the positive, so the courts were the principal agencies on which the people relied for protection and advancement of their interests. In various forms, from the popular assemblies of Rome, to the *folkmoot* of Anglo-Saxon England, to contemporary tribunals, courts are best able, on this approach, to understand the foundations of social relations and the rhythms to which they work. By contrast the political constitution comes from an image of society structured by status and property, the agencies of government commissioned to preserve it. Beneath appealing images of the body politic, united, harmonious and stable, all in their place working together for the common good, lie relationships of power and privilege, out of which the doctrines of constitutional history emerged. There was no political arena because there was no need for one, the body politic preordained and perfectly ordered. The reality was different, the people, down to the most common, naturally occupy the lowest organ, the feet. Just as naturally they want to improve their lives, secure needs and advance utilities, and so the body politic gives way to the political arena. As the struggle heightens, the power of the people becomes unstoppable and concessions have to be made. The body politic proves obsolete, its heir the representative invested with constitutional authority.

---

[33] These matters are well discussed in S Hindle, *The State and Social Change in Early Modern England, 1550–1640* (Basingstoke, Palgrave, 2002) ch 3.

[34] ibid 93.

[35] T Stretton, 'The People and the Law' in K Wrightson (ed), *A Social History of England 1500–1750* (Cambridge, Cambridge University Press, 2017) 201.

[36] On the Court of Requests, see Joliffe (n 31).

[37] Discussed in DJ Galligan, 'The Indirect Origins of the Juridical Constitution' (unpublished, 2011).

A glance at history casts some light on relations between the people and the courts today. The political process is part of the great scramble, the main arena in which the people promote their interests and influence policy. The people are aware of the defects and the limitations, the unevenness and the imbalance of the scramble. They know other avenues are open and that in certain matters the courts offer help where the political process fails them. They see the courts are designed to protect their rights according to the law and constitution. They see that may mean refining the law, giving content to abstract standards, and filling in gaps. To the objection that law-making is the domain of the political process, they offer two replies. One historical that the courts have always made policy and law in this limited and incremental manner. The other calls on constitutional practice. Constitutions normally authorise courts to interpret its terms, some of which are bound to be open and abstract. Perhaps most tellingly the people insist there is more to the constitution than the official discourse; insist on a prior sense of constitution embedded in their sentiments and dispositions and in their social relationships. A sense of constitution that sees through the misleading image of representation and the fiction of the people ruling themselves. They know the limitations of the political process. Casting a cold eye on government, the people conclude that elected representatives have primary responsibility for settling policies and making law. They also accept that judges are suitably qualified, experienced and disinterested to settle such matters as they occur in the course of litigation. And to that the people find no credible objection on constitutional grounds. That is not to license the courts to make law and policy at large; but within the confines of the case, guided by the context of ideas, values and standards, restrained and tempered by a sense of their rightful place in the constitutional order, to decide the issue of policy necessary to the decision.

A final word on competence. Having sketched out a constitutionally justifiable role for the courts in deciding policy matters, there remains the issue of their suitability as institutions to decide policy. Three brief points. First, a model of policy-making, a rather ideal model, has the following features. The issue is announced and made widely known and submissions are invited from the public at large, from institutions and associations both public and private. Perhaps a hearing is arranged; tentative policies are proposed; the reasons given; the costs and benefits assessed. The likely impact is calculated; other options considered and why one is preferred over others explained. Further submissions are then invited and the final policy is announced with reasons. The model can be seen most faithfully in the practices of some administrative and regulatory agencies, from where in other contexts it fades away in favour of unbounded discretion.[38] The model sets exacting standards which often prove too onerous at even the highest parliamentary level of legislation, while the lower levels of government

---

[38] For discussion of administrative processes, see Galligan (n 12).

are at risk of making policy in ignorance of the model. Secondly, the competence of the courts is to be judged not in isolation or by a standard of perfection but by enquiring into the comparative competence of the various agencies including courts. Thirdly, the courts have ways of receiving submissions from sources other than the parties, ways of enabling other persons and groups with an interest to join in the judicial process.

And so, friend or foe, ally or enemy, what are we to conclude? For some the fisherman gets it just right, captures an eternal truth and faithfully records the people's sentiment of scepticism. But there is another sector which sees the courts as part of a community's endeavour to achieve common purposes, to protect and advance the well-being of all its members. Its place is not defined by a set of ideas fixed in advance and rigid in application. Nor is the scope of its place perfectly defined and marked off from that of other institutions. There are guiding axioms and social and cultural understandings, a sense of constitution, and a disposition of self-restraint. Courts conscientiously so charged, despite imperfections and failures, deserve the respect and possibly the alliance and friendship of the people.

Bibliography

Addink, H, *Good Governance: Concept and Context* (Oxford, Oxford University Press, 2019).

Alter, K, *Establishing the Supremacy of European Law* (Oxford, Oxford University Press, 2001).

Agmon-Gonnen, M, 'Judicial Independence: The Threat from Within' (2005) 38 *Israel Law Review* 120.

Anderson, P, 'Ever Closer Union' [2021] *London Review of Books* 7.

Arnull, A, *The European Union and Its Court of Justice* (Oxford, Oxford University Press, 2006).

Bailleux, J, 'Michel Gaudet A Law Entrepreneur: The Role of the Legal Service of the European executives in the Invention of EU Law and the *Common Market Law Review*' (2013) 50 *CML Rev* 359.

Baker, JH, *An Introduction to English Legal History* (Butterworth, London, 2002).

Barak, A 'The Constitutional Revolution: Protected Human Rights' (1992) 1 *Mishpat u'Mimshal – Law and Government in Israel* 3.

Barak, A, *The Judge in a Democracy* (Princeton, NJ, Princeton University Press, 2006).

Barak-Erez, D 'Israel: The Security Barrier – Between International Law, Constitutional Law and Domestic Judicial Review' (2006) 4 *International Journal of Constitutional Law* 540.

Barnard, C, 'The Calm after the Storm. Time to Reflect on European Scholarship after *Viking* and *Laval*' in A Bogg, C Colstello and A Davies (eds), *Research Handbook on EU Labour Law* (Cheltenham, Edward Elgar, 2020).

Barnard, C and Butlin, F, 'Free Movement vs Fair Movement: Brexit and Managed Migration' (2018) 55 *CML Rev* 203.

Barnard, C and Leinarte, E, 'The Court of Justice in Times of Politicisation: "Law as a Mask and Shield" revisited' (2020) 27 *Journal of European Public Policy* 382.

Bradley, A, 'Judges and the Media – The Kilmuir Rules' [1986] *PL* 383.

Beers, D, 'A Tale of Two Transitions: Exploring the Origins of Post-Communist Judicial Culture the Romanian and Czech Republics' (2010) 18 *Demokratizatsiya* 28.

Bendor, A, 'Justiciability of the Israeli Fight Against Terrorism' (2007) 39 *George Washington International Law Review* 149.

Bickel, A, *The Least Dangerous Branch: The Supreme Court* (New Haven, CT, Yale University Press, 1986).

Benvenuti, S and Paris, D, 'Judicial Self-Government in Italy: Merits, Limits, and the Reality of an Export Model' (2018) 19 *German Law Review* 1641.

Bickel, A, *The Least Dangerous Branch* (New Haven, CT, Yale University Press, 1962).

Bickel, A, *The Supreme Court and the Idea of Progress* (New Haven, CT, Harper & Row, 1970).

Bingham, T, *The Rule of Law* (London, Penguin, 2010).

Bobek, M, 'Global Solutions, Local Problems: A Critical Study of Judicial Council in Central and Eastern Europe' (2007) 15 *German Law Review* 1257.

Bobek, M, 'The Fortress of Judicial Independence and the Mental Transitions of the Central European Judiciaries' (2008) 14 *European Public Law* 99.

Bobek, M, 'More Heads, More Reason: A Comparative Reflection on The role of the Enlarged Judicial Formation in Apex Jurisdictions', address to Centre for European Studies (2020).

Botero, S, 'Judicial Impact and Court Promoted Monitoring in Argentina' (2018) 50 *Comparative Politics* 169.

Bradford, A, *The Brussels Effect* (Oxford, Oxford University Press, 2020).

Brazier, R, 'Government and the Law: Ministerial Responsibility for Legal Affairs' [1989] *PL* 61.

Brinks, D and Forbath, W, 'The Role of Courts and Constitutions in the New Politics of Welfare in Latin America' in R Peerenboom and T Ginsburg (eds), *Law and Development of Middle-Income Countries: Avoiding the Middle-Income Trap* (New York, Cambridge University Press, 2014).

Burke, E, *The Writings and Speeches of Edmund Burke* [1729–97] (Oxford, Oxford University Press, 1981–2015).

Burley, A-M and Walter, M, 'Europe Before the Court: A Political Theory of Legal Integration' (1993) 47 *International Organization* 41.

Butt, D, 'Transformative Constitutionalism and Socio-economic Rights: Report of a Lecture by the Chief Justice of South Africa' (Oxford, Foundation for Law Justice & Society, 2008).

Caldiera, GA and Gibson, JL, 'The Etiology of Public Support for the Supreme Court' (1992) 36 *American Journal of Political Science* 835.

Cass, T, *The Limits of Judicial Independence* (Cambridge, Cambridge University Press, 2010).

Couso, J, 'The Transformation of Constitutional Discourse and the Judicialization of Politics in Latin America' in J Couso, A Huneeus, and R Sieder (eds), *Cultures of Legality: Judicialization and Political Activism in Latin America* (New York, Cambridge University Press, 2010).

Czarnota, A, 'Rule of Lawyers or Rule of Law? On Constitutional Crisis and the Rule of Law in Poland' in *Governance and Constitutionalism: Law, Politics and International Neutrality* (London and New York: Routledge, 2018).

Dahl, R, 'Decision-making in a Democracy: The Role of the Supreme Court as a National Policy-maker' (1957) 6 *Journal of Public Law* 279.

Daly, P 'Judicial Independence and Accountability in the British Constitution' (2019) *European Journal of Constitutional Law* 141.

Dickson, B, 'Operations and Practice: A Comparison of the Role of the Supreme Court in Canada and the United States' (1980) 3 *Canada United States Law Journal* 86.

Díez, J, *The Politics of Gay Marriage in Latin America* (New York, Cambridge University Press, 2015).

Dotan, Y, 'Judicial Rhetoric, Government Lawyers, and Human Rights: The Case of the Israeli High Court of Justice During the Intafada' (1999) 33 *Law and Society Review* 319.

Doughty, J, Reed, L, and Magrath, P, *Transparency in the Family Courts: Publicity and Privacy in Practice* (London: Bloomsbury Professional, 2018).

Dworkin, R, *Taking Rights Seriously* (Duckworth, London, 1978).

Dworkin, R, *Freedom's Law: The Moral Reading of the American Constitution* (Oxford, Oxford University Press, 1999).

Elkins, R, 'Judicial Supremacy and the Rule of Law' (2003) 119 *LQR* 127.

Elkins, R and Gee, G, '*Miller*, Constitutional Realism and the Politics of Brexit' in M Elliot, J Williams and A Young (eds), *UK Constitution after Miller: Brexit and Beyond* (Oxford, Hart Publishing, 2018).

Elliott, M, *The Constitutional Foundations of Judicial Review* (Oxford, Hart Publishing, 2001).

Entrikin, JL, 'Global Judicial Transparency Norms' (2019) 18 *Washington University Global Studies Law Review* 55.

Epp, C, *The Rights Revolution: Lawyers, Activists, and the Supreme Courts in Comparative Perspective* (Chicago, University of Chicago Press, 1998).

Figueroa, E, 'Transparency in Administrative Courts: From the Outside Looking In' (2015) 35 *Journal of the National Association of Administrative Law Judiciary* 1.

Frankenburg, G, 'Constitutional Transfers and Experiments in the Nineteenth Century' in *Order from Transfer: Comparative Constitutional Design and Legal Culture* (London: Edward Elgar, 2013).

Franklin, C, 'Behavioural Factors Affecting Judicial Independence' in S Burbank and B Friedman (eds), *Judicial Independence at the Crossroads: An Interdisciplinary Approach* (London, Sage, 2002).

Freestone, D, 'The Supremacy of Community Law in National Courts' (1979) 42 *MLR* 220.

Friedland, M, *A Place Apart: Judicial Independence and Accountability in Canada* (Ottawa, Canadian Judicial Council, 1995).

Fuller, LL, 'The Forms and Limits of Adjudication' (1978) 92 *Harvard Law Review* 353.

Galligan, DJ, 'Judicial Review and Democratic Principles: Two Theories' (1983) *Australian Law Journal*, reprinted in M Tushnet (ed), *Bills of Rights* (London, Routledge, 2007).

Galligan, DJ, *Discretionary Powers: A Legal Study of Official Discretion* (Oxford, Clarendon Press, 1987).

Galligan, DJ, *Due Process and Fair Procedures* (Oxford, Clarendon Press, 1997).

Galligan, DJ, *Law in Modern Society* (Oxford, Clarendon Press, 2007).

Galligan, DJ, 'The Indirect Origins of the Juridical Constitution' (Oxford, Annual Lecture in Law Justice & Society, Foundation for Law Justice & Society, 2011).

Galligan, DJ, *Judging Judges* (Oxford, Policy Brief, Foundation for Law Justice & Society, 2012).

Galligan, DJ, 'The Sovereignty Deficit of Modern Constitutions' (2013) 33 *OJLS* 345.

Galligan, DJ, 'The People, The Constitution, and the Idea of Representation' in DJ Galligan and M Versteeg (eds), *Social and Political Foundations of Constitutions* (New York, Cambridge University Press, 2013).

Galligan, DJ, 'The Levellers, the People, and the Constitution' in DJ Galligan (ed), *Constitutions and the Classics* (Oxford, Oxford University Press, 2014).

Galligan, DJ, 'Magna Carta: A Mess of Pottage, A Beggarly Thing' (Meeting of the American Bar Association, London, 2015).

Galligan, DJ and Matczak, M, 'Empirical Study of Judicial Discretion in Polish Administrative Courts' in R Coman and J-M De Wade (eds), *Judicial Reform in Central and Eastern European Countries* (Brugge, Vanden Books, 2007).

Gargarella, R (ed), *Por una justicia dialógica. El Poder Judicial como promotor de la deliberación democrática* (Buenos Aires, Siglo XXI, 2014).

Gavison, R, 'The Constitutioanl Revolution: A Reality or Self-fulfilling Prophecy' (1997) 28 *Mishpatin* 21.

Gee, G, 'Defending Judicial Independence in the British Constitution' in A Dodek and L Sossin (eds), *Judicial Independence in Context* (Toronto, Irwin Law, 2010).

Gee, G, 'Guarding the Guardians: The Chief Executive of the UK Supreme Court' [2013] *PL* 538.

Gee, G, 'What Are Lord Chancelllors For?' [2014] *PL* 11.

Gee, G, *The Politics of Judicial Independence in the UK's Changing Constitution* (Cambridge, Cambridge University Press, 2015).

Gibson, LG, Caldeira, A and Spence, LK, 'Measuring Attitudes towards the United States Supreme Court' (2003) 47 *Americn Journal of Political Science* 353.

Ginsburg, T and Versteeg, M, 'Why Do Countries Adopt Constitutional Review?' (2014) 30 *Journal of Law, Economics, and Organization* 587.

Gloppen, S, Garagella, R and Skaar, E, *Democratization and the Judiciary: The Accountability Function of Courts in New Democracies* (Frank Cass, London, 2004).

Gonzalez-Ocantos, E, *Shifting Legal Visions: Judicial Change and Human Rights Trials in Latin America* (New York, Cambridge University Press, 2016).

Gonzalez-Ocantos, E, 'Communicative Entrepreneurs: The Case of the Inter-American Court of Human Rights' Dialogue with National Judges' (2018) 62 *International Studies Quarterly* 737.

Gonzalez-Ocantos, E and Dinas, E, 'Compensation and Compliance: Source of Public Acceptance of the UK Supreme Court's Brexit Decision' (2019) 53(3) *Law & Society Review* 889.

Gonzalez-Ocantos, E and Baraybar, V, 'Lava Jato Beyond Borders: The Uneven Performance of Anticorruption Judicial Efforts in Latin America' (2019) 15 *Taiwan Journal of Democracy* 63.

Gonzalez-Ocantos, E and Sandholtz, W 'Constructing a Regional Human Rights Legal Order: The Inter-American Court, National Courts, and Judicial Dialogue, 1988–2014' (2020) *International Journal of Constitutional*, available at SSRN: https://ssrn.com/abstract=3661877.

Greene, JE, *The Eyes of the People: Democracy in an Age of Spectatorship* (New York, Oxford University Press, 2010).

Guarnieri, C and Pederzoli, P, *The Power of Judges* (Oxford, Oxford University Press, 2002).

Hailbronner, M, 'Transformative Constitutionalism: Not Only in the Global South' (2017) 65 *American Journal of Comparative Law* 527.

Hamburger, P, *Law and Judicial Duty* (Cambridge, MA, Harvard University Press, 2008).

Handberg, R, 'Public Opinion and the US Supreme Court 1935–1981' (1984) 59 *International Social Science Review* 3.

Hardin, R, *Indeterminacy and Society* (Princeton, NJ, Princeton University Press, 2003).

Harel, A, 'The Rule of Law and Judicial Review: Reflections on the Israeli Constitutional Revolution' in D Dyzenhaus (ed), *Recrafting the Rule of Law: Recrafting the Legal Order* (Oxford, Hart Publishing, 1999).

Harpaz, G, 'When Does a Court Deviate from its own Principles: The Adjudication by the Israeli Supreme Court in the Occupied Palestinian Territories' (2015) *Leiden Journal of International Law* 31.

Hart Ely, J, *Democracy and Distrust: A Theory of Judicial Review* (Cambridge, MA, Harvard University Press, 1980).

Heald, D, *Transparency, the Key to Better Governance* (Oxford, Oxford University Press, 2006).

Helfer, L and Slaughter, A-M, 'Toward a Theory of Effective Supranational Adjudication' (1997) 107 *Yale Law Journal* 272.

Helmke, G, *Institutions on the Edge: The Origins and Consequences of Inter-branch Crises in Latin America* (New York, Cambridge University Press, 2017).

Helmke, G and Staton, J, 'The Puzzling Judicial Politics of Latin America: A Theory of Litigation, Judicial Decisions and Interbranch Conflict' in G Helmke and J Ríos Figueroa (eds), *Courts in Latin America* (New York, Cambridge University Press, 2011).

Hendley, K, 'Telephone Law and the Rule of Law: The Russian Case' (2009) 1 *Hague Journal of the Rule of Law.*

Hilbink, L, *Judges Beyond Politics in Democracy and Dictatorship: Lessons from Chile* (New York, Cambridge University Press, 2007).

Hilbink, L, 'The Origins of Positive Judicial Independence' (2012) 64 *World Politics* 587.

Hindle, S, *The State and Social Change in Early Modern England 1550–1640* (Basingstoke, Palgrave, 2002).

Hirschl, R, *Towards Juristocracy: The Origins and Consequences of the New Constitutionalism* (Cambridge, MA and London, Harvard University Press, 2004).

Hoffmann, L, 'Judges, Interpretation, and Self-government' in R Ekins, P Yowell and NW Barber (eds), *Lord Sumption and the Limits of Law* (Oxford, Hart Publishing, 2016).

Hofnung, M, 'The Unintended Consequences of Unplanned Constitutional Reform: Constitutional Politics in Israel' (1996) 44 *American Journal of Comparative Law* 585.

Hofnung, M and Weinshall-Margel, K, 'Judicial Setbacks, Material Gains: Terror Litigation at the Israeli High Court of Justice' (2010) 7 *Journal of Empirical Legal Studies* 664.

Horsley, T, *The Court of Justice of the European Union as Institutional Actor: Judicial Law-making and Its Limits* (Cambridge, Cambridge University Press, 2018).

House of Lords Constitution Committee (2014) *The Office of Lord Chancellor.*

Hume, D, *Essays Moral Political and Literary* [1741], ed EF Miller (Indianapolis, IN, Liberty Press, 1985).

Iancu, B, 'Perils of Sloganized Constitutional Concepts, Notably that of "Judicial Independence"' (2017) 13 *European Constitutional Law Review* 582.

Iancu, B, 'Changed Vocabularies: A Few Semantic Ambiguities of Network Constitutionalism' in *New Developments in Constitutional Law: Essays in Honour of Andras Sajo* (The Hague: Eleven International Publishing, 2018).

Iancu, B *'Quad licet Jovi non licet bovi?* The Venice Commission as Norm Enterpreneur' (2019) 11 *Hague Journal of the Rule of Law* 189.

Iancu, B and Tanasescu, ES, *Governance and Constitutionalism: Law, Politics, and Institutional Neutrality* (London and New York: Routledge, 2018).

Joliffe, JEA, *The Constitutional History of Medieval England* (Adam and Charles Black, London, 1937).

Jones, P, 'Political Equality and Majority Rule' in D Miller and L Siedentop (eds), *The Nature of Political Theory* (Oxford, Clarendon Press, 1983).

Kapiszewski, D, *High Courts and Economic Governance in Argentina and Brazil* (New York, Cambridge University Press, 2012).

Kaufman, I, 'Chilling Judicia Indepndence' (1979) 88 *Yale Law Journal* 689.

King, J, 'Institutional Approaches to Judicial Restraint' (2008) 28 *OJLS* 409.

Klare, KE, 'Legal Culture and Transformative Constitutionalism' (1998) 14 *South African Journal of Human Rights* 146.

Kibet, E and Fombad, C 'Transformative Constitutionalism and the Adjudication of Constitutional Rights in Africa' (2017) 17 *African Human Rights Law Journal* 340.

Klarman, J, *From Jim Crow to Civil Rights: The Supreme Court and the Struggle for Racial Equality* (Oxford, Oxford University Press, 2006).

Knights, M, *Representation and Misrepresentation* (Oxford, Oxford University Press, 2005).

Kornhauser, L, 'Is Judicial Independence a Useful Concept' in SB Burbank and B Friedman (eds), *Judicial Independence at the Crossroads: An Interdisciplinary Approach* (London, Sage, 2002).

Kosaf, D, *Perils of Judicial Self-government in Transitional Societies* (Oxford, Oxford University Press, 2016).

Kosaf, D, 'Politics of Judicial Independence and Judicial Accountability in Czechia' (2017) 13 *European Constitutional Law Review* 96.

Kosaf, D and Lixinski, L, 'Domestic Judicial Design by International Human Rights Courts' (2015) 109 *American Journal of International Law* 713.

Kosaf, D and Sipulova, K, 'The Strasbourg Court Meets Abusive Constitutionalism: Baka v Hungary and the Rule of Law' (2018) 10 *Hague Journal of the Rule or Law* 83.

Kosaf, D and Vyhnanek, L. 'The Constitutional Court of Czechia' in *The Max Planck Handbook in European Public Law*, vol III (2019).

Kosaf, D and Sipulova, K, 'How to Fight Court-packing' (2020) 6 *Constitutional Studies* 133.

Kramer, L 'Judicial Supremacy and the End of Judicial Restraint' (2012) 100 *California Law Review* 621.

Lange, P, 'Transformative Constitutionalism' (2006) 17 *Stellenbosch Law Review* 352.

Lenaerts, K 'How the ECJ Thinks: A Study of Judicial Legitimacy' (2013) 36 *Fordham International Law Journal* 1302.

Le Sueur, A, 'The Judicial Review Debate: From Partnership to Friction' (1996) 31 *Government and Opposition* 8.

Le Sueur, A (ed), *Building the UK's New Supreme Court* (Oxford, Oxford University Press, 2004).

Leuch, B, 'The *Cassis de Dijon* Judgement and the European Commission' in A Albors-Llorens, C Bernard and B Leucht (eds), *Cassis de Dijon: Forty Years On* (Oxford, Hart Publishing, 2021).

Levitsky, S and Ziblat, D, *How Democracies Die: What History Tells Us About Our Future* (London: Penguin Books, 2017).

Lindquist, SA, *Measuring Judicial Activism* (Oxford: Oxford University Press, 2009).

Lindseth, P, 'Law, History, and Memory: Republican Moments and the Legitimacy of Constitutional Review in France' [1997] *Columbia Journal of European Law* 3.

McCloskey, RG, *The American Supreme Court*, rev edn, ed S Levinson (Chicago, University of Chicago Press, 2016).

Mohallem, M, 'Horizontal Judicial Dialogue on Human Rights: The Practice of Constitutional Courts in South America' in A Muller (ed), *Judicial Dialogue and Human Rights* (Cambridge, Cambridge University Press, 2017).

Monahan, P, *Politics and the Constitution: The Charter, Federalism and the Supreme Court of Canada* (Toronto, Carswell, 1987).

O'Brien, P, 'Enemies of the People: Judges, the Media, and the Mythical Lord Chancellor' [2017] *PL* 143.

Peretti, T, 'Does Judicial Independence Exist? The Lessons of Social Science Research' in S Burbank and B Friedman (eds), *Judicial Independence at the Crossroads: An Interdisciplinary Approach* (London, Sage, 2002).

Perez, AT, 'Judicial Self-government and Judicial Independence: Political Capture of the General V Council of the Judiciary in Spain' (2018) 19 *German Law Review* 1769.

Phelan, W, *Great Judgements of the Court of Justice* (Cambridge, Cambridge University Press, 2019).

Popeva, M, *Politicized Justice in Emerging Democracies: A Study of Courts in Russia and Ukraine* (New York, Cambridge University Press, 2012).

Poze, DE, 'The Irony of Judicial Elections' (2008) 108 *Columbia Law Review* 265.

Prassl, J, 'Business Freedoms and Employment Rights in the European Union' [2015] *Cambridge Yearbook of European Legal Studies* 189.

Ramseyer, E, 'The Puzzling (In)dependence of Courts: A Comparative Perspective' (1994) 23 *Journal of Legal Studies* 721.

Rasmussen, H, *On Law and Policy in the European Court of Justice: A Comparative Study in Judicial Policymaking* (Dordrecht, Martinus Nijhoff, 1986).

Rasmussen, M, 'The Origins of a Legal Revolution – The Early History of the European Court of Justice' (2008) 14 *Journal of European Integration History* 77.

Reichman, A, 'Judicial Independence in Times of War' [2011] *Utah Law Review* 63.

Reynolds, S, *Kingdoms and Communities in Western Europe 900–1300* (Oxford, Clarendon Press, 1997).

Robertson, D, *Judicial Discretion in the House of Lords* (Oxford, Clarendon Press, 1998).

Rodríguez-Garavito, C, 'Latin American Constitutionalism: Social and Economic Rights: Beyond the Courtroom: The Impact of Judicial Activism on Socioeconomic Rights in Latin America' (2011) 89 *Texas Law Review* 1669.

Rodríguez-Garavito, C and Rodríguez-Franco, F, *Radical Deprivation on Trial: The Impact of Judicial Activism on Socioeconomic Rights in the Global South* (New York, Cambridge University Press, 2015).

Rosenbaum, S, 'Courts as Political Players' (2019) 8 *Israel Journal of Health Policy Research* 32.

Rosenberg, J, *Trial of Strength: The Battle Between Ministers and Judges over Who Makes the Law* (London: Richard Chen, 1997).

Rosenberg, J, *Enemies of the People: How Judges Shape Society* (Bristol, Bristol University Press, 2020).

Saati, A, 'Participatory Constitution-making as a Transnational Legal Norm' (2017) 2 *UC Irvine Journal of International, Trans-national, and Comparative Law* 113.

Sadurski, W, *Poland's Constitutional Breakdown* (Oxford, Oxford University Press, 2020).

Sales, P, 'Legislative Intention, Interpretation, and the Principle of Legality' (2019) 40 *Statute Law Review* 53.

Sales, P and Elkins, R, 'Rights-consistent Interpretation of the Human Rights Act 1998' (2011) 127 *Law Quarterly Review* 217.

Scheb, JM, 'Public Holds US Supreme Court in High Regard' (1993) 77 *Judicature* 273.

Scheppele, KL, 'Autocratic Legalism Symposium: The Limits of Constitutionalism' (2018) 85 *University of Chicago Law Review* 545.

Schwartz, H, *The Struggle for Constitutional Justice in Post-Communist Europe* (Chicago, University of Chicago Press, 2004).

Sega, JA and Spaeth HJ, *The Supreme Court and the Attitudinal Model Revisited* (Cambridge, Cambridge University Press, 2002).

Selejan-Gutan, R, 'Perils of a "Perfect Euro-Model" of Judicial Council' (2018) 19 *German Law Review* 1707.

Shakespeare, W, *The Tragedy of King Lear; The First Part of the Contention of the Two Famous Houses of York and Lancaster (Henry VI Part II); Pericles Prince of Tyre* in *The Complete Works of Shakespeare*, ed S Wells and G Taylor (Oxford, Oxford University Press, 1990).

Shamir, E, 'Landmark Case and the Reproduction of Legitimacy: The Case of Israel's High Court of Justice' (1990) 24 *Law and Society Review* 781.

Shapiro, M, *Courts: A Comparative and Political Analysis* (Chicago, University of Chicago Press, 2013).

Sharpe, R, *Good Judgment: Making Judicial Decisions* (Toronto, University of Toronto Press, 2018).

Sharpe, R and McMahon, P, *The Persons Case; The Origins and the Legacy of the Fight for Legal Personhood* (Toronto, University of Toronto Press, 2007).

Sharpe, R and Bradfield, M, 'Crisis in Pakistan' in A Dodek and L Sossin (eds), *Judicial Independence in Context* (Toronto, Irwin Law, 2010).

Shavez, RB, *The Rule of Law in Nascent Democracies: Judicial Politics in Argentina* (Stanford, CA, Stanford University Press, 2004).

Shetreet, S, 'Judicial Independence and Accountability in Israel' (1984) 33 *ICLQ* 979.

Shetreet, S, 'Creating a Culture of Judicial Independence: The Practical Challenge and the Conceptual and the Conceptual Infrastructure' in S Shetreet and C Forsyth (eds), *The Culture of Judicial Independenc: Conceptual Foundations and Practical Challenges* (Leiden, Nijhoff, 2012).

Shetreet, S, *Judges on Trial: The Independence and Accountability of the English Judiciary* (Cambridge, Cambridge University Press, 2013).

Smilov, D, 'EU Enlargement and the Constitutional Principle of Judicial Independence' in W Sadurski, A Czarnota, M Krygier (eds), *Spreading Democracy and the Rule of Law* (Dordrecht, Springer, 2006).

Sommer, H 'The Non-Enumerated Rights: On the Scope of the Constitutional Revolution' (1997) 28 *Mishpatin* 341.

Stevens, R, *The Independence of the Judiciary: The View from the Lord Chancellor's Office* (Oxford, Clarendon Press, 1993).

Sipulova, K, 'The Czech Constitutional Curt' in K Pozcza (ed), *Constitutional Politics and the Judiciary* (London, Routledge, 2019).

Sipulova, K and Kosaf, D, 'The Strasbourg Court Meets Abusive Constitutionalism: Baka v Hungary and the Rule or Law' (2018) 10 *Hague Journal of the Rule of Law* 83.

Sipulova, K and Kosaf, D, 'How to Fight Court-packing' (2020) 6 *Constitutional Studies* 133.

Sipulova, K, Spac, S and Urbanikova, M, 'Capturing the Judiciary from Inside: The Story of Judicial Self-governance in Slovakia' (2018) 19 *German Law Journal* 1741.

Smith, A, *Lectures on Jurisprudence* [1763], ed RL Meek, DD Raphael and PG Stein (Indianapolis, IN, Liberty Fund, 1972–73, 1978).

Staton, JK, *Judicial Power and Strategic Communication in Mexico* (Cambridge, Cambridge University Press, 2010).

Stein, E, 'Lawyers, Judges, and the Making of a Transnational Constitution' (1981) 75 *American Journal of International Law* 1.

Stretton, T, 'The People and the Law' in K Wrightson (ed), *A Social History of England 1500–1750* (Cambridge, Cambridge University Press, 2017).

Stone Sweet, A, *Governing with Judges: Constitutional Politics in Europe* (Oxford, Oxford University Press, 2000).

Sunstein, C, Schkade, D, Ellman, A and Sawicki, A, *Are Judges Political – An Empirical Analysis of the Federal Judiciary* (Washington DC, Brookings Institute, 2006).

Taylor, MM 'Beyond Judicial Reform: Courts as Political Agents in Latin America' (2006) 41 *Latin American Research Review* 269.

Treanor, WM 'Case of the Prisoners and the Origins of Judicial Review' (1994) 143 *University of Pennsylvania Law Review* 491.

Thomas, Lord, *The Judiciary Within the State – The Relationship Between the Branches of the State* (Michael Ryle Memorial Lecture, 2017).

Trochev, A and Ellet, R, 'Judges and Their Allies' (2014) 2 *Journal of Law and Courts* 67.

Vanberg, G, 'Establishing Judicial Independence in West Germany' (2000) 32 *Comparative Politics* 333.

Vanberg, G 'Constitutional Courts in Comparative Perspective: A Theoretical Assessment' (2015) 18 *Annual Review of Politial Science* 167.

Vauchez, A 'The Strange Non-Death of Statism: Tracing the Ever Protracted Rise of Judicial-Self in France' (2018) 19 *German Law Review* 1613.

Vico, G, *The New Science* [1774] (London, Penguin Books, 1999).

Vilhena, O, Baxi, U and Viljoen, F, *Comparing the Apex Courts of Brazil, India, and South Africa* (Pretoria, Pretoria University Press, 2013).

Von Bogdandy, A, MacGregor, F, Antioniazzi, MM, Puovesan, F and Soley, X (eds), *Transformative Constitutionalism in Latin America: The Emergence of a New Ius Commune* (Oxford: Oxford university Press, 2013).

Waldron, J, 'The Constitutional Conception of Democracy' in *Law and Disagreement* (Oxford, Oxford University Press, 1999).

Waldron, J, 'The Core of the Case Against Judicial Review' (2006) 115 *Yale Law Journal* 1346.

Wall, S, *Reluctant European* (Oxford, Oxford University Press, 2019).

Warr, J, *A Spark in the Ashes* [1648–49], ed S Sedley and L Kaplan (London, Verso, 1992).

Watson, G, 'The Judge and Court Administration' in AM Linden (ed), *The Canadian Judiciary* (Toronto, Osgoode Hall Law School, 1976).

Weatherall, S, 'After Keck: Some Thoughts on How to Clarify the Clarification' (1996) 33 *CML Rev* 885.

Weatherall, S, 'Use and Abuse of the EU's Charter of Fundamental Rights' (2014) 10 *European Review of Contract Law* 167.

Weber, M, *Economy and Society*, ed G Roth and C Wittich (Berkeley, University of California Press, 1968).

White, S, 'Parliaments, Constitutional Conventions, and Popular Sovereignty' (2017) 19 *British Journal of Politics and International Relations* 320.

Wigmore, JH, *Evidence in Trials at Common Law*, rev JH Chadbourn (Boston, MA, Little, Brown, 1976).

Wilson, B and Rodríguez-Cordero, JC, 'Legal Opportunity Structures and Social Movements The Effects of Institutional Change on Costa Rican Politics' (2006) 15 *Comparative Political Studies* 63.

Wood, GS, *The Creation of the American Republic 1776* (Chapel Hill, University of North Carolina Press, 1998).

Woodhouse, D, *The Office of the Lord Chancellor* (Oxford, Hart Publishing, 2001).

Zoll, F and Wirtham, L, 'Judicial Independence and Accountability: Withstanding Political Stress in Poland' (2019) *Fordham International Law Journal* 875.

Index